North Sea Waypoint Directory

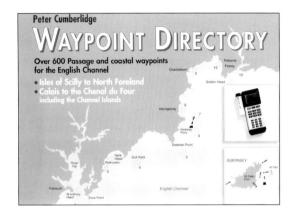

By the same author:

Waypoint Directory
Isles of Scilly to North Foreland
Calais to the Chenal du Four and Channel Islands

ISBN 0-7136-4117-7

This first *Waypoint Directory* is an invaluable reference for anyone navigating by GPS, Loran or Decca, whether under sail or power. It contains 55 coastal approach charts for the English and French sides of the English Channel, showing the positions and details of over 600 carefully chosen waypoints. Alongside each waypoint chart is an easy-to-read table giving the latitude and longitude of each waypoint, as well as details of the coastal dangers to take into account when using the waypoints. All the charts are drawn to scale, giving at-a-glance advice on the best routes to take anywhere in the English Channel. The *Waypoint Directory* is an indispensable aid for route planning and navigation on both yachts and motorboats.

'We used this book on a cruise to Brittany and the Channel Islands, where it earned its place in the library several times over.'
Yachting Monthly

'A good book to have on board, but also very useful for forward passage planning' *The Boatman*

Peter Cumberlidge

North Sea Waypoint Directory

Over 1000 passage and coastal waypoints
plus 90 landfall charts

• Thames Estuary to the Humber
• Dover Strait to the Elbe and Esbjerg
  including the Frisian Islands

Charts devised by Jane Cumberlidge and drawn by Michelle Harris

Adlard Coles Nautical • London

Published 1999 by Adlard Coles Nautical
an imprint of A & C Black (Publishers) Ltd
35 Bedford Row, London WC1R 4JH

Copyright © Peter Cumberlidge 1999

ISBN 0-7136-4799-X

A CIP catalogue record for this book is available from
the British Library

Typeset in 11 on 12.5pt Baskerville
Printed in Hong Kong by Wing King Tong Co. Ltd.

Contents

Outline maps vi
Introduction 3

Dover Strait 14
Dover to North Foreland 18
North Foreland to Tongue Sand and Princes Channel 20
Whitstable Bay and East approaches to the Swale 22
North Foreland to North Edinburgh Channel 24
Princes and North Edinburgh Channels to The Warp 26
The Thames Sea Reach and Medway approaches 30
North Edinburgh Channel to the River Crouch 32
Approaches to the River Blackwater 36
SW approaches to Harwich and Walton Backwaters 38
Harwich entrance 40
Harwich entrance to the River Deben 42
North Edinburgh Channel to the East Swin 44
Kentish Knock to Sunk Head 48
Outer approaches to Harwich 50
Outer approaches to the Thames Estuary (south) 52
Outer approaches to the Thames Estuary (north) 56
Outer approaches to the River Deben 60
Shipway Channel and North Shipwash 62
Outer approaches to Orford Haven 64
Southwold to Lowestoft 66
Approaches to Lowestoft 68
Lowestoft to Great Yarmouth 70
Great Yarmouth to Cockle Gatway 74
Cockle Gatway to Sheringham Shoal 78
Approaches to Blakeney and Wells-next-the-Sea 80
Approaches to Brancaster and Burnham Overy Staithe 82
Outer approaches to The Wash 84
The Wash 86
Inner Dowsing to Mablethorpe 88

Mablethorpe to Spurn Head and the River Humber 90
Calais and Cap Gris-Nez 92
Calais to Gravelines 94
Gravelines to Dunkerque 96
East approaches to Dunkerque 98
Nieuwpoort to Oostende 100
Oostende to Zeebrugge 102
West approaches to the Westerschelde 104
North-west approaches to the Westerschelde 106
Approaches to Vlissingen (Flushing) 108
West approaches to the Roompot 110
North-west approaches to the Oosterschelde barrier 112
North approaches to Geul van de Banjaard 114
Approaches to Stellendam 116
Inner approaches to the Hook of Holland 118
Goeree to IJmuiden – Outer approaches to the Hook of Holland 120
Outer approaches to Zeegat van Texel 124
Zeegat van Texel – south approach channel 126
Zeegat van Texel and approaches to Den Helder 128
Zeegat van Texel – north approach channel 130
Den Helder to Den Oever 132
Texel to Terschelling 134
Approaches to Zeegat van Terschelling 136
Approaches to West Terschelling harbour and the Vliestroom 138
Waddenzee approaches to Harlingen 140
Terschelling to Ameland 142
Ameland to Borkum 144
Outer approaches to Schiermonnikoog and Lauwersoog 146
Inner approaches to Schiermonnikoog and Lauwersoog 148
West approaches to Borkum 150

Outer approaches to Borkum and the Eems 152
Inner approaches to Borkum 156
Borkum to Eemshaven 158
River Eems – Eemshaven to Campen lighthouse 160
River Eems – approaches to Delfzijl 162
Osterems entrance – Borkum to Juist and Memmert 164
Outer approaches to Norderney 166
Approaches to Norderneyer Seegat 168
Norderney to Spiekeroog 170
West approaches to Die Jade and Die Weser – Spiekeroog to Wangerooge 172
Outer approaches to Helgoland 174
Outer approaches to Die Jade, Die Weser and Die Elbe 176
Outer entrance to Die Jade and Die Weser 178
Die Jade to Wilhelmshaven 180
Die Elbe entrance – Elbe light float to Scharhörn and Grosser Vogelsand 182
Die Elbe – Scharhörn to Cuxhaven 184
Norderelbe – outer approaches 186
Norderelbe – Buschsand to Zehnerloch 188
Outer approaches to the Eider River, Norderpiep and Süderpiep 190
Approaches to Norderpiep and Süderpiep 192
Entrance to the Eider River 194
Approaches to Hever and Schmaltief 196
Outer approaches to Rütergat, Amrum and Vortrapptief 198
Rütergat and south approaches to Amrum and Föhr 200
Outer approaches to Sylt 202
Lister Tief and RΩmΩ 204
Approaches to Esbjerg and FanΩ 206

Index 208

Outline maps

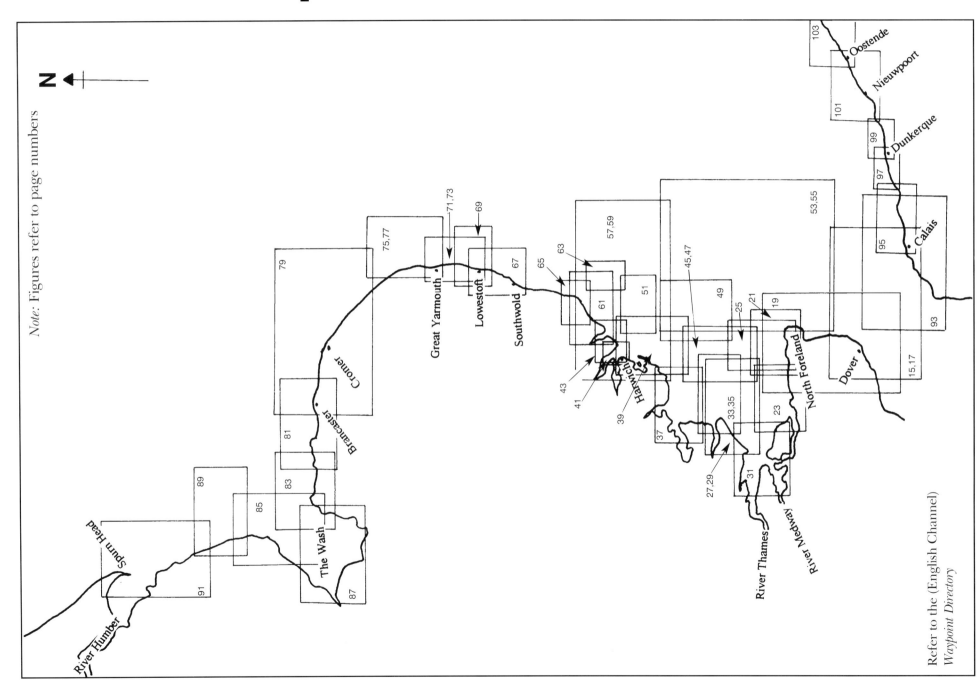

Note: Figures refer to page numbers

Refer to the (English Channel)
Waypoint Directory

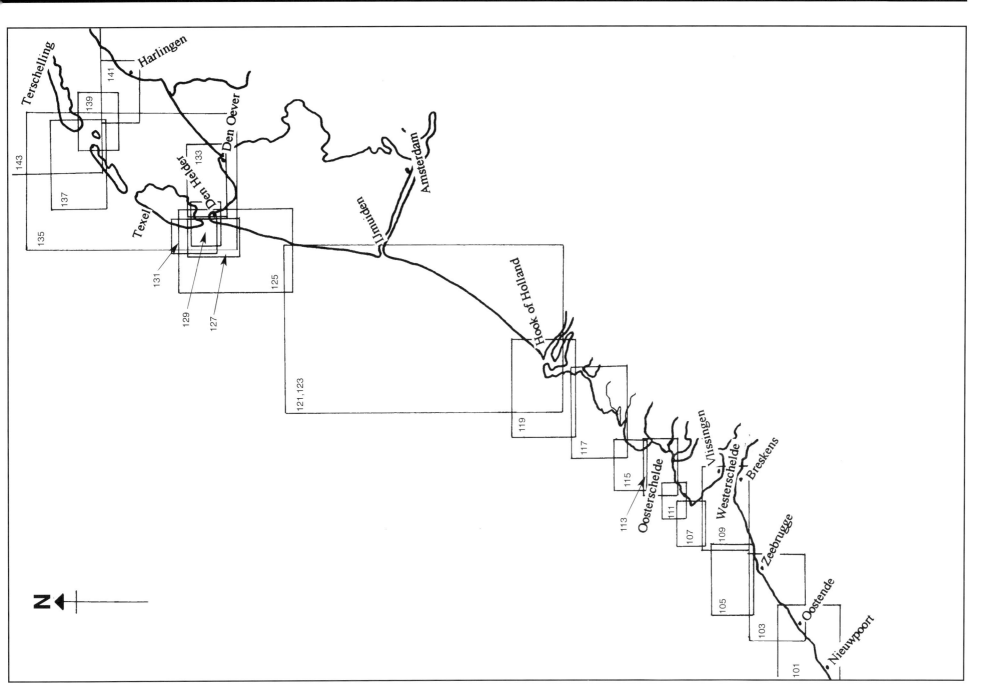

N

Terschelling
Harlingen
141
139
143
137
135
Den Oever
Den Helder
133
Texel
131
129
127
125
Amsterdam
IJmuiden
121,123
Hook of Holland
119
117
Vlissingen
115
Oosterschelde
113
Westerschelde
111
Breskens
107
109
Zeebrugge
105
Oostende
103
Nieuwpoort
101

1

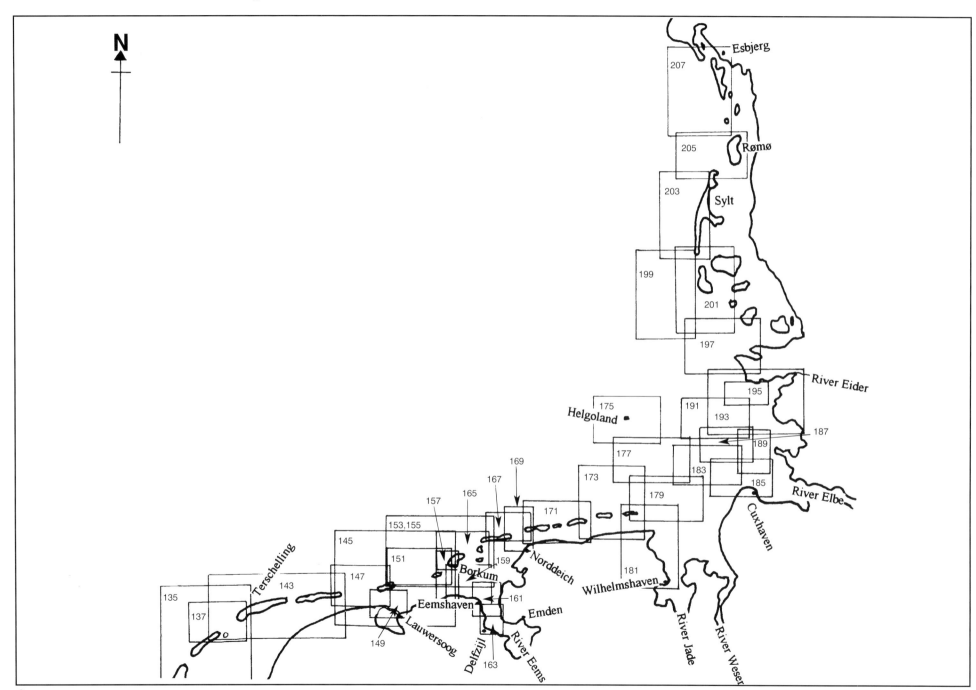

Introduction

ELECTRONIC NAVIGATION

All navigation, 'manual' or electronic, has the common purpose of moving a craft safely from place to place and keeping track of where you are on the way. The aims of modern navigation are identical to those of traditional navigation. Technology simply enables us to do this more easily, accurately and, on the whole, more safely. Remember the basic objectives of any navigation:

1 Planning a safe route;
2 Position fixing and monitoring your route;
3 Safe pilotage and avoiding traffic.

Principles of seamanship do not change for electronic navigation. Linked to the basic skills and an awareness of error must be a sense of strategy and an understanding of the potential risks posed by a particular sea area at a given time in the conditions likely to be prevailing.

Even using GPS or Decca, you still need to give a wide berth to dangerous reefs and banks, passing down-tide or to leeward if possible. You should be wary of certain headlands in wind-over-tide conditions, and cautious about approaching rocky coasts at night, in murky visibility or in strong onshore winds.

You have to allow for possible weather shifts, make best use of tides, plan landfalls carefully and work out alternative bolt-holes. Flexibility is easier with modern electronics, but navigators must always be a bit pessimistic, ready for possible changes of course or destination in case of mechanical problems or a threatening forecast.

It certainly makes sense for navigators to use any modern equipment to best advantage. There is nothing wrong with making GPS, Decca or Loran central to your navigation, so long as:

(a) Equipment is carefully installed to reduce the risk of power failure, aerial problems or damage by seawater or corrosion;
(b) You keep a regular record of displayed latitude and longitude, at least every hour for a displacement boat and more frequently aboard high-speed boats, so that if all systems fail you can carry on navigating manually.

GPS (GLOBAL POSITIONING SYSTEM)

This latest satellite navigation system was developed by the US Defense Department and is based on a network of twenty-four satellites, of which five are usually within 'view' of most locations at any particular time. The system works by measuring differences between the times that signals are sent from the satellites and the times they are received by the GPS set. From these time differences are calculated the distances between the satellites and the receiver. Since the satellites always know where they are, an accurate position can be calculated for the receiver.

Three satellite position lines provide a two-dimensional fix of latitude and longitude, while four or more position lines can give a three-dimensional fix of latitude, longitude and altitude. Yacht GPS sets are usually set up for two-dimensional fixes, since they are normally used at sea level.

Because the system was devised by the military, there are intentionally two levels of accuracy it can provide – precision accuracy for military use and coarse accuracy for general use. The master transmitting station in the US deliberately degrades signal accuracy by making variable adjustments, and this is the 'Selective Availability' which reduces position-fixing accuracy to within

about a 100 metre radius of your true position.

For most practical purposes this is an extremely acceptable accuracy, especially when you think this facility is obtainable anywhere on the globe. However, the slight fuzziness induced by Selective Availability means that you cannot necessarily rely totally on GPS in such tight corners as you can with Decca. Whereas, with Decca, you might safely be able to pick your way into an Essex river in quite thick fog, you would probably be pushing your luck using ordinary GPS. However, the civilian modification known as Differential GPS, which restores accuracy to within about 10 metres, is now widely available and means buying a slightly different type of aerial.

Mounting a GPS antenna

A GPS antenna should be sited to give a clear view of the horizon, but does not, unlike a Loran or Decca aerial, need to be as high as possible. The most convenient position for a GPS antenna aboard a yacht is often on one side of the pushpit, well clear of the boom, mainsheet or topping lift. The most convenient location aboard a motor boat is normally somewhere on the flybridge or wheelhouse roof, well above any parts of the boat that could interfere with line-of-sight reception. A GPS antenna should be mounted clear of the transmitting plane of a radar scanner.

Hand-held GPS sets also like a clear horizon, and best results will be obtained from the cockpit of a yacht or the flybridge of a motor boat.

Ease of data entry

All GPS sets from reputable manufacturers will provide reliable position-fixing within the limits of system accuracy. However, sets differ considerably in the ease with which waypoint data can be entered and navigational information presented. If you buy a GPS set simply on price, you may find that keying in waypoint positions and identifiers is extremely laborious, involving many key strokes and much use of the +/– function. The course and distance to the next waypoint may also be difficult to read, or perhaps mixed up with all kinds of extraneous data on the display.

Ease of use is an important consideration at sea, and you should try entering a whole set of waypoint positions into a wide range of GPS sets before deciding to buy.

Starting up

If a new GPS set is taken to any position in the world and simply switched on, it may take anything from several minutes to a quarter of an hour to provide a fix from this unprepared start. This process can be greatly speeded up by telling the set more or less where it is in space and time by keying in your approximate latitude, longitude, altitude, date and time. This start-up routine should also be followed if the set has been transported more than about 100 miles since it was last used. In the normal course of use, however, a GPS, Decca or Loran set will remember the last position before it was switched off and use this to 'initialise' and work out the first fix when it is switched on again.

THE LORAN–C SYSTEM

The Loran–C navigation system works on a principle similar to Decca, but uses pulse signals instead of a continuous wave transmission. This gives the system a much greater range than Decca. The Loran–C groundwave signal can normally be received accurately at between 800 and 1200 nautical miles, and the pulses can also travel as 'skywaves' at much greater range, albeit with less accuracy.

Four new Loran–C chains are replacing the old Norwegian chain to provide extensive coverage over UK and NW European waters. The transmissions are subject to similar propagation errors as the Decca system, but can function with reasonable accuracy at much greater range. Using the groundwave signals, Loran–C has an accuracy of about 100 metres when you are 200 nautical miles from the transmitters, to between 250 metres and a mile when you are operating at 500 miles range.

Mounting a Loran aerial

Loran aerials should be mounted as high as possible on board for best results, although aerial height is not so critical with this system as with Decca.

THE DECCA SYSTEM

The Decca Navigator System covers UK and NW European waters, but the UK Decca chains of transmitters now have a limited life and it will not be too long before the system is phased out. Although Decca offered restricted coverage compared with the GPS satellite system, it did have the advantage of excellent accuracy and repeatability within its own area. While the system continues, provided you are receiving a strong signal and have a reliable aerial installation and power supply, it is feasible to use Decca safely in very tight navigational corners if you are overtaken by poor visibility.

DUAL SYSTEMS

Fail-safe thinking

The best manufacturers produce reliable, sophisticated and accurate navigation systems that can

be linked together into a full facility network. It is we, the navigators, that now need to become more professional in our thinking about electronic navigation. At the same time, we also need to adopt considerably higher standards for their installation.

It is instructive to compare boat navigation with aviation. Air navigation is almost all done by instruments, and pilots, even of light aircraft, are accustomed to relying on instruments as a matter of routine. However, aviation systems are generally installed, checked and maintained to a much higher standard than most yacht systems, and the practice of system duplication for safety is well accepted.

This is an important objective when more and more yachtsmen are coming to rely increasingly on electronics. The two principles of duplication and independence are central in the specification of aircraft systems, and it seems reasonable to follow this example aboard yachts.

Duplication and independence can apply not only to main items of equipment, but also to the auxiliaries which support them, such as power supplies, wiring, switching and aerials. There is little point, for example, in installing both a GPS and a Decca set for added safety, if both are powered by the same battery through the same supply circuit. That would be like having two engines fed by a single fuel tank, making both engines equally vulnerable to water or dirt in the common fuel system.

If possible, it makes sense to install a separate 'GPS' battery, with the Decca perhaps supplied from the normal services battery and with the engine starting battery separate again.

Separate aerials

Aerials are always potentially vulnerable, especially on smaller boats, whether you are talking about GPS, Decca, VHF or Navtex. If you decide to duplicate position-fixing systems, it makes sense to continue the principle of independence and mount the two aerials in different parts of the boat if possible. Decca and Loran benefit from aerial height, so these whips are best mounted either at a masthead or up on a radar arch.

A GPS aerial does not need to be so high and is physically much smaller, so it is suitable for mounting on the pushpit of a sailing yacht and perhaps on the side of the flybridge aboard a motor boat, or up on a radar arch or, for a boat without a flybridge, somewhere safe and open on the wheelhouse roof.

With these well separated locations, in the case of one aerial being damaged, the other would be likely to survive. For this reason, you are more vulnerable using combined aerial units, which are marketed on the basis that a single aerial system can cope with all your reception requirements. A whole range of vital equipment would then depend on a single component, which is always dubious practice at sea.

Duplicating prime equipment

Many boat owners still consider it extravagant to double up on main items of electronics, and yet this is really no more than prudent seamanship when you are relying heavily on electronics for navigation. You wouldn't go cruising, for example, without at least one spare anchor or a couple of spare alternator belts. At present, we have the advantage of at least two independently operated systems of navigation – GPS and the new Loran chains for Northern European and Mediterranean waters.

The cost of equipment duplication is becoming increasingly reasonable, although one has to bear in mind that the working life of the Decca chains is now very limited. However, four new Loran–C

chains have recently improved the Loran coverage over north-west Europe and the British Isles. There is therefore plenty of scope for navigation system duplication using GPS and Loran–C.

In fact many boat owners have already had duplicate systems running for some time using Decca and GPS. Those who were still using Decca while its future was under discussion could suddenly find a Decca station going off air for maintenance, or perhaps the boat would enter a local area of poor resolution. Decca signal propagation was always less reliable at night, or towards dawn and dusk, when the red signal light was apt to come and go intermittently. Then it was certainly reassuring to have a constant GPS display alongside the Decca to compare notes.

Using regular manual back-up

Even with fully duplicated position-fixing systems, it is vital to keep a regular note of the minimum data that would enable you to carry on navigating manually should all your equipment fail. The minimum safe record would be to write down every hour, against the time, your course and log reading, and then your latitude and longitude by Decca or GPS, having first checked that both displays are giving practically the same readings.

Any significant discrepancy between Decca and GPS positions should be investigated at once, when you will have to make a judgement about which position is likely to be the more reliable.

By keeping up this minimum log as a routine, you will never be more than an hour away from an accurate position, and you can quickly use your course steered and present log reading to work out an estimated position if your GPS and Decca both go down.

ELECTRONIC NAVIGATION IN PRACTICE

The power of Decca, GPS and Loran systems comes not just from the amazing facility of having your position displayed continuously to two decimal places of a minute, but also from the sophisticated passage planning software which has introduced the concepts of 'waypoint' and 'cross-track error', and brings into sharp focus the idea of 'course and speed made good'.

The displays of 'distance to next waypoint' and 'bearing to next waypoint' are important features, and electronic navigators now visualise, and hence plan, their passages in a different kind of way. Destinations are more precise, with waypoints normally specified to two decimal places of a minute.

One side-effect of such accurate navigation comes from greatly increased expectations of a precisely ordered passage. Even fairly minor incidents or problems causing deviations from plan can now instil a sense of 'distress', whereas they would once have been accepted as a normal part of passage-making and being at sea. Remember that you are not necessarily in danger just because a system has failed and you suddenly don't know exactly where you are.

Allowing for tide

Tide does not vanish because you are using a precise position-fixing system. For passage-making in tidal waters, you still have to assess the net tidal effect in advance, as you would if navigating the traditional way. Indeed, a full understanding of tidal streams is important for interpreting changing displays, especially 'cross-track error' displays.

Novice navigators sometimes regard 'cross-track error' as a navigational error or an off-course warning needing immediate correction, but this is usually not the case on a longish passage. Cross-track error is not an error if, for example, the tide is setting west for the first half of a Channel crossing, then slack for an hour, then setting east for the second half.

Working out the best course to start steering involves the same calculations as if you were navigating by traditional methods. The tidal vectors are compounded for the estimated duration of your passage, and the course to steer laid off on the chart in the usual way.

Monitoring tide

Accurate position-fixing systems allow you to monitor the effect of tidal streams quite precisely. With Decca, GPS or Loran interfaced to an electronic compass and log, some systems can display the tidal direction and rate you are experiencing at any given time, by calculating the vector difference between the course steered and speed through the water and your actual course and speed made good.

Even without this facility, an experienced navigator can soon tell from the 'cross-track error' and 'bearing to next waypoint' displays whether he is experiencing more or less tide than predicted and can then adjust his course in good time.

Landfall procedures

The satisfaction of a good landfall never palls, although a landfall on instruments has a different quality to the traditional style of arrival where you were often not too sure which section of coast would lift above the horizon.

Using GPS or Decca, especially linked to a chart plotter, you make a landfall more gradually, well in advance of seeing land. The flashing blip edges closer to your approach waypoint, converging with the video outline of the coast. The first

radar echoes of the coast may turn up long before you glimpse land over the bow. A radar scan somehow has a genuine solid feel about it, a real but invisible sighting. Yet even knowing your position every step of the way, it is always exhilarating when the first smudge of land appears ahead.

As you draw closer inshore, even if using a good plotter, you should plot the GPS latitude and longitude on a large-scale chart from time to time, rather than rely on the 'distance and bearing to next waypoint' display; remember that an approach waypoint may be slightly in error, and this might not show up until you get close in amongst hazards.

A traditional danger about landfalls is that, suddenly, the passage may feel almost over and the navigator starts to relax, imagining himself to have arrived just as the boat is entering the most risky part of the trip. This tendency is equally relevant to instrument landfalls, sometimes more so because a navigator using GPS usually feels certain about his position and confident about picking up whatever marks he has set as waypoints. Guard against over-confidence and keep double-checking the navigation until you really do arrive.

Heavy weather

Good electronics really come into their own in heavy weather, especially with position-fixing systems duplicated for peace of mind. The main requirement for navigation in heavy weather is that your passage planning be even more conscientious than usual.

The classic landfall risk, of trying to reach a nearby harbour which is inherently unsafe in the prevailing conditions, can actually be increased when you have accurate position-fixing systems – when anything seems possible. This is a question of seamanship rather than navigation, but there

are cases every season where skippers using Decca or GPS have diverted, in deteriorating weather, for dangerous entrances they would never have considered if navigating by traditional methods.

Even with high technology, prudent seamanship should rule the day. Beware of closing a tide-swept rocky coast in rising onshore winds, or making for a shallow river mouth where the seas are liable to break over a bar. Don't risk being guided with digital accuracy into a traditional seaman's death-trap.

The danger of 'auto-steering'

Perhaps one of the greatest hazards from fully integrated systems is the increasing risk from boats being steered on autopilot directly from the GPS or Decca computer – that is, when you select a particular waypoint and tell the boat to go there automatically. This auto-track facility must be used with great caution, not only in terms of always keeping a good lookout at sea, but also in the care given to data input so that you are not sent off in an inadvertently dangerous direction. All kinds of dramatic nightmare scenarios can be imagined when technology gives you the facility, as it were, to dial-a-destination.

WAYPOINT THINKING

Although navigators have always used buoys and other seamarks as signposts on passage, the waypoint concept has a wider meaning since its incorporation into GPS, Decca and Loran sailplan systems. Waypoints are used to represent both tangible navigation marks along a route and more arbitrary positions which serve as convenient turning-points between successive stages of a passage.

Fig 1 shows examples of three different types of waypoint, using a coastal passage eastwards round Tangle Point and Bull Head.

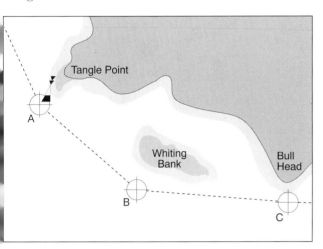

Waypoint A is the south-cardinal buoy off Tangle Point, either its actual latitude and longitude or a position slightly to seaward of the buoy. Waypoint B is a clearing waypoint set a safe distance to seaward of Whiting Bank so that the passage legs approaching and leaving B both lie in safe water. Waypoint C is a headland waypoint whose distance offshore will depend on how steep the coast is, and whether there are any tidal overfalls or crabpots to avoid.

Once you start using waypoints as a matter of routine, it soon becomes apparent that different types of waypoint tend to be used in slightly different circumstances.

Seamark waypoints

Seamark waypoints may be buoys, beacons, lightfloats, lightships, and so on. Some navigators set actual positions for seamark waypoints, to maximise the chance of finding the mark. Others prefer offset waypoints, to be sure of staying in safe water – and, in poor visibility, to reduce the risk of collision with the waypoint!

Clearing waypoints

Danger clearing waypoints are set a safe but arbitrarily judged distance clear of navigational dangers such as sandbanks, reefs, headlands or races off headlands. Because clearing waypoints are often positions at which you change course, they must be set so that your tracks approaching and leaving the waypoint both lie in safe water, i.e. with no dangerous cutting of corners.

The distance off for clearing waypoints may depend on weather and sea-state, wind direction, visibility, whether the headland is an area for crabpots, the type of boat (deep or shallow draught) and her general manoeuvrability and cruising speed.

Setting the right distance off involves judgement. You don't want to shave a danger area too close, yet taking too wide a sweep adds extra distance and time which may be crucial later in the passage – even half an hour at sea can have a significant bearing on events in the lottery of changing weather and sea conditions.

Turning waypoints

Some waypoints are arbitrarily chosen positions at which it is simply convenient to change course – for example, off a bulge in the coast where the shoreline changes direction, or perhaps on the edge of a traffic separation scheme within which your course is constrained at right-angles to the direction of the scheme.

Departure waypoints

When starting an open sea passage, navigators have always taken a final departure from some convenient known point, such as an outer channel buoy or a fix position off a headland. You should also set departure waypoints when using Decca or GPS, rather than allowing the system to take its own departure from wherever you switch on. The cross-track error display will then make full sense, relating to the open sea track once you are properly on passage.

Landfall waypoints

These are carefully chosen positions out in safe water, perhaps within a few miles of the coast you are heading for. Landfall waypoints may be seamarks, such as fairway buoys or outer channel buoys, but they may also just be convenient positions on the chart which are far enough offshore to be safe destinations in any weather, but close enough inshore that you can identify landmarks and get your bearings before starting to approach the coast.

When specifying landfall waypoints, much depends on the type of coastline you are approaching: whether steep-to or gradually shoaling, whether it is free of offshore dangers or littered with rocks or sandbanks, whether it is high and fairly easy to identify or low and featureless.

Also consider what the tide will be doing as you approach the coast. Where streams are powerful, such as in the Dover Strait, or in the great estuaries of the Elbe or the Westerschelde, it is usually best to arrive a little uptide of your destination. It is easier to drop down ½ mile with a 3-knot tide than push back against it.

Approach waypoints

You need to have done your homework for the final approach and carefully worked out any inshore waypoints that will be useful, for example, in leading along a harbour entrance channel or into a river mouth in poor visibility. It doesn't make sense to use Decca or GPS to arrive precisely at an outer fairway buoy and then risk getting lost in the more intricate approach buoyage simply through lack of preparation.

It is usually best to have entered a complete set of waypoints for a passage, a door-to-door route which can, if necessary, take you right up to the marina entrance. Such detailed waypoint planning will be appreciated if the weather turns foul during a landfall, when the coast you have successfully found and identified vanishes in driving rain, along with the next critical buoy you thought you had just spotted a mile away.

Of course you need to be careful using waypoints close inshore and along narrow channels, since the normal limits of system accuracy can take you the wrong side of a buoy as easily as the right side. However, close-quarters waypoints can at least set you off in the right direction towards the next mark, until you identify it for certain by eye.

Bear in mind the outer limits of accuracy of the navigation system you are using. Although absolute accuracies quoted in GPS brochures and manuals may be of the order of 20 metres, similar to the repeatable accuracies quoted for Decca, the actual GPS accuracy achieved in practice may be much coarser than this.

For GPS, you should reckon on a circle of accuracy between 50 and 100 metres diameter, but sometimes up to 300 metres under worst conditions of Selective Availability of the satellite system.

Marking waypoints on the chart

Having decided on a set of waypoints for a passage, I always like to pencil them on the charts, using the now conventional waypoint symbol and with the Decca or GPS identifier written against each waypoint, for example P1, P2, P3, P4 etc, or the relevant reference numbers from a *Waypoint Directory*.

Entering and checking waypoints

Using electronic systems as primary means of position-fixing, it is vital to double-check, slowly and carefully, that you have entered your selected waypoints accurately. One wrong digit can lead you into trouble, and a slight error in a waypoint position can be more dangerous than a large error which may often reveal itself as such in good time.

Make sure you key in the decimal point correctly, and check that you are entering latitude when your system is expecting latitude, and longitude when it is expecting longitude. All the longitudes in the book are east of Greenwich, so you need to know whether your program assumes east or west longitude as a default entry – remember to change this if necessary with the +/– or E/W key.

Once all the waypoints for a passage have been entered, you should always scroll them across the display to double-check the latitudes and longitudes against your list. Check and double-check. The example below, from a passage that was described to me by a much chastened skipper, shows what can happen when a single digit is entered incorrectly (Fig 2).

Because, in this case, the waypoint position had been entered only slightly incorrectly, the previous stages of this passage across the southern North Sea had seemed perfectly correct to the navigator, with the West Hinder tower turning up in the right place at the right time and the crew feeling confident, on their last leg, that they were nicely 'on the glide-path' for Nieuwpoort.

However, the visibility closed to less than ½ a mile after the West Hinder. At this stage, the skipper was apparently making for two waypoints that he had set in order to cross the shipping lanes more or less at right-angles and then pass safely east of the shallowest parts of the Oost Dyck and Outer Ratel banks. They had cleared the Oost

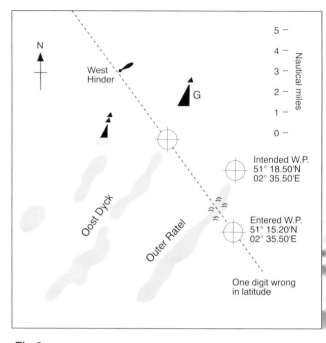

Fig 2

Dyck as planned, but it was the Outer Ratel waypoint which had been wrongly entered. The tide was fairly well down and the wind was a moderate north-westerly.

Everything still seemed under control on board, with the Decca counting down reassuringly, to two decimal places, towards the next waypoint. I certainly recognise that comfortable feeling as navigator when your instruments tally nicely with where you think you are and everything appears to be properly in place. It is usually then, before complacence sets in, that an experienced navigator starts to get edgy.

This particular crew had a nasty shock when, in murky visibility, they found themselves surrounded by turbid sand-coloured water and steep breaking seas. The echo-sounder reading fell back to less than 3 metres as the boat crossed the shallowest part of the Outer Ratel bank. Then the 'waypoint passed' bleeper went off at a position, it later transpired, a good 2 miles south-west of where the navigator had intended to be.

There was just enough water to float them over the bank, but conditions were rough for a while, several crests broke into the cockpit, and things were thrown into confusion as the navigator felt well and truly lost. Wisely, once clear of broken water, he hove-to for ten minutes or so to study the chart, check the last waypoint and work out what had gone wrong. Then he plotted a new zigzag route to clear the even shallower banks off Nieuwpoort and the relieved crew arrived safely a couple of hours later.

This incident was interesting not just because it underlined the danger of entering a waypoint incorrectly, but also because it illustrated the marked and sudden change between the skipper feeling completely in control as he navigated by instruments, and then totally lost and disorientated when reality did not match what the displays were telling him.

That kind of extreme jolt did not happen so often before electronic systems were widely used, because most small boat navigators felt uncertain and partly lost most of the time. They were never quite sure where they were, but at least they knew they weren't sure. When using modern navigation systems, therefore, it is still a good idea to retain or cultivate a sceptical sense of uncertainty about your position and how things are going. Old hands seem to develop the habit of running double-checks on any piece of navigational information, whatever its source.

In this case, a simple check against the compass could have indicated that something was amiss. After passing the West Hinder, the navigator simply followed the Decca 'course to next waypoint', correcting the helm to port or star-board depending on the cross-track error display. There is nothing wrong with this for short legs when the tide is not too strong, but it would have made sense to compare the 'course to next waypoint' with the course the chart indicated they should have been steering. This would have immediately shown that the Decca was asking them to steer too far to the south. From the Oost Dyck waypoint, there should have been a positive course alteration to port towards the Outer Ratel waypoint.

A gradually increasing discrepancy between a charted course and GPS displayed 'course to next waypoint' is usually the result of a cross-tide, but if you know what the stream should be doing and the difference between the displayed and charted courses to steer develops as expected, you have a welcome consistency between different sources of information which improves the reliability of the navigational conclusions you can draw. The habit of looking for consistency, or inconsistency, between different sources of navigational information is just as important as it always was, perhaps more important now that we are tending to use electronic systems as the primary method of navigation.

Conclusions on choosing and using waypoints

Waypoint thinking has become a normal part of navigation for those who use electronics as a matter of course, but it is always important to remember that GPS, Decca or Loran sailplan displays depend crucially on the care and accuracy with which waypoints are specified, stored and handled.

Although some traditional navigational methods and skills are falling naturally into disuse, many new kinds of expertise are emerging, the most important of which centre on the business of passage-planning and setting up the ship's navigation system so that it can handle likely changes of route without significant reprogramming or data entry at sea. The key consideration here lies in specifying safe individual waypoints that can also be incorporated into safe and efficient waypoint networks.

Although the process of setting a waypoint may seem routine, there can be many strategic implications in the selection of even a single waypoint, especially off a tricky coast. How a number of waypoints then fit together to form a route can be critical to the value and flexibility of a passage plan.

CHART PLOTTERS

State of the art
Of all marine electronics, video chart plotters have attracted the greatest research effort in the last few years and will continue to do so for some time. Electronic plotters are now set to move from their earlier rather gimmicky status to becoming practical tools for navigation at sea. This *Waypoint Directory* is equally valuable when used with chart plotters as it is with more straightforward GPS or Loran–C sets.

There is already great diversity in the style and quality of cartography available. Most plotters are permanently installed with a world map and you buy plug-in chart cartridges to provide navigational fine detail for different sea areas. Different manufacturers have devised their own types of chart cartridge, none of which are compatible with each other. When you buy a plotter, you therefore have to use the particular chart cartridges and system of cartography supplied for it. The best-known names in digital cartography are probably C-Map, Furuno, G-Chart, Livechart and Navionics.

Although digital cartography is becoming more detailed, clearer and more akin to real paper charts, there is always a degree of simplification compared with what is shown on, for example, the largest-scale Admiralty chart of the same area.

At present, these simplifications are a fact of life, but they will gradually reduce as software and display technology improve. It is these simplifications you have to assess when buying a chart plotter, and they are even more important than the general ease of operation of the hardware. When comparing different systems of cartography, look first for some obvious points:

- whether major familiar landmarks are shown, as they would be on an Admiralty chart;
- whether you can easily distinguish drying areas from, say, 5-metre or 10-metre contour lines;
- whether the drying heights, or at least the shallowest drying heights, of dangerous banks and shoals are shown;
- whether you can easily distinguish different types of buoy or beacon, and whether the most important buoys and beacons appear and can be recognised on a medium-scale display, without you having to zoom right in to pick up this detail.
- whether you can easily distinguish between drying reefs, drying mud or drying sandbanks – there are important practical differences;
- whether important leading lines and leading lights are clearly shown.

Zooming, scrolling and re-compiling

An important practical difference between different types of cartography is the ease with which you can zoom-into selected sea areas or scroll the chart north, south, east or west, and then, having zoomed or scrolled, the speed or otherwise at which the new section of chart compiles itself on the screen. Some systems take ages to redraw the new section, while others are very slick and rapid. You get what you pay for in this respect, since faster microchips and more working memory are more expensive.

Operating procedures

After clear and accurate cartography, perhaps the most important features a chart plotter can offer are the quick and easy setting of waypoints, the easy combination of waypoints into routes and passage plans, and the facility for easily editing or changing waypoints, routes and passage plans under way as circumstances require. You should readily be able to move, add or delete waypoints in any order.

Remember that fewer keys on the keyboard may look like elegant design, but often means that data entry is more complicated, with double keystrokes and much use of 'soft' keys or the +/– key.

Size of display

As a rule, the larger display a chart plotter has, the more effective it can be as a practical navigational tool, so long as the cartography is up to standard. The most effective displays for larger boats are the customised 12-inch VGA colour monitors, although some of the very compact units suitable for sports boats manage to fit effective displays onto much smaller screens.

Look for the effective use of different shades of grey on LCD displays, which can improve clarity and make it easier to identify buoys and dangers. Also check how effective the display and keyboard lighting is for night use.

Whichever chart plotter you choose and install, be sure to have all the necessary paper charts on board as well. They still provide the definitive information and are clear, fully detailed, easy to read, extremely good value and do not fade away when your batteries go flat.

Paper chart plotters

For longer passage-making and more extensive cruising, many navigators favour one of the excellent paper chart plotters, such as the Yeoman or Geografix Vision. Both these systems use an intelligent chart table, or digitising mat, onto which a standard paper chart is clipped.

The Yeoman has been refined over many years now, but was originally designed simply as an electronic chart table. Once the system has been referenced to that particular chart, an electronic puck can automatically sense its position when moved across the chart table, displaying the latitude and longitude of the puck cross-wires on an integral LCD. Thus you can move the puck to any point on the chart and read off its position directly. Conversely, you can key in a required latitude and longitude and then move the puck across the chart until the four directional reference lights all go out, thereby homing onto the position directly.

The Yeoman can be interfaced to most GPS, Decca or Loran sets with an NMEA 0183 data output, so that a GPS/Decca/Loran position can be plotted directly on a traditional chart using the puck. Accurate waypoints, conversely, can be read directly off the chart and entered into a GPS, Decca or Loran sailplan.

The Geografix Vision system includes an integral GPS and the equivalent of the Yeoman puck – the 'graphic display unit' – has a more sophisticated transparent LCD screen. As you move the GDU across the chart table, the boat's present position and recent track appear on the LCD superimposed on the chart in the right place. Selected waypoints also appear as they come within the area of the LCD.

Both these systems appeal to navigators who like the best of both worlds – the benefits of electronic position-fixing and passage-planning coupled with precise, instantaneous reference to traditional charts. Video chart plotters still have to advance in quality to approach the seamanlike qualities of these highly practical paper chart plotters. It is certainly significant that the Yeoman system is now fitted to British offshore lifeboats.

PC chart plotters and Admiralty ARCS charts

Various software companies produce chart-plotting and passage-planning software for personal computers, laptops or notebooks, but there are not many 'marinised' computers or monitors on the market suitable for the rigours of life aboard a yacht or motor boat at sea.

The most recent and impressive developments in PC charts are the ARCS charts (Admiralty Raster Chart Service) now produced by the British Admiralty. These high-quality electronic charts cover the full range of Admiralty paper charts worldwide, and are the only official electronic equivalent of Admiralty paper charts.

Computer chart systems have been used aboard commercial ships as 'navigational aids' for some time, but the Dutch shipping authorities have recently approved an experiment in which three Dutch tankers will operate with ARCS charts as their primary navigation system, carrying selected paper charts as a back-up. This is a major step forward for electronic charting, bringing these systems into the official mainstream of navigation.

The complete range of Admiralty charts is contained on eleven CDs, and it won't be long before weekly updates can be sent directly by satellite communication to ships anywhere in the world. Yacht or motor boat owners would prob-

ably only buy corrections each season, supplied on an Update CD.

Admiralty ARCS charts are not the final answer to electronic charting since the more software-versatile Vector charts will certainly be developed to greater sophistication in the future. For the present, however, ARCS charts provide the official standard by which the quality and detail of other chart plotter displays should be judged. Even if you can't run to a full PC system on your boat, ARCS charts can be referred to at home or in the office, and would be useful for cruise- and passage-planning.

Each waypoint chart in this book gives recommendations, on the left-hand page, for the appropriate Admiralty paper and equivalent ARCS charts to use in the sea area concerned. The catalogue numbers for electronic ARCS charts are identical to the equivalent traditional paper charts.

USING THE WAYPOINT DIRECTORY

This *Directory* has been compiled for the convenience of anyone who uses electronic systems for navigating within the southern North Sea, including the Thames Estuary, whether under sail or power. As I have indicated, choosing and specifying waypoints, especially landfall waypoints, needs care and consideration. The waypoints presented in this *Directory* have certainly been set with safety in mind, but they have also been chosen to be practical in all kinds of passage-making circumstances, whether yachts are coasting in a local area between successive waypoints, or whether the navigator is arriving on a particular stretch of coast after a longish passage.

It is not enough to present waypoints in a long

list with rather vague labels. A navigator has to see where a waypoint lies in relation to a harbour entrance, in relation to coastal dangers, and in relation to other waypoints. Each double-page spread in this book therefore deals with a particular section of coast, with a chart on the right-hand page showing the location of all the chosen waypoints in that area, and the positions of these waypoints given in a table on the left-hand page.

Of course the latitude and longitude of every waypoint is given to two decimal places of a minute, ready for immediate entry into a Decca or GPS sailplan. However, it is also important for a navigator to know exactly where each waypoint can be located and plotted on an Admiralty chart. Therefore, the charted position of every waypoint is also included in the tables, precisely related by bearing and distance to some readily identifiable landmark or seamark. You therefore know exactly which waypoint you are dealing with and can readily judge whether it is safe and suitable for your purpose.

Also on the left-hand page of each spread, I give a brief résumé of the significant dangers for that area, together with the relevant Admiralty charts, so that the navigator has these summarised conveniently to hand.

DATUM OF CHARTED POSITIONS

The latitudes and longitudes of all the waypoints in this *Directory* have been taken from and cross-checked with the most recent large-scale charts of the areas concerned. However, remember that positions derived from GPS are based on the world datum known as WGS 84 (World Geodetic System 84) whereas most Admiralty charts of UK waters are based on datum OSGB 36 (Ordnance Survey of Great Britain 1936) and those covering French, Dutch and German waters are generally referred to as ED 50 (European Datum 1950). Admiralty charts always give the datum to which the chart refers, in the notes immediately under the title. Also given, in a note titled 'Satellite-Derived Positions', are the corrections required to convert between GPS datum and charted position datum.

In practice, this correction can often be ignored for normal offshore yacht navigation, but it becomes more critical if you are trying to use GPS for close-quarters navigation. Around the Dover Strait, for example, the distance between WGS 84 datum and charted position datum is of the order of 150 metres, a perfectly acceptable level of accuracy in clear visibility and fair weather when you have time to identify buoys by eye and steer towards them as required. However, the current 'Selective Availability' of full GPS accuracy means that, for most of the time in the southern North Sea, a position computed by a yacht GPS without differential enhancement may only be accurate to about +/– 300 metres. The difference between GPS and charted datum therefore becomes highly significant if you are navigating towards a narrow buoyed channel in poor visibility.

Selecting the correct datum

Each waypoint table in this book specifies the datum to which all latitudes and longitudes in that particular table are referred. Most GPS receivers allow you to specify position output in different chart datums, so automatic correction simply involves selecting the correct datum on your set. If your GPS does not have this facility, you can easily make a simple arithmetic correction using the datum differences and worked example shown in 'Satellite-Derived Positions' notes on the relevant Admiralty chart.

GENERAL CAUTION

All the waypoints in this *Directory* have been chosen and specified with great care, to be safe, suitable and convenient when used in conjunction with Decca or GPS, either for making a landfall on the relevant section of coast or for cruising between sections. However, it is never necessarily safe to approach any waypoint from all directions. Navigators must always refer to the appropriate large-scale Admiralty charts when planning landfalls or passages in any of the areas covered by this *Directory*.

On the question of published accuracy, it is also important to remember that, while the marked positions of all waypoints and the accuracy of their latitudes and longitudes have been exhaustively checked before publication, the small risk of errors can never be eliminated entirely. This *Waypoint Directory* is presented in good faith as a considerable aid and convenience to navigators, but neither the author nor the publishers can hold themselves responsible for any accident or misadventure allegedly attributable, wholly or partly, to the use of any waypoint contained herein, whether or not there was any author's or publisher's error in specifying or printing the waypoint positions or their latitudes and longitudes.

All navigators at sea are ultimately responsible for their own safety and must assure themselves of the accuracy and relevance of published information before acting upon it. In particular, any published waypoint from whatever source must always be used in a seamanlike manner, and its accuracy and suitability for a specific navigational purpose verified by reference to the largest-scale Admiralty charts of the area.

ACKNOWLEDGEMENTS

The waypoint charts in this book were devised by Jane Cumberlidge, drawn by Michelle Harris and with reference mainly to the latest published British Admiralty charts. Our thanks are due to the Hydrographic Office for their help in supplying reference material. In particular I would like to thank Roger Teale, Senior Product Manager (Charts) at the Hydrographic Office, Taunton, for his assistance.

Most of the waters covered by this book involve quite intricate pilotage through areas well-littered with sandbanks and offshore shoals. It is therefore important always to navigate with the latest corrected charts on board. For each of the waypoint areas in this book I have recommended the best large-scale British Admiralty or foreign charts to use in conjunction with the *North Sea Waypoint Directory*.

Passage notes
and landfall charts

WP No	Waypoint name and position	Latitude	Longitude
1–1	Gull Stream south, between S Brake and W Goodwin buoys	51°15.35'N	01°27.17'E
1–2	East Goodwin clearing, ½ M due E of E-card buoy	51°16.00'N	01°36.40'E
1–3	South Goodwin LANBY, actual position	51°07.95'N	01°28.59'E
1–4	Dover west entrance, midway between outer pierheads	51°06.69'N	01°19.82'E
1–5	South Falls S-card buoy, actual position	51°13.82'N	01°44.05'E
1–6	SW Sandettié W-card buoy, actual position	51°09.70'N	01°45.71'E
1–7	Varne LANBY, actual position	51°01.25'N	01°24.00'E
1–8	Colbart N-card buoy, actual position	50°57.44'N	01°23.40'E
1–9	Ruytingen SW green buoy, actual position	51°04.98'N	01°46.87'E
1–10	Dyck red buoy, actual position	51°02.96'N	01°57.87'E
1–11	Calais CA6 red approach buoy, actual position	50°58.30'N	01°45.70'E
1–12	Calais entrance, midway between outer pierheads	50°58.37'N	01°50.52'E

COASTAL DANGERS

Refer to Admiralty charts 323 and 1892

The Varne

The narrow Varne shoal lies 8 miles off Folke-stone and runs NE–SW for just over 6 miles, but the centre strip, with less than 5 metres depth, is only 2 miles long. The shoal is guarded at its NE end by the Varne LANBY and by buoys else-where. With minimum depths of 3–3.5 metres, the Varne produces dangerous seas in fresh and heavy weather, when you should stay outside the buoys altogether. In calm conditions with some rise of tide, most boats can cut over the shoal, especially at the deeper ends, although there are few circumstances when this can serve any advantage.

Le Colbart

A few miles south of the Varne, another long nar-row shoal stretches for almost 9 miles between Colbart N-cardinal buoy and the SW Colbart S-cardinal buoy. Several parts of this shoal have less than 3 metres depth and one small patch near the middle has only 1.6 metres. Le Colbart has no buoys along its east or west sides and should be given a wide berth in anything other than calm conditions.

Inshore banks NE of Cap Gris-Nez

A broad area of inshore banks extends NE from Cap Gris-Nez for nearly 7 miles. Parts of Banc à la Ligne almost dry at LAT, while La Barrière, further NE, has soundings down to 2 metres. Take care to stay outside these banks if coasting between Calais and Boulogne, or perhaps if creeping inshore to dodge the worst of a SW-going tide after having crossed the shipping lanes bound from Dover to Calais.

About 6 miles WSW of Calais entrance, various shoal patches lie up to 1½ miles seaward of Cap Blanc Nez – a prominent rise in the cliffs some

130 metres high. Le Rouge Riden bank has a minimum depth of 1.3 metres, and a shallow wreck, with only 0.2 metres over it, lies about ¼ mile inside CA3 (Les Quénocs) green buoy. When coasting between Cap Gris-Nez and Calais approaches, aim to stay outside CA1 and CA3 green buoys.

Ridens de la Rade

This narrow bank runs WSW–ENE off Calais, forming a partial natural breakwater up to 1 mile offshore. The shallowest depths are about 0.8 metres at LAT, ½ a mile seaward of Calais break-waters, with a wider shoal area further east over 1 mile off the hoverport.

In reasonable weather, with sufficient rise of tide, it is safe for boats to cut across Ridens de la Rade, especially when leaving Calais near high water. However, the bank is dangerous in fresh to strong onshore winds, or in fresh north-easterlies or south-westerlies when the tide is weather-going.

Goodwin Sands

The Goodwins are probably the most notorious dangers in the English Channel. These extensive drying sands lie up to 7 miles offshore between Ramsgate and South Foreland. The Goodwins should be avoided in all circumstances, and are well marked on their east, north and south sides.

The well-used channel between the Goodwins and the Kent coast is partly sheltered by the banks in onshore winds. The wide, southern entrance to this channel lies between South Foreland and the South Goodwin LANBY. Working north, you need to pick up Goodwin Fork S-cardinal buoy and then the narrow gate between South Brake red buoy and West Goodwin green buoy. From this gate, you can make good north true for 4 miles, passing safely east of Brake Sand, until you join the Ramsgate entrance channel.

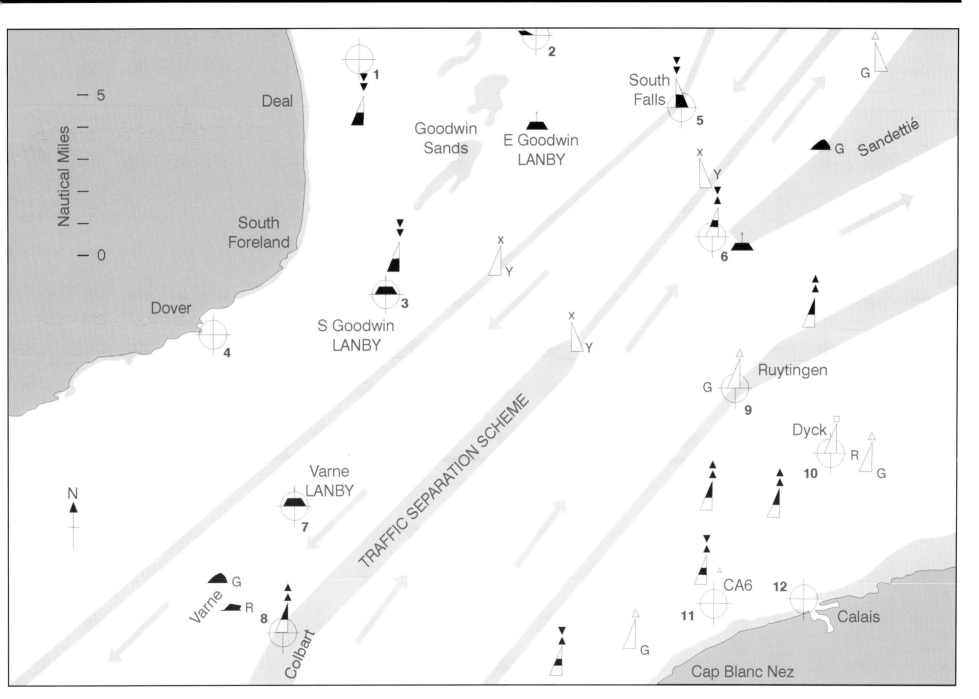

Deal

Goodwin
Sands

E Goodwin
LANBY

South
Falls

Sandettié

South
Foreland

Dover

S Goodwin
LANBY

Ruytingen

Dyck

Varne
LANBY

TRAFFIC SEPARATION SCHEME

N

Varne

CA6

Calais

Colbart

Cap Blanc Nez

Nautical Miles

— 5

— 0

1

2

3

4

5

6

7

8

9

10

11

12

G

X
Y

X
Y

X
Y

G

R

G

R

G

G

15

WP No	Waypoint name and position	Latitude	Longitude
1–1	Gull Stream south, between S Brake and W Goodwin buoys	51°15.35'N	01°27.17'E
1–2	East Goodwin clearing, ½ M due E of E-card buoy	51°16.00'N	01°36.40'E
1–3	South Goodwin LANBY, actual position	51°07.95'N	01°28.59'E
1–4	Dover west entrance, midway between outer pierheads	51°06.69'N	01°19.82'E
1–5	South Falls S-card buoy, actual position	51°13.82'N	01°44.05'E
1–6	SW Sandettié W-card buoy, actual position	51°09.70'N	01°45.71'E
1–7	Varne LANBY, actual position	51°01.25'N	01°24.00'E
1–8	Colbart N-card buoy, actual position	50°57.44'N	01°23.40'E
1–9	Ruytingen SW green buoy, actual position	51°04.98'N	01°46.87'E
1–10	Dyck red buoy, actual position	51°02.96'N	01°57.87'E
1–11	Calais CA6 red approach buoy, actual position	50°58.30'N	01°45.70'E
1–12	Calais entrance, midway between outer pierheads	50°58.37'N	01°50.52'E

Datum OSGB 36 The waypoint latitudes and longitudes in this table refer to Ordnance Survey of Great Britain (1936) Datum

Gull Stream is a buoyed channel running SW–NE for just over 5 miles between the West Goodwin buoy and the north entrance between Gull E-cardinal buoy and Goodwin Knoll green buoy.

Boats heading for Calais from Ramsgate can either come inside the Goodwins and thence via the South Goodwin LANBY, or outside via the East Goodwin buoy and LANBY. In any event, the TSS must be crossed at right-angles. Since Ramsgate has snug waiting pontoons in the Royal Harbour, you can leave at any convenient time.

Brake Sand

The Brake is a nasty area of banks stretching from ½ a mile to nearly 4 miles south of Ramsgate entrance. The shallowest drying area is about 2 miles south of Ramsgate. Making between Quern N-cardinal buoy and the gateway formed by South Brake red buoy and West Goodwin green, boats should leave the Brake safely to the west.

Alternatively, pass inside Brake Sand via the Ramsgate Channel, using B1 and B2 green conical buoys to clear the west edge of the shoals.

Traffic Separation Scheme

The Dover Strait is one of the busiest seaways in the world. All movements are monitored closely by the Channel Navigation Information Service run by Dover Coastguard and the French 'CROSSMA' station at Cap Gris-Nez.

Passage planning usually centres around the legal requirement to cross the Traffic Separation Scheme at right-angles and choosing the best point of entry to the TSS for the tidal stream and sea conditions. Remember that it is course steered that counts when crossing the lanes, not your track. You should be *heading* at right-angles to the main traffic flow.

Clear of the lanes, you can head for the Calais approach channel, which runs close along the French coast inside the long Ridens de la Rade

bank. Take great care to avoid cross-Channel ferries in this approach corridor, and when entering or leaving Calais or Dover harbours.

Dover Strait tides

The Dover Strait tides, squeezed between South Foreland and Cap Gris-Nez, are stronger than most strangers anticipate. Spring rates exceed 3½ knots in the middle of the narrows and off Cap Gris-Nez, and sometimes touch 4 knots off Dover Harbour. The wind is often a notch fresher in the Strait than in the more open water on either side, steepening the sea when the tide is weather-going. In the narrows, the strongest part of the NE-going stream occurs an hour after high water at Dover. The strongest part of the SW-going stream occurs about 4 hours before HW Dover.

Slack water in the narrows occurs at around 0420 hours after HW Dover and 0140 hours before HW Dover. The slack water stand between the last of the SW-going stream and the first of the NE-going is barely ½ hour, while the changeover between the NE-going stream and the SW-going is more gradual.

Note that conditions just off Dover Harbour can be very rough locally, especially off the west entrance at springs in strong south-westerlies. There are also some unusual local eddies just off and within Dover Harbour, caused by the breakwaters jutting well out into the Channel tide.

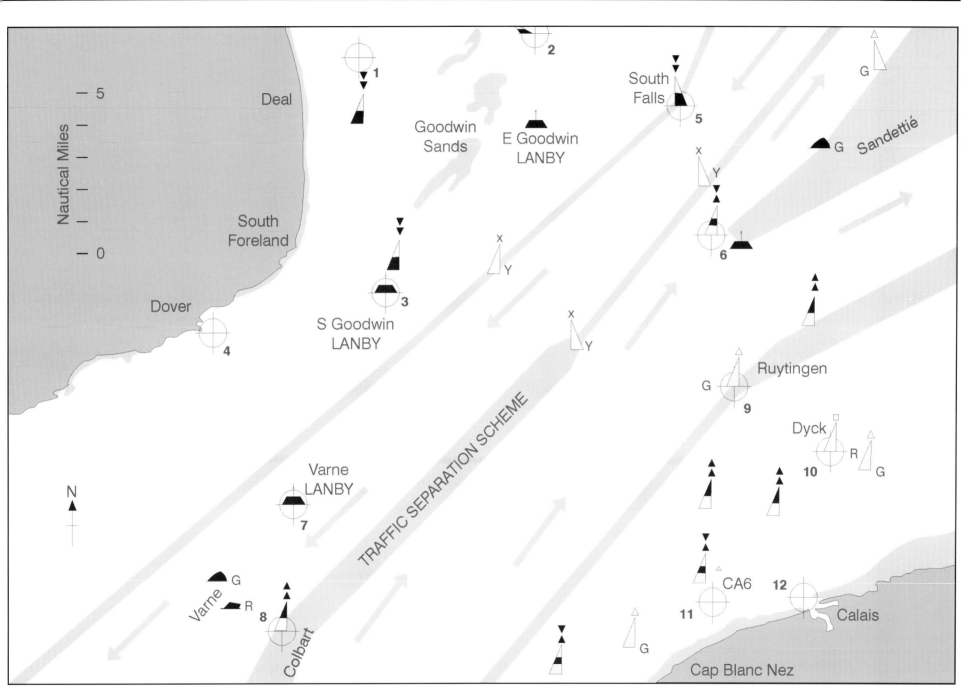

Deal

Goodwin
Sands

E Goodwin
LANBY

South
Falls

Sandettié

South
Foreland

S Goodwin
LANBY

Dover

Ruytingen

Dyck

Varne
LANBY

TRAFFIC SEPARATION SCHEME

Nautical Miles

5

0

N

Varne

Colbart

CA6

Calais

Cap Blanc Nez

1
2
3
4
5
6
7
8
9
10
11
12

G
G
X
Y
X
Y
X
Y
G
G
R
G

WP No	Waypoint name and position	Latitude	Longitude
2–1	Dover west approach, 1½ ca SE of Admiralty pierhead	51°06.45'N	01°19.94'E
2–2	Dover east approach, 1 ca 100°T from E Arm pierhead	51°07.25'N	01°20.87'E
2–3	South Goodwin LANBY, actual position	51°07.95'N	01°28.59'E
2–4	East Goodwin clearing, ½ M due E of E-card buoy	51°16.00'N	01°36.40'E
2–5	Gull Stream south, between S Brake and W Goodwin buoys	51°15.35'N	01°27.17'E
2–6	Gull Stream mid, between Brake red buoy and NW Goodwin	51°16.83'N	01°28.55'E
2–7	Goodwin Knoll green conical buoy, actual position	51°19.55'N	01°32.30'E
2–8	Ramsgate Quern, 2 ca due E of N-card buoy	51°19.37'N	01°26.52'E
2–9	Ramsgate entrance, midway between outer pierheads	51°19.50'N	01°25.51'E
2–10	North Foreland, 1 M due E of lighthouse	51°22.46'N	01°28.40'E
2–11	Elbow N-card buoy, actual position	51°23.20'N	01°31.68'E

Datum OSGB 36 The waypoint latitudes and longitudes in this table refer to Ordnance Survey of Great Britain (1936) Datum

COASTAL DANGERS
Refer to Admiralty charts 323 and 1828

Goodwin Sands
The Goodwins are probably the most notorious dangers in the English Channel. These extensive drying sands lie up to 7 miles offshore between Ramsgate and South Foreland. The Goodwins should be avoided in all circumstances, and are well marked on their east, north and south sides.

The well-used channel between the Goodwins and the Kent coast is partly sheltered by the banks in onshore winds. The wide, southern entrance to this channel lies between South Foreland and the South Goodwin LANBY. Working north, you need to pick up Goodwin Fork S-cardinal buoy and then the narrow gate between South Brake red buoy and West Goodwin green buoy. From this gate, you can make good north true for 4 miles, passing safely east of Brake Sand, until you join the Ramsgate entrance channel.

Gull Stream is a buoyed channel running SW–NE for just over 5 miles between the West Goodwin buoy and the north entrance between Gull E-cardinal buoy and Goodwin Knoll green buoy.

Brake Sand
The Brake is a nasty area of banks stretching from ½ mile to nearly 4 miles south of Ramsgate entrance. The shallowest drying area is about 2 miles south of Ramsgate. Making between Quern N-cardinal buoy and the gateway formed by South Brake red buoy and West Goodwin green, boats should leave the Brake safely to the west. Alternatively, pass inside Brake Sand via the Ramsgate Channel, using B1 and B2 green conical buoys to clear the west edge of the shoals.

Traffic Separation Scheme
The Dover Strait is one of the busiest seaways in the world. All movements are monitored closely by the Channel Navigation Information Service run by Dover Coastguard and the French 'CROSSMA' station at Cap Gris-Nez. It is a legal requirement to cross the Traffic Separation Scheme at right-angles – remember that it is course steered that counts when crossing the lanes, not your track. You should be *heading* at right-angles to the main traffic flow.

Fast-moving ferries
Watch out for fast-moving cross-Channel ferries in this area, especially near the entrances to Dover and Ramsgate. Yachts should avoid navigating anywhere near the Dover Strait in poor visibility.

Strong tides
The Dover Strait tides are stronger than most strangers anticipate. Spring rates can reach 4 knots off Dover Harbour. Winds are often a notch fresher in the Strait, steepening the sea when the tide is weather-going. Conditions just off Dover Harbour can be very rough locally, especially off the west entrance at springs in strong south-west-erlies. There are also some unusual local eddies just off and within Dover Harbour, caused by the breakwaters jutting well out into the Channel stream.

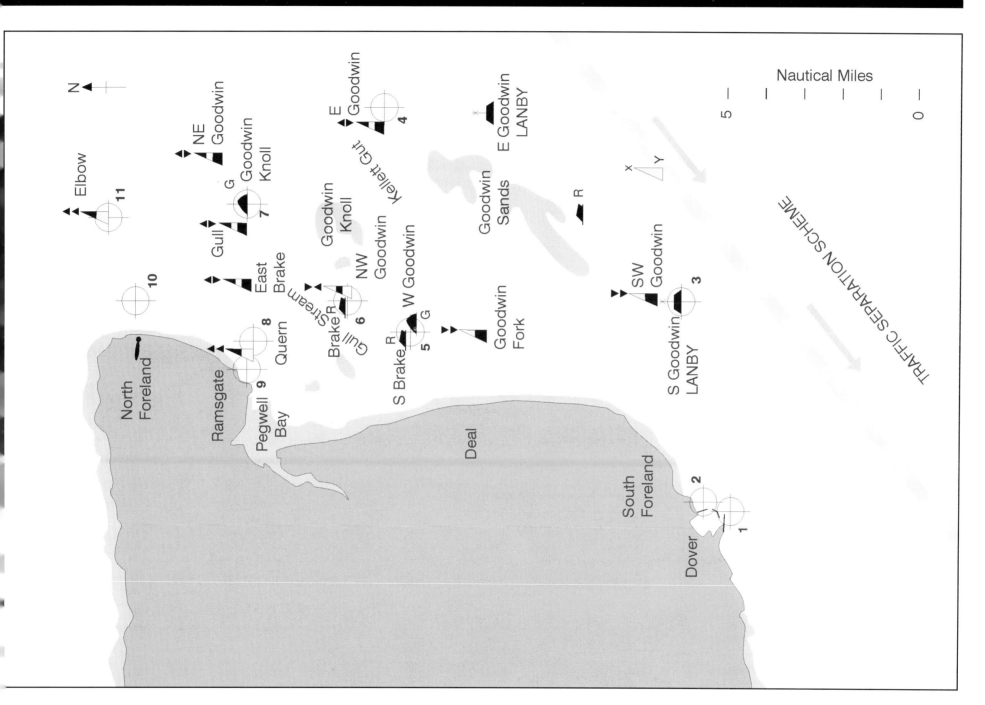

Nautical Miles

TRAFFIC SEPARATION SCHEME

N

Elbow
11
NE Goodwin
Goodwin Knoll
7
G
Gull
East Brake
10
Brake
Gull Stream
R
R
8
Quern
9
Ramsgate
Pegwell Bay
North Foreland
NW Goodwin
Goodwin Knoll
S Brake
R
W Goodwin
G
5
6
E Goodwin
4
Kellett Gut
Goodwin Sands
E Goodwin LANBY
R
x
Y
Goodwin Fork
SW Goodwin
x
3
S Goodwin LANBY
Deal
South Foreland
Dover
2
1

5

0

WP No	Waypoint name and position	Latitude	Longitude
3–1	North Foreland, 1 M due E of lighthouse	51°22.46'N	01°28.40'E
3–2	Elbow N-card buoy, actual position	51°23.20'N	01°31.68'E
3–3	White Ness clearing, ¾ M 060°T from White Ness	51°23.55'N	01°27.58'E
3–4	Longnose, 100 m due N of Longnose red buoy	51°24.18'N	01°26.18'E
3–5	E Margate red buoy, actual position	51°27.00'N	01°26.50'E
3–6	E Margate inner, ½ M 250°T from East Margate red buoy	51°26.83'N	01°25.74'E
3–7	Tongue Sand Tower E, ½ M due E of Tongue Sand Tower	51°29.54'N	01°22.91'E
3–8	Tongue Sand Tower W, ¾ M due W of Tongue Sand Tower	51°29.54'N	01°20.90'E
3–9	East Tongue red buoy, actual position	51°28.73'N	01°18.72'E
3–10	South Shingles, 2 ca due S of S-card buoy	51°28.99'N	01°16.12'E
3–11	North Tongue, 2 ca due N of North Tongue red buoy	51°28.99'N	01°13.20'E
3–12	Queens Channel east, 1½ M south of Tongue Sand Tower	51°28.04'N	01°22.10'E
3–13	Queens Channel middle, 0.9 M due S of E Tongue red buoy	51°27.83'N	01°18.72'E
3–14	Queens Channel west, 1.8 M due S of N Tongue red buoy	51°26.99'N	01°13.20'E
3–15	Margate offing, 1½ M due E of SE Margate E-card buoy	51°24.10'N	01°22.88'E
3–16	SE Margate, 1½ ca due S of E-card buoy	51°23.95'N	01°20.50'E
3–17	Gore Channel, 1½ ca due S of South Margate green buoy	51°23.73'N	01°16.75'E
3–18	Margate Hook, ¼ M due S of S-card beacon	51°23.89'N	01°14.40'E
3–19	Hook Spit narrows, 100 m due S of Hook Spit green buoy	51°23.98'N	01°12.69'E
3–20	NE Spit E-card buoy, actual position	51°27.90'N	01°30.00'E

Datum OSGB 36 The waypoint latitudes and longitudes in this table refer to Ordnance Survey of Great Britain (1936) Datum

COASTAL DANGERS
Refer to Admiralty charts 1605, 1607 and 1828

Margate Sand
This is the nearest of the Thames Estuary banks to North Foreland, lying 3 miles off the North Kent coast opposite Margate. Parts of Margate Sand dry to over 2½ metres and strangers should not attempt to cut across them under any conditions. The east end of Margate Sand is guarded at some distance by the East Margate red buoy, which you can pass up to 1 mile inside in quiet conditions.

Boats skirting Margate Sand either pass to the east and north, via the Queens Channel, or keep well to the south, following the North Kent coast through the South Channel, the Gore and the Horse Channel.

Margate Hook
The narrow sandbank known as Margate Hook lies a mile off the North Kent coast south-west of Margate Sand. The south edge of Margate Hook is marked (from east to west) by the SE Margate E-cardinal buoy, S Margate green buoy, Margate Hook S-cardinal beacon and Hook Spit green buoy. The South Channel and Gore Channel lead close south of these buoys and at the west end of Margate Hook you cut between Hook Spit green buoy and East Last red buoy into the Horse Channel and the shallow waters of the Kentish Flats.

Tongue Sand
Tongue Sand lies on the north side of Queens Channel and only small patches of it dry. The east tip is marked by East Tongue red buoy and the north edge by North Tongue red buoy. When using the Queens Channel be sure to leave Tongue Sand well clear to the north, since the bank is unmarked on its south side.

Tongue Sand Tower, a curious relic of the last war, actually lies a good 3 miles to the east of Tongue Sand, and 2 miles just north of east from the East Tongue red buoy.

Shingles Bank
The Shingles Bank is an extensive shoal area right in the middle of the southern part of the Thames Estuary. Patches of the Shingles dry to between ½ and 1 metre, but most parts have at least ½ metre depth at LAT. In quiet weather with sufficient rise of tide, boats that know the area can cut across the deepest parts of the Shingles.

The Princes Channel runs east–west about 1 mile south of the Shingles. Approaching the Princes Channel from seaward, you would normally leave Tongue Sand Tower and its buoys to the north, then leave East Tongue red buoy to port, South Shingles S-cardinal bell buoy to starboard and then North Tongue red buoy to port.

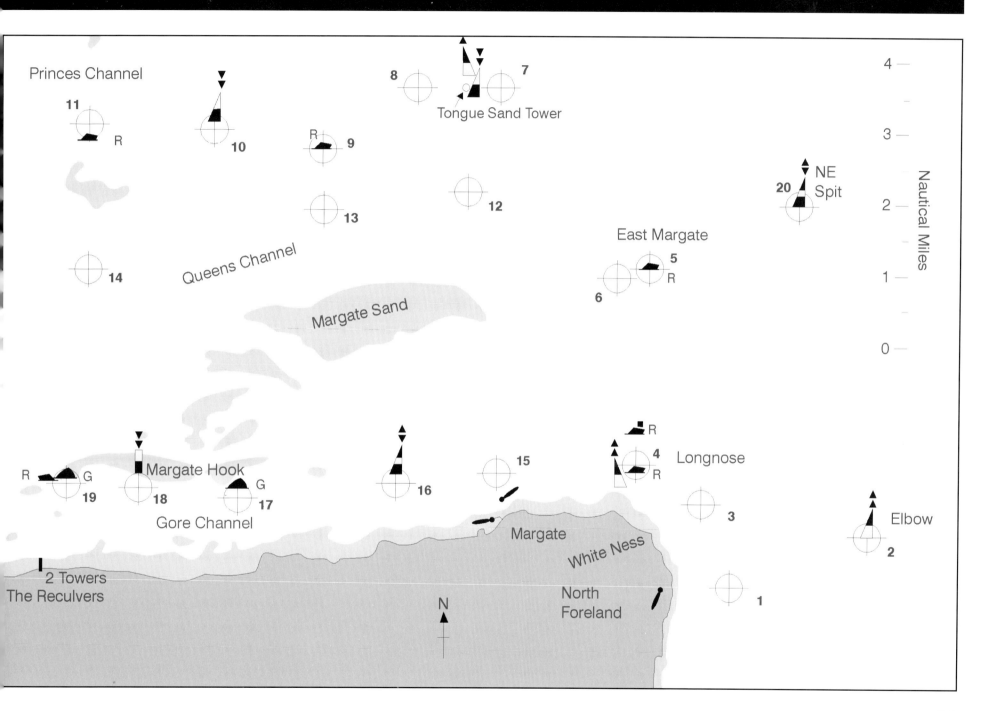

Princes Channel

11

R

10

R 9

8 7

Tongue Sand Tower

NE
20 Spit

East Margate

12

5
R
6

14

Queens Channel

Margate Sand

4 — Nautical Miles

3 —

2 —

1 —

0 —

R

15

R

4
R

Longnose

R G

Margate Hook

G

3

Elbow

19 18 17

16

2

Gore Channel

Margate

White Ness

2 Towers

The Reculvers

N

North
Foreland

1

21

Whitstable Bay and East approaches to the Swale

WP No	Waypoint name and position	Latitude	Longitude
4–1	Hook Spit narrows, 100 m due S of Hook Spit green buoy	51°23.98'N	01°12.69'E
4–2	Copperas Channel, 1 M 330°T from the Reculvers Tower	51°23.61'N	01°11.29'E
4–3	Horse Channel, 2.3 M 325°T from the Reculvers Tower	51°24.64'N	01°09.97'E
4–4	Herne Bay offing, 2¼ M due N of Herne Bay clock tower	51°24.62'N	01°07.68'E
4–5	Studhill Bay offing, 3 M 315°T from Herne Bay clock tower	51°24.49'N	01°04.31'E
4–6	Whitstable Street, 1½ ca due N of N-card buoy	51°23.98'N	01°01.70'E
4–7	East Swale approach, 1 ca SE of Columbine Spit green buoy	51°23.76'N	01°00.25'E
4–8	East Swale outer, midway Ham Gat and Pollard Spit buoys	51°23.00'N	00°58.54'E
4–9	East Swale inner, 100 m SE from Sand End green buoy	51°21.36'N	00°56.07'E
4–10	Queens Channel west, 1.8 M due S of N Tongue red buoy	51°26.99'N	01°13.20'E
4–11	Kentish Flats, 1¼ M SW of Pan Sand S-card buoy	51°27.08'N	01°08.63'E
4–12	Spaniard, ¼ M due S of Spaniard E-card buoy	51°25.95'N	01°04.10'E
4–13	Four Fathoms E, 1½ M 260°T from Spaniard E-card buoy	51°25.96'N	01°01.74'E
4–14	Four Fathoms middle, 1 M 195°T from Middle Sand RW beacon	51°25.98'N	00°59.71'E
4–15	Four Fathoms W, 1 ca due S of the Spile green buoy	51°26.30'N	00°55.80'E
4–16	East Cant, 3 ca due S of 'F' beacon	51°27.14'N	00°52.60'E
4–17	Medway fairway buoy, actual position	51°28.80'N	00°52.92'E
4–18	West Oaze, 1 ca due S of W-card buoy	51°28.94'N	00°55.52'E
4–19	SW Oaze, 1 ca due S of S-card buoy	51°28.93'N	00°57.03'E
4–20	Red Sand Towers, 6 ca due N of the most northerly tower	51°29.23'N	00°59.52'E
4–21	S Oaze, ¼ M due S of green buoy	51°29.75'N	01°00.80'E
4–22	East Redsand, actual position of red buoy	51°29.38'N	01°04.14'E
4–23	Shivering Sands south, 3 ca due S of the most southerly tower	51°29.55'N	01°04.91'E
4–24	South Girdler west, 1¼ M 205°T from Girdler red buoy	51°28.02'N	01°05.67'E
4–25	Princes Channel west, midway West Girdler and Girdler buoys	51°29.39'N	01°06.70'E
4–26	SE Girdler, 3 ca due S of green buoy	51°29.17'N	01°10.00'E
4–27	North Tongue, 2 ca due N of North Tongue red buoy	51°28.99'N	01°13.20'E
4–28	Sea Reach yellow buoy, actual position	51°29.42'N	00°52.67'E

Datum OSGB 36 The waypoint latitudes and longitudes in this table refer to Ordnance Survey of Great Britain (1936) Datum

COASTAL DANGERS
Refer to Admiralty charts 1607 and 2571

Margate Hook
This narrow sandbank lies 1 mile off the North Kent coast south-west of Margate Sand. The south edge of Margate Hook is marked (from east to west) by the SE Margate E-cardinal buoy, S Margate green buoy, Margate Hook S-cardinal beacon and Hook Spit green buoy. The South and Gore Channels lead south of these buoys and at the west end of Margate Hook you cut between Hook Spit green and East Last red buoys into Horse Channel and the shallow Kentish Flats.

Tongue Sand
Tongue Sand lies on the north side of Queens Channel and only small patches dry. The east tip is marked by East Tongue red buoy and the north edge by North Tongue red buoy. When using the Queens Channel be sure to leave Tongue Sand well clear to the north, since the bank is unmarked on its south side.

Tongue Sand Tower, a curious relic of the last war, actually lies a good 3 miles to the east of Tongue Sand, and 2 miles just north of east from the East Tongue red buoy.

Studhill and Clite Hole Bank
A wide area of shallow water extends for nearly 2 miles off the North Kent coast between Herne Bay and Whitstable. Studhill and Clite Hole Bank have soundings down to about 1 metre at LAT and the bottom in these areas is strewn with cement boulders. This area should be avoided altogether below half-tide and is unsuitable for anchoring at any state of tide (see note on oyster beds below).

Whitstable Street
A long narrow sandspit, known as Whitstable Street, extends just west of north from the Whitstable shore for about 1 mile. The spit dries to 1 metre in parts and would normally only constitute a potential hazard for shoal draught boats making for the small drying harbour at Whitstable.

Whitstable Oyster Beds
Oyster beds are worked in the entrance to the East Swale and in the whole area of shallow coastal water east of Whitstable as far as Reculver Boats must avoid grounding or anchoring in this area and their owners are liable to pay compensation if any of the oyster beds are damaged.

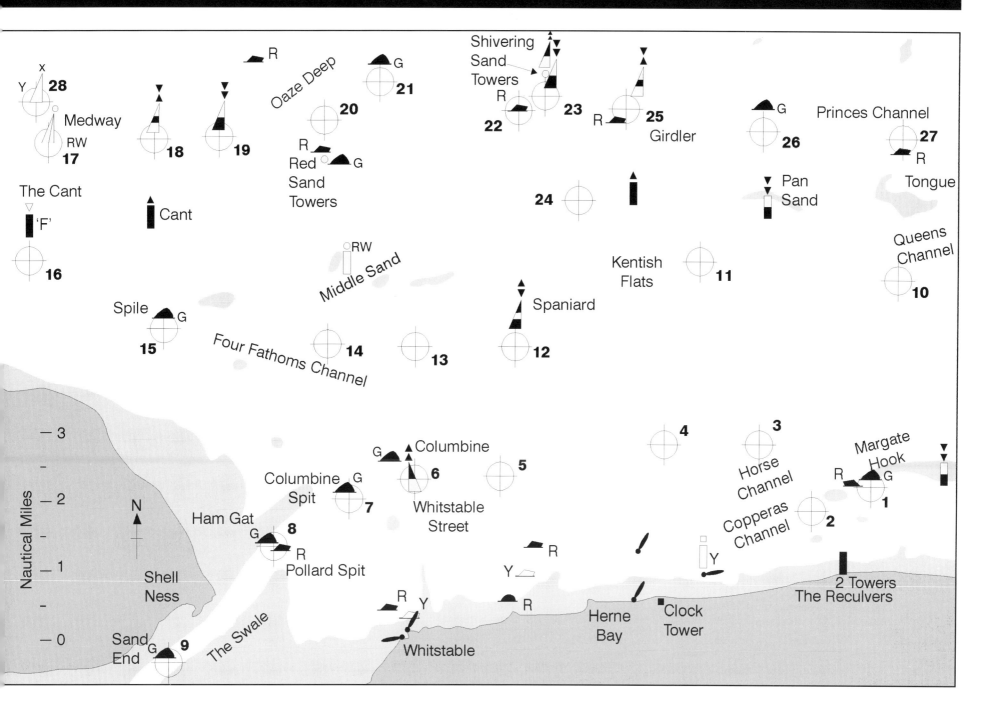

Y x **28**

Medway

RW

17

The Cant

▽
'F'

16

Cant

▼
18

▼
19

R

Oaze Deep

20

R
Red
Sand
Towers

G

G
21

RW
Middle Sand

Spile G
15

Four Fathoms Channel

14

13

Spaniard
12

Kentish
Flats
11

24

Shivering
Sand
Towers
R

22

23

R

R
25
Girdler

Pan
Sand

G
26

Princes Channel

G

27
R

Tongue

Queens
Channel

10

Columbine
G
6

Columbine
Spit
G
7

Whitstable
Street

5

4

3

Horse
Channel

Copperas
Channel

2

Margate
Hook
R
G
1

▼
▼

Nautical Miles

— 3

— 2

N

Ham Gat
G
8
R
Pollard Spit

Shell
Ness

— 1

R

Y

R

Y

2 Towers
The Reculvers

Herne
Bay

Clock
Tower

— 0

Sand
End
G
9

The Swale

Whitstable

WP No	Waypoint name and position	Latitude	Longitude
5–1	North Foreland, 1 M due E of lighthouse	51°22.46'N	01°28.40'E
5–2	White Ness clearing, ¾ M 060°T from White Ness	51°23.55'N	01°27.58'E
5–3	Longnose, 100 m due N of Longnose red buoy	51°24.18'N	01°26.18'E
5–4	Margate offing, 1½ M due E of SE Margate E-card buoy	51°24.10'N	01°22.88'E
5–5	SE Margate, 1½ ca due S of E-card buoy	51°23.95'N	01°20.50'E
5–6	Gore Channel, 1½ ca due S of South Margate green buoy	51°23.73'N	01°16.75'E
5–7	E Margate red buoy, actual position	51°27.00'N	01°26.50'E
5–8	E Margate inner, ½ M 250°T from East Margate red buoy	51°26.83'N	01°25.74'E
5–9	Queens Channel east, 1½ M S of Tongue Sand Tower	51°28.04'N	01°22.10'E
5–10	Queens Channel middle, 0.9 M due S of E Tongue red buoy	51°27.83'N	01°18.72'E
5–11	East Tongue red buoy, actual position	51°28.73'N	01°18.72'E
5–12	South Shingles, 2 ca due S of S-card buoy	51°28.99'N	01°16.12'E
5–13	Tongue Sand Tower E, ½ M due E of Tongue Sand Tower	51°29.54'N	01°22.91'E
5–14	Tongue Sand Tower W, ¾ M due W of Tongue Sand Tower	51°29.54'N	01°20.90'E
5–15	Outer Tongue fairway buoy, actual position	51°30.70'N	01°26.50'E
5–16	S Edinburgh SE, 2 M 345°T from S Shingles S-card buoy	51°31.14'N	01°15.28'E
5–17	Edinburgh SE, between Edinburgh red and No 1 S-card buoys	51°31.48'N	01°21.72'E
5–18	Edinburgh SE inner, between Patch and SE Long Sand buoys	51°32.24'N	01°21.07'E
5–19	Edinburgh E middle, between Edinburgh No 2 and No 3 buoys	51°32.93'N	01°20.37'E
5–20	Edinburgh middle, between Edinburgh No 4 and No 5 buoys	51°33.32'N	01°19.41'E
5–21	Edinburgh W middle, between Edinburgh No 6 and No 7 buoys	51°33.47'N	01°18.21'E
5–22	Edinburgh W, between Edinburgh No 8 and No 9 buoys	51°33.32'N	01°16.68'E
5–23	Shingles Patch, 3 ca N of N-card buoy	51°33.28'N	01°15.48'E
5–24	Long Sand NW, 1½ M 245°T from NW Long Sand beacon	51°34.09'N	01°15.96'E

Datum OSGB 36 The waypoint latitudes and longitudes in this table refer to Ordnance Survey of Great Britain (1936) Datum

COASTAL DANGERS

Refer to Admiralty charts 1605 and 1607

Margate Sand

This is the nearest of the Thames Estuary banks to North Foreland, lying 3 miles off the North Kent coast opposite Margate. Parts of Margate Sand dry to more than 2½ metres and strangers should not try to cut across them under any conditions. The east end of Margate Sand is guarded at some distance by the East Margate red buoy, which you can pass up to 1 mile inside in quiet conditions.

Boats skirting Margate Sand either pass to the east and north, via the Queens Channel, or keep well to the south, following the North Kent coast through the South Channel, the Gore and Horse Channel.

Tongue Sand

Tongue Sand lies on the north side of Queens Channel and only small patches dry. The east tip is marked by East Tongue red buoy and the north edge by North Tongue red buoy. When using the Queens Channel be sure to leave Tongue Sand well clear to the north, since the bank is unmarked on its south side.

Tongue Sand Tower, a curious relic of the last war, actually lies a good 3 miles east of Tongue Sand, and 2 miles seaward of East Tongue red buoy. Approaching Princes Channel from seaward, you would normally leave Tongue Sand Tower and its buoys to the north, East Tongue red buoy to the south, then leave South Shingles S-cardinal bell buoy to the north.

Long Sand

Long Sand is part of a vast finger of banks and shoals stretching north-east from the seaward edge of North Edinburgh Channel for a good 18 miles out to Long Sand Head. Vessels passing through the well-buoyed North Edinburgh Channel leave the inner part of Long Sand to the north-east and Shingles Patch to the south-west. Fisherman's Gat, a deep, unmarked fairway about 1 mile wide, cuts across the bottom of the 'finger' just NE of the inner part of Long Sand; this channel should be used with care.

Shingles Patch

This wide shoal area lies on the south-west side of North Edinburgh Channel and much of it has less than 1 metre depth at LAT. Shingles Patch is marked on its north side by the North Shingles red buoy, Shingles Patch N-cardinal buoy, and the red buoys of the North Edinburgh Channel. The south-east edge of Shingles Patch is unmarked.

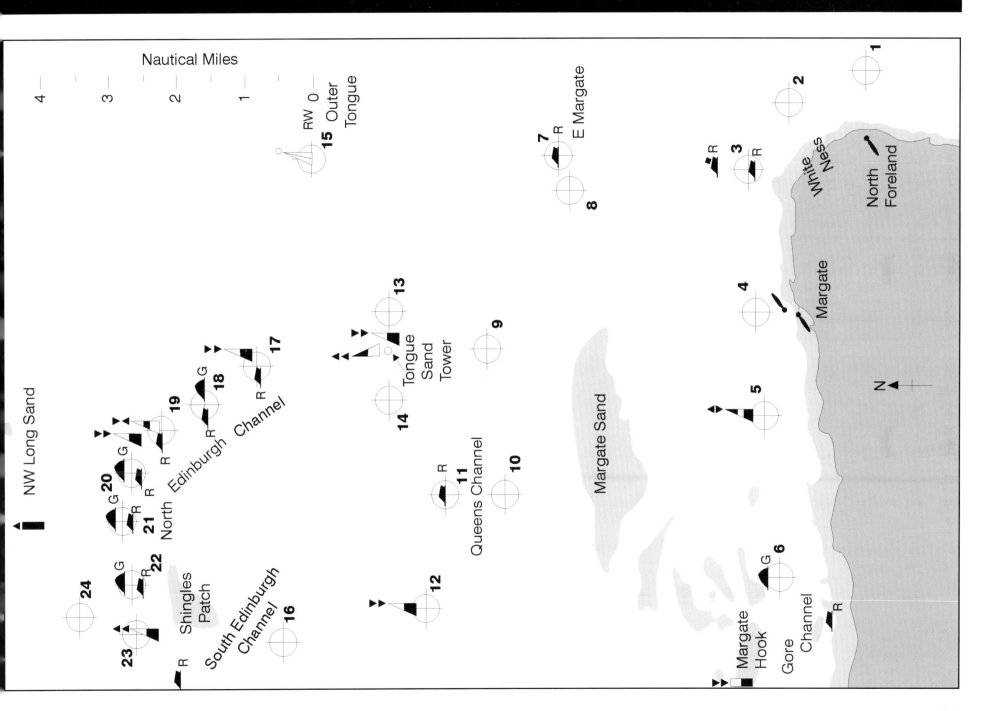

Nautical Miles

NW Long Sand

RW 0
15 Outer Tongue

E Margate
R
7

R
8

R
3
R

White Ness

North Foreland

Margate

N

4

13

17
G
R
18

19
R
G
20
R
G
21
R

North Edinburgh Channel

Tongue Sand Tower

14

5

9

Queens Channel
R
11

10

Margate Sand

22
G
R

24

23
R

Shingles Patch

South Edinburgh Channel

16

12

6
G

Margate Hook

Gore Channel
R

WP No	Waypoint name and position	Latitude	Longitude
6–1	South Shingles, 2 ca due S of S-card buoy	51°28.99'N	01°16.12'E
6–2	North Tongue, 2 ca due N of N Tongue red buoy	51°28.99'N	01°13.20'E
6–3	SE Girdler, 3 ca due S of green buoy	51°29.17'N	01°10.00'E
6–4	Princes Channel west, midway West Girdler and Girdler buoys	51°29.39'N	01°06.70'E
6–5	South Girdler west, 1¼ M 205°T from Girdler red buoy	51°28.02'N	01°05.67'E
6–6	Shivering Sands south, 3 ca due S of the most southerly tower	51°29.55'N	01°04.91'E
6–7	East Redsand, actual position of red buoy	51°29.38'N	01°04.14'E
6–8	S Oaze, ¼ M due S of green buoy	51°29.75'N	01°00.80'E
6–9	Red Sand Towers, 6 ca due N of the most northerly tower	51°29.23'N	00°59.52'E
6–10	SW Oaze, 1 ca due S of S-card buoy	51°28.93'N	00°57.03'E
6–11	West Oaze, 1 ca due S of W-card buoy	51°28.94'N	00°55.50'E
6–12	Edinburgh W, between Edinburgh No 8 and No 9 buoys	51°33.32'N	01°16.68'E
6–13	Shingles Patch, 3 ca N of N-card buoy	51°33.28'N	01°15.48'E
6–14	Long Sand NW, 1½ M 245°T from NW Long Sand beacon	51°34.09'N	01°15.96'E
6–15	North Shingles, 1½ ca due N of North Shingles red buoy	51°32.82'N	01°14.34'E
6–16	Mid Shingles, 4 ca due N of Mid Shingles red buoy	51°32.33'N	01°12.08'E
6–17	NW Shingles, 4 ca due N of NW Shingles N-card buoy	51°31.64'N	01°09.82'E
6–18	SE Knob, 1 ca due S of SE Knob green buoy	51°30.77'N	01°06.53'E
6–19	Shivering Sands north, 4 ca due N of the most northerly tower	51°30.31'N	01°04.90'E
6–20	Knob fairway buoy, actual position	51°30.68'N	01°04.39'E
6–21	Black Deep SW, midway No 9 S-card and No 10 red buoys	51°34.91'N	01°15.45'E

COASTAL DANGERS

Refer to Admiralty charts 1183, 1605, 1607 and 1975

Tongue Sand

Tongue Sand lies on the north side of Queens Channel and only small patches dry. The east tip is marked by East Tongue red buoy and the north edge by North Tongue red buoy. Be sure to leave Tongue Sand well clear to the south as you come through Princes Channel. The edge of the shallow water is normally obvious from tidal eddies and overfalls.

Shingles Bank

The Shingles Bank is an extensive shoal area right in the middle of the southern part of the Thames Estuary. Patches of the Shingles dry to between ½ and 1 metre, but most parts have at least ½ metre depth at LAT. In quiet weather with sufficient rise of tide, yachts that know the area can cut across the deepest parts of the Shingles.

The Princes Channel runs east–west about 1 mile south of the Shingles. Approaching the Princes Channel from seaward, you would normally leave Tongue Sand Tower and its buoys to the north, then leave East Tongue red buoy to port, South Shingles S-cardinal bell buoy to starboard and North Tongue red buoy to port.

Shingles Patch

This wide shoal area lies on the south-west side of North Edinburgh Channel and much of it has less than ½ metre depth at LAT. Shingles Patch is marked on its north side by the North Shingles red buoy, Shingles Patch N-cardinal buoy and the red buoys of the North Edinburgh Channel. However, the south-east edge of Shingles Patch is unmarked.

SW Sunk

Sunk Sand is a long narrow shoal separating Black Deep from the East Swin. SW Sunk is the south-west extremity of the Sunk Sand, more or less opposite Black Deep No 7 green buoy. The largest drying part of the SW Sunk is just under 1 mile long and dries to about ½ metre. Smaller drying patches, just above datum, string out to the south-west to link up with the Knock John Sand. A narrow swatchway cuts through this shoal area just south of the SW Sunk beacon, providing a useful shortcut for boats crossing the estuary between Black Deep and Barrow Deep. Depths are liable to change through this swatchway (you should always refer to the latest edition of Admiralty chart 1975), but the cut is normally passable for most boats with 2 hours rise of tide.

Knock John Sand

This long narrow shoal forms a natural continuation of the Sunk Sand at its inshore end. The longest drying area is about 2 miles long, with drying heights between ½ and 1½ metres. Knock John Tower stands 4 cables east of the most south-westerly drying patch.

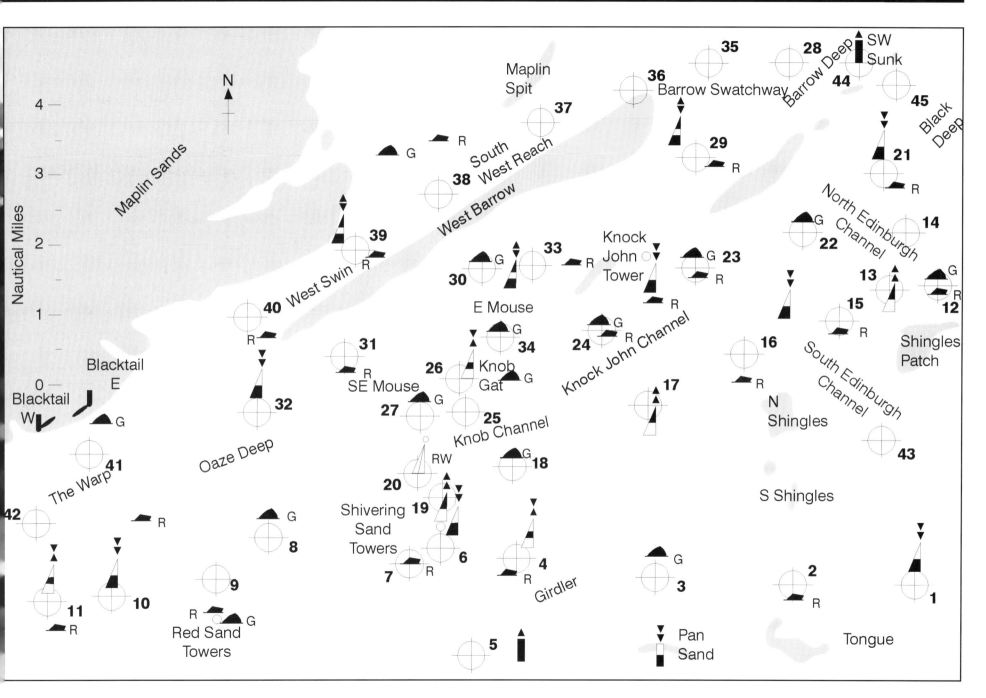

Maplin Sands

Maplin Spit

N

4

3

Nautical Miles

2

1

0

Blacktail E

Blacktail W

35

28

Barrow Deep

SW Sunk

36

Barrow Swatchway

44

45

Black Deep

37

South West Reach

G

R

29

R

21

R

38

West Barrow

North Edinburgh Channel

14

West Swin

39

R

Knock John Tower

22

13

G

R

12

30

G

33

R

23

G

R

15

R

West Swin

40

R

E Mouse

34

G

24

G

R

Knock John Channel

16

R

South Edinburgh Channel

Shingles Patch

31

R

26

Knob Gat

G

17

N Shingles

SE Mouse

32

27

G

25

Knob Channel

18

G

S Shingles

Oaze Deep

20

RW

19

41

The Warp

42

R

8

G

Shivering Sand Towers

6

4

R

3

G

2

R

1

9

7

R

Girdler

11

R

10

R

G

Red Sand Towers

5

Pan Sand

Tongue

27

WP No	Waypoint name and position	Latitude	Longitude
6–22	Knock John East, 2 ca due S of No 11 green buoy	51°34.10'N	01°13.50'E
6–23	Knock John, midway No 1 green and Knock John red buoys	51°33.59'N	01°10.95'E
6–24	Knock John west, midway No 4 red buoy and No 5 green buoy	51°32.69'N	01°08.75'E
6–25	Knob Gat south, ½ M due S of Knob Gat W-card buoy	51°31.56'N	01°05.53'E
6–26	Knob Gat, 100 m due W of Knob Gat W-card buoy	51°32.06'N	01°05.44'E
6–27	SE Mouse, 2 ca due S of SE Mouse green buoy	51°31.45'N	01°04.41'E
6–28	Barrow Deep SW, 1 M due W of the SW Sunk beacon	51°36.52'N	01°13.22'E
6–29	West Barrow outer, midway No 8 red and No 9 E-card buoys	51°35.16'N	01°10.94'E
6–30	West Barrow middle, 1 ca due S of No 11 green buoy	51°33.62'N	01°05.84'E
6–31	West Barrow inner, 1 ca due N of No 14 red buoy	51°32.29'N	01°02.65'E
6–32	SW Barrow, 2 ca due S of SW Barrow S-card buoy	51°31.60'N	01°00.53'E
6–33	North Knob W, ½ M NE of No 12 E-card buoy	51°33.63'N	01°07.10'E
6–34	East Mouse, 100 metres SE of East Mouse green buoy	51°32.63'N	01°06.36'E
6–35	Barrow Swatchway east, 2.2 M due W of the SW Sunk beacon	51°36.52'N	01°11.27'E
6–36	Barrow Swatchway middle, 1 M 325°T from No 9 E-card buoy	51°36.14'N	01°09.49'E
6–37	Barrow Swatchway west, 2 M 280°T from No 9 E-card buoy	51°35.67'N	01°07.21'E
6–38	South West Reach, ¾ M due S of Maplin Bank red buoy	51°34.71'N	01°04.80'E
6–39	West Swin, midway Maplin E-card and West Swin red buoys	51°33.91'N	01°02.84'E
6–40	SW Swin, 4 ca NW of SW Swin red buoy	51°32.97'N	01°00.31'E
6–41	Blacktail Spit, ¾ M due S of Blacktail East beacon	51°31.02'N	00°56.56'E
6–42	The Warp middle, 1.4 M due S of Blacktail West beacon	51°30.04'N	00°55.30'E
6–43	South Edinburgh SE, 2 M 345°T from S Shingles S-card buoy	51°31.14'N	01°15.28'E
6–44	SW Sunk beacon, actual position	51°36.52'N	01°14.84'E
6–45	SW Sunk beacon, SE approach, 7 ca 120°T from SW Sunk bn	51°36.16'N	01°15.82'E

Datum OSGB 36 The waypoint latitudes and longitudes in this table refer to Ordnance Survey of Great Britain (1936) Datum

Maplin Sands

This famous expanse of drying sands extends a good 3 miles off the Essex shore between Shoebury Ness and Foulness Point. The south edge of the Maplins is fairly well marked by buoys and beacons along The Warp channel, but the east edge has only the NE Maplin green buoy, Maplin Edge green buoy and the Maplin E-cardinal buoy. Parts of the Maplin Sands are designated areas for firing practice from the Shoeburyness Artillery Ranges. Red flags or lights are displayed when these ranges are in use.

Poor visibility

Boats should avoid making passages through this part of the Thames Estuary in poor visibility, even with the aid of GPS and radar. The tidal streams run quickly through the deep-water channels and set across many of the sands, and it is easy to mistake buoys in mist or heavy rain. Fast-moving shipping will also be a danger under these conditions.

West Barrow

The long West Barrow Sand dries for about 6 miles, with drying heights ranging from about 1–2½ metres and several wrecks are still partly exposed. The West Barrow separates the south-west part of Barrow Deep from the West Swin and is not a sandbank to be trifled with.

At the north-east tip of West Barrow Sand, the narrow Barrow Swatchway cuts through between Barrow Deep and South West Reach, but this short cut is unmarked and must be used with care when the sands are covered. At low water springs, with the West and East Barrow completely exposed, the Barrow Swatchway is obvious and straightforward, carrying 4–5 metres once you are through the narrowest part at the east end.

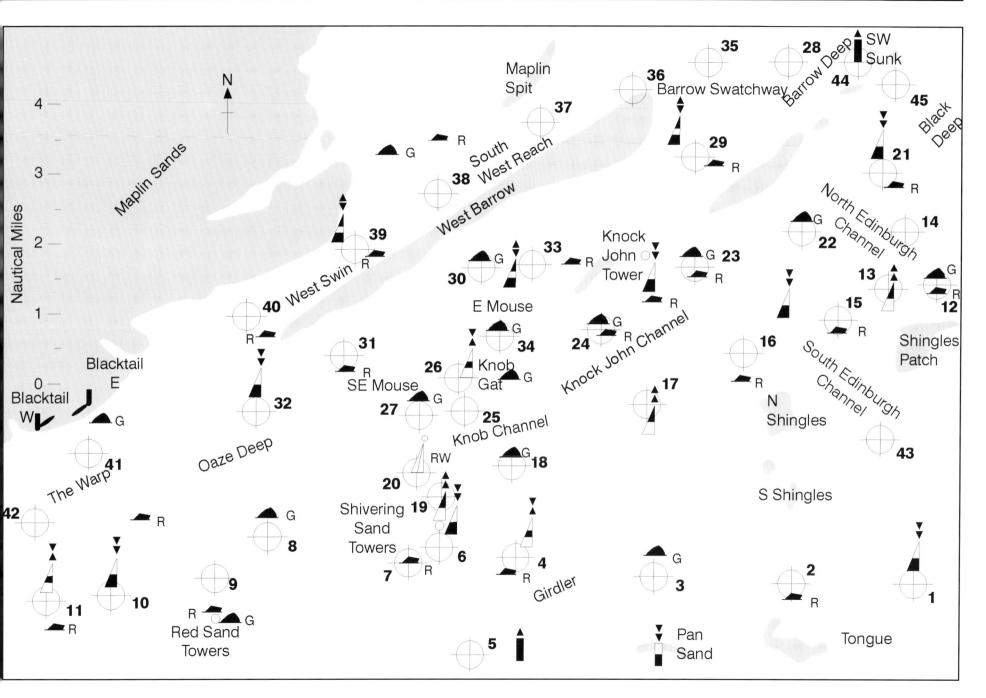

Maplin
Spit

35

28 Barrow Deep

SW
Sunk

36 Barrow Swatchway

44

45

Black
Deep

37

Maplin Sands

G   R

South
West Reach

29

R

21

R

38 West Barrow

North Edinburgh
Channel

14

Nautical Miles

West Barrow

39

G   **33**

Knock
John
Tower

23

22

13

G

30 West Swin

R

G

R

R

12

R   **40** West Swin

R

E Mouse

G

34

24

G

Knock John Channel

15

Shingles
Patch

Blacktail
E

R

31

R

26 Knob
Gat

G

R

16

R

South Edinburgh
Channel

Blacktail
W

G

SE Mouse

27

32

G

25 Knob Channel

G   **18**

17

N
Shingles

Oaze Deep

RW

20

43

41

The Warp

19 Shivering
Sand
Towers

S Shingles

42

R

G

8

6

4

G

2

1

7

R

R

Girdler

3

R

11

10

9

R   G

Red Sand
Towers

5

▼ Pan
□
■ Sand

Tongue

WP No	Waypoint name and position	Latitude	Longitude
7–1	The Warp middle, 1.4 M due S of Blacktail West beacon	51°30.04'N	00°55.30'E
7–2	East Shoebury, 6 ca due S of East Shoebury beacon	51°30.28'N	00°53.03'E
7–3	Shoebury middle, 3 ca due S of Shoebury beacon	51°29.97'N	00°49.36'E
7–4	West Shoebury, 1 ca due S of West Shoebury green buoy	51°30.10'N	00°45.83'E
7–5	Southend east, ½ M 130°T from the east Southend pierhead	51°30.52'N	00°44.12'E
7–6	Southend pier, 1 ca due S of the east Southend pierhead	51°30.74'N	00°43.50'E
7–7	Leigh outer, 100 m due S of Leigh green buoy	51°30.99'N	00°42.67'E
7–8	Leigh inner, midway Ray Gut red and green buoys	51°31.25'N	00°42.30'E
7–9	Leigh Creek entrance, 1.3 M 300°T from Leigh green buoy	51°31.69'N	00°40.87'E
7–10	West Oaze, 1 ca due S of W-card buoy	51°28.94'N	00°55.52'E
7–11	Four Fathoms west, 1 ca due S of the Spile green buoy	51°26.30'N	00°55.80'E
7–12	East Cant, 3 ca due S of 'F' beacon	51°27.14'N	00°52.60'E
7–13	Medway fairway buoy, actual position	51°28.80'N	00°52.92'E
7–14	Medway outer approach, midway No 1 and No 2 buoys	51°28.38'N	00°50.61'E
7–15	Medway inner approach, midway No 3 and No 4 buoys	51°28.12'N	00°49.42'E
7–16	Medway entrance, midway No 7 and No 8 buoys	51°27.83'N	00°47.66'E
7–17	Sheerness NE, midway No 9 and No 10 buoys	51°27.67'N	00°46.78'E
7–18	Little Nore, 1 ca due N of West Cant red buoy	51°27.29'N	00°45.61'E
7–19	Grain Edge, 100 m SE of Grain Edge green buoy	51°27.55'N	00°45.64'E
7–20	Nore Swatch, 100 m NE of Nore Swatch red buoy	51°28.30'N	00°45.71'E
7–21	Garrison Point, midway Garrison Pt and Grain Hard green buoy	51°26.88'N	00°44.50'E
7–22	Sheerness Inner, midway North Kent and South Kent buoys	51°26.02'N	00°43.67'E
7–23	West Swale outer, 3 ca 010°T from Queenborough Spit buoy	51°26.08'N	00°44.11'E
7–24	Sea Reach yellow buoy, actual position	51°29.42'N	00°52.67'E
7–25	Yantlet No 2 fairway buoy, actual position	51°29.37'N	00°49.84'E
7–26	Yantlet No 3 fairway buoy, actual position	51°29.30'N	00°46.63'E
7–27	Yantlet No 5 fairway buoy, actual position	51°29.92'N	00°41.55'E
7–28	Yantlet No 7 yellow buoy, actual position	51°30.07'N	00°37.15'E

Datum OSGB 36 The waypoint latitudes and longitudes in this table refer to Ordnance Survey of Great Britain (1936) Datum

COASTAL DANGERS

Refer to Admiralty charts 1183, 1185 and 3683

Maplin Sands

This famous expanse of drying sands extends three miles off the Essex shore between Shoebury Ness and Foulness Point. The south edge of the Maplins is fairly well marked by buoys and beacons along The Warp channel, but the east edge has only the NE Maplin green buoy, Maplin Edge green buoy and the Maplin E-cardinal buoy. Parts of the Maplin Sands are designated areas for firing practice from the Shoeburyness Artillery Ranges. Red flags or lights are displayed when these ranges are in use.

The Cant

This broad area of shallow water lies off the north coast of the Isle of Sheppey and the bottom is littered with numerous obstructions and pieces of wreckage. Soundings vary from about 1–3 metres, although the Cant shoal, marked by a beacon, has only 0.4 metres over it. The area is safely navigable above half-tide and the Four Fathoms Channel leads into it from the south-east, but should be avoided near low water.

Cheyney Spit

A shoal spur, with soundings between 0.8 and 2 metres, extends north for just over 1 mile from the north end of the Isle of Sheppey. This is a possible hazard if you are cutting into the River Medway from the Four Fathoms Channel.

Grain Spit

This wide area of drying mud flats bulges out for a good mile from the north-east side of the Isle of Grain, with drying heights from about ½–3½ metres. Take care to avoid Grain Spit if you are cutting round the Isle of Grain between the Yantlet Channel and the River Medway.

Sheerness Middle Sand

This tongue of shallow water extends eastwards from the drying part of Grain Spit for nearly 2 miles. Yachts cutting between the Yantlet Channel and the River Medway can cross the middle part of Sheerness Middle Sand at most states of tide, using Grain Edge green buoy and Nore Swatch red buoy as safe water marks. However, you should stay well clear of the tip of Sheerness Middle sand, where a dangerous wreck, the Richard Montgomery, is marked by yellow buoys.

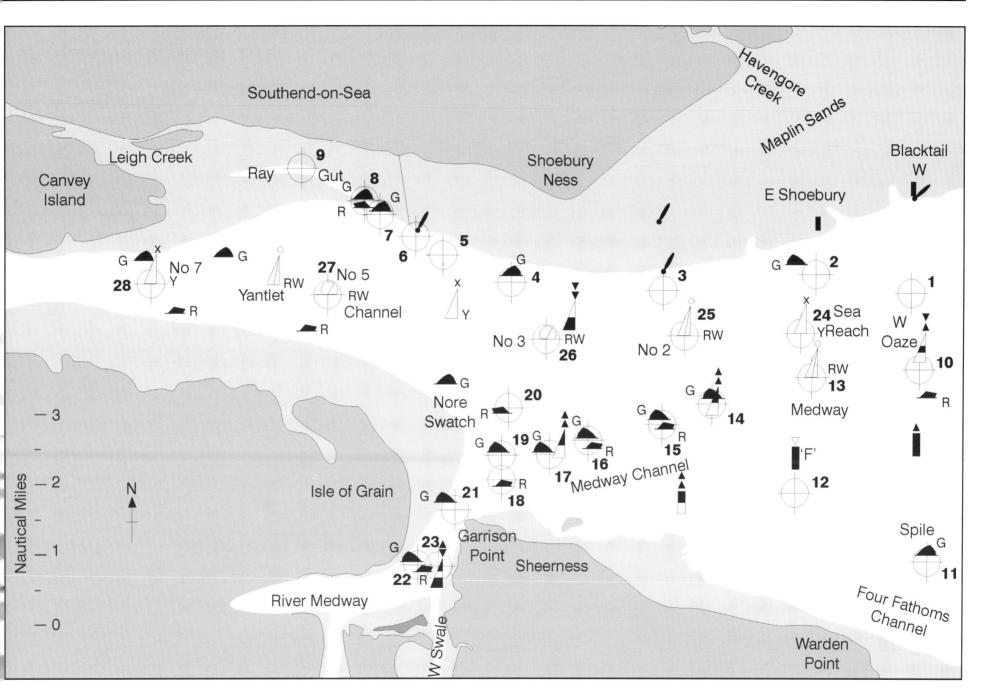

Southend-on-Sea

Havengore
Creek

Maplin Sands

Leigh Creek

Canvey
Island

Ray   Gut   **9**

8

Shoebury
Ness

Blacktail
W

E Shoebury

G

G

R

7

6

5

G

4

3

G **2**

1

G

X

No 7

G

RW

27 No 5

28

Y

Yantlet

RW

Channel

R

X

Y

R

No 3

RW

26

25

RW

No 2

x

24 Sea
Y Reach

W
Oaze

10

RW

13

R

Medway

Nore
Swatch

G

20

R

G

19

G

G

17 Medway Channel

16

R

G

R

15

G

14

'F'

12

G

21

R

18

Spile

G

11

Isle of Grain

N

Nautical Miles

— 3

— 2

— 1

— 0

G

23

22

R

Garrison
Point

Sheerness

River Medway

W Swale

Warden
Point

Four Fathoms
Channel

WP No	Waypoint name and position	Latitude	Longitude
8–1	Edinburgh W, between Edinburgh No 8 and No 9 buoys	51°33.32'N	01°16.68'E
8–2	Shingles Patch, 3 ca N of N-card buoy	51°33.28'E	01°15.48'E
8–3	Long Sand NW, 1½ M 245°T from NW Long Sand beacon	51°34.09'N	01°15.96'E
8–4	Black Deep SW, midway No 9 S-card and No 10 red buoys	51°34.91'N	01°15.45'E
8–5	Knock John east, 2 ca due S of No 11 green buoy	51°34.10'N	01°13.50'E
8–6	Knock John, midway No 1 green and Knock John red buoys	51°33.59'N	01°10.95'E
8–7	North Knob W, ½ M NE of No 12 E-card buoy	51°33.68'N	01°07.10'E
8–8	West Barrow middle, 1 ca due S of No 11 green buoy	51°33.62'N	01°05.84'E
8–9	West Barrow outer, midway No 8 red and No 9 E-card buoys	51°35.16'N	01°10.94'E
8–10	Barrow Deep, midway No 6 red and No 7 green buoys	51°37.53'N	01°14.31'E
8–11	Barrow Deep SW, 1 M due W of the SW Sunk beacon	51°36.52'N	01°13.22'E
8–12	Barrow Swatchway east, 2.2 M due W of the SW Sunk beacon	51°36.52'N	01°11.27'E
8–13	Barrow Swatchway middle, 1 M 325°T from No 9 E-card buoy	51°36.14'N	01°09.49'E
8–14	Barrow Swatchway west, 2 M 280°T from No 9 E-card buoy	51°35.67'N	01°07.21'E
8–15	South West Reach, ¾ M due S of Maplin Bank red buoy	51°34.71'N	01°04.80'E
8–16	West Swin, midway Maplin E-card and West Swin red buoys	51°33.91'N	01°02.84'E
8–17	Middle Deep SW, 1 M due N of the Barrow beacon	51°38.13'N	01°08.23'E
8–18	Barrow beacon, actual position	51°37.13'N	01°08.23'E
8–19	NE Maplin green buoy, actual position	51°37.43'N	01°04.90'E
8–20	NE Maplin SE, 7 ca SE of the NE Maplin green buoy	51°36.94'N	01°05.70'E
8–21	Maplin Edge, midway Maplin Edge green and Maplin Bank red	51°35.39'N	01°04.28'E
8–22	East Barrow NE, 6 ca 290°T from Barrow No 5 green buoy	51°40.22'N	01°15.38'E
8–23	East Barrow inner, 1.2 M 260°T from Barrow No 5 green buoy	51°39.80'N	01°14.37'E
8–24	Middle Deep NE, 9 ca due S of N-Middle N-card buoy	51°40.10'N	01°12.00'E

COASTAL DANGERS

Refer to Admiralty charts 1183, 1605, 1607, 1609, 1975 and 3750

SW Sunk

Sunk Sand is a long narrow shoal separating Black Deep from East Swin. SW Sunk is the south-west extremity of Sunk Sand, opposite Black Deep No 7 green buoy. The largest drying part of SW Sunk is just under 1 mile long and dries to about half a metre. Smaller drying patches, just above datum, string out to the south-west to link up with the Knock John Sand. A narrow swatchway cuts through this shoal area just south of the SW Sunk beacon, providing a useful short cut for yachts crossing the estuary between Black Deep and Barrow Deep. Depths are liable to change through this swatchway (always refer to the latest edition of Admiralty chart 1975), but this cut is normally passable for most yachts with 2 hours rise of tide.

Knock John Sand

This long narrow shoal forms a natural continuation of the Sunk Sand at its inshore end. The longest drying area is about two miles long, with drying heights between ½ and 1½ metres. Knock John Tower stands 4 cables east of the most south-westerly drying patch.

West Barrow

The long West Barrow Sand dries for about 6 miles, with drying heights ranging from about 1–2½ metres and several wrecks still partly exposed. The West Barrow separates the south-west part of Barrow Deep from the West Swin and is not a sandbank to be trifled with.

At the north-east tip of West Barrow Sand, the narrow Barrow Swatchway cuts through between Barrow Deep and South West Reach, but this short cut is unmarked and must be used with care when the sands are covered. At low water springs, with the West and East Barrow completely exposed, the Barrow Swatchway is obvious and straightforward, carrying 4–5 metres once you are through the narrowest part at the east end.

Maplin Sands

This famous expanse of drying sands extends a good three miles off the Essex shore between Shoebury Ness and Foulness Point. The south edge of the Maplins is fairly well marked by buoys and beacons along The Warp channel, but the east edge has only the NE Maplin green buoy, Maplin Edge green buoy and the Maplin E-cardinal buoy. Parts of the Maplin Sands are designated areas for firing practice from the Shoeburyness Artillery Ranges. Red flags or lights are displayed when these ranges are in use.

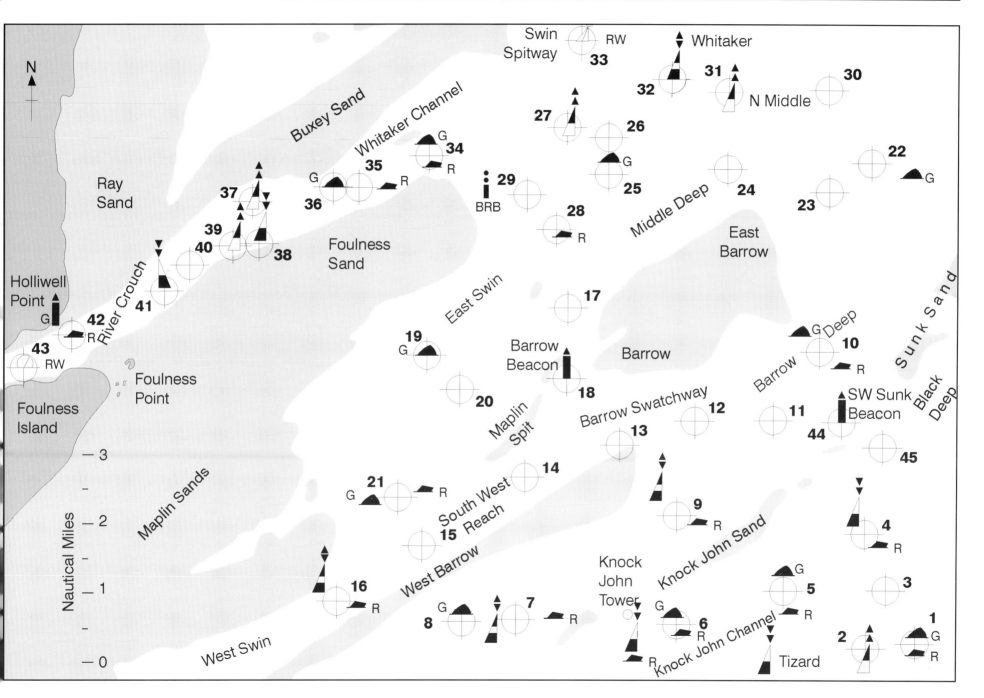

N

Swin Spitway **33** RW

Whitaker **31** **32**

N Middle **30**

Buxey Sand

Whitaker Channel **34** G **35** R

27 **26**

22 G

Ray Sand

36 G R

29 BRB

25 **24** **23**

37

39 **40** **38**

Foulness Sand

Middle Deep

East Barrow

Holliwell Point G **42** R

River Crouch

41

43 RW

Foulness Point

Foulness Island

28 R

17

East Swin

19 G **20**

Barrow Beacon **18**

Barrow

G Deep **10** R

Barrow **11**

S u n k S a n d

Maplin Spit

Barrow Swatchway **12**

SW Sunk Beacon **44**

Black Deep

13

45

Nautical Miles

— 3

21 G R **14**

South West **15** Reach

9 R

4 R

Maplin Sands

— 2

West Barrow

16 R

Knock John Sand

Knock John Tower

5 **3**

— 1

8 G **7** R

G **6** R

Knock John Channel

1 G R

2

Tizard

— 0

West Swin

West Swin

WP No	Waypoint name and position	Latitude	Longitude
8–25	South Whitaker, 2 ca due S of S Whitaker green buoy	51°40.00'N	01°09.13'E
8–26	Whitaker Spit outer, 3½ ca due N of S Whitaker green buoy	51°40.55'N	01°09.13'E
8–27	Whitaker Channel approach, 100 m N of No 6 N-card buoy	51°40.72'N	01°08.17'E
8–28	West Hook Middle, 1 ca NW of West Hook Middle red buoy	51°39.23'N	01°07.91'E
8–29	Whitaker Spit inner, 6 ca 080°T from Whitaker Spit beacon	51°39.71'N	01°07.25'E
8–30	NE Middle, 1½ M 080°T from N-Middle N-card buoy	51°41.28'N	01°14.39'E
8–31	North Middle, 2 ca due N of N-Middle N-card buoy	51°41.20'N	01°12.00'E
8–32	Whitaker E-card buoy, actual position	51°41.41'N	01°10.60'E
8–33	Swin Spitway red-and-white fairway buoy, actual position	51°41.94'N	01°08.43'E
8–34	Whitaker Channel entrance, midway Ridge and Swallow Tail	51°40.29'N	01°04.91'E
8–35	Whitaker Channel inner, midway Foulness and S Buxey buoys	51°39.83'N	01°03.24'E
8–36	South Buxey green buoy, actual position	51°39.82'N	01°02.60'E
8–37	Sunken Buxey, 1 ca due N of N-card buoy	51°36.60'N	01°00.70'E
8–38	Buxey No 1, close south of S-card buoy	51°39.01'N	01°00.86'E
8–39	Buxey No 2, close north of N-card buoy	51°38.96'N	01°00.25'E
8–40	Crouch approach, ½ M 050°T from Outer Crouch S-card	51°38.68'N	00°59.23'E
8–41	Outer Crouch, 100 m due S of Outer Crouch S-card buoy	51°38.30'N	00°58.61'E
8–42	River Crouch entrance, 100 m NW of Crouch red buoy	51°37.64'N	00°56.42'E
8–43	Inner Crouch red-and-white fairway buoy, actual position	51°37.19'N	00°55.24'E
8–44	SW Sunk beacon, actual position	51°36.52'N	01°14.84'E
8–45	SW Sunk beacon, SE approach, 7 ca 120°T from SW Sunk bn	51°36.16'N	01°15.82'E

Datum OSGB 36 The waypoint latitudes and longitudes in this table refer to Ordnance Survey of Great Britain (1936) Datum

Foulness Sand

This broad expanse of drying sand extends for 5 miles NE from Foulness Point as far as the Whitaker black-red-black beacon. Drying heights are mostly between one and two metres and the sands are left to port as you follow the Whitaker Channel into the River Crouch.

Buxey Sand

On the north side of the Whitaker Channel, Buxey Sand extends for 5 miles NE-SW opposite Foulness Sand and is left to starboard as you enter the Crouch. The drying heights are slightly less than for Foulness Sand and a narrow tidal cut, the Ray Sand Channel, leads across the inner part of Buxey Sand between the Blackwater and the Crouch. Shoal draught boats can use this cut within a couple of hours of high water.

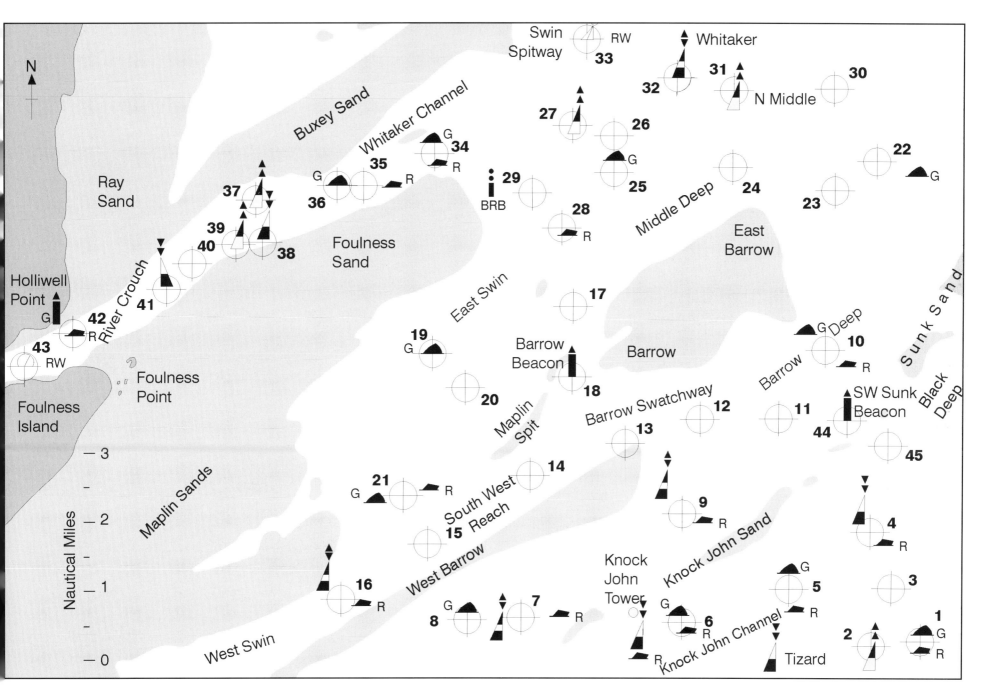

N

Swin
Spitway
RW
33

Whitaker

31

32

N Middle

30

Buxey Sand

Whitaker Channel

27

26

G **34**
R

35

G **36**

R

G **25**

22

G

Ray
Sand

37

39

40

38

Foulness
Sand

29
BRB

28
R

Middle Deep

24

East
Barrow

23

Sunk Sand

Holliwell
Point
G

River Crouch

41

42
R

43
RW

Foulness
Point

Foulness
Island

East Swin

17

19
G

Barrow
Beacon

Barrow

G Deep
10
R

Barrow

Black Deep

Maplin Sands

Nautical Miles

— 3

—

— 2

—

— 1

—

— 0

20

Maplin
Spit

Barrow Swatchway

12

11

SW Sunk
Beacon
44

45

21
G

R

South West
15 Reach

14

13

West Barrow

Knock John Sand

9

R

4

R

16
R

Knock
John
Tower

Knock John Channel

5

3

8
G

7

R

G
6
R

R

2

1
G
R

West Swin

R Knock John Channel

Tizard

35

WP No	Waypoint name and position	Latitude	Longitude
9–1	North Middle, 2 ca due N of N-Middle N-card buoy	51°41.20'N	01°12.00'E
9–2	Middle Deep NE, 9 ca due S of N-Middle N-card buoy	51°40.10'N	01°12.00'E
9–3	Whitaker E-card buoy, actual position	51°41.41'N	01°10.60'E
9–4	South Whitaker, 2 ca due S of S Whitaker green buoy	51°40.00'N	01°09.13'E
9–5	Whitaker Spit outer, 3½ ca due N of S Whitaker green buoy	51°40.55'N	01°09.13'E
9–6	Whitaker Spit inner, 6 ca 080°T from Whitaker Spit beacon	51°39.71'N	01°07.25'E
9–7	West Hook Middle, 1 ca NW of West Hook Middle red buoy	51°39.23'N	01°07.91'E
9–8	Whitaker Channel approach, 100 m N of No 6 N-card buoy	51°40.72'N	01°08.17'E
9–9	Whitaker Channel entrance, midway Ridge and Swallow Tail	51°40.29'N	01°04.91'E
9–10	Whitaker Channel inner, midway Foulness and S Buxey buoys	51°39.83'N	01°03.24'E
9–11	S Buxey green buoy, actual position	51°39.82'N	01°02.60'E
9–12	Sunken Buxey, 1 ca due N of N-card buoy	51°36.60'N	01°00.70'E
9–13	Swin Spitway red-and-white fairway buoy, actual position	51°41.94'N	01°08.43'E
9–14	Wallet Spitway red-and-white fairway buoy, actual position	51°42.84'N	01°07.41'E
9–15	Knoll, 100 m NE of the Knoll N-card buoy	51°43.89'N	01°05.23'E
9–16	North Eagle, 1 ca due N of N-card buoy	51°44.79'N	01°04.41'E
9–17	Eagle, 2 ca SW of the Eagle green buoy	51°43.97'N	01°03.68'E
9–18	NW Knoll, midway NW Knoll red and Colne Bar green buoys	51°44.45'N	01°02.46'E
9–19	Blackwater approach, 2 ca SW of Bench Head green buoy	51°44.52'N	01°00.97'E
9–20	Blackwater outer, 1.45 M 060°T from Sales Point	51°45.22'N	00°58.48'E
9–21	Blackwater mouth, 9 ca due N of Sales Point	51°45.40'N	00°56.46'E
9–22	Nass, 100 m NE of the Nass E-card beacon	51°45.84'N	00°55.00'E
9–23	Mersea Quarters, 100 m N of No 6 red buoy	51°45.93'N	00°54.31'E
9–24	Blackwater inner, 7 ca 215°T from the Nass E-card beacon	51°45.23'N	00°54.29'E
9–25	Bradwell approach, 2 ca 320°T from marina tidal beacon	51°44.68'N	00°53.13'E
9–26	Bradwell outer, Bradwell marina tidal beacon, actual position	51°44.53'N	00°53.35'E
9–27	Thirslet, 1 ca SE of Thirslet green buoy	51°43.63'N	00°50.61'E
9–28	Colne approach, midway Colne Pt and inner Bench Hd buoys	51°45.97'N	01°01.96'E
9–29	Colne outer, 100 m due E of No 8 red buoy	51°46.94'N	01°01.17'E
9–30	Colne inner, 1½ ca E of Mersea Stone on Brightlingsea L/Line	51°47.94'N	01°00.72'E
9–31	Gunfleet SW, 2 M 100°T from Knoll N-card buoy	51°43.50'N	01°08.35'E
9–32	Wallet SW, 1.7 M 185°T from Clacton-on-Sea pierhead	51°45.32'N	01°09.30'E
9–33	Clacton offing, 1.6 M 130°T from Clacton-on-Sea pierhead	51°45.99'N	01°11.50'E
9–34	Gunfleet Middle, 2¾ M 135°T from Clacton-on-Sea pierhead	51°45.05'N	01°12.66'E

Datum OSGB 36 The waypoint latitudes and longitudes in this table refer to Ordnance Survey of Great Britain (1936) Datum

COASTAL DANGERS
Refer to Admiralty charts 1975 and 3741

Buxey Sand
On the north side of the Whitaker Channel, Buxey Sand extends for 5 miles NE–SW opposite Foulness Sand and is left to starboard as you enter the Crouch. The drying heights are slightly less than for Foulness Sand and a narrow tidal cut, the Ray Sand Channel, leads across the inner part of Buxey Sand between the Blackwater and the Crouch. Shoal draught boats can use this cut within a couple of hours of high water.

The Spitway
At the NE tip of Buxey Sand, the shallow Spitway provides the main through-route between the Blackwater and the Crouch. Depths vary as the sands shift, but you can normally reckon on a metre at LAT. In quiet weather, most yachts will have no problem with 1 hour's rise of tide, but the more the better. The way through the Spitway is marked by two red-and-white fairway buoys, one each side of the shoal area – Wallet Spitway buoy to the north and Swin Spitway buoy to the south.

Bachelors Spit
The main channel into the Blackwater is well buoyed, but yachts using Ray Sand Channel between the Crouch and Blackwater must watch out for the unmarked shoals on Bachelors Spit, which extends well east from St Peter's and Dengie Flats on the south side of the Blackwater entrance.

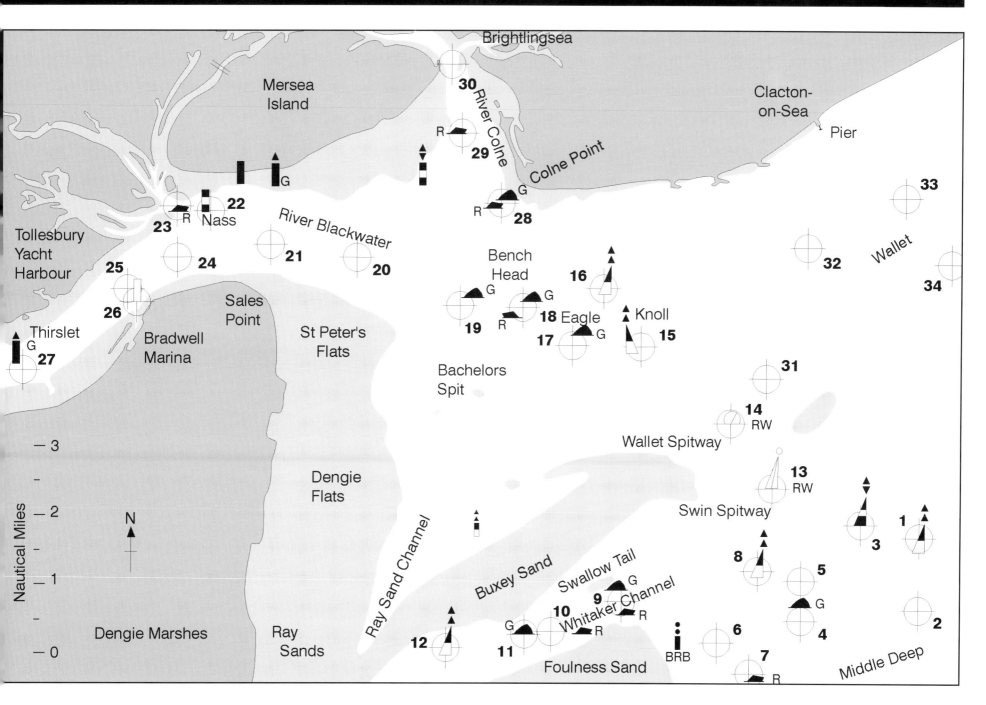

Brightlingsea

Mersea
Island

30 River Colne

Clacton-
on-Sea

Pier

R
29

R
G
28

G
22

33

23 R Nass

River Blackwater

32

Wallet

34

Tollesbury
Yacht
Harbour

24

21

20

25

Sales
Point

Bench
Head

16

G
26

Bradwell
Marina

St Peter's
Flats

G
19

R
18
Eagle

G
17

Knoll

15

Thirslet
G
27

Bachelors
Spit

31

14
RW

— 3

Dengie
Flats

Wallet Spitway

13
RW

— 2

N

Ray Sand Channel

Swin Spitway

1

3

Nautical Miles

Buxey Sand

Swallow Tail

8

5

— 1

G
9
Whitaker Channel

R

G

10

12

G
11

R

6

4

2

— 0

Dengie Marshes

Ray
Sands

Foulness Sand

BRB

7
R

Middle Deep

37

WP No	Waypoint name and position	Latitude	Longitude
10–1	Wallet SW, 1.7 M 185°T from Clacton-on-Sea pierhead	51°45.32'N	01°09.30'E
10–2	Clacton offing, 1.6 M 130°T from Clacton-on-Sea pierhead	51°45.99'N	01°11.50'E
10–3	Gunfleet Middle, 2¾ M 135°T from Clacton-on-Sea pierhead	51°45.05'N	01°12.66'E
10–4	Gunfleet NW, 1½ ca NW of Wallet No 4 red buoy	51°46.62'N	01°17.17'E
10–5	Wallet Middle, 1.7 M 120°T from Holland Haven radar mast	51°47.66'N	01°15.35'E
10–6	Frinton offing, 3¼ M due S of The Naze Tower	51°48.60'N	01°17.39'E
10–7	Wallet NE, 1.8 M 145°T from Walton-on-the Naze pierhead	51°49.09'N	01°18.58'E
10–8	Gunfleet south, 3½ M 245°T from Gunfleet Spit S-card buoy	51°43.81'N	01°16.67'E
10–9	Gunfleet Spit, 2 ca due S of Gunfleet Spit S-card buoy	51°45.10'N	01°21.80'E
10–10	East Swin middle, 1.4 M due S of Gunfleet Spit S-card buoy	51°43.90'N	01°21.80'E
10–11	Gunfleet North, 1½ ca NW of Wallet No 2 red buoy	51°48.96'N	01°22.94'E
10–12	Goldmer Gat, 2½ M due W of NE Gunfleet E-card buoy	51°49.90'N	01°23.87'E
10–13	South Cork, 2 ca due S of South Cork S-card buoy	51°51.10'N	01°24.20'E
10–14	Medusa green buoy, actual position	51°51.20'N	01°20.45'E
10–15	Stone Banks, 3 ca due W of Stone Banks red buoy	51°53.17'N	01°18.86'E
10–16	Pye End fairway buoy, actual position	51°55.00'N	01°18.00'E
10–17	Landguard SW, 1 M 157°T from Blackman's Head red beacon	51°55.19'N	01°18.55'E
10–18	Cliff Foot clearing, 4 ca due E of Blackman's Head red beacon	51°56.10'N	01°18.56'E
10–19	Pitching Ground, 1½ ca due S of Pitching Ground red buoy	51°55.24'N	01°21.15'E
10–20	Landguard SE, midway Rolling Ground and Beach End buoys	51°55.55'N	01°19.58'E
10–21	Landguard east, 4 ca NW of Platters S-card buoy	51°55.90'N	01°20.62'E

Datum OSGB 36 The waypoint latitudes and longitudes in this table refer to Ordnance Survey of Great Britain (1936) Datum

COASTAL DANGERS
Refer to Admiralty charts 1183, 1975 and 2052

Gunfleet Sand
The long finger of Gunfleet Sand runs approximately ENE–WSW for more than 10 miles, from the Spitway opposite Buxey Sand out to the deeper water of the Goldmer Gat. The main drying parts of Gunfleet Sand lie more or less opposite Walton-on-the-Naze some 4–5 miles offshore, but the whole length of the Gunfleet forms a partial natural breakwater about 4 miles offshore between Clacton-on-Sea and Walton-on-the-Naze. The broad channel between Gunfleet and the coast is known as the Wallet and forms the usual route for boats between the Blackwater and Harwich approaches.

The drying parts of Gunfleet Sand dry to barely 1 metre, but the whole length of the shoal has soundings of less than 1 metre except at the NE tip. The main drying parts of Gunfleet are marked by Wallet No 2 and No 4 red buoys, and the NE extremity is guarded by the NE Gunfleet E-cardinal buoy. Do not attempt to cross any part of Gunfleet Sand without local knowledge.

Cork Sand
The narrow sliver of Cork Sand extends just west of south for about 3 miles from near the south edge of the main Harwich approach channel. The southern part dries to just over 1 metre. Cork Sand provides a natural barrier between the main east approaches to Harwich and the shallow 'back-door' route from the south via the Medusa Channel. Cork Sand is guarded at its north tip by the Cork N-cardinal beacon and on the south side by the South Cork S-cardinal buoy.

West Rocks
This area of rocky shoals, the centre of which is almost awash at datum, lies between the south tip of Cork Sand and the South Cork S-cardinal buoy. Always keep south of this buoy when you are approaching the Medusa Channel from the south-east.

Stone Banks
This patchy area of shoals is left to starboard as you approach the Medusa Channel from the south. These shoals, with a least depth of 1.9 metres, are guarded by Stone Banks red buoy, but care must be taken in poor visibility not to stray east of a direct line between the Medusa green buoy and Stone Banks red buoy.

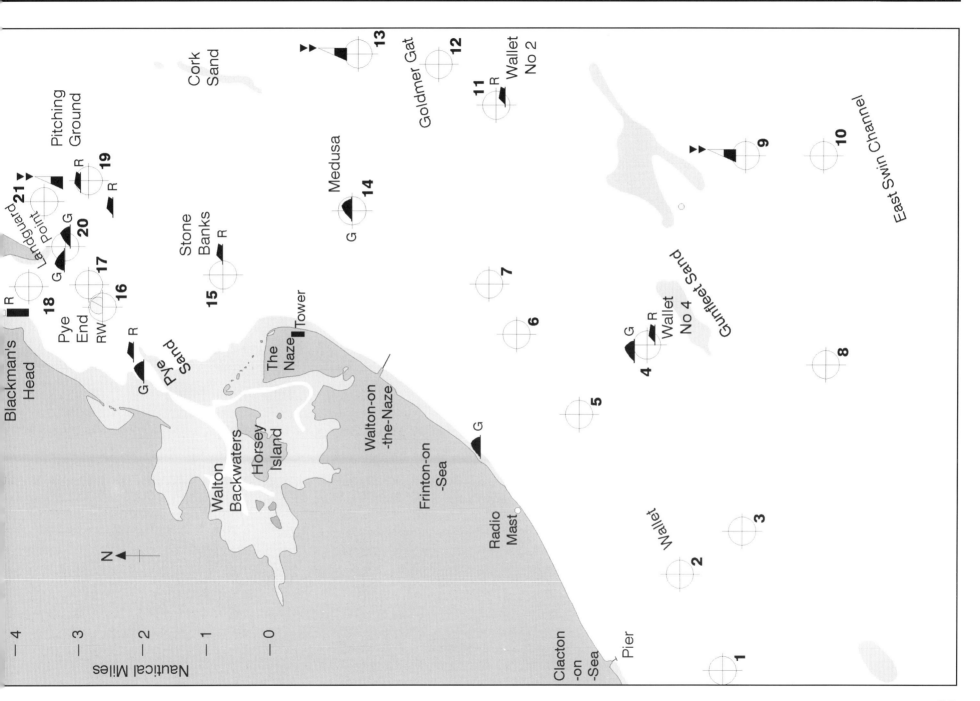

WP No	Waypoint name and position	Latitude	Longitude
11–1	Pye End fairway buoy, actual position	51°55.00'N	01°18.00'E
11–2	Landguard SW, 1 M 157°T from Blackman's Head red beacon	51°55.19'N	01°18.55'E
11–3	Landguard buoy, 100 m SW of Landguard N-card buoy	51°55.31'N	01°18.92'E
11–4	Inner Ridge, 1 ca due S of Inner Ridge red buoy	51°52.21'N	01°19.69'E
11–5	Landguard SE, midway Rolling Ground and Beach End buoys	51°55.55'N	01°19.58'E
11–6	Cliff Foot buoy, 1 ca due W of Cliff Foot red buoy	51°55.69'N	01°18.49'E
11–7	Cliff Foot clearing, 4 ca due E of Blackman's Head red beacon	51°56.10'N	01°18.56'E
11–8	Harwich entrance, 1 ca due W of the North Shelf red buoy	51°56.65'N	01°18.54'E
11–9	Guard, 100 m NE of the Guard red buoy	51°57.07'N	01°17.94'E
11–10	Shotley Spit, 100 m SE of the Shotley Spit S-card buoy	51°57.23'N	01°17.73'E
11–11	College red buoy, actual position	51°57.52'N	01°17.43'E
11–12	Pepys red buoy, actual position	51°57.72'N	01°17.00'E
11–13	Orwell red buoy, actual position	51°58.14'N	01°16.65'E
11–14	Ganges green buoy, actual position	51°57.07'N	01°17.12'E
11–15	Shotley Point Marina, midway between the entrance beacons	51°57.23'N	01°16.83'E
11–16	Bristol green buoy, actual position	51°57.02'N	01°16.32'E

Datum OSGB 36 The waypoint latitudes and longitudes in this table refer to Ordnance Survey of Great Britain (1936) Datum

COASTAL DANGERS
Refer to Admiralty charts 2052 and 2693

Pye Sand and Sunken Pye
As you approach Harwich from the south by the Medusa Channel, leaving Stone Banks red buoy fairly close to the east, a wide area of very shallow water opens up to the west in Pennyhole Bay and the approaches to the Walton Backwaters. Pye Sand and the Sunken Pye are two particularly shallow areas of hard sand that must be left well clear to the west as you come through the Medusa Channel. Soundings over Sunken Pye are between ½ and 1 metre and the NE extremity of these shoals is marked by the Pye End red-and-white fairway buoy, which you must reach before turning to approach the Walton Backwaters.

Halliday Rock Flats
The shallow area around Sunken Pye effectively continues north towards the Dovercourt shore across Halliday Rock Flats. This whole bight between the outer Harwich breakwater and the entrance to the Backwaters has soundings mostly well under 1 metre, with patches of less than ½ metre. Near low water, therefore, you need to keep well over to the east of Pye End buoy if approaching Harwich from the south.

Cliff Foot Rocks
This cluster of rocky patches lies a couple of cables SE of the outer breakwater, off Blackman's Head. Their least depth is 1.3 metres. Although guarded by Cliff Foot and South Shelf red buoys, Cliff Foot Rocks are quite close to the recom-mended approach track for boats coming in and out of Harwich, which lies just the 'wrong' side of the buoys. Be careful, therefore, to avoid these shoals near low water.

The Guard
A shoal area juts well out from the north end of Harwich town waterfront, just as you round the point to enter the River Stour. A patch with only 0.3 metres over it lies nearly 2 cables offshore. Although this shoal is guarded by the red channel buoys, you will be just the 'wrong' side of these buoys if following the recommended approach track for boats coming in and out of Harwich. Be careful to avoid The Guard near low water.

Shipping in Harwich approaches
Harwich and Felixstowe are busy commercial ports and large ships and ferries are continually on the move in the Harwich approach channel. Take great care not to impede shipping and always use the recommended approach track for boats, which lies just the 'wrong' side of the red buoys on the west and south sides of the deep-water channel.

Crab-pot floats
The shallow waters off the Naze and near the Medusa Channel contain a good many crab-pots, so take particular care in this area in poor visibility. Where possible, avoid using the Medusa Channel at night. If leaving Harwich this way towards the end of the day for a night passage across the North Sea, it is advisable to get well clear of the Medusa Channel and Goldmer Gat before dusk.

Nautical Miles

N

Port of Felixstowe

Felixstowe Dock

RoRo

Container Terminal

Landguard Point

Beach End

5

G

G

G

R

4

Landguard

3

N Shelf

R

G

R

G

R

8

7

6

2

Pye End

RW

1

Sunken Pye

Cliff Foot Rocks

R

Guard

9

Shotley Spit

10

R

College

11

R

Pepys

12

R

River Orwell

Orwell

13

R

G

Shotley Point Marina

Bristol

G

15

G

14

Ganges

River Stour

RoRo

Harwich

Blackman's Head

Small Craft Moorings

16

G

WP No	Waypoint name and position	Latitude	Longitude
12–1	Pye End fairway buoy, actual position	51°55.00'N	01°18.00'E
12–2	Landguard SW, 1 M 157°T from Blackman's Head red beacon	51°55.19'N	01°18.55'E
12–3	Landguard buoy, 100 m SW of Landguard N-card buoy	51°55.31'N	01°18.92'E
12–4	Inner Ridge, 1 ca due S of Inner Ridge red buoy	51°52.21'N	01°19.69'E
12–5	Landguard SE, midway Rolling Ground and Beach End buoys	51°55.55'N	01°19.58'E
12–6	Cliff Foot buoy, 1 ca due W of Cliff Foot red buoy	51°55.69'N	01°18.49'E
12–7	Cliff Foot clearing, 4 ca due E of Blackman's Head red beacon	51°56.10'N	01°18.56'E
12–8	Harwich entrance, 1 ca due W of the North Shelf red buoy	51°56.65'N	01°18.54'E
12–9	Guard, 100 m NE of the Guard red buoy	51°57.07'N	01°17.94'E
12–10	Pitching Ground, 1½ ca due S of Pitching Ground red buoy	51°55.24'N	01°21.15'E
12–11	Landguard East, 4 ca NW of Platters S-card buoy	51°55.90'N	01°20.62'E
12–12	Platters S-card buoy, actual position	51°55.62'N	01°21.07'E
12–13	Felixstowe offing, 1 M SE of St John's church spire	51°56.91'N	01°21.99'E
12–14	Wadgate Ledge green buoy, actual position	51°56.08'N	01°22.21'E
12–15	Felixstowe Ledge green buoy, actual position	51°56.29'N	01°24.52'E
12–16	Washington green buoy, actual position	51°56.49'N	01°26.70'E
12–17	South Channel W, 3½ ca due S of No 6 yellow buoy	51°55.29'N	01°22.96'E
12–18	Cork Sand N, 1½ ca due N of Cork Sand N-card beacon	51°55.34'N	01°25.31'E
12–19	Cork Sand red buoy, actual position	51°55.43'N	01°25.95'E
12–20	Harwich South Channel outer, 4 ca SE of No 2 yellow buoy	51°55.62'N	01°28.10'E
12–21	Woodbridge Haven fairway, 8 ca 150°T from south Martello Tr	51°58.04'N	01°23.97'E
12–22	Woodbridge Haven E, 1.2 M 160°T from Bawdsey Radio Tr	51°58.46'N	01°25.25'E
12–23	Cutler south clearing, 2½ M 140°T from Bawdsey Radio Tr	51°57.67'N	01°27.19'E
12–24	Cutler east clearing, 2 ca due E of the Cutler green buoy	51°58.50'N	01°27.94'E
12–25	Woodbridge Haven NE, 1.4 M 095°T from Bawdsey Radio Tr	51°59.45'N	01°26.84'E

Datum OSGB 36 The waypoint latitudes and longitudes in this table refer to Ordnance Survey of Great Britain (1936) Datum

COASTAL DANGERS
Refer to Admiralty chart 2693

Cliff Foot Rocks
This cluster of rocky patches (least depth 1.3 metres) lies 2 cables SE of Harwich outer breakwater, off Blackman's Head. Although guarded by Cliff Foot and South Shelf red buoys, Cliff Foot Rocks are close to the recommended approach track for boats coming in and out of Harwich, which follows just the 'wrong' side of the buoys. Be careful, therefore, to avoid these shoals near low water.

Shipping in Harwich approaches
Harwich and Felixstowe are busy commercial ports and large ships and ferries are continually on the move in the Harwich approach channel. Take care not to impede shipping and always use the recommended approach track for boats, which lies just the 'wrong' side of the red buoys on the west and south sides of the deep-water channel.

Cork Sand
The north end of Cork Sand lies close to the recommended track for boats entering Harwich from the east. Be sure to pass north of Cork Sand N-cardinal beacon as you come through the South Channel along the track, even though you will pass just the 'wrong' side of Cork Sand red buoy.

Landguard Point
A wide shoal area extends east and north-east from Landguard Point for about 1 mile, following the line of the shore. Soundings are less than ½ metre in parts. Watch out for these shoals if you are following the coast in either direction between Landguard Point and Woodbridge Haven.

A small 0.8 metre shoal known as Platters and a wreck with ½ metre over it at LAT lie a few cables west and north-west of Wadgate Ledge green buoy. Both are significant within 2 hours of low water. Waypoints 12–11 and 12–13 can be used to lead you between these dangers and the Landguard Point shallows.

Woodbridge Haven entrance
The shingle banks and bar at the entrance to Woodbridge Haven are notoriously mobile and the buoys are moved from time to time to reflect changes in the channel. It is best to approach after half-flood and to leave, if possible, 1 hour before high water. The entrance should be avoided altogether in fresh onshore winds, especially with a spring ebb running.

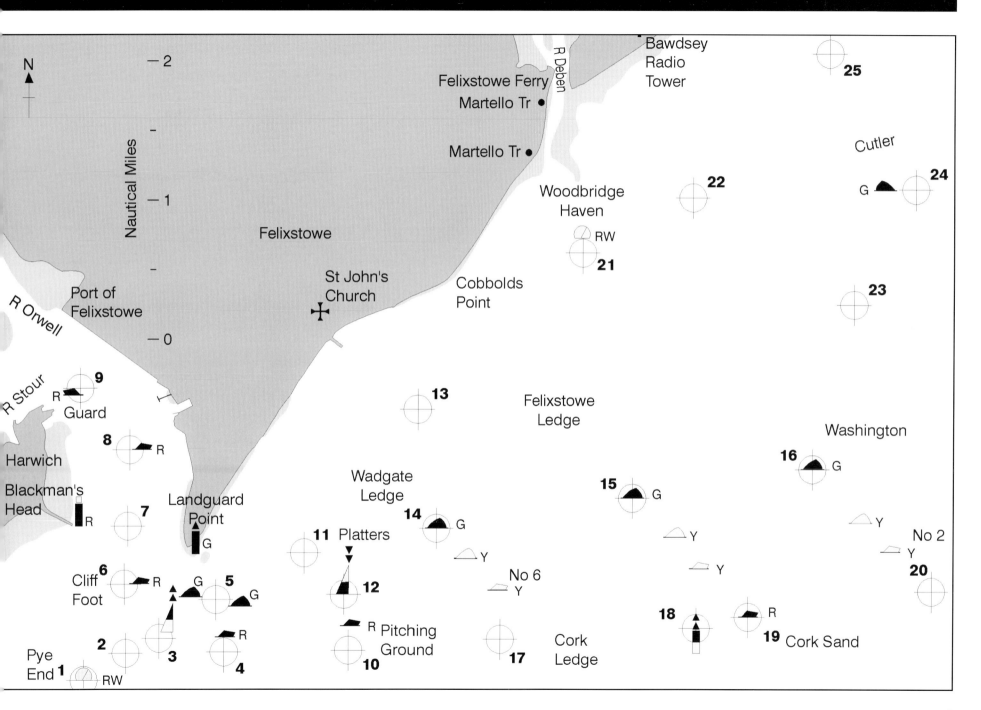

N

Nautical Miles

— 2

— 1

—

— 0

R Orwell

R Stour

Port of
Felixstowe

Felixstowe

St John's
Church

Cobbolds
Point

Felixstowe Ferry
Martello Tr ●

Martello Tr ●

R Deben

Bawdsey
Radio
Tower

25

Cutler

Woodbridge
Haven

RW

21

22

G **24**

23

9
R Guard

8
R

13

Felixstowe
Ledge

Washington

16 G

Harwich

Blackman's
Head

R

7

Landguard
Point

G

Wadgate
Ledge

14 G

11 Platters

12

R Pitching
Ground

No 6
Y

15 G

Y

Y

Y

No 2

Y

20

Cliff
Foot

6
R

G **5**
G

R

18

19 Cork Sand

R

Pye
End **1**
RW

2

3

4

10

17

Cork
Ledge

43

WP No	Waypoint name and position	Latitude	Longitude
13–1	Edinburgh Middle, between Edinburgh No 4 and No 5 buoys	51°33.32'N	01°19.41'E
13–2	Edinburgh W Middle, between Edinburgh No 6 and No 7 buoys	51°33.47'N	01°18.21'E
13–3	Edinburgh W, between Edinburgh No 8 and No 9 buoys	51°33.32'N	01°16.68'E
13–4	Shingles Patch, 3 ca N of N-card buoy	51°33.28'N	01°15.48'E
13–5	Long Sand NW, 1½ M 245°T from NW Long Sand beacon	51°34.09'N	01°15.96'E
13–6	Black Deep SW, midway No 9 S-card and No 10 red buoys	51°34.91'N	01°15.45'E
13–7	SW Sunk beacon, SE approach, 7 ca 120°T from SW Sunk bn	51°36.16'N	01°15.82'E
13–8	SW Sunk beacon, actual position	51°36.52'N	01°14.84'E
13–9	Barrow Deep, midway No 6 red and No 7 green buoys	51°37.53'N	01°14.31'E
13–10	East Barrow NE, 6 ca 290°T from Barrow No 5 green buoy	51°40.22'N	01°15.38'E
13–11	East Barrow inner, 1.2 M 260°T from Barrow No 5 green buoy	51°39.80'N	01°14.37'E
13–12	Middle Sunk south, midway Black Deep No 7 and No 8 buoys	51°36.63'N	01°18.90'E
13–13	Black Deep middle, midway No 5 and No 6 buoys	51°39.02'N	01°23.81'E
13–14	Little Sunk east, midway Little Sunk and Long Sand beacons	51°41.68'N	01°27.23'E
13–15	Barrow Deep NE, midway No 4 W-card and No 5 green buoys	51°39.92'N	01°16.97'E
13–16	East Swin south, midway No 3 E-card and No 2 red buoys	51°41.98'N	01°21.69'E
13–17	NE Middle, 1½ M 080°T from N Middle N-card buoy	51°41.28'N	01°14.39'E
13–18	NE Middle swatchway, 1.8 M east of N Middle N-card buoy	51°41.00'N	01°14.89'E
13–19	East Swin SW, 1.4 M 285°T from No 3 E-card bell buoy	51°42.39'N	01°18.17'E
13–20	Gunfleet south, 3½ M 245°T from Gunfleet Spit S-card buoy	51°43.81'N	01°16.67'E
13–21	East Swin middle, 1.4 M due S of Gunfleet Spit S-card buoy	51°43.90'N	01°21.80'E
13–22	Gunfleet Spit, 2 ca due S of Gunfleet Spit S-card buoy	51°45.10'N	01°21.80'E
13–23	East Swin NE, 1.6 M due N of West Sunk W-card buoy	51°45.90'N	01°25.90'E
13–24	Gunfleet NW, 1½ ca NW of Wallet No 4 red buoy	51°46.62'N	01°17.17'E

COASTAL DANGERS

Refer to Admiralty charts 1183, 1607 and 1975

Gunfleet Sand

The long finger of Gunfleet Sand runs ENE–WSW for more than 10 miles from the Blackwater approaches out to the deeper water of Goldmer Gat. The main drying parts of Gunfleet lie opposite Walton-on-the-Naze, 4–5 miles offshore. These areas dry to about 1 metre and the whole length of the bank has soundings of less than a metre except at the NE tip, where the NE Gunfleet E-cardinal buoy guards the seaward approach.

The south edge of Gunfleet Sand borders the East Swin, or King's Channel, and is marked only by Gunfleet Spit E-cardinal bell buoy, 1 mile south-east of the old Gunfleet lighthouse opposite the largest drying part of the sand. Do not attempt to cross any part of Gunfleet Sand without local knowledge.

Sunk Sand

This long narrow bank stretches north-east for 13 miles from the SW Sunk beacon, separating Black Deep from Barrow Deep and the East Swin. SW Sunk lies opposite Black Deep No 7 green buoy. The largest drying part of the SW Sunk is just under 1 mile long and dries to about ½ metre. A narrow swatchway cuts through the shoals just south of the SW Sunk beacon, providing a useful route for boats crossing the estuary between Black Deep and Barrow Deep. Depths are liable to change through this swatchway (always refer to the latest edition of Admiralty chart 1975), but the cut is normally passable for most craft with 2 hours rise of tide.

Middle Sunk lies 2½ miles north-east of the SW Sunk beacon and dries to almost 2 metres. Little Sunk is the most seaward drying part of the Sunk Sand, running more or less between Black Deep No 1 and No 3 green buoys. The SW end of Little Sunk is marked by a beacon and in quiet weather you can cut across the bank at this point by passing a couple of cables south of Little Sunk beacon.

The seaward extremity of Sunk Sand is guarded by Sunk Head N-cardinal buoy, which lies close north-east of the ruined base of the old Sunk Head Tower. The tower foundations have only 2.▮ metres over them at LAT.

Long Sand

Long Sand is part of a vast finger of banks and shoals stretching north-east from the seaward edge of North Edinburgh Channel for a good 18 miles out to Long Sand Head. Vessels passing through the well-buoyed North Edinburgh Channel leave the inner part of Long Sand to the north-east. Fisherman's Gat, a deep, unmarked fairway about 1 mile wide, cuts across the bottom of the 'finger' just NE of the inner part of Long Sand.

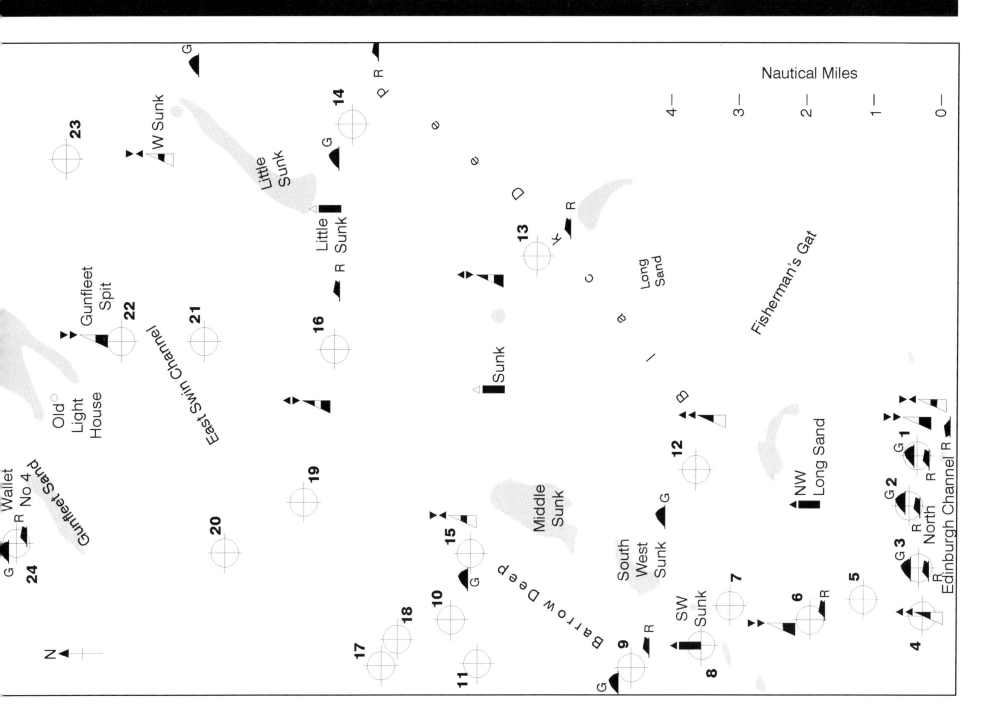

Nautical Miles

4 3 2 1 0

W Sunk

Little Sunk

14

G

R

R

23

Gunfleet Spit 22

21

16

19

Old Light House

East Swin Channel

Little Sunk R Sunk

13

R

Long Sand

Fisherman's Gat

Sunk

Wallet R No4

Gunfleet Sand

24 G

20

Middle Sunk

17 18

10

15 G

Barrow Deep

South West Sunk

SW Sunk

12 G

B

NW Long Sand

North R Edinburgh Channel R

G 1

G 2

G 3

9 R

7

6 R

5

11

8 G

4

N

WP No	Waypoint name and position	Latitude	Longitude
13–1	Edinburgh Middle, between Edinburgh No 4 and No 5 buoys	51°33.32'N	01°19.41'E
13–2	Edinburgh W Middle, between Edinburgh No 6 and No 7 buoys	51°33.47'N	01°18.21'E
13–3	Edinburgh W, between Edinburgh No 8 and No 9 buoys	51°33.32'N	01°16.68'E
13–4	Shingles Patch, 3 ca N of N-card buoy	51°33.28'N	01°15.48'E
13–5	Long Sand NW, 1½ M 245°T from NW Long Sand beacon	51°34.09'N	01°15.96'E
13–6	Black Deep SW, midway No 9 S-card and No 10 red buoys	51°34.91'N	01°15.45'E
13–7	SW Sunk beacon, SE approach, 7 ca 120°T from SW Sunk bn	51°36.16'N	01°15.82'E
13–8	SW Sunk beacon, actual position	51°36.52'N	01°14.84'E
13–9	Barrow Deep, midway No 6 red and No 7 green buoys	51°37.53'N	01°14.31'E
13–10	East Barrow NE, 6 ca 290°T from Barrow No 5 green buoy	51°40.22'N	01°15.38'E
13–11	East Barrow inner, 1.2 M 260°T from Barrow No 5 green buoy	51°39.80'N	01°14.37'E
13–12	Middle Sunk south, midway Black Deep No 7 and No 8 buoys	51°36.63'N	01°18.90'E
13–13	Black Deep middle, midway No 5 and No 6 buoys	51°39.02'N	01°23.81'E
13–14	Little Sunk east, midway Little Sunk and Long Sand beacons	51°41.68'N	01°27.23'E
13–15	Barrow Deep NE, midway No 4 W-card and No 5 green buoys	51°39.92'N	01°16.97'E
13–16	East Swin south, midway No 3 E-card and No 2 red buoys	51°41.98'N	01°21.69'E
13–17	NE Middle, 1½ M 080°T from N Middle N-card buoy	51°41.28'N	01°14.39'E
13–18	NE Middle swatchway, 1.8 M east of N Middle N-card buoy	51°41.00'N	01°14.89'E
13–19	East Swin SW, 1.4 M 285°T from No 3 E-card bell buoy	51°42.39'N	01°18.17'E
13–20	Gunfleet south, 3½ M 245°T from Gunfleet Spit S-card buoy	51°43.81'N	01°16.67'E
13–21	East Swin middle, 1.4 M due S of Gunfleet Spit S-card buoy	51°43.90'N	01°21.80'E
13–22	Gunfleet Spit, 2 ca due S of Gunfleet Spit S-card buoy	51°45.10'N	01°21.80'E
13–23	East Swin NE, 1.6 M due N of West Sunk W-card buoy	51°45.90'N	01°25.90'E
13–24	Gunfleet NW, 1½ ca NW of Wallet No 4 red buoy	51°46.62'N	01°17.17'E

Datum OSGB 36 The waypoint latitudes and longitudes in this table refer to Ordnance Survey of Great Britain (1936) Datum

The seaward drying parts of Long Sand are marked on their west side by the red channel buoys of Black Deep, but the east side of Long Sand is unmarked for the 19 miles between North Edinburgh Channel and Long Sand Head N-cardinal bell buoy, which guards the seaward extremity of the shoals.

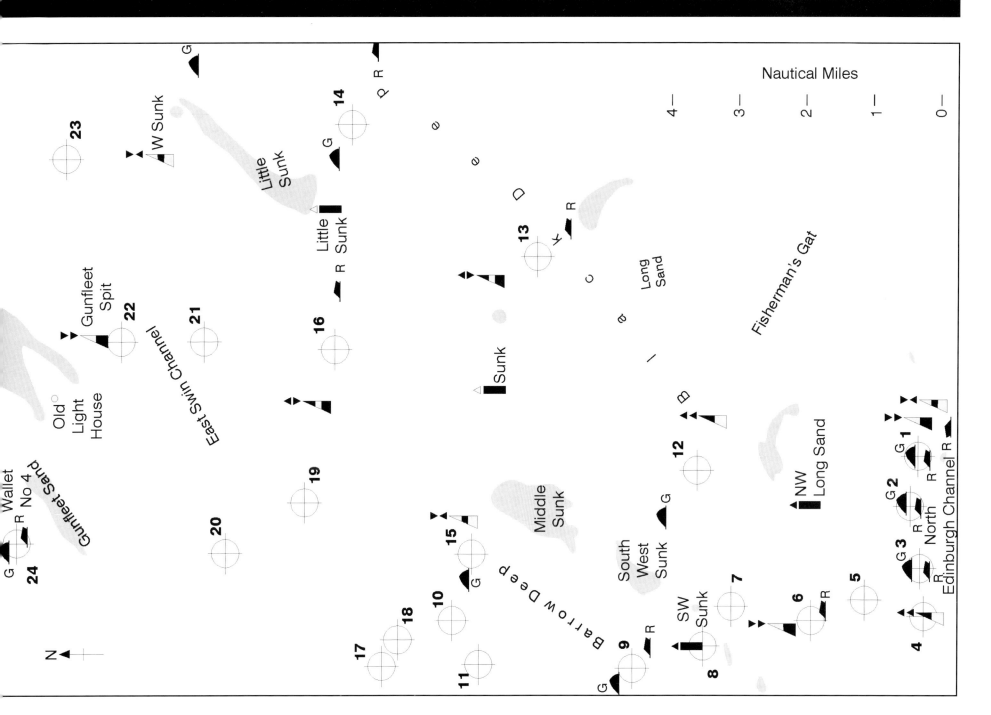

Nautical Miles

4 — 3 — 2 — 1 — 0 —

23

W Sunk

G 14
R

Little
Sunk

Little
Sunk G

R

13
R
Long
Sand

Fisherman's Gat

Gunfleet
Spit 22

Old
Light
House

East Swin Channel

21

16

Sunk

19

Middle
Sunk

South
West
Sunk

B

NW
Long Sand

Long Sand

12
G

Wallet
R No 4

Gunfleet Sand
G
24

N

17

18

10
G

15

Barrow Deep

11

G R

SW
Sunk

9

8
G

7

6
R

5

G 2
G 1
R
R North R

G 3
R
Edinburgh Channel R

4

47

WP No	Waypoint name and position	Latitude	Longitude
14–1	Black Deep N outer, midway Sunk Head buoy and No 2 buoy	51°46.10'N	01°31.49'E
14–2	Black Deep N inner, 8 cables E of Black Deep No 1 green buoy	51°44.01'N	01°29.51'E
14–3	Little Sunk east, midway Little Sunk and Long Sand beacons	51°41.68'N	01°27.23'E
14–4	Sunk Head Tower N clearing, ½ M due N of N-card buoy	51°47.11'N	01°30.62'E
14–5	Sunk Head inner N clearing, 1.2 M 235°T from N-card buoy	51°45.92'N	01°29.01'E
14–6	East Swin NE outer, 1.6 M NW of Sunk Head N-card buoy	51°47.74'N	01°28.80'E
14–7	Long Sand Head N clearing, 2 M due W of N-card buoy	51°47.87'N	01°36.31'E
14–8	Long Sand Head N-card buoy, actual position	51°47.87'N	01°39.54'E
14–9	Long Sand Head NE clearing, 1 M 160°T from N-card buoy	51°46.93'N	01°40.10'E
14–10	Long Sand Head E clearing, 3½ M 190°T from N-card buoy	51°44.42'N	01°38.56'E
14–11	Knock Deep NE, 3½ M due E of the Long Sand beacon	51°41.45'N	01°35.20'E
14–12	Knock Deep middle, 4 M 155°T from the Long Sand beacon	51°37.83'N	01°32.29'E
14–13	Knock Deep SW, 6.2 M due E of the NW Long Sand beacon	51°34.70'N	01°28.10'E
14–14	Kentish Knock E-card whistle buoy, actual position	51°38.50'N	01°40.50'E
14–15	South Knock S-card bell buoy, actual position	51°34.74'N	01°36.12'E
14–16	South Knock east clearing, 1 M due E of S-card bell buoy	51°34.74'N	01°37.73'E

Datum OSGB 36 The waypoint latitudes and longitudes in this table refer to Ordnance Survey of Great Britain (1936) Datum

COASTAL DANGERS

Refer to Admiralty charts 1183 and 1975

Sunk Sand

Sunk Sand is a long narrow bank stretching north-east for 13 miles from the SW Sunk beacon, separating Black Deep from Barrow Deep and the East Swin. Middle Sunk lies 2½ miles north-east of the SW Sunk beacon and dries to almost 2 metres. Little Sunk is the most seaward drying part of the Sunk Sand, running more or less between Black Deep No 1 and No 3 green buoys. The SW end of Little Sunk is marked by a beacon and in quiet weather you can cut across the bank at this point by passing a couple of cables south of Little Sunk beacon.

The seaward extremity of Sunk Sand is guarded by Sunk Head N-cardinal buoy, which lies close north-east of the ruined base of the old Sunk Head Tower. The tower foundations have only 2.1 metres over them at LAT.

Long Sand

Long Sand is part of a vast finger of banks and shoals stretching north-east from the seaward edge of North Edinburgh Channel for a good 18 miles out to Long Sand Head. Vessels passing through the well-buoyed North Edinburgh Channel leave the inner part of Long Sand to the north-east. Fisherman's Gat, a deep, unmarked fairway about 1 mile wide, cuts across the bottom of the 'finger' just NE of the inner part of Long Sand.

The seaward drying parts of Long Sand are marked on their west side by the red channel buoys of Black Deep, but the east side of Long Sand is unmarked for the 19 miles between North Edinburgh Channel and Long Sand Head N-cardinal bell buoy, which guards the seaward extremity of the shoals.

Kentish Knock

The infamous Kentish Knock is the most seaward of the Thames Estuary banks and in many ways the most dangerous, as the large number of wrecks marked on the chart will testify. Kentish Knock runs almost north–south and is 8 miles long. There are several drying patches and a good many areas where the depth is less than ½ metre at LAT.

The bank is marked on the east side by Kentish Knock E-cardinal whistle buoy and at the south-east tip by the South Knock S-cardinal bell buoy, but these two buoys are nearly 5 miles apart and great care must be taken anywhere in this area in poor or even moderate visibility. There is no buoy at the north end of the bank, where soundings fall quickly from about 12 metres down to 3 metres and then to less than ½ metre.

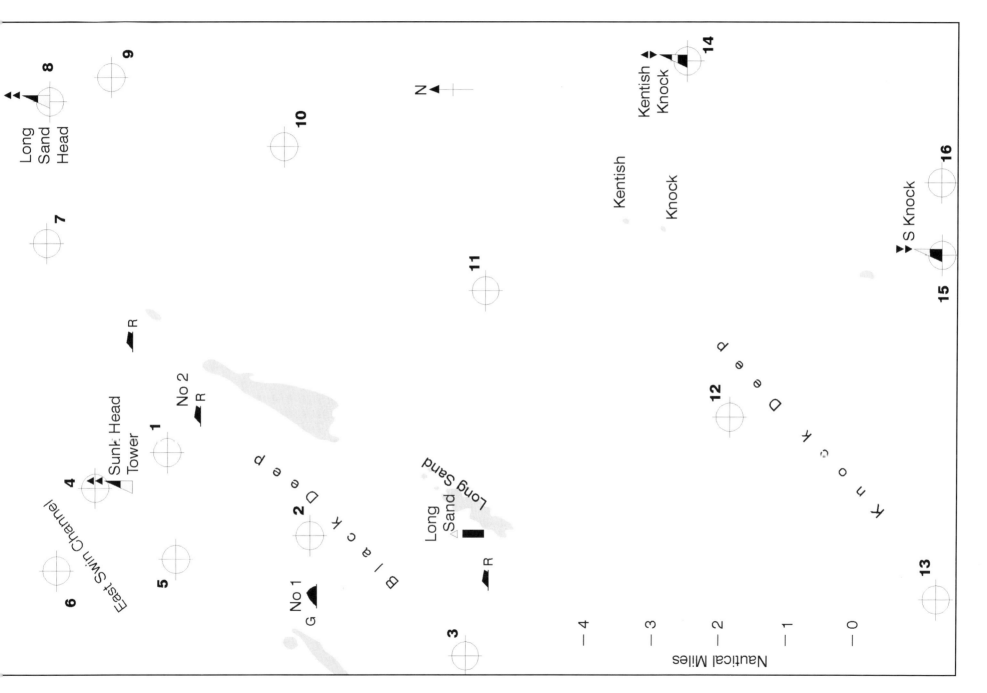

Long Sand Head

8

9

Kentish Knock

14

N

10

Kentish

Knock

7

16

S Knock

15

11

R

No 2
R

Sunk Head
Tower

1

12

Deep

Long Sand

Long Sand

4

R

Black Deep

2

Knock Deep

East Swin Channel

5

R

13

6

No 1

G

3

— 4

— 3

— 2

— 1

— 0

Nautical Miles

WP No	Waypoint name and position	Latitude	Longitude
15–1	Cork Sand N, 1½ ca due N of Cork Sand N-card beacon	51°55.34'N	01°25.31'E
15–2	Cork Sand red buoy, actual position	51°55.43'N	01°25.95'E
15–3	Harwich South Channel outer, 4 ca SE of No 2 yellow buoy	51°55.62'N	01°28.10'E
15–4	Felixstowe Ledge green buoy, actual position	51°56.29'N	01°24.52'E
15–5	Washington green buoy, actual position	51°56.49'N	01°26.70'E
15–6	Shipway red-and-white fairway buoy, actual position	51°56.72'N	01°30.78'E
15–7	Cross South, ½ M due S of Cross yellow channel buoy	51°55.70'N	01°30.58'E
15–8	Haven fairway, 1 ca SW of Haven red-and-white fairway buoy	51°55.65'N	01°32.54'E
15–9	Haven NE, 7 ca 045°T from Haven red-and-white fairway buoy	51°56.23'N	01°33.48'E
15–10	Rough N-card buoy, actual position	51°55.16'N	01°31.11'E
15–11	Cork Hole, 1 M 160°T from Cork Sand N-card beacon	51°54.25'N	01°25.88'E
15–12	Roughs Tower west clearing, 3 ca due W of Roughs Tower	51°53.68'N	01°28.46'E
15–13	Roughs Tower east clearing, 3 ca due E of Roughs Tower	51°53.68'N	01°29.45'E
15–14	SW Tail of Rough, 1¼ M 220°T from Roughs Tower	51°52.73'N	01°27.63'E
15–15	SW Shipwash W-card buoy, actual position	51°54.72'N	01°34.32'E
15–16	North Threshold, 1 ca due W of yellow channel buoy	51°54.47'N	01°33.40'E
15–17	Shiphead red buoy, actual position	51°53.75'N	01°34.00'E
15–18	South Shipwash S-card buoy, actual position	51°52.68'N	01°34.17'E
15–19	South Threshold yellow channel entrance buoy, actual position	51°52.45'N	01°33.29'E
15–20	Fort Massac SW, 3 ca SW of W Fort Massac W-card buoy	51°53.12'N	01°32.24'E

Datum OSGB 36 The waypoint latitudes and longitudes in this table refer to Ordnance Survey of Great Britain (1936) Datum

down to ½ metre or less in parts. When approaching Harwich from the east, care must be taken to avoid these shoals and it is safest to pass south of, or at least close to, the South Shipwash S-cardinal buoy.

Shipping in Harwich approaches

Harwich and Felixstowe are busy commercial ports and large ships and ferries are continually on the move in the Harwich deep-water approach channel. Take care not to impede shipping and always use the recommended approach track for boats, which lies just the 'wrong' side of the red buoys on the south side of the deep-water channel. Yachts approaching Harwich from the south-east would normally pass within 1 mile east of Roughs Tower and its buoys before heading for Cork Sand red buoy and the start of the recommended approach track.

COASTAL DANGERS
Refer to Admiralty chart 2052

Cork Sand

The narrow sliver of Cork Sand extends just west of south for about 3 miles from near the south edge of the main Harwich approach channel. The southern part dries to just over 1 metre. Cork Sand provides a natural barrier between the main east approaches to Harwich and the shallow 'back-door' route from the south via the Medusa Channel. Cork Sand is guarded at its north tip by the Cork N-cardinal beacon and on the south side by the South Cork S-cardinal buoy.

The north end of Cork Sand lies close to the recommended track for boats entering Harwich from the east. Be sure to pass north of Cork Sand N-cardinal beacon as you come through the South Channel along the track, even though you will pass just the 'wrong' side of Cork Sand red buoy.

Shipwash

The south part of the long Shipwash bank is guarded by the SW Shipwash W-cardinal buoy, Shiphead red buoy and South Shipwash S-cardinal buoy. The southern section of the bank has some of the shallowest water, with soundings

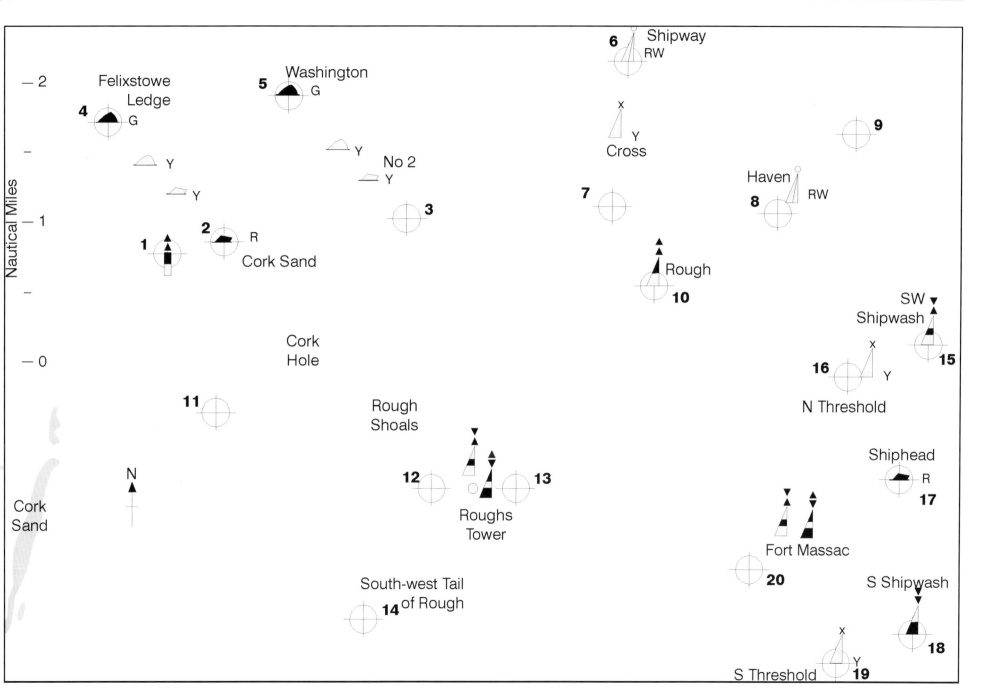

— 2

Nautical Miles

Felixstowe
Ledge
4 G

Washington
5 G

6 Shipway
RW

x
Y
Cross

9

— 1

Y

No 2
Y
Y

7

Haven
8 RW

3

1

2 R
Cork Sand

Rough
10

SW
Shipwash
15

— 0

Cork
Hole

16 Y

N Threshold

11

Rough
Shoals

Shiphead
17 R

N

12 **13**

Roughs
Tower

Fort Massac
20

S Shipwash

Cork
Sand

South-west Tail
14 of Rough

x
Y
S Threshold **19**

18

51

WP No	Waypoint name and position	Latitude	Longitude
16–1	East Goodwin clearing, ½ M due E of E-card buoy	51°16.00'N	01°36.40'E
16–2	Inter Bank yellow separation zone buoy, actual position	51°16.45'N	01°52.33'E
16–3	'MDW' S-card buoy, actual position	51°19.10'N	01°59.40'E
16–4	'F2' yellow separation zone bell buoy, actual position	51°20.40'N	01°56.30'E
16–5	Mid Falls red bell buoy, actual position	51°18.60'N	01°47.10'E
16–6	NE-Goodwin E-card buoy, actual position	51°20.30'N	01°34.27'E
16–7	North Foreland, 1 M due E of lighthouse	51°22.46'N	01°28.40'E
16–8	Elbow N-card buoy, actual position	51°23.20'N	01°31.68'E
16–9	CS5 yellow separation zone buoy, actual position	51°23.00'N	01°50.00'E
16–10	Sandettié deep-water route north light float, actual position	51°23.85'N	02°00.58'E
16–11	Falls Head N-card buoy, actual position	51°28.17'N	01°50.05'E
16–12	Drill Stone E-card bell buoy, actual position	51°25.80'N	01°43.05'E
16–13	Longnose, 100 m due N of Longnose red buoy	51°24.18'N	01°26.18'E
16–14	E Margate red buoy, actual position	51°27.00'N	01°26.50'E
16–15	NE Spit E-card buoy, actual position	51°27.90'N	01°30.00'E
16–16	Outer Tongue fairway buoy, actual position	51°30.70'N	01°26.50'E
16–17	Knock Deep SW, 6.2 M due E of the NW Long Sand beacon	51°34.70'N	01°28.10'E
16–18	South Knock S-card bell buoy, actual position	51°34.74'N	01°36.12'E
16–19	South Knock east clearing, 1 M due E of S-card bell buoy	51°34.74'N	01°37.73'E
16–20	Knock Deep middle, 4 M 155°T from the Long Sand beacon	51°37.83'N	01°32.29'E
16–21	Kentish Knock E-card whistle buoy, actual position	51°38.50'N	01°40.50'E
16–22	Little Sunk east, midway Little Sunk and Long Sand beacons	51°41.68'N	01°27.23'E
16–23	Knock Deep NE, 3½ M due E of the Long Sand beacon	51°41.45'N	01°35.20'E

COASTAL DANGERS

Refer to Admiralty charts 323, 1183 and 1406

Sunk Sand

Sunk Sand is a long narrow bank stretching north-east for 13 miles from the SW Sunk beacon, separating Black Deep from Barrow Deep and the East Swin. Middle Sunk lies 2½ miles north-east of the SW Sunk beacon and dries to almost 2 metres. Little Sunk is the most seaward drying part of the Sunk Sand, running more or less between Black Deep No 1 and No 3 green buoys. The SW end of Little Sunk is marked by a beacon and in quiet weather you can cut across the bank at this point by passing a couple of cables south of Little Sunk beacon.

The seaward extremity of Sunk Sand is guarded by Sunk Head N-cardinal buoy, which lies close north-east of the ruined base of the old Sunk Head Tower. The tower foundations have only 2.1 metres over them at LAT.

Long Sand

Long Sand is part of a vast finger of banks and shoals stretching north-east from the seaward edge of North Edinburgh Channel for a good 18 miles out to Long Sand Head. Vessels passing through the well-buoyed North Edinburgh Channel leave the inner part of Long Sand to the north-east. Fisherman's Gat, a deep, unmarked fairway about a mile wide, cuts across the bottom of the 'finger' just NE of the inner part of Long Sand.

The seaward drying parts of Long Sand are marked on their west side by the red channel buoys of Black Deep, but the east side of Long Sand is unmarked for the 19 miles between North Edinburgh Channel and Long Sand Head N-cardinal bell buoy, which guards the seaward extremity of the shoals.

Kentish Knock

The infamous Kentish Knock is the most seaward of the Thames Estuary banks and in many ways the most dangerous, as the large number of wrecks marked on the chart will testify. Kentish Knock runs almost north–south and is 8 miles long. There are several drying patches and a good many areas where the depth is less than ½ metre at LAT.

The bank is marked on the east side by Kentish Knock E-cardinal whistle buoy and at the south-east tip by the South Knock S-cardinal bell buoy, but these two buoys are nearly 5 miles apart and great care must be taken anywhere in this area in poor or even moderate visibility. There is no buoy at the north end of the bank, where soundings fall quickly from about 12 metres down to 3 metres and then to less than ½ metre.

Goodwin Sands

The Goodwins are probably the most notorious dangers in the English Channel. They are extensive drying sands lying up to 7 miles offshore between Ramsgate and South Foreland. The Goodwins should be avoided in all circumstances, and are well marked on their east, north and south sides.

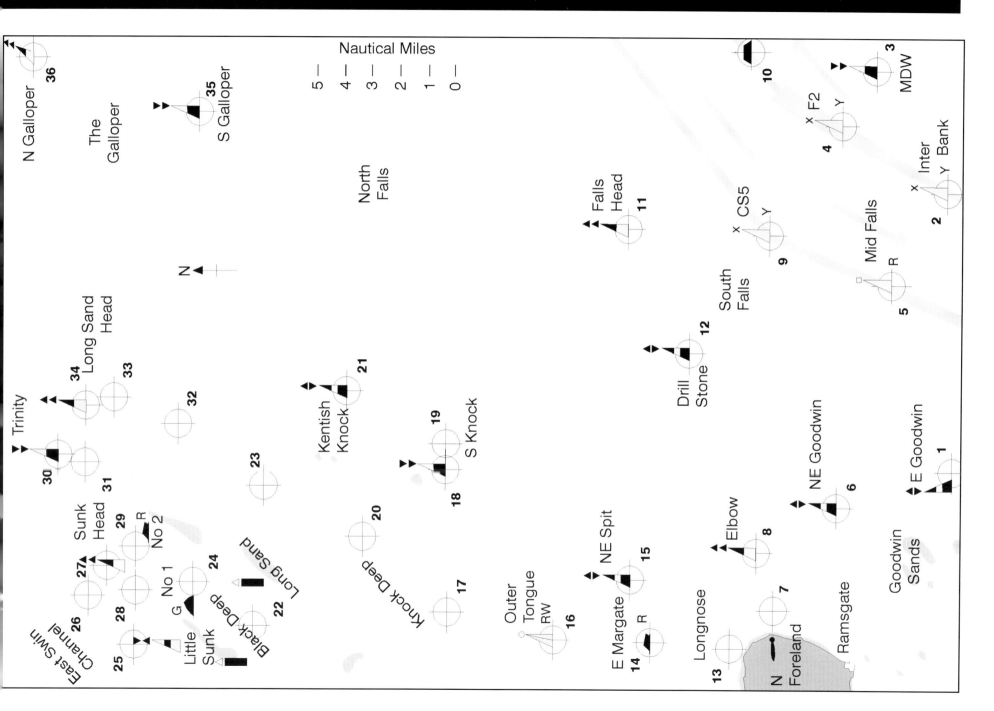

Nautical Miles

5 —
4 —
3 —
2 —
1 —
0 —

N Galloper
36

The
Galloper

S Galloper
35

North
Falls

Long Sand
Head

Trinity

34
33
32

30
31

Sunk
Head
29
R
No 2

27
No 1
G
24

Little
Sunk
22

Black Deep
Long Sand

East Swin
Channel
26
28
25

Kentish
Knock
21

S Knock
19
18

23

20

Knock Deep
17

Outer
Tongue
RW
16

NE Spit
15

E Margate
R
14
13

Longnose
7

N
Foreland

Ramsgate

Goodwin
Sands

Elbow
8

NE Goodwin
6

E Goodwin
1

Falls
Head
11

x CS5
Y
9

South
Falls

Drill
Stone
12

Mid Falls
R
5

x F2
Y
4

x Inter
Y Bank
2

MDW
3

10

N

53

WP No	Waypoint name and position	Latitude	Longitude
16–24	Black Deep N inner, 8 ca E of Black Deep No 1 green buoy	51°44.01'N	01°29.51'E
16–25	East Swin NE, 1.6 M due N of West Sunk W-card buoy	51°45.90'N	01°25.90'E
16–26	East Swin NE outer, 1.6 M NW of Sunk Head N-card buoy	51°47.74'N	01°28.80'E
16–27	Sunk Head Tower N clearing, ½ M due N of N-card buoy	51°47.11'N	01°30.62'E
16–28	Sunk Head inner N clearing, 1.2 M 235°T from N-card buoy	51°45.92'N	01°29.01'E
16–29	Black Deep N outer, midway Sunk Head buoy and No 2 buoy	51°46.10'N	01°31.49'E
16–30	Trinity S-card buoy, actual position	51°49.02'N	01°36.50'E
16–31	Long Sand Head N clearing, 2 M due W of N-card buoy	51°47.87'N	01°36.31'E
16–32	Long Sand Head E clearing, 3½ M 190°T from N-card buoy	51°44.42'N	01°38.56'E
16–33	Long Sand Head NE clearing, 1 M 160°T from N-card buoy	51°46.93'N	01°40.10'E
16–34	Long Sand Head N-card buoy, actual position	51°47.87'N	01°39.54'E
16–35	South Galloper S-card whistle buoy, actual position	51°43.95'N	01°56.53'E
16–36	North Galloper N-card buoy, actual position	51°50.00'N	01°59.50'E

Datum OSGB 36 The waypoint latitudes and longitudes in this table refer to Ordnance Survey of Great Britain (1936) Datum

The well-used channel between the Goodwins and the Kent coast is partly sheltered by the banks in onshore winds. The wide, southern entrance to this channel lies between South Foreland and the South Goodwin light-float. Working north, you need to pick up Goodwin Fork S-cardinal buoy and then the narrow gate between South Brake red buoy and West Goodwin green buoy. From this gate, you can make good north true for 4 miles, passing safely east of Brake Sand, until you join the Ramsgate entrance channel.

Gull Stream is a buoyed channel running SW–NE for just over 5 miles between the West Goodwin buoy and the north entrance between Gull E-cardinal buoy and Goodwin Knoll green buoy.

The Galloper

Galloper bank is a narrow shoal about 5 miles long, marked at its north end by the North Galloper N-cardinal buoy and at its south end by South Galloper S-cardinal buoy. The least depth is about 2½ metres and boats should avoid crossing the Galloper unless conditions are particularly calm. A nasty sea breaks over the Galloper in heavy weather from any quarter.

Noord Hinder shipping lanes

The shipping lanes shown on this chart are part of the Noord Hinder South traffic separation scheme. Yachts and other craft should stay out of these lanes as far as possible and should only cross them at right-angles. Shipping is busy through these lanes, which take traffic bound to and from Rotterdam and the German ports.

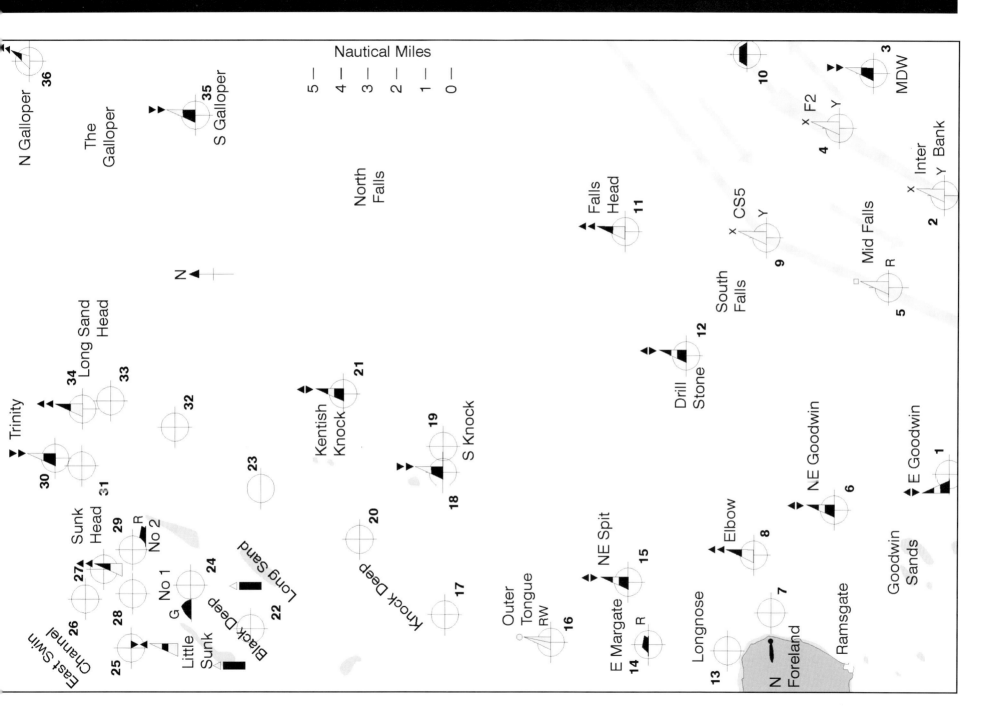

Nautical Miles

5 —
4 —
3 —
2 —
1 —
0 —

N Galloper **36**

The Galloper

S Galloper **35**

North Falls

Falls Head **11**

x F2
Y
4

MDW **3**

x Inter
x
Y Bank
2

10

x CS5
Y
9

Mid Falls
R
5

South Falls

Drill Stone **12**

N

Long Sand Head

34
33

Trinity
30
31
32

Kentish Knock **21**

S Knock
19
18

NE Goodwin **6**

E Goodwin **1**

Sunk Head
29
No 2 R
27
28
No 1
G
Black Deep
24
Long Sand
22

Knock Deep
20
17

NE Spit **15**

E Margate
R
14

Elbow **8**

Longnose **13**

N Foreland

Ramsgate

Goodwin Sands

East Swin Channel
26
25
Little Sunk

Outer Tongue RW **16**

7

WP No	Waypoint name and position	Latitude	Longitude
17–1	South Galloper S-card whistle buoy, actual position	51°43.95'N	01°56.53'E
17–2	North Galloper N-card buoy, actual position	51°50.00'N	01°59.50'E
17–3	Inner Gabbard S-card buoy, actual position	51°51.20'N	01°52.40'E
17–4	Long Sand Head N-card buoy, actual position	51°47.87'N	01°39.54'E
17–5	Long Sand Head NE clearing, 1 M 160°T from N-card buoy	51°46.93'N	01°40.10'E
17–6	Long Sand Head E clearing, 3½ M 190°T from N-card buoy	51°44.42'N	01°38.56'E
17–7	Knock Deep NE, 3½ M due E of the Long Sand beacon	51°41.45'N	01°35.20'E
17–8	Trinity S-card buoy, actual position	51°49.02'N	01°36.50'E
17–9	Long Sand Head N clearing, 2 M due W of N-card buoy	51°47.87'N	01°36.31'E
17–10	Black Deep N outer, midway Sunk Head buoy and No 2 buoy	51°46.10'N	01°31.49'E
17–11	Black Deep N inner, 8 ca E of Black Deep No 1 green buoy	51°44.01'N	01°29.51'E
17–12	Little Sunk east, midway Little Sunk and Long Sand beacons	51°41.68'N	01°27.23'E
17–13	Sunk Head Tower N clearing, ½ M due N of N-card buoy	51°47.11'N	01°30.62'E
17–14	Sunk Head inner N clearing, 1.2 M 235°T from N-card buoy	51°45.92'N	01°29.01'E
17–15	East Swin NE outer, 1.6 M NW of Sunk Head N-card buoy	51°47.74'N	01°28.80'E
17–16	East Swin NE, 1.6 M due N of West Sunk W-card buoy	51°45.90'N	01°25.90'E
17–17	Gunfleet Spit, 2 ca due S of Gunfleet Spit S-card buoy	51°45.10'N	01°21.80'E
17–18	East Swin Middle, 1.4 M due S of Gunfleet Spit S-card buoy	51°43.90'N	01°21.80'E
17–19	East Swin South, midway No 3 E-card and No 2 red buoys	51°41.98'N	01°21.69'E
17–20	East Swin SW, 1.4 M 285°T from No 3 E-card bell buoy	51°42.39'N	01°18.17'E
17–21	Gunfleet South, 3½ M 240°T from Gunfleet Spit S-card buoy	51°43.81'N	01°16.67'E
17–22	NE Middle swatchway, 1.8 M east of N Middle N-card buoy	51°41.00'N	01°14.89'E
17–23	NE Middle, 1½ M 080°T from N Middle N-card buoy	51°41.28'N	01°14.39'E
17–24	Gunfleet NW, 1½ ca NW of Wallet No 4 red buoy	51°46.62'N	01°17.17'E

COASTAL DANGERS
Refer to Admiralty charts 1183, 2052 and 1406

Shipwash
The long Shipwash bank lies about 8 miles offshore opposite the Harwich approaches and is almost 9 miles from north to south. The north end is guarded by the North Shipwash N-cardinal buoy and the seaward edge by the East Shipwash E-cardinal buoy. The Shipway channel lies just inside the Shipwash and the west edge of the bank is guarded by the NW Shipwash red buoy.

The south part of the long Shipwash bank is guarded by the SW Shipwash W-cardinal buoy, Shiphead red buoy and South Shipwash S-cardinal buoy. The southern section of the bank has some of the shallowest water, with soundings down to ½ metre or less in parts. When approaching Harwich from the east, care must be taken to avoid these shoals and it is safest to pass south of, or at least close to, the South Shipwash S-cardinal buoy.

Woodbridge Haven entrance
The shingle banks and bar at the entrance to Woodbridge Haven are notoriously mobile and the buoys are moved from time to time to reflect changes in the channel. It is best to approach after half-flood and to leave, if possible, 1 hour before high water. The entrance should be avoided altogether in fresh onshore winds, especially with a spring ebb running.

Shipping in Harwich approaches
Harwich and Felixstowe are busy commercial ports and large ships and ferries are continually on the move in the Harwich deep-water approach channel. Take care not to impede shipping and always use the recommended approach track, which lies just the 'wrong' side of the red buoys on the south side of the deep-water channel. Boats approaching Harwich from the south-east would normally pass within a mile east of Roughs Tower and its buoys before heading for Cork Sand red buoy and the start of the recommended approach track.

Gunfleet Sand
The long finger of Gunfleet Sand runs ENE–WSW for more than 10 miles from the Blackwater approaches out to the deeper water of Goldmer Gat. The main drying parts of Gunfleet lie opposite Walton-on-the-Naze, 4–5 miles offshore. These areas dry to about 1 metre and the whole length of the bank has soundings of less than 1 metre except at the NE tip, where the NE Gunfleet E-cardinal buoy guards the seaward approach.

The south edge of Gunfleet Sand borders the East Swin, or King's Channel, and is marked only by Gunfleet Spit E-cardinal bell buoy, 1 mile south-east of the old Gunfleet lighthouse opposite the largest drying part of the sand. Do not attempt to cross any part of Gunfleet Sand without local knowledge.

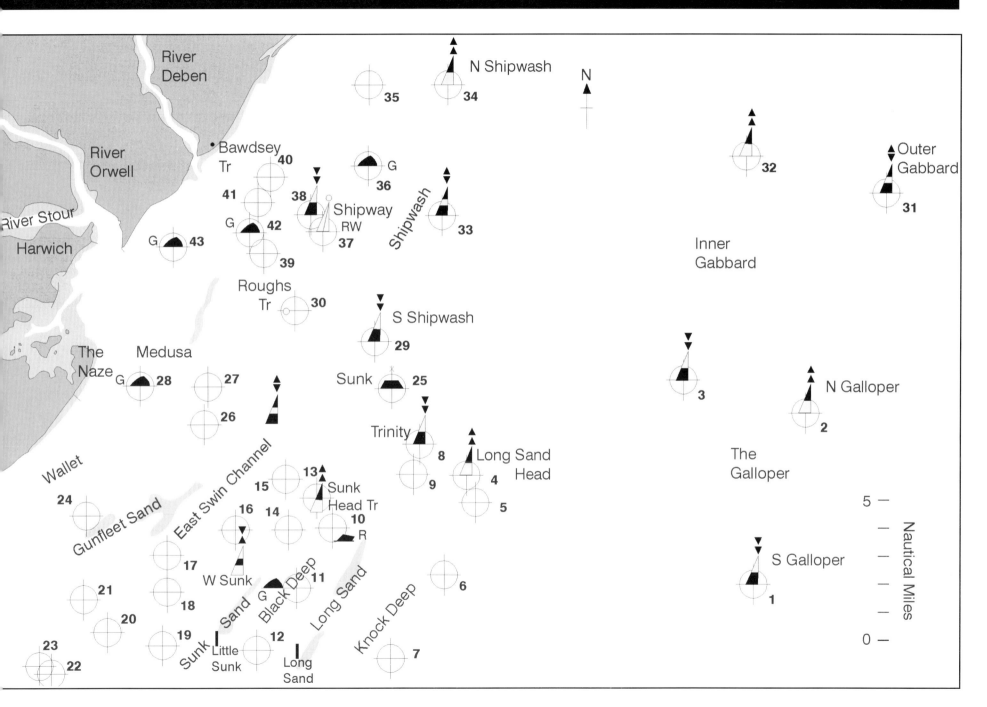

River Deben

N Shipwash

35

34

N

River Orwell

Bawdsey Tr

40

River Stour

G

36

41

38

Shipway RW

Shipwash

32

Outer Gabbard

Harwich

G 42

37

33

31

G 43

39

Inner Gabbard

Roughs Tr 30

S Shipwash

29

The Naze

Medusa

27

Sunk 25

3

N Galloper

G 28

26

Trinity

2

8 Long Sand Head

The Galloper

Wallet

East Swin Channel

13

Sunk Head Tr

9

4

5

24

Gunfleet Sand

15

14

10

R

5 —

16

W Sunk

Nautical Miles

17

Black Deep 11

Long Sand

Knock Deep

6

S Galloper

21

1

18

G Sand

20

19

Sunk

12

23

Little Sunk

Long Sand

7

0 —

22

WP No	Waypoint name and position	Latitude	Longitude
17–25	Sunk LANBY, actual position	51°51.00'N	01°35.00'E
17–26	Goldmer Gat, 2½ M due W of NE Gunfleet E-card buoy	51°49.90'N	01°23.87'E
17–27	South Cork, 2 ca due S of South Cork S-card buoy	51°51.10'N	01°24.20'E
17–28	Medusa green buoy, actual position	51°51.20'N	01°20.45'E
17–29	South Shipwash S-card buoy, actual position	51°52.68'N	01°34.17'E
17–30	Roughs Tower east clearing, 3 ca due E of Roughs Tower	51°53.68'N	01°29.45'E
17–31	Outer Gabbard E-card whistle buoy, actual position	51°57.80'N	02°04.30'E
17–32	North Inner Gabbard N-card buoy, actual position	51°59.10'N	01°56.10'E
17–33	East Shipwash E-card buoy, actual position	51°57.05'N	01°38.00'E
17–34	North Shipwash N-card buoy, actual position	52°01.70'N	01°38.35'E
17–35	Sledway NE, 3 M due W of North Shipwash N-card buoy	52°01.70'N	01°33.46'E
17–36	Mid Bawdsey green buoy, actual position	51°58.85'N	01°33.71'E
17–37	Shipway red-and-white fairway buoy, actual position	51°56.72'N	01°30.78'E
17–38	South Bawdsey S-card whistle buoy, actual position	51°57.20'N	01°30.33'E
17–39	Harwich South Channel outer, 4 ca SE of No 2 yellow buoy	51°55.62'N	01°28.10'E
17–40	Cutler east clearing, 2 ca due E of the Cutler green buoy	51°58.50'N	01°27.94'E
17–41	Cutler south clearing, 2½ M 140°T from Bawdsey Radio Tower	51°57.67'N	01°27.19'E
17–42	Washington green buoy, actual position	51°56.49'N	01°26.70'E
17–43	Wadgate Ledge green buoy, actual position	51°56.08'N	01°22.21'E

Datum OSGB 36 The waypoint latitudes and longitudes in this table refer to Ordnance Survey of Great Britain (1936) Datum

Fisherman's Gat, a deep, unmarked fairway about 1 mile wide, cuts across the bottom of the 'finger' just NE of the inner part of Long Sand.

The seaward drying parts of Long Sand are marked on their west side by the red channel buoys of Black Deep, but the east side of Long Sand is unmarked for the 19 miles between North Edinburgh Channel and Long Sand Head N-cardinal bell buoy, which guards the seaward extremity of the shoals.

The Galloper

Galloper bank is a narrow shoal about 5 miles long, marked at its north end by the North Galloper N-cardinal buoy and at its south end by South Galloper S-cardinal buoy. The least depth is about 2½ metres and boats should avoid crossing the Galloper unless conditions are particularly calm. A nasty sea breaks over the Galloper in heavy weather from any quarter.

Sunk Sand

Sunk Sand is a long narrow bank stretching north-east for 13 miles from the SW Sunk beacon, separating Black Deep from Barrow Deep and the East Swin. Middle Sunk lies 2½ miles north-east of the SW Sunk beacon and dries to almost 2 metres. Little Sunk is the most seaward drying part of the Sunk Sand, running more or less between Black Deep No 1 and No 3 green buoys. The SW end of Little Sunk is marked by a beacon and in quiet weather you can cut across the bank at this point by passing a couple of cables south of Little Sunk beacon.

The seaward extremity of Sunk Sand is guarded by Sunk Head N-cardinal buoy, which lies close north-east of the ruined base of the old Sunk Head Tower. The tower foundations have only 2.1 metres over them at LAT.

Long Sand

Long Sand is part of a vast finger of banks and shoals stretching north-east from the seaward edge of North Edinburgh Channel for a good 18 miles out to Long Sand Head. Vessels passing through the well-buoyed North Edinburgh Channel leave the inner part of Long Sand to the north-east.

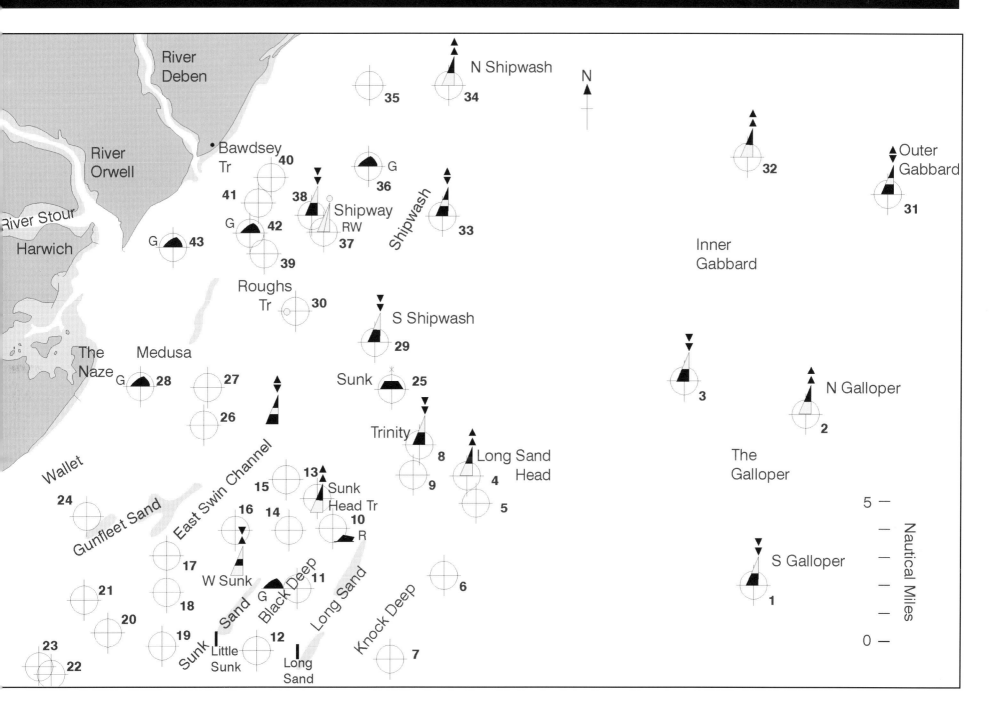

River Deben

River Orwell

River Stour

Harwich

Bawdsey

Roughs Tr

The Naze

Medusa

Wallet

Gunfleet Sand

East Swin Channel

Sunk Sand

W Sunk

Black Deep

G

Little Sunk

Long Sand

Knock Deep

Long Sand

Sunk Head Tr

Shipway RW

Shipwash

Sunk

Trinity

Long Sand Head

N Shipwash

S Shipwash

N

Inner Gabbard

Outer Gabbard

N Galloper

The Galloper

S Galloper

Nautical Miles

5 —

0 —

35   34   32   31

40   36   33

41   38   G   30

G   42   29   3

G   43   39   25   2

28   27   8

26   13   4   6

15   Sunk   9   5

16   14   10   R

17   11   1

21   18   20   12

23   19   7

22

59

WP No	Waypoint name and position	Latitude	Longitude
18–1	Washington green buoy, actual position	51°56.49'N	01°26.70'E
18–2	Shipway red-and-white fairway buoy, actual position	51°56.72'N	01°30.78'E
18–3	Shipway channel south, 1¼ M due E of Shipway fairway buoy	51°56.75'N	01°32.78'E
18–4	South Bawdsey S-card whistle buoy, actual position	51°57.20'N	01°30.33'E
18–5	Cutler south clearing, 2½ M 140°T from Bawdsey Radio Tr	51°57.67'N	01°27.19'E
18–6	Cutler east clearing, 2 ca due E of the Cutler green buoy	51°58.50'N	01°27.94'E
18–7	Woodbridge Haven E, 1.2 M 160°T from Bawdsey Radio Tr	51°58.46'N	01°25.25'E
18–8	Woodbridge Haven fairway, 8 ca 150°T from south Martello Tr	51°58.04'N	01°23.97'E
18–9	Bawdsey Bank S clearing, 5¼ M due E of Bawdsey Radio Tr	51°59.57'N	01°33.15'E
18–10	Sledway south, 3.3 M due E of Bawdsey Radio Tr	51°59.57'N	01°29.96'E
18–11	Cutler north clearing, 2 M 085°T from Bawdsey Radio Tr	51°59.74'N	01°27.83'E
18–12	Woodbridge Haven NE, 1.4 M 095°T from Bawdsey Radio Tr	51°59.45'N	01°26.84'E
18–13	Mid Bawdsey green buoy, actual position	51°58.85'N	01°33.71'E
18–14	Sledway middle, 4.6 M 202°T from Orford Ness lighthouse	52°00.75'N	01°31.78'E
18–15	Orford Haven S outer, 6 M 225°T from Orford Ness lighthouse	52°00.77'N	01°27.67'E

Datum OSGB 36 The waypoint latitudes and longitudes in this table refer to Ordnance Survey of Great Britain (1936) Datum

COASTAL DANGERS
Refer to Admiralty charts 2052 and 2693

Woodbridge Haven entrance
The shingle banks and bar at the entrance to Woodbridge Haven are notoriously mobile and the buoys are moved from time to time to reflect changes in the channel. It is best to approach the mouth of the River Deben after half-flood and to leave, if possible, 1 hour before high water. The entrance should be avoided altogether in fresh onshore winds, especially with a spring ebb running. Harwich entrance is only 5 miles to the south-west and can be approached safely in practically any weather.

Bawdsey Bank
The Bawdsey Bank lies about 6 miles ENE of Woodbridge Haven entrance and has a least depth of 2 metres. Although in quiet to moderate weather it is perfectly safe to cross Bawdsey Bank, especially above half-tide, the sea breaks over parts of the bank in an easterly swell, when the area should be given a wide berth.

Cutler Bank
The narrow Cutler Bank lies just over 2 miles east of Woodbridge Haven entrance and runs roughly NNE–SSW for 1½ miles. The least depth over the shoal itself is 2.3 metres, but a shallow wreck has only 1.2 metres over it at LAT. The wreck is marked on its east (offshore) side by the Cutler green buoy, which is unlit.

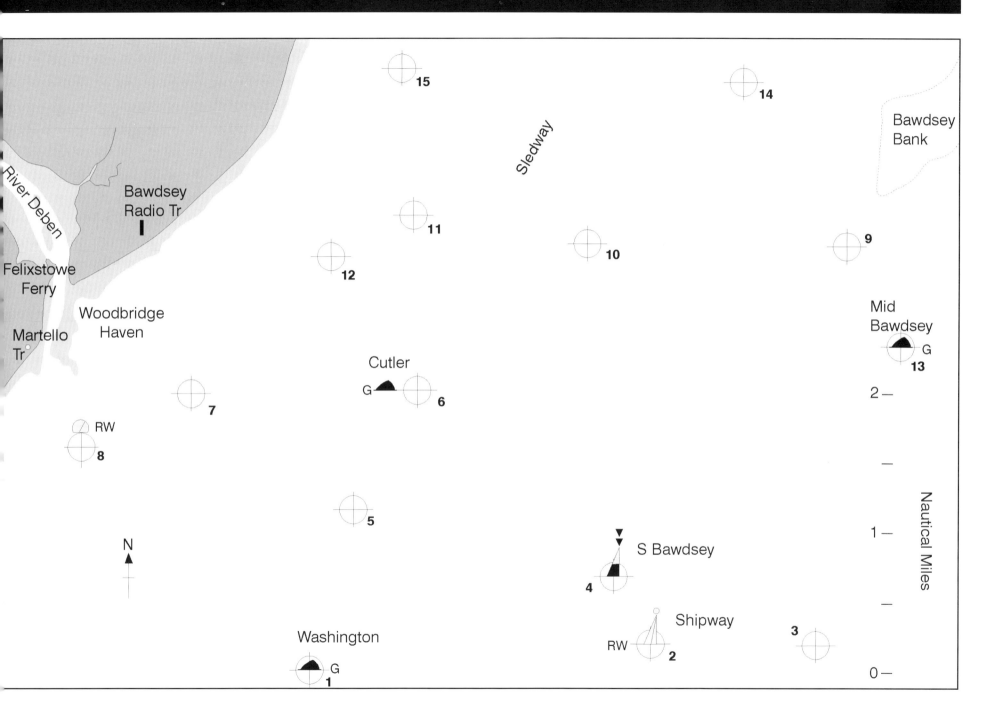

River Deben

Bawdsey
Radio Tr

Felixstowe
Ferry

Martello
Tr

Woodbridge
Haven

Sledway

Bawdsey
Bank

15

14

11

10

9

12

Mid
Bawdsey

13
G

Cutler
G
6

7

2 —

RW

8

5

N

S Bawdsey

4

1 —

Nautical Miles

Shipway

RW

2

3

Washington

G
1

0 —

WP No	Waypoint name and position	Latitude	Longitude
19–1	Shipway channel south, 1¼ M due E of Shipway fairway buoy	51°56.75'N	01°32.78'E
19–2	Haven NE, 7 ca 045°T from Haven red-and-white fairway buoy	51°56.23'N	01°33.48'E
19–3	East Shipwash E-card buoy, actual position	51°57.05'N	01°38.00'E
19–4	Mid Bawdsey green buoy, actual position	51°58.85'N	01°33.71'E
19–5	Shipway middle, 6 ca 110°T from Mid Bawdsey green buoy	51°58.64'N	01°34.63'E
19–6	NW Shipwash red buoy, actual position	51°58.33'N	01°36.32'E
19–7	Shipway NE, 4.4 M 165°T from Orford Ness lighthouse	52°00.78'N	01°36.45'E
19–8	Bawdsey Bank NE, 3.7 M 175°T from Orford Ness lighthouse	52°01.29'N	01°35.10'E
19–9	NE Bawdsey green buoy, actual position	52°01.70'N	01°36.20'E
19–10	North Shipwash N-card buoy, actual position	52°01.70'N	01°38.35'E
19–11	Shipway N entrance, 3½ M 145°T from Orford Ness lighthouse	52°02.12'N	01°37.87'E
19–12	Bawdsey Bank S clearing, 5¼ M due E of Bawdsey Radio Tr	51°59.57'N	01°33.15'E
19–13	Sledway middle, 4.6 M 202°T from Orford Ness lighthouse	52°00.75'N	01°31.78'E
19–14	Sledway NE, 2½ M due S from Orford Ness lighthouse	52°02.50'N	01°34.54'E

Datum OSGB 36 The waypoint latitudes and longitudes in this table refer to Ordnance Survey of Great Britain (1936) Datum

Local direction of buoyage
Because the Shipway is effectively an approach channel for the ports of Harwich and Felixstowe, the local direction of buoyage in the Shipway is from north to south. Therefore the NW Shipwash is left to port when you are coming down the Shipway from north to south, and the Mid Bawdsey green buoy is left to starboard.

COASTAL DANGERS
Refer to Admiralty chart 2052

Bawdsey Bank
The Bawdsey Bank lies about 6 miles ENE of Woodbridge Haven entrance and has a least depth of 2 metres. Although in quiet to moderate weather it is perfectly safe to cross Bawdsey Bank, especially above half-tide, the sea breaks over parts of the bank in an easterly swell, when the area should be given a wide berth.

Shipwash
The long Shipwash bank lies about 8 miles offshore opposite the Harwich approaches and is almost 9 miles from north to south. The north end is guarded by the North Shipwash N-cardinal buoy and the seaward edge by the East Shipwash E-cardinal buoy. The Shipway channel lies just inside the Shipwash and the west edge of the bank is guarded by the NW Shipwash red buoy.

When approaching Harwich from the northeast, you can avoid the Shipwash by picking up waypoint 19–10, leaving the North Shipwash N-cardinal to the east and then following the Shipway Channel inside the Shipwash bank.

Traffic in the Shipway Channel
Keep clear of shipping using the Shipway Channel and watch out for ships manoeuvring at slower speed near the south end of the Shipway when embarking pilots for Harwich.

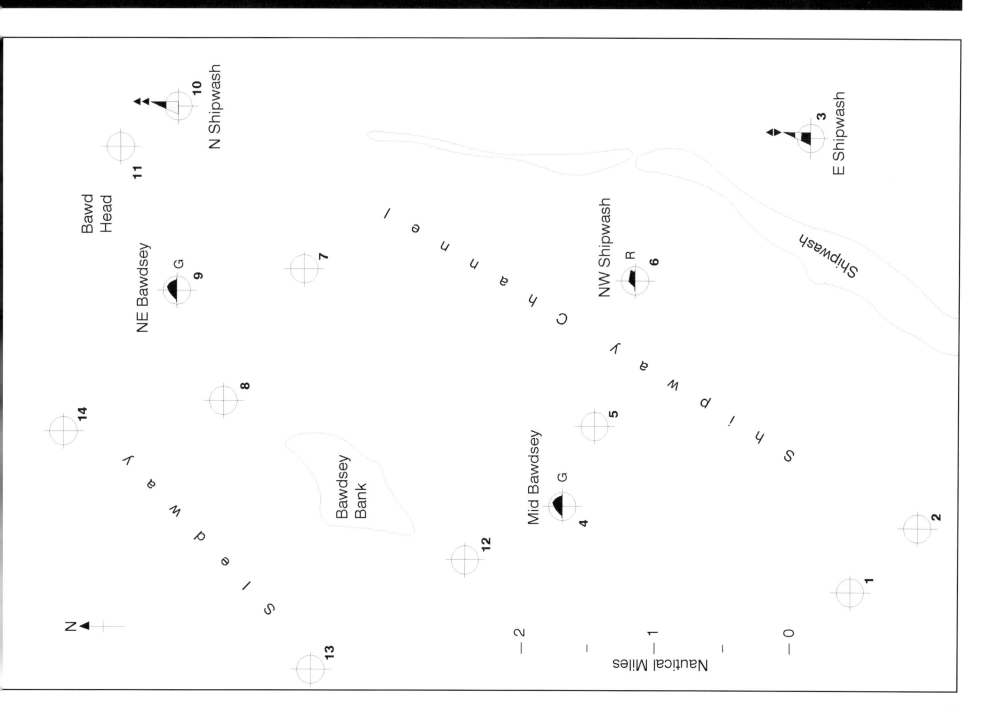

WP No	Waypoint name and position	Latitude	Longitude
20–1	Shipway NE, 4.4 M 165°T from Orford Ness lighthouse	52°00.78'N	01°36.45'E
20–2	NE Bawdsey green buoy, actual position	52°01.70'N	01°36.20'E
20–3	North Shipwash N-card buoy, actual position	52°01.70'N	01°38.35'E
20–4	Shipway N entrance, 3½ M 145°T from Orford Ness lighthouse	52°02.12'N	01°37.87'E
20–5	Bawdsey Bank NE, 3.7 M 175°T from Orford Ness lighthouse	52°01.29'N	01°35.10'E
20–6	Sledway middle, 4.6 M 202°T from Orford Ness lighthouse	52°00.75'N	01°31.78'E
20–7	Sledway NE, 2½ M due S from Orford Ness lighthouse	52°02.50'N	01°34.54'E
20–8	Whiting S clearing, 2 ca 200°T from SW Whiting S-card buoy	52°00.90'N	01°30.79'E
20–9	Whiting NE clearing, NE Whiting E-card buoy, actual position	52°03.76'N	01°33.90'E
20–10	Orford Ness inner, 7 ca SE true from Orford Ness lighthouse	52°04.50'N	01°35.40'E
20–11	Orford Ness outer, 1.7 M SE true from Orford Ness lighthouse	52°03.80'N	01°36.52'E
20–12	Hollesley Bay NE, ½ M SW true from Orford Ness lighthouse	52°04.65'N	01°33.97'E
20–13	Hollesley Bay middle, 3 M 222°T from Orford Ness lighthouse	52°02.77'N	01°31.34'E
20–14	Hollesley Bay SW, 5 M 222°T from Orford Ness lighthouse	52°01.29'N	01°29.18'E
20–15	Orford Haven S outer, 6 M 225°T from Orford Ness lighthouse	52°00.77'N	01°27.67'E
20–16	Orford fairway, 7 ca due E of middle Bawdsey Beach Martello Tr	52°01.53'N	01°27.68'E

Datum OSGB 36 The waypoint latitudes and longitudes in this table refer to Ordnance Survey of Great Britain (1936) Datum

COASTAL DANGERS

Refer to Admiralty charts 2052 and 2695

Orford Haven entrance

The shallow entrance to Orford Haven – the mouth of the River Ore – is well known for its constantly shifting shingle banks. The exact directions for the entrance are likely to change from year to year, especially after periods of heavy winter storms from the east. Up-to-date directions can be obtained at the beginning of each season from either the Aldeburgh Yacht Club or the Alde and Ore Association at Woodlands, Priory Road, Snape IP17 1SD.

In any event, strangers should only approach Orford Haven in quiet offshore weather in the absence of swell. It is said that the best time to enter or leave the river is from about 1 hour after low water, when there should be enough depth over the bar, but the worst of the shingle banks will still be uncovered and therefore easier to avoid.

Whiting Bank

The Whiting Bank runs approximately NNE–SSW and lies between 1 and 2 miles offshore opposite the long sandspit that separates the River Ore from the sea. The Whiting is about 2½ miles long and the shallowest parts have only 1 metre depth at LAT. Steep seas break over the bank in heavy onshore weather and overfalls are active when a fresh wind is blowing against the tide.

The Whiting Bank is marked at its north end by the NE Whiting E-cardinal buoy and at its south end by the SW Whiting S-cardinal buoy. The fairway inside the bank is known as the Hollesley Channel, for which Whiting Hook red buoy marks the west edge of the bank. The much wider channel outside Whiting Bank is called the Sledway.

Bawdsey Bank

The Bawdsey Bank lies about 4 miles ESE of Orford Haven entrance and has a least depth of 2 metres. Although in quiet to moderate weather it is perfectly safe to cross Bawdsey Bank, especially above half-tide, the sea breaks over parts of the bank in an easterly swell, when the area should be given a wide berth.

Shipwash

The long Shipwash bank lies about 8 miles offshore opposite the Harwich approaches and is almost 9 miles from north to south. The north end is guarded by the North Shipwash N-cardinal buoy and the seaward edge by the East Shipwash E-cardinal buoy. The Shipway channel lies just inside the Shipwash and the west edge of the bank is guarded by the NW Shipwash red buoy.

When approaching Harwich from the north-east, you can avoid the Shipwash by picking up waypoint 19–10, leaving the North Shipwash N-cardinal to the east and then following the Shipway Channel inside the Shipwash bank.

Local direction of buoyage

Because the Shipway is effectively an approach channel for the ports of Harwich and Felixstowe, the local direction of buoyage in the Shipway is from north to south. Therefore the NW Shipwash is left to port when you are coming down the Shipway from north to south, and the Mid Bawdsey green buoy is left to starboard. The direction of buoyage in the Sledway is also from north to south.

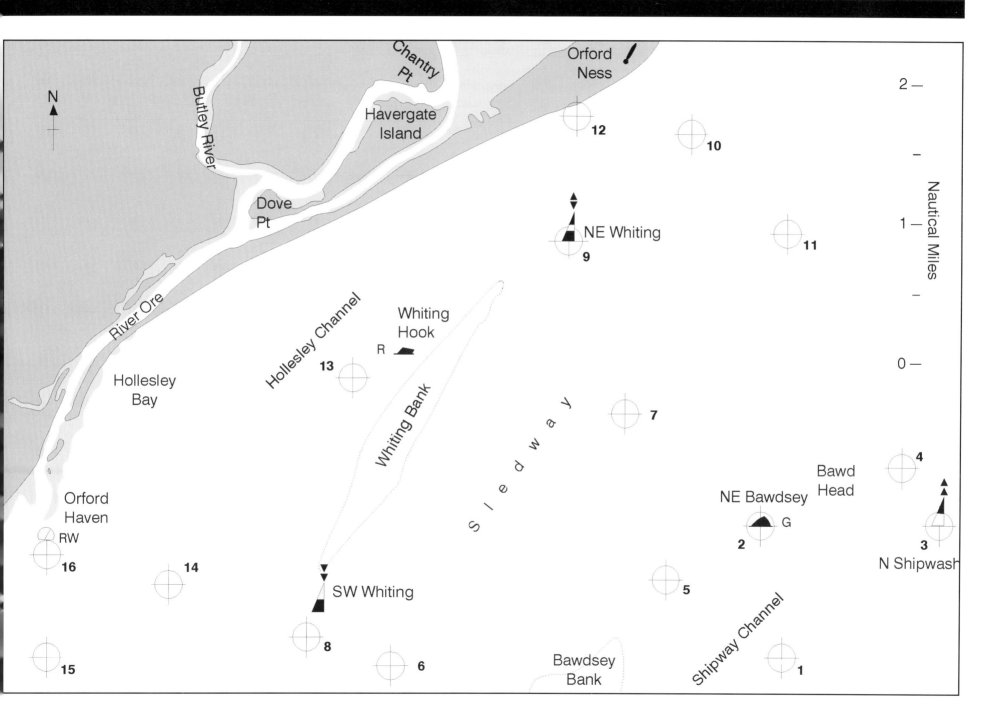

N

Chantry Pt

Orford Ness

Butley River

Havergate Island

12

10

Dove Pt

NE Whiting

9

11

River Ore

Whiting Hook

Hollesley Channel

R

13

Whiting Bank

Hollesley Bay

S l e d w a y

7

4

Bawd Head

NE Bawdsey

G

2

3

Orford Haven

RW

16

14

SW Whiting

5

N Shipwash

8

15

6

Bawdsey Bank

Shipway Channel

1

Nautical Miles

2 —

—

1 —

—

0 —

WP No	Waypoint name and position	Latitude	Longitude
21–1	Southwold approach, ¾ M 120°T from Southwold S pierhead	52°18.36'N	01°41.63'E
21–2	Southwold entrance, midway north and south pierhead lights	52°18.75'N	01°40.62'E
21–3	East Barnard outer, ½ M due E true from E-card buoy	52°25.12'N	01°47.30'E
21–4	East Barnard E-card buoy, actual position	52°25.12'N	01°46.49'E
21–5	Barnard inner, 9 ca due W true from E-card buoy	52°25.12'N	01°45.02'E
21–6	Newcome outer, ½ M E true from Newcome Sand red buoy	52°26.40'N	01°47.98'E
21–7	Newcome Sand red buoy, actual position	52°26.40'N	01°47.15'E
21–8	Stanford Channel S, midway Stanford and South Holm buoys	52°27.33'N	01°47.06'E
21–9	Stanford Channel N, 9 ca E true from Lowestoft N pierhead light	52°28.28'N	01°46.98'E
21–10	North Newcome red buoy, actual position	52°28.28'N	01°46.43'E
21–11	East Newcome red buoy, actual position	52°28.50'N	01°49.30'E
21–12	Pakefield Road, 1 M 190°T from Claremont pierhead light	52°26.89'N	01°44.70'E
21–13	Lowestoft South Road, 2 ca 135°T from Claremont pierhead Lt	52°27.72'N	01°45.21'E
21–14	Lowestoft entrance, 100 m 135°T from Lowestoft N pierhead Lt	52°28.25'N	01°45.57'E

Datum OSGB 36 The waypoint latitudes and longitudes in this table refer to Ordnance Survey of Great Britain (1936) Datum

COASTAL DANGERS
Refer to Admiralty charts 1543, 2695 and 1536

Southwold entrance
The shallow entrance to the River Blyth leads across a coastal bar, with depths less than ½ metre, and then between two jetties into the partly drying lower reaches of Southwold harbour. Not far upstream, an attractive, deeper stretch of the river is flanked each side by wooden staging for local fishing boats and yachts. The land on either side is low and flat. These staging berths are well sheltered, especially up at Blackshore Quay where you will find the harbour office and sailing club, a chandler, diesel fuel and the Harbour Inn. The river entrance itself, however, must always be treated with care.

It is best to approach Southwold after half-flood, an hour or two before high water. The ebb can run up to 6 knots and helps to create steep confused seas at the entrance in onshore winds. Strangers should not try to enter Southwold in any strong winds from the east, whatever the state of tide. Three flashing red lights are shown at night if conditions are dangerous to enter.

Barnard shoal
The Barnard is the most southerly of the numerous banks and shoals in the approaches to Lowestoft. The shallowest part is about 1 mile long and extends up to ½ mile offshore between Benacre Ness and Kessingland village. Soundings are generally ½ metre or less, but an isolated 1.9 metre patch lies 6 cables west of the East Barnard E-cardinal buoy.

Between Benacre Ness and Lowestoft, the coastal approaches are generally shallow with several more pronounced shoals and banks.

Coming from the south, the simplest strategy is to stay outside East Barnard E-cardinal buoy and Newcome Sand red buoy before following the main Stanford Channel into Lowestoft. However, just seaward of the shallowest part of Barnard shoal, a deeper cut follows the coast not quite 1 mile *inside* the East Barnard buoy, leading you north inside Newcome Sand to Pakefield Road, Lowestoft South Road and the inner approach to Lowestoft harbour.

Newcome Sand
This wide area of shoals SSE of Lowestoft entrance extends nearly 1½ miles from north to south and ¾ mile from east to west. The shallowest parts of Newcome Sand have depths between ½ and 1 metre. These shoals are dangerous in heavy onshore weather at any state of tide, and fresh winds against the stream cause boisterous overfalls.

In quiet weather you can cut inside Newcome Sand through Pakefield Road, but if in doubt stay outside Newcome Sand red buoy before following the main Stanford Channel into Lowestoft.

South Holm sand
The long southern tail of Holm Sand is left to seaward as you approach Lowestoft from the south through the Stanford Channel. The southern tip of this shoal is marked by South Holm S-cardinal buoy. Between this buoy and the SW Holm green buoy, depths over the southern part of Holm Sand fall steadily from 4.9 to 0.7 metres.

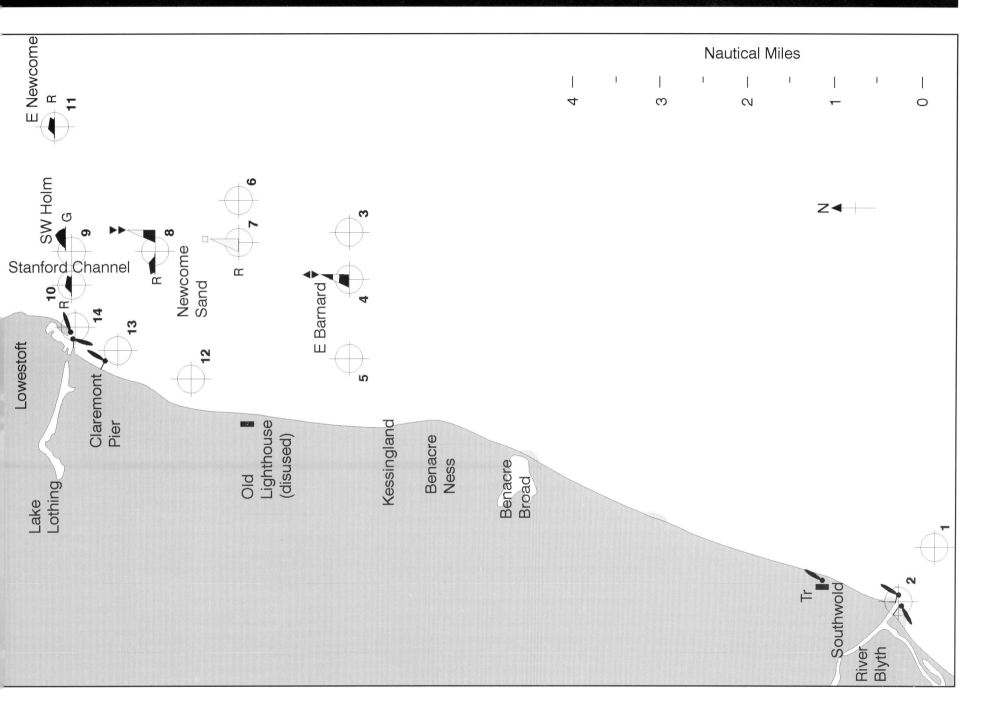

Nautical Miles

E Newcome
R
11

SW Holm
G
9

Stanford Channel
R
10
R
14
13

Newcome
Sand
R
8
R

6

7

3

E Barnard
4

5

12

Lowestoft

Lake
Lothing

Claremont
Pier

Old
Lighthouse
(disused)

Kessingland

Benacre
Ness

Benacre
Broad

Tr

Southwold

River
Blyth

1

2

N

4

3

2

1

0

WP No	Waypoint name and position	Latitude	Longitude
22–1	Newcome outer, ½ M E true from Newcome Sand red buoy	52°26.40'N	01°47.98'E
22–2	Newcome Sand red buoy, actual position	52°26.40'N	01°47.15'E
22–3	Stanford Channel outer, 4 M due E of Pakefield S water tower	52°27.24'N	01°50.33'E
22–4	Stanford Channel S, midway Stanford and South Holm buoys	52°27.33'N	01°47.06'E
22–5	Stanford Channel N, 9 ca E true from Lowestoft N pierhead light	52°28.28'N	01°46.98'E
22–6	North Newcome red buoy, actual position	52°28.28'N	01°46.43'E
22–7	East Newcome outer, 3 ca due E of East Newcome red buoy	52°28.50'N	01°49.79'E
22–8	East Newcome red buoy, actual position	52°28.50'N	01°49.30'E
22–9	East Newcome inner, 3 ca due W of East Newcome red buoy	52°28.50'N	01°48.81'E
22–10	Lowestoft North Road, 2 ca W true from W Holm green buoy	52°29.80'N	01°46.86'E
22–11	Lowestoft Ness offing, 6½ ca due E from the Ness	52°28.83'N	01°46.95'E
22–12	Holm Sand E clearing, 3.4 M 065°T from Lowestoft S pierhead	52°29.70'N	01°50.51'E
22–13	Pakefield Road, 1 M 190°T from Claremont pierhead light	52°26.89'N	01°44.70'E
22–14	Lowestoft South Road, 2 ca 135°T from Claremont pierhead Lt	52°27.72'N	01°45.21'E
22–15	Lowestoft entrance, 100 m 135°T from Lowestoft N pierhead Lt	52°28.25'N	01°45.57'E

Datum OSGB 36 The waypoint latitudes and longitudes in this table refer to Ordnance Survey of Great Britain (1936) Datum

COASTAL DANGERS
Refer to Admiralty chart 1536

Barnard shoal
The Barnard is the most southerly of the numerous banks and shoals in the approaches to Lowestoft. The shallowest part is about 1 mile long and extends up to ½ mile offshore between Benacre Ness and Kessingland village. Soundings are generally ½ metre or less, but an isolated 1.9 metre patch lies 6 cables west of the East Barnard E-cardinal buoy.

Between Benacre Ness and Lowestoft, the coastal approaches are generally shallow with several more pronounced shoals and banks. Coming from the south, the simplest strategy is to stay outside East Barnard E-cardinal buoy and Newcome Sand red buoy before following the main Stanford Channel into Lowestoft. However, just seaward of the shallowest part of Barnard shoal, a deeper cut follows the coast not quite 1 mile *inside* the East Barnard buoy, leading you north inside Newcome Sand to Pakefield Road, Lowestoft South Road and the inner approach to Lowestoft harbour.

Newcome Sand
This wide area of shoals SSE of Lowestoft entrance extends nearly 1½ miles from north to south and ¾ mile from east to west. The shallowest parts of Newcome Sand have depths between ½ and 1 metre. These shoals are dangerous in heavy onshore weather at any state of tide, and fresh winds against the stream cause boisterous overfalls.

In quiet weather you can cut inside Newcome Sand through Pakefield Road, but if in doubt stay outside Newcome Sand red buoy before following the main Stanford Channel into Lowestoft.

Holm Sand
The long southern tail of Holm Sand is left to seaward as you approach Lowestoft from the south through the Stanford Channel. The southern tip of this shoal is marked by South Holm S-cardinal buoy. Between this buoy and the SW Holm green buoy, depths over the southern part of Holm Sand fall steadily from 4.9 to 0.7 metres.

The main drying part of Holm Sand lies to the north of Lowestoft harbour entrance, although this ½ mile long patch is just above datum and only shows on a low spring tide. This drying area is not quite 1½ miles offshore and acts as a partial natural breakwater to Lowestoft North Road, a broad fairway and shipping anchorage to the north of Lowestoft entrance.

Lowestoft North Road leads north to a slightly wide fairway, known as Corton Road, also partly sheltered from seaward by the long northern arm of Holm Sand which tails north for a good 3 miles beyond the main drying part of the bank and for 5 miles north of Lowestoft entrance.

The northern shoals of Holm Sand are marked on their west side by NW Holm green buoy, on their seaward side by East Holm and NE Holm red buoys, and at the north tip by Holm Sand N-cardinal buoy. Much of this northern part of the bank has soundings between 1 and 1½ metres at LAT and should not be crossed except in calm weather with sufficient rise of tide. The sea breaks dangerously over Holm Sand in heavy onshore weather and overfalls are kicked up in fresh wind-over-tide conditions.

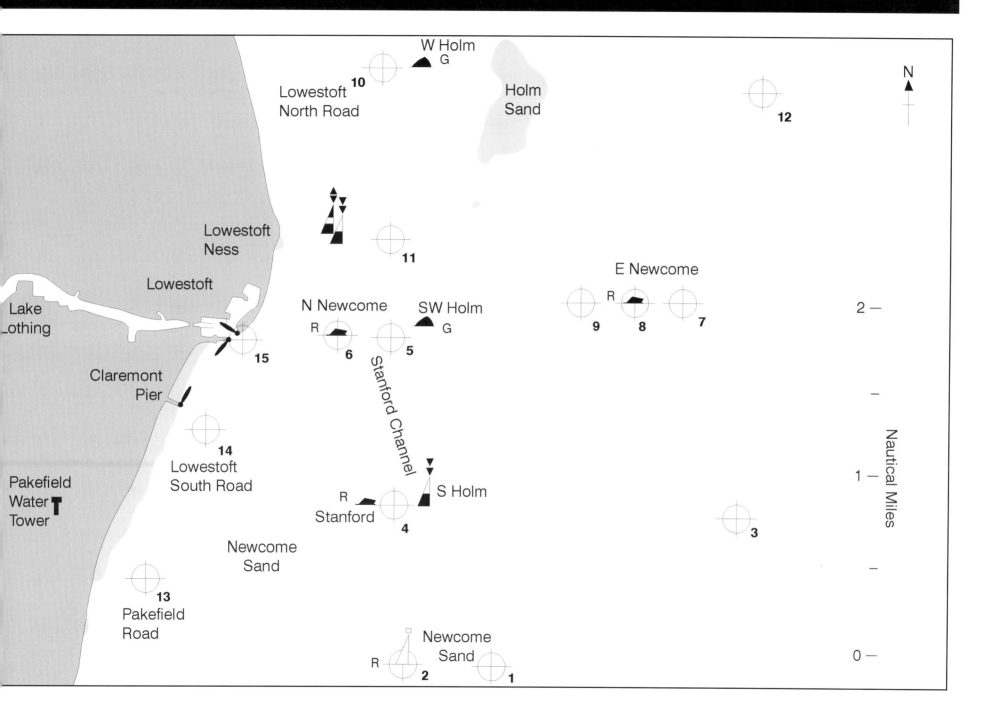

W Holm
G

Lowestoft ¹⁰
North Road

Holm
Sand

12

N

Lowestoft
Ness

Lowestoft

11

E Newcome

Lake
Lothing

N Newcome

SW Holm

R

R

G

9   8   7

2 —

R

6   5

15

Stanford Channel

Claremont
Pier

14

Lowestoft
South Road

Pakefield
Water
Tower

S Holm

R

Stanford

4

1 —

Nautical Miles

3

Newcome
Sand

13

Pakefield
Road

Newcome
Sand

R

2   1

0 —

69

Lowestoft to Great Yarmouth

WP No	Waypoint name and position	Latitude	Longitude
23–1	Stanford Channel outer, 4 M due E of Pakefield water tower	52°27.24'N	01°50.33'E
23–2	Stanford Channel S, midway Stanford and South Holm buoys	52°27.33'N	01°47.06'E
23–3	Stanford Channel N, 9 ca E true from Lowestoft N pierhead light	52°28.28'N	01°46.98'E
23–4	North Newcome red buoy, actual position	52°28.28'N	01°46.43'E
23–5	East Newcome red buoy, actual position	52°28.50'N	01°49.30'E
23–6	Pakefield Road, 1 M 190°T from Claremont pierhead light	52°26.89'N	01°44.70'E
23–7	Lowestoft South Road, 2 ca 135°T from Claremont pierhead light	52°27.72'N	01°45.21'E
23–8	Lowestoft entrance, 100 m 135°T from Lowestoft N pierhead light	52°28.25'N	01°45.57'E
23–9	Lowestoft Ness offing, 6½ ca due E from the Ness	52°28.83'N	01°46.95'E
23–10	Lowestoft North Road, 2 ca W true from W Holm green buoy	52°29.80'N	01°46.86'E
23–11	Holm Sand E clearing, 3.4 M 065°T from Lowestoft S pierhead	52°29.70'N	01°50.51'E
23–12	East Holm outer, 4 ca due E of East Holm red buoy	52°31.06'N	01°50.07'E
23–13	East Holm red buoy, actual position	52°31.06'N	01°49.42'E
23–14	Corton E-card buoy, actual position	52°31.11'N	01°51.49'E
23–15	Corton outer, 1 M due E of Corton E-card buoy	52°31.11'N	01°53.13'E
23–16	South Corton S-card buoy, actual position	52°32.15'N	01°50.13'E
23–17	Holm Channel outer, midway S Corton and E Holm buoys	52°31.60'N	01°49.78'E
23–18	Holm Channel inner, midway Holm green and Holm Sand buoys	52°33.48'N	01°47.55'E
23–19	Holm Sand north, 3 ca due N of Holm Sand N-card buoy	52°33.75'N	01°47.02'E
23–20	Corton Road, 1.1 M due E of Corton church tower	52°31.27'N	01°46.31'E
23–21	NW Holm, 4 ca due W of NW Holm green buoy	52°31.91'N	01°46.15'E
23–22	Great Yarmouth entrance, 70 m 135°T from north pierhead light	52°34.33'N	01°44.54'E
23–23	Great Yarmouth outer, ½ M due E from south pierhead light	52°34.30'N	01°45.20'E
23–24	West Corton, 1 ca SW of West Corton W-card buoy	52°34.40'N	01°46.30'E
23–25	South Cross SE, 5 M due E from Great Yarmouth S pierhead light	52°34.30'N	01°52.52'E
23–26	South Cross inner, 4.4 M 080°T from Britannia pierhead light	52°37.22'N	01°51.66'E
23–27	SW Scroby, 3 ca due W of SW Scroby green buoy	52°35.80'N	01°45.89'E
23–28	Yarmouth Road, 8 ca 065°T from Britannia pierhead light	52°36.80'N	01°45.76'E
23–29	Scroby Elbow, ¼ M NW of Scroby Elbow green buoy	52°37.50'N	01°46.20'E

COASTAL DANGERS

Refer to Admiralty chart 1536

Newcome Sand

This wide area of shoals SSE of Lowestoft entrance extends nearly 1½ miles from north to south and ¾ mile from east to west. The shallowest parts of Newcome Sand have depths between ½ and 1 metre. These shoals are dangerous in heavy onshore weather at any state of tide, and fresh winds against the stream cause boisterous overfalls.

In quiet weather you can cut inside Newcome Sand through Pakefield Road, but if in doubt stay outside Newcome Sand red buoy before following the main Stanford Channel into Lowestoft.

Holm Sand

The long southern tail of Holm Sand is left to seaward as you approach Lowestoft from the south through the Stanford Channel. The southern tip of this shoal is marked by South Holm S-cardinal buoy. Between this buoy and the SW Holm green buoy, depths over the southern part of Holm Sand fall steadily from 4.9 to 0.7 metres.

The main drying part of Holm Sand lies to the north of Lowestoft harbour entrance, although this ½ mile long patch is just above datum and only shows on a low spring tide. This drying area is not quite 1½ miles offshore and acts as a partial natural breakwater to Lowestoft North Road, a broad fairway and shipping anchorage to the north of Lowestoft entrance.

Lowestoft North Road leads north to a slightly wide fairway, known as Corton Road, also partly sheltered from seaward by the long northern arm of Holm Sand which tails north for a good 3 miles beyond the main drying part of the bank and for 5 miles north of Lowestoft entrance.

The northern shoals of Holm Sand are marked on their west side by NW Holm green buoy, on their seaward side by East Holm and NE Holm red buoys, and at the north tip by Holm Sand N-cardinal buoy. Much of this northern part of the bank has soundings between 1 and 1½ metres at LAT and should not be crossed except in calm weather with sufficient rise of tide. The sea breaks dangerously over Holm Sand in heavy onshore weather and overfalls are kicked up in fresh wind-over-tide conditions.

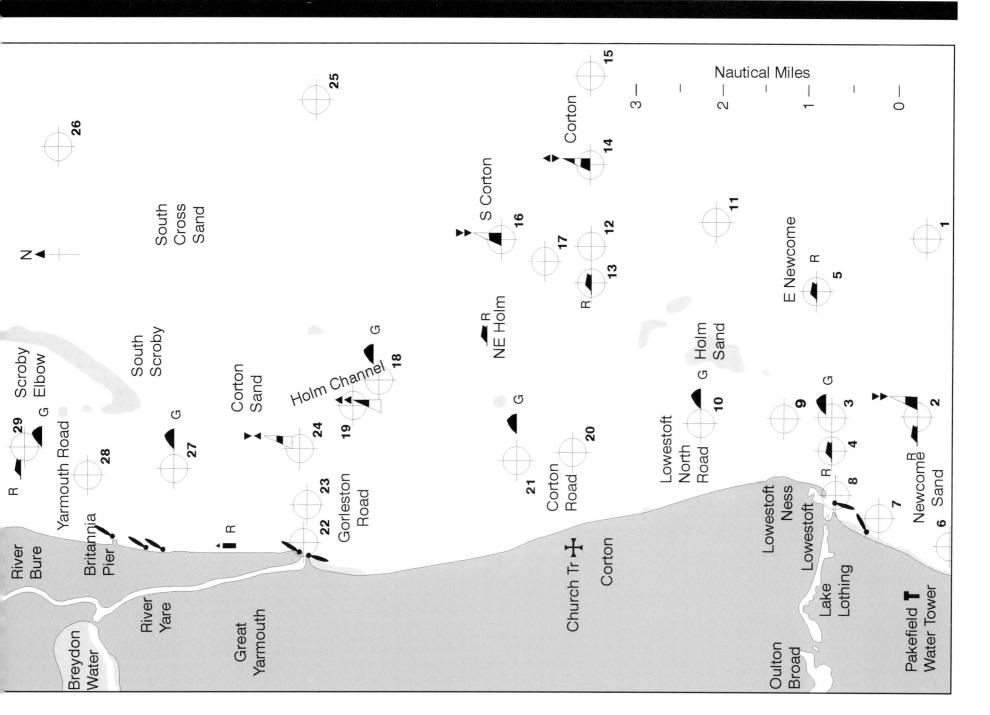

River Bure

Breydon Water

Scroby Elbow
G
29 R
29

Yarmouth Road

Britannia Pier

River Yare

South Scroby

G
27

28

Great Yarmouth

South Cross Sand

26

25

N

Corton Sand

R

22 23

Gorleston Road

Holm Channel

24

19

18 G

G
21

20 G

Corton Road

Church Tr ✝

Corton

NE Holm
R

S Corton
16

17

13 R

12

Corton
14

15

Nautical Miles

3 —
2 —
1 —
0 —

11

Lowestoft North Road

Holm Sand
10 G

9 G

3

4 R

E Newcome
R
5

Lowestoft Ness

Lowestoft

Lake Lothing

Oulton Broad

2

7

8 R

6 Newcome Sand
R

Pakefield ⊤ Water Tower

WP No	Waypoint name and position	Latitude	Longitude
23–1	Stanford Channel outer, 4 M due E of Pakefield water tower	52°27.24'N	01°50.33'E
23–2	Stanford Channel S, midway Stanford and South Holm buoys	52°27.33'N	01°47.06'E
23–3	Stanford Channel N, 9 ca E true from Lowestoft N pierhead light	52°28.28'N	01°46.98'E
23–4	North Newcome red buoy, actual position	52°28.28'N	01°46.43'E
23–5	East Newcome red buoy, actual position	52°28.50'N	01°49.30'E
23–6	Pakefield Road, 1 M 190°T from Claremont pierhead light	52°26.89'N	01°44.70'E
23–7	Lowestoft South Road, 2 ca 135°T from Claremont pierhead light	52°27.72'N	01°45.21'E
23–8	Lowestoft entrance, 100 m 135°T from Lowestoft N pierhead light	52°28.25'N	01°45.57'E
23–9	Lowestoft Ness offing, 6½ ca due E from the Ness	52°28.83'N	01°46.95'E
23–10	Lowestoft North Road, 2 ca W true from W Holm green buoy	52°29.80'N	01°46.86'E
23–11	Holm Sand E clearing, 3.4 M 065°T from Lowestoft S pierhead	52°29.70'N	01°50.51'E
23–12	East Holm outer, 4 ca due E of East Holm red buoy	52°31.06'N	01°50.07'E
23–13	East Holm red buoy, actual position	52°31.06'N	01°49.42'E
23–14	Corton E-card buoy, actual position	52°31.11'N	01°51.49'E
23–15	Corton outer, 1 M due E of Corton E-card buoy	52°31.11'N	01°53.13'E
23–16	South Corton S-card buoy, actual position	52°32.15'N	01°50.13'E
23–17	Holm Channel outer, midway S Corton and E Holm buoys	52°31.60'N	01°49.78'E
23–18	Holm Channel inner, midway Holm green and Holm Sand buoys	52°33.48'N	01°47.55'E
23–19	Holm Sand north, 3 ca due N of Holm Sand N-card buoy	52°33.75'N	01°47.02'E
23–20	Corton Road, 1.1 M due E of Corton church tower	52°31.27'N	01°46.31'E
23–21	NW Holm, 4 ca due W of NW Holm green buoy	52°31.91'N	01°46.15'E
23–22	Great Yarmouth entrance, 70 m 135°T from north pierhead light	52°34.33'N	01°44.54'E
23–23	Great Yarmouth outer, ½ M due E from south pierhead light	52°34.30'N	01°45.20'E
23–24	West Corton, 1 ca SW of West Corton W-card buoy	52°34.40'N	01°46.30'E
23–25	South Cross SE, 5 M due E from Great Yarmouth S pierhead light	52°34.30'N	01°52.52'E
23–26	South Cross inner, 4.4 M 080°T from Britannia pierhead light	52°37.22'N	01°51.66'E
23–27	SW Scroby, 3 ca due W of SW Scroby green buoy	52°35.80'N	01°45.89'E
23–28	Yarmouth Road, 8 ca 065°T from Britannia pierhead light	52°36.80'N	01°45.76'E
23–29	Scroby Elbow, ¼ M NW of Scroby Elbow green buoy	52°37.50'N	01°46.20'E

Datum OSGB 36 The waypoint latitudes and longitudes in this table refer to Ordnance Survey of Great Britain (1936) Datum

Corton Sand

The shoal areas known as Corton Sand lie opposite and south-east of Great Yarmouth entrance. The south part of Corton Sand is just over 1 mile seaward of the north part of Holm Sand and its shallowest parts are almost awash at datum. All these sandbanks off the Norfolk coast are liable to shift to some extent, but the outer part of Corton is particularly mobile. Its southern tip is marked by South Corton S-cardinal bell buoy and the Holm Channel (with least depth about 6 metres) cuts between this bell buoy and the two red buoys marking the seaward edge of north Holm Sand.

The inner, more northern part of Corton Sand lies more or less opposite Great Yarmouth entrance and has depths of less than ½ metre in parts. Steep overfalls build over this area with a weather-going tide.

South Cross Sand

This narrow tail of shoals 2 miles long is a natural extension of the outer part of Corton Sand, but has depths between 6 and 9 metres. Steep overfalls build over South Cross Sand with a weather-going tide.

South Scroby Sand

The South Scroby Sand forms a natural continuation north from the inner part of Corton Sand, and thereafter runs into the Middle Scroby and North Scroby Sands. This long cordon of banks and shoals lies from 1–1½ miles offshore and stretches northwards from Great Yarmouth entrance for about 8 miles, acting as a partial breakwater for Yarmouth Road and Caister Road. The drying part of South Scroby Sand is over 1½ miles long, with drying heights between 0.2 and 1.6 metres. In any significant weather, the sea breaks heavily over the northern tip of this drying area.

General warning

There are few occasions when it would be wise to cut across any of the banks in this area and strangers are advised to stay in the main, deep-water channels when approaching Lowestoft or Great Yarmouth. This is an unforgiving stretch of coast, especially in onshore weather, and considerable caution is required. You should always navigate with the latest version of Admiralty chart 1536.

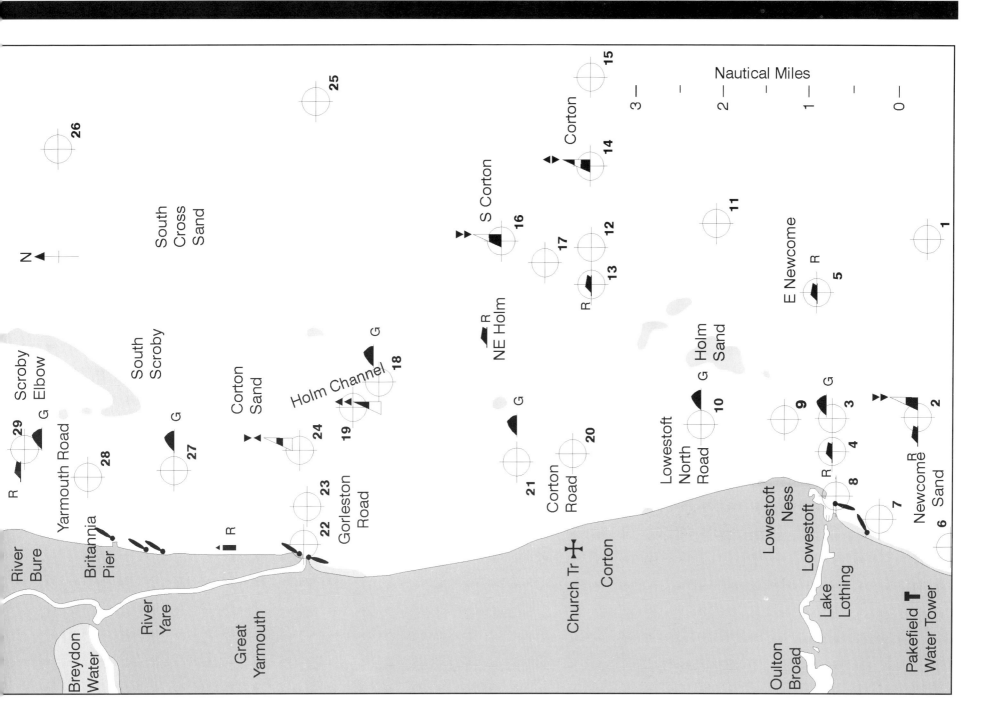

Nautical Miles

River Bure

Breydon Water

River Yare

Great Yarmouth

Britannia Pier

Yarmouth Road

Scroby Elbow

South Scroby

South Cross Sand

Corton Sand

Holm Channel

Gorleston Road

Corton Road

NE Holm

S Corton

Corton

Church Tr

Corton

Lowestoft North Road

Holm Sand

Lowestoft Ness

Lowestoft

Lake Lothing

Oulton Broad

Newcome Sand

E Newcome

Pakefield Water Tower

N

29 R
G Elbow
28
27 G
26
25
24
23
22
21
20
19
18 G
17
16
15
14
13 R
12
11
10
9
8 R
7
6 R
5 R
4
3 G
2
1
R NE Holm
G
R

WP No	Waypoint name and position	Latitude	Longitude
24–1	Great Yarmouth outer, ½ M due E from south pierhead light	52°34.30'N	01°45.20'E
24–2	Great Yarmouth entrance, 70 m 135°T from north pierhead light	52°34.33'N	01°44.54'E
24–3	West Corton, 1 ca SW of West Corton W-card buoy	52°34.40'N	01°46.30'E
24–4	SW Scroby, 3 ca due W of SW Scroby green buoy	52°35.80'N	01°45.89'E
24–5	Yarmouth Road, 8 ca 065°T from Britannia pierhead light	52°36.80'N	01°45.76'E
24–6	Scroby Elbow, ¼ M NW of Scroby Elbow green buoy	52°37.50'N	01°46.20'E
24–7	Caister Road, 1½ M due E of Caister-on-Sea church tower	52°38.96'N	01°46.00'E
24–8	Caister Road north, midway N Caister and NW Scroby buoys	52°40.38'N	01°46.05'E
24–9	Caister Shoal inner S, ¾ M due E of Caister-on-Sea church tower	52°38.96'N	01°44.78'E
24–10	Caister Shoal inner N, 1½ M 020°T from Caister radio mast	52°41.00'N	01°43.87'E
24–11	Hemsby outer, 100 m due E of Hemsby red buoy	52°41.86'N	01°45.08'E
24–12	Hemsby Hole, 1 M 115°T from Winterton disused lighthouse	52°42.33'N	01°43.32'E
24–13	Cockle Gatway S, ¼ M due W of North Scroby N-card buoy	52°42.50'N	01°44.37'E
24–14	Cockle Gatway N, Cockle E-card buoy actual position	52°44.00'N	01°43.70'E
24–15	South Cross SE, 5 M due E from Great Yarmouth S pierhead Lt	52°34.30'N	01°52.52'E
24–16	South Cross outer, 5.6 M due E of Britannia pierhead light	52°36.47'N	01°52.75'E
24–17	South Cross inner, 4.4 M 080°T from Britannia pierhead light	52°37.22'N	01°51.66'E
24–18	East Cross Sand red buoy, actual position	52°40.02'N	01°53.77'E
24–19	NE Cross Sand E-card buoy, actual position	52°43.00'N	01°53.75'E
24–20	Barley Picle SE, 4.8 M due E of Caister radio mast	52°39.59'N	01°50.89'E

Datum OSGB 36 The waypoint latitudes and longitudes in this table refer to Ordnance Survey of Great Britain (1936) Datum

COASTAL DANGERS
Refer to Admiralty charts 1536 and 1543

Corton Sand
The shoal areas known as Corton Sand lie opposite and south-east of Great Yarmouth entrance. The south part of Corton Sand is just over 1 mile seaward of the north part of Holm Sand and its shallowest parts are almost awash at datum. All these sandbanks off the Norfolk coast are liable to shift to some extent, but the outer part of Corton is particularly mobile. Its southern tip is marked by South Corton S-cardinal bell buoy and the Holm Channel (with least depth about 6 metres) cuts between this bell buoy and the two red buoys marking the seaward edge of north Holm Sand.

The inner, more northern part of Corton Sand lies more or less opposite Great Yarmouth entrance and has depths of less than ½ metre in parts at LAT. Steep overfalls build over this area in fresh wind-over-tide conditions.

South Cross Sand
This narrow tail of shoals 2 miles long is a natural extension of the outer part of Corton Sand, but has depths between 6 and 9 metres. Steep over-falls build over South Cross Sand with a weather-going tide.

Middle Cross Sand
Middle Cross Sand lies 5 miles offshore opposite the North Scroby and Middle Scroby Sands and about 2 miles further seaward. Least depths over Middle Cross are 2.7 metres in the north part and 3.3 metres over the long southern tail. Overfalls build up over Middle Cross Sand with a strong weather-going tide. The seaward side of these shoals is guarded by East Cross Sand red buoy and NE Cross Sand E-cardinal buoy.

South Scroby Sand
The South Scroby Sand forms a natural continuation north from the inner part of Corton Sand, and thereafter runs into the Middle Scroby and North Scroby Sands. This long cordon of banks and shoals lies from 1–1½ miles offshore and stretches northwards from Great Yarmouth entrance for about 8 miles, acting as a partial breakwater for Yarmouth Road and Caister Road.

The drying part of South Scroby Sand is over 1½ miles long, with drying heights between 0.2 and 1.6 metres. In any significant weather, the sea breaks heavily over the northern tip of this drying area.

Middle and North Scroby
The Middle and North Scroby Sands extend north from the drying part of South Scroby, following the line of the coast about 1½ miles offshore. There are one or two drying patches, but depths range mostly between 1 and 3 metres. In any significant weather, the sea breaks heavily over these shoals.

NE Cross Sand

Nautical Miles

N

Winterton Overfalls

Barley Picle

Middle Cross Sand

Middle Scroby

South Cross Sand

Cockle

N Scroby

Cockle Shoal

North Scroby

Mast

G

Caister Road

G

South Scroby

G

Corton Sand

W Corton

Cockle Gatway

Hemsby Hole

Caister Shoal

Caister-on-Sea

Radio Mast

Tr

River Bure

Yarmouth Road

Breydon Water

Britannia Pier

River Yare

Great Yarmouth

WP No	Waypoint name and position	Latitude	Longitude
24–1	Great Yarmouth outer, ½ M due E from south pierhead light	52°34.30'N	01°45.20'E
24–2	Great Yarmouth entrance, 70 m 135°T from north pierhead light	52°34.33'N	01°44.54'E
24–3	West Corton, 1 ca SW of West Corton W-card buoy	52°34.40'N	01°46.30'E
24–4	SW Scroby, 3 ca due W of SW Scroby green buoy	52°35.80'N	01°45.89'E
24–5	Yarmouth Road, 8 ca 065°T from Britannia pierhead light	52°36.80'N	01°45.76'E
24–6	Scroby Elbow, ¼ M NW of Scroby Elbow green buoy	52°37.50'N	01°46.20'E
24–7	Caister Road, 1½ M due E of Caister-on-Sea church tower	52°38.96'N	01°46.00'E
24–8	Caister Road north, midway N Caister and NW Scroby buoys	52°40.38'N	01°46.05'E
24–9	Caister Shoal inner S, ¾ M due E of Caister-on-Sea church tower	52°38.96'N	01°44.78'E
24–10	Caister Shoal inner N, 1½ M 020°T from Caister radio mast	52°41.00'N	01°43.87'E
24–11	Hemsby outer, 100 m due E of Hemsby red buoy	52°41.86'N	01°45.08'E
24–12	Hemsby Hole, 1 M 115°T from Winterton disused lighthouse	52°42.33'N	01°43.32'E
24–13	Cockle Gatway S, ¼ M due W of North Scroby N-card buoy	52°42.50'N	01°44.37'E
24–14	Cockle Gatway N, Cockle E-card buoy actual position	52°44.00'N	01°43.70'E
24–15	South Cross SE, 5 M due E from Great Yarmouth S pierhead Lt	52°34.30'N	01°52.52'E
24–16	South Cross outer, 5.6 M due E of Britannia pierhead light	52°36.47'N	01°52.75'E
24–17	South Cross inner, 4.4 M 080°T from Britannia pierhead light	52°37.22'N	01°51.66'E
24–18	East Cross Sand red buoy, actual position	52°40.02'N	01°53.77'E
24–19	NE Cross Sand E-card buoy, actual position	52°43.00'N	01°53.75'E
24–20	Barley Picle SE, 4.8 M due E of Caister radio mast	52°39.59'N	01°50.89'E

Datum OSGB 36 The waypoint latitudes and longitudes in this table refer to Ordnance Survey of Great Britain (1936) Datum

Caister Shoal

This narrow bank lies just over ½ mile offshore opposite Caister-on-Sea. The shallowest part is about 1 mile long and has depths of between about ½ and 1½ metres. Caister Shoal is guarded on its seaward side by the North Caister and Mid Caister red buoys, but there are no buoys on the inshore side. In quiet weather you can cut inside Caister Shoal by keeping only 3–4 cables off the coast, but you should stay outside with any swell running. The sea breaks heavily over Caister Shoal in onshore weather.

Nautical Miles

NE Cross Sand

Middle Cross Sand

South Cross Sand

Barley Picle

Winterton Overfalls

Cockle

N Scroby
Cockle Shoal

Hemsby Hole

Cockle Gatway

North Scroby

Middle Scroby

Caister Road

Caister Shoal

Caister-on-Sea

Radio Mast

Tr

South Scroby

Yarmouth Road

Britannia Pier

River Bure

Breydon Water

Corton Sand

W Corton

River Yare

Great Yarmouth

Mast

R

G

G

G

G

R

R

R

R

N

1
2
3
4
5
6
7
8
9
10
11
12
13
14
15
16
17
18
19
20

WP No	Waypoint name and position	Latitude	Longitude
25–1	Cockle Gatway N, Cockle E-card buoy, actual position	52°44.00'N	01°43.70'E
25–2	Cockle Gatway S,¼ M due W of North Scroby N-card buoy	52°42.50'N	01°44.37'E
25–3	NE Cross Sand E-card buoy, actual position	52°43.00'N	01°53.75'E
25–4	Barley Picle north, 5 M E of Winterton-on-Sea church tower	52°42.90'N	01°49.60'E
25–5	Haisborough Gat NW, 2.2 M 295°T from Newarp light-float	52°49.29'N	01°52.50'E
25–6	S Haisbro clearing, 4 ca due S of S Haisbro S-card bell buoy	52°50.40'N	01°48.39'E
25–7	Would outer, 6.5 M 045°T from Happisburgh lighthouse	52°53.80'N	01°39.88'E
25–8	Would middle, 4.3 M 035°T from Happisburgh lighthouse	52°52.70'N	01°36.40'E
25–9	Would inner, 2½ M due N true from Happisburgh lighthouse	52°51.68'N	01°32.30'E
25–10	Cromer offing, 8.3 M 040°T from Cromer lighthouse	53°01.82'N	01°27.97'E
25–11	Cromer outer, 4.6 M 040°T from Cromer lighthouse	52°58.97'N	01°23.98'E
25–12	Cromer inner, 2.2 M 040°T from Cromer lighthouse	52°57.15'N	01°21.45'E
25–13	Hewett Gas Field south, 19 M 084°T from Cromer lighthouse	52°57.50'N	01°50.58'E
25–14	Hewett Gas Field west, 13 M 053°T from Cromer lighthouse	53°03.28'N	01°36.38'E
25–15	N Haisbro, 3 ca due W of N Haisbro N-card buoy	53°00.20'N	01°31.90'E
25–16	Sheringham NE, 8 ca N of E Sheringham E-card buoy	53°03.00'N	01°15.00'E
25–17	Sheringham NW, 1.2 M N of W Sheringham W-card buoy	53°04.14'N	01°06.86'E
25–18	Sheringham SE, 3.3 M 318°T from Cromer lighthouse	52°57.93'N	01°15.46'E
25–19	Blakeney Overfalls NE, 2 ca N of Blakeney Overfalls red buoy	53°03.22'N	01°01.50'E
25–20	Blakeney east outer, 4.3 M 020°T from Blakeney church tower	53°01.08'N	01°04.03'E
25–21	Blakeney east inner, 2 M 020°T from Blakeney church tower	52°58.92'N	01°02.71'E

Datum OSGB 36 The waypoint latitudes and longitudes in this table refer to Ordnance Survey of Great Britain (1936) Datum

COASTAL DANGERS
Refer to Admiralty charts 106 and 108

Cockle Gatway
Cockle Gatway is the narrow channel inside the north tip of North Scroby Sand. It forms the north entrance to the long roadstead hemmed between the Norfolk coast and the 15 mile string of banks and shoals from North Scroby down to Holm Sand and the entrance to Lowestoft.

Cockle Shoal is effectively an extension of North Scroby Sand and forms a kind of bar across this north entrance with LAT depths of over 5 metres.

Because this bar lies at the end of a long, partially confined roadstead, the tide can run quite swiftly through Cockle Gatway, in excess of 3½ knots at springs. A strong tide over the shoaling bottom causes short steep overfalls through the Gatway, especially when the stream is weather-going. Hemsby red buoy is left close to the west as you come through Cockle Gatway; the North Scroby N-cardinal whistle buoy is normally left to the east.

Cockle E-cardinal bell buoy lies just over 1 mile offshore opposite Winterton Ness and boats can pass ¼ mile inside it when coasting.

Coastal shoals off Winterton Ness
An area of coastal shoals extends about ¾ mile offshore near Winterton Ness, with least depths under 2½ metres. Boats should keep a good 1½ miles offshore when passing Winterton Ness, and it is convenient to pass outside the Cockle E-cardinal bell buoy for this purpose.

Haisborough Sand
This long shoal runs more or less NW–SE and lies 8 miles offshore opposite that rather austere stretch of Norfolk coast between Winterton Ness and Cromer. Most of the shallowest part of Haisborough has less than 2 metres depth at LAT. There are several areas with well under 1 metre depth and a few small drying patches, or patches almost awash.

Haisborough Sand is marked at either end by cardinal buoys and on its landward edge by the Mid Haisborough green buoy. Most boats coasting between Great Yarmouth and either The Wash or the Humber would normally pass inside Haisborough Sand, through The Would.

North Hewett Gas Field
The four massive rigs of the North Hewett Gas Field lie between 5 and 10 miles north and northeast of Haisborough Sand and should be given a wide berth if you stray into this area. The working lights of the gas rigs are conspicuous and rather eerie at night.

Sheringham Shoal
This narrow bank about 4 miles long lies just over 5 miles offshore opposite Sheringham village. The bank runs parallel to the coast and is marked at each end by east and west cardinal buoys. The shallowest part of Sheringham Shoal has a least depth of about 2½ metres. Steep seas break over the shoal in heavy onshore weather.

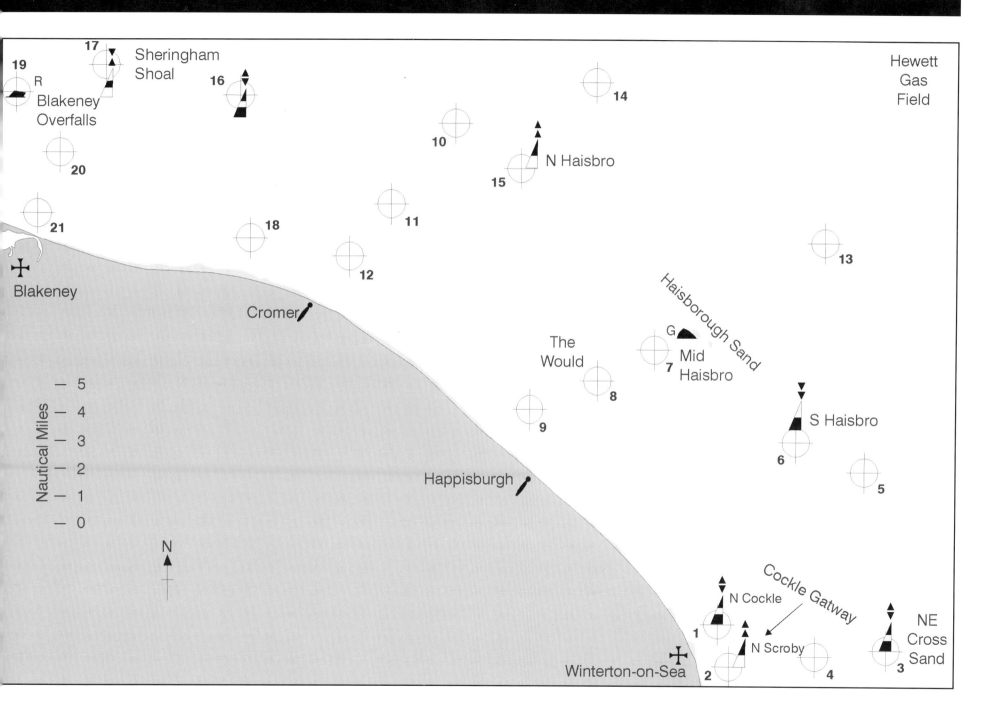

19 R

Blakeney
Overfalls

17 Sheringham
Shoal

16

20

14 Hewett
Gas
Field

10

N Haisbro

15

21

18

11

12

Blakeney

Cromer

Haisborough Sand

The
Would

G Mid
Haisbro

7

13

8

9

S Haisbro

6

5

Nautical Miles

— 5
— 4
— 3
— 2
— 1
— 0

N

Happisburgh

Cockle Gatway

N Cockle

1

N Scroby

NE
Cross
Sand

2

4

3

Winterton-on-Sea

WP No	Waypoint name and position	Latitude	Longitude
26–1	Blakeney Overfalls NE, 2 ca N of Blakeney Overfalls red buoy	53°03.22'N	01°01.50'E
26–2	Blakeney east outer, 4.3 M 020°T from Blakeney church tower	53°01.08'N	01°04.03'E
26–3	Blakeney east inner, 2 M 020°T from Blakeney church tower	52°58.92'N	01°02.71'E
26–4	Blakeney Point inner, 3 M 325°T from Blakeney church tower	52°59.49'N	00°58.73'E
26–5	Blakeney Point outer, 4.3 M 340°T from Blakeney church tower	53°01.09'N	00°59.17'E
26–6	Blakeney approach 3.6 M 325°T from Blakeney church tower	53°00.00'N	00°58.14'E
26–7	Blakeney entrance, 2.9 M 322°T from Blakeney church tower	52°59.33'N	00°58.62'E
26–8	The Bink clearing, 3.2 M 010°T from Wells church tower	53°00.21'N	00°52.26'E
26–9	Wells offing, 4½ M due N of Wells church tower	53°01.55'N	00°51.35'E
26–10	Wells fairway, 3.1 M 340°T from Wells church tower	52°59.98'N	00°49.59'E
26–11	Blakeney Overfalls NW, 6½ M 010°T from Wells church tower	53°03.45'N	00°53.22'E

Datum OSGB 36 The waypoint latitudes and longitudes in this table refer to Ordnance Survey of Great Britain (1936) Datum

COASTAL DANGERS

Refer to Admiralty chart 108

Sheringham Shoal

This narrow bank about 4 miles long lies just over 5 miles offshore opposite Sheringham village. The bank runs parallel to the coast and is marked at each end by east and west cardinal buoys.

The shallowest part of Sheringham Shoal has a least depth of about 2½ metres. Steep seas break over the shoal in heavy onshore weather.

Blakeney Overfalls

This broad bank is about 2½ miles long by nearly 1 mile wide and lies 3 miles offshore opposite Blakeney Point. The least depth over the shallow west end of Blakeney Overfalls is about 2 metres.

As its name suggests, this area is a mass of short steep overfalls during the strongest hours of the tide, especially when the stream is weather-going. Steep dangerous seas break over the bank in heavy onshore weather, especially in strong northerlies and north-easterlies.

Blakeney Harbour approaches

Blakeney is a small Norfolk fishing village and its shallow harbour is approached by a narrow buoyed channel that curves around the low dunes of Blakeney Point. The channel and outer sands are often shifting and the buoys are moved frequently to take account of this. Strangers should only approach Blakeney in flat calm conditions with good visibility, aiming to enter about 1 hour before local high water.

Never try to approach Blakeney after high water, when a false move may leave you grounded on the sands and exposed to the risk of deteriorating weather. It is better to be a bit early on the tide than too late.

Wells-next-the-Sea

The shallow harbour at Wells is slightly easier to enter than Blakeney, but strangers should not attempt to go in when the wind is onshore. Calm conditions and good visibility are advisable for a first visit. Aim to be near the Wells fairway buoy about 1½ hours before local high water and then head SSE to pick up the outer channel buoys that guard the edge of West Sands and Bob Hall's Sand.

Never try to approach Wells after high water, when a false move may leave you grounded on the sands and exposed to the risk of deteriorating weather.

General warning

The north coast of Norfolk and the approaches to The Wash provide few corners of refuge for boats, which need to be highly self-sufficient when cruising this area. The small harbours of Blakeney and Wells are only accessible in quiet conditions and you should always have an alternative plan in case of deteriorating weather. In strong westerlies, Great Yarmouth is the only safe bet. In strong easterlies, you can find shelter at King's Lynn in the south-east corner of The Wash, although great care must be taken when approaching the banks and channels of The Wash in any difficult weather.

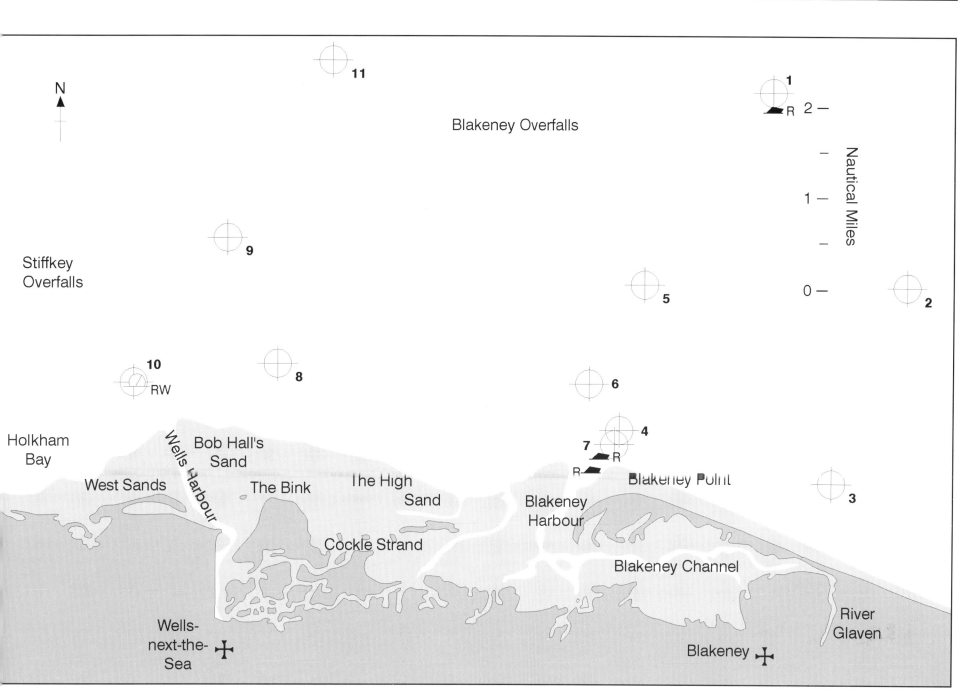

N

Blakeney Overfalls

1

R 2 —

— Nautical Miles

1 —

Stiffkey
Overfalls

9

5

0 —

2

10

RW

8

6

4

7

R

R

Blakeney Point

3

Holkham
Bay

Wells Harbour

Bob Hall's
Sand

West Sands

The Bink

The High
Sand

Blakeney
Harbour

Cockle Strand

Blakeney Channel

River
Glaven

Wells-
next-the-
Sea

Blakeney

Approaches to Brancaster and Burnham Overy Staithe

WP No	Waypoint name and position	Latitude	Longitude
27–1	Burnham approach, 3.4 M 310°T from Wells church tower	52°59.24'N	00°47.04'E
27–2	Bridgirdle, 2 ca due N of Bridgirdle red buoy	53°01.92'N	00°44.10'E
27–3	Sledway inner, 4.3 M due N of Titchwell church spire	53°02.07'N	00°37.43'E
27–4	Sledway outer, 6 ca NE of the Woolpack red buoy	53°03.09'N	00°32.25'E
27–5	Brancaster Road, 2.3 M N of Burnham Deepdale church tower	53°00.24'N	00°41.25'E
27–6	Brancaster Road SW, 2 M N of Brancaster church tower	52°59.79'N	00°38.37'E
27–7	Brancaster channel, 9 ca 340°T from Brancaster church tower	52°58.64'N	00°37.90'E
27–8	Thornham approach, 1.8 M 350°T from Thornham ruined tower	52°59.38'N	00°34.40'E
27–9	The Bays, 1.9 M 350°T from Holme-next-the-Sea church tower	52°59.50'N	00°31.98'E
27–10	Middle Bank SW, 2.7 M 333°T from Holme-next-the-Sea tower	53°00.04'N	00°30.50'E

Datum OSGB 36 The waypoint latitudes and longitudes in this table refer to Ordnance Survey of Great Britain (1936) Datum

COASTAL DANGERS
Refer to Admiralty charts 108 and 1200

Stiffkey Overfalls
This broad shallow area lies 2–3 miles north of Holkham Bay and the entrance to Burnham Overy Staithe. The least depth over Stiffkey Overfalls is about 2 metres and short steep seas build up here with a weather-going tide.

Approach to Burnham Overy Staithe
The drying inlet leading to Burnham Overy Staithe is only suitable for shallow-draught boats that can take the ground easily and safely. If you don't have bilge keels or a lifting keel, stay well clear. In any case, Burnham should only be entered in calm conditions. If you do decide to nudge in, approach the entrance about 1¼ hours before local high water.

Approach to Brancaster Harbour
The main buoyed approach channel into Brancaster Harbour leads eastwards close along the shore, starting just west of the prominent golf club. Brancaster is only suitable for shallow-draught boats that can take the ground easily and safely, but the approach channel is slightly more straightforward than the entrance to Burnham Overy Staithe. Even so, you should only try to enter Brancaster Harbour in quiet conditions, aiming to reach the outer buoys about 1½ hours before local high water.

Burnham Flats
This extensive shallow area stretches a good 5 miles offshore opposite Burnham Overy Staithe, with depths between 1 and 4½ metres at LAT. Brancaster Road, a deeper roadstead about 2 miles long, lies well inside Burnham Flats just 1 mile north of Scolt Head. The seas are short and steep over Burnham Flats in fresh onshore winds, and with a weather-going tide. Most boats

coasting between Cromer and The Wash would normally take the Sledway channel inside Burnham Flats at about half-tide.

Woolpack
The wide Woolpack shoal lies west of Burnham Flats and just north of the Sledway channel. Much of the Woolpack has less than ½ metre at LAT and one or two patches dry. Most boats coasting between Cromer and The Wash would normally take the Sledway channel just south of the Woolpack at about half-tide.

Middle Bank and Gore Middle
These two drying banks are joined together and lie 1½ miles north of Gore Point in the north-east corner of The Wash. Gore Middle dries up to 1.3 metres and the Middle Bank up to 2.2 metres.

Most boats coasting between Cromer and The Wash would normally take the Sledway channel well north of Middle Bank and Gore Middle, but in quiet weather shallow-draught boats can cut close south of these banks through The Bays. For this short cut, always use the latest Admiralty charts 108 and 1200.

General warning
The north coast of Norfolk and the approaches to The Wash provide few corners of refuge for boats, which need to be highly self-sufficient when cruising this area. The small harbours of Blakeney and Wells are only accessible in quiet conditions near high water and you should always have an alternative plan in case of deteriorating weather.

In strong westerlies Great Yarmouth is the only safe bet. In strong easterlies, you can find shelter at King's Lynn in the south-east corner of The Wash, although great care must be taken when approaching the banks and channels of The Wash in any difficult weather.

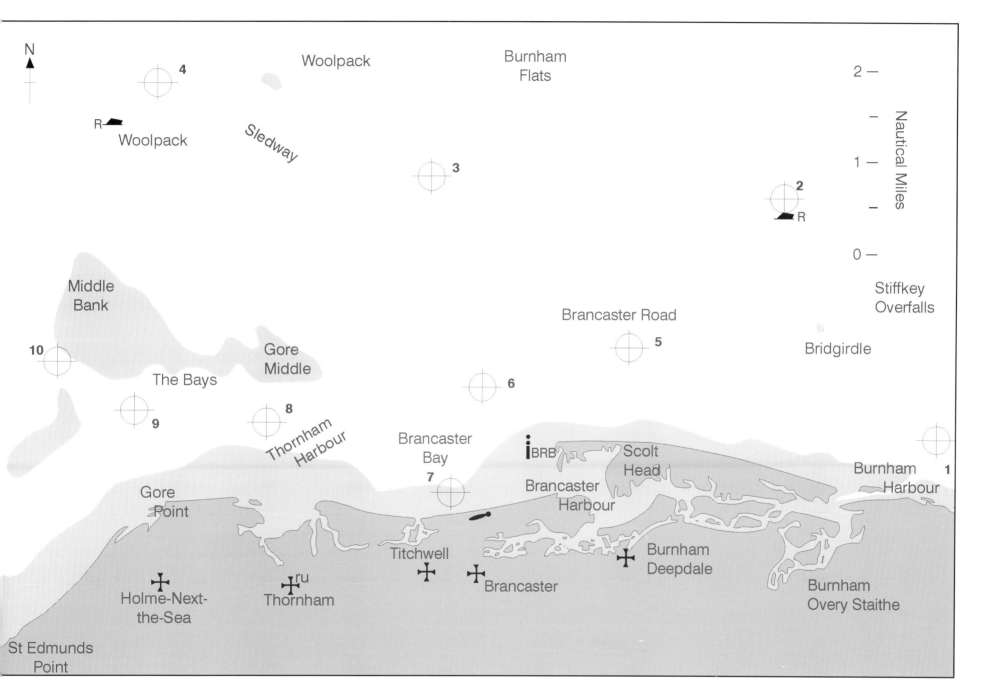

N

Woolpack

Burnham
Flats

4

R Woolpack

Sledway

3

2

R

Nautical Miles

2 —

—

1 —

—

0 —

Stiffkey
Overfalls

Middle
Bank

Brancaster Road

5

Bridgirdle

10

Gore
Middle

The Bays

6

9

8

Thornham
Harbour

Brancaster
Bay

BRB

Scolt
Head

Burnham
Harbour

1

7

Gore
Point

Brancaster
Harbour

Titchwell

ru
Thornham

Brancaster

Burnham
Deepdale

Holme-Next-
the-Sea

Burnham
Overy Staithe

St Edmunds
Point

WP No	Waypoint name and position	Latitude	Longitude
28–1	Sledway inner, 4.3 M due N of Titchwell church spire	53°02.07'N	00°37.43'E
28–2	Sledway outer, 6 ca NE of the Woolpack red buoy	53°03.09'N	00°32.25'E
28–3	Brancaster Road SW, 2 M N of Brancaster church tower	52°59.79'N	00°38.37'E
28–4	Thornham approach, 1.8 M 350°T from Thornham ruined tower	52°59.38'N	00°34.40'E
28–5	The Bays, 1.9 M 350°T from Holme-next-the-Sea church tower	52°59.50'N	00°31.98'E
28–6	Middle Bank SW, 2.7 M 333°T from Holme-next-the-Sea tower	53°00.04'N	00°30.50'E
28–7	Roaring Middle light-float, actual position	52°58.61'N	00°21.15'E
28–8	Sunk W-card buoy, actual position	52°56.27'N	00°23.51'E
28–9	No 1 N-card bell-buoy, actual position	52°56.00'N	00°20.00'E
28–10	North Well red-and-white fairway buoy, actual position	53°03.00'N	00°28.00'E
28–11	Lynn Knock, 2 ca due E of Lynn Knock green buoy	53°04.40'N	00°27.68'E
28–12	Lynn Knock west, 1¼ M due W of Lynn Knock green buoy	53°04.40'N	00°25.25'E
28–13	Woolpack, 3 ca due W of the Woolpack red buoy	53°02.67'N	00°31.05'E
28–14	Burnham Flats, ¼ M NE of Burnham Flats W-card buoy	53°07.71'N	00°35.32'E
28–15	Burnham Flats outer, 1 M NE Burnham Flats W-card buoy	53°08.23'N	00°36.21'E
28–16	Skegness offing, 3.2 M due E of Skegness gas holder	53°08.45'N	00°25.07'E
28–17	Ingoldmells offing, 3.4 M due E of Ingoldmells church tower	53°11.62'N	00°25.75'E
28–18	Inner Dowsing SW, 1.2 M due W of S Inner Dowsing bell buoy	53°12.10'N	00°31.78'E
28–19	Scott Patch, ¾ M SE of Scott Patch E-card buoy	53°10.58'N	00°37.38'E

Datum OSGB 36 The waypoint latitudes and longitudes in this table refer to Ordnance Survey of Great Britain (1936) Datum

COASTAL DANGERS
Refer to Admiralty charts 108 and 1200

Woolpack
The wide Woolpack shoal lies west of Burnham Flats and just north of the Sledway channel. Much of the Woolpack has less than ½ metre at LAT and one or two patches dry. Most boats coasting between Cromer and The Wash would normally take the Sledway channel just south of the Woolpack at about half-tide.

Middle Bank and Gore Middle
These two drying banks are joined and lie 1½ miles north of Gore Point in the north-east corner of The Wash. Gore Middle dries up to 1.3 metres and the Middle Bank up to 2.2 metres.

Most boats coasting between Cromer and The Wash would normally take the Sledway channel well north of Middle Bank and Gore Middle, but in quiet weather shallow-draught boats can cut close south of these banks through The Bays. For this short cut, always use the latest Admiralty charts 108 and 1200.

Sunk Sand
This extensive drying sandbank lies in the north-east corner of The Wash opposite Hunstanton and Gore Point. The south-west corner of the Sunk is guarded only by Sunk W-cardinal buoy, so take care when arriving in The Wash from the north-east.

Long Sand
This long drying bank lies on the west side of The Wash, with drying heights up to 2.7 metres. About 5 miles long by 1 mile wide, Long Sand has no buoys guarding its seaward edge, so take care when approaching The Wash from the north-east. A direct line between North Well red-and-white fairway buoy and Roaring Middle red-and-white light-float leads safely into The Wash a good mile clear of Long Sand. The buoyed channel known as Boston Deep leads inside Long Sand and provides the normal coasting route between Skegness and Boston.

Dogs Head Sands
The sandbanks known as the Inner Dogs Head (dries up to 3.3 metres) and the Outer Dogs Head (dries up to 3.7 metres) extend northwards from near the north-east edge of Long Sand towards Gibraltar Point. The Inner and Outer Knock shoals lie west and north from the Outer Dogs Head. A buoyed channel, the Wainfleet Swatchway, leads from close off Skegness past Gibraltar Point inside Inner Knock and thus well inside Outer Dogs Head and Inner Dogs Head.

General warning
The approaches to The Wash provide few corners of refuge for boats, which need to be highly self-sufficient when cruising this area. You should always have an alternative plan in case of deteriorating weather, bearing in mind the wind direction and the height over tide over the various banks and shoals.

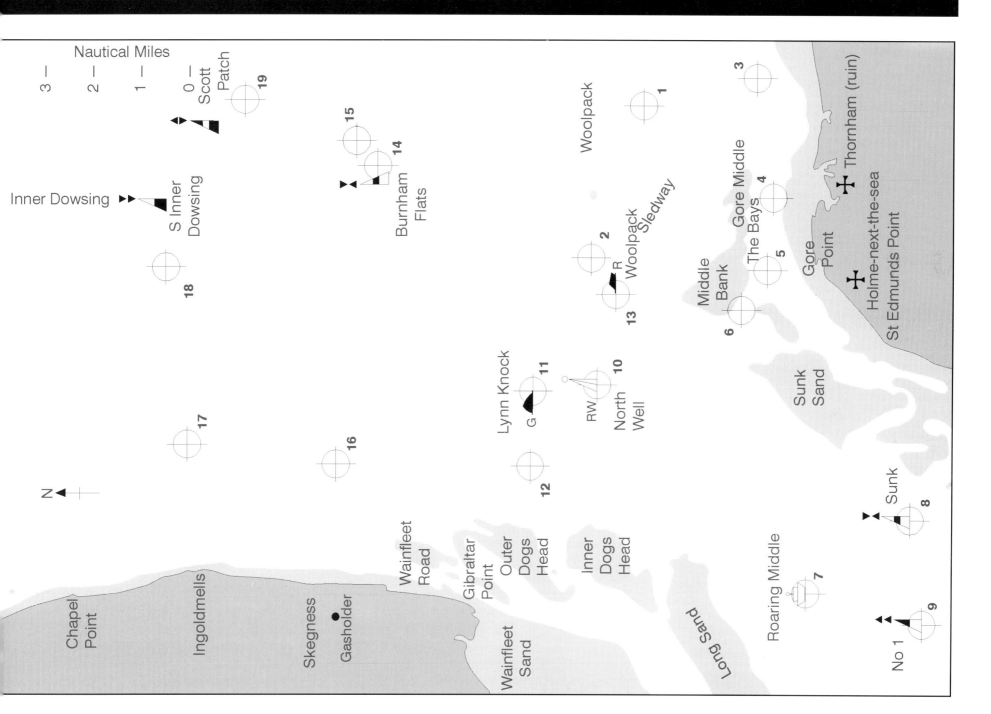

Nautical Miles

3 —
2 —
1 —
0 —

Scott Patch
19

Inner Dowsing

S Inner Dowsing

18

15

14

Burnham Flats

Woolpack

1

3

Woolpack Sledway

2

R Woolpack
13

Gore Middle
4

The Bays
5

Middle Bank

Gore Point
6

Holme-next-the-sea

St Edmunds Point

Thornham (ruin)

17

Lynn Knock
G **11**

RW
North Well
10

16

12

N

Chapel Point

Ingoldmells

Skegness
● Gasholder

Wainfleet Road

Gibraltar Point

Outer Dogs Head

Inner Dogs Head

Wainfleet Sand

Long Sand

Roaring Middle
7

Sunk
8

No 1
9

Sunk Sand

85

The Wash

WP No	Waypoint name and position	Latitude	Longitude
29–1	The Bays, 1.9 M 350°T from Holme-next-the-Sea church tower	52°59.50'N	00°31.98'E
29–2	Middle Bank SW, 2.7 M 333°T from Holme-next-the-Sea tower	53°00.04'N	00°30.50'E
29–3	Roaring Middle light float, actual position	52°58.61'N	00°21.15'E
29–4	Sunk W-card buoy, actual position	52°56.27'N	00°23.51'E
29–5	Cork Hole Channel, 3.6 M 245°T from Hunstanton water tower	52°54.29'N	00°24.44'E
29–6	No 1 N-card bell buoy, actual position	52°56.00'N	00°20.00'E
29–7	Teetotal Channel, midway No 2 red and No 3 green buoys	52°54.60'N	00°19.56'E
29–8	Bar Flat E-card buoy, actual position	52°55.10'N	00°16.46'E
29–9	Old Lynn Channel, 1.6 M 190°T from Bar Flat E-card buoy	52°53.53'N	00°16.00'E
29–10	Wisbech Channel, 3 M 353°T from Trial Bank light	52°53.54'N	00°14.10'E
29–11	Boston Roads fairway, 2.8 M 306°T from No 1 N-card buoy	52°57.65'N	00°16.26'E
29–12	Freeman Channel east, 7.3 M due N true from Trial Bank light	52°57.85'N	00°14.70'E
29–13	Boston Lower Road, 4.2 M due E of Fishtoft church tower	52°57.76'N	00°08.83'E
29–14	The Well, 3½ M 226°T from North Well fairway buoy	53°00.54'N	00°23.80'E
29–15	Sunk Sand west, 4.3 M 327°T from Hunstanton water tower	52°59.42'N	00°26.00'E

Datum OSGB 36 The waypoint latitudes and longitudes in this table refer to Ordnance Survey of Great Britain (1936) Datum

COASTAL DANGERS
Refer to Admiralty charts 108 and 1200

Middle Bank
This drying sandbank is joined to Gore Middle and lies 1½ miles north of Gore Point in the north-east corner of The Wash. Middle Bank dries up to 2.2 metres and Gore Middle, just to the east, dries up to 1.3 metres. Most boats coasting between Cromer and The Wash would normally take the Sledway channel well north of Middle Bank and Gore Middle.

Sunk Sand
This extensive drying sandbank lies in the north-east corner of The Wash opposite Hunstanton and Gore Point. The south-west corner of the Sunk is guarded only by Sunk W-cardinal buoy, so take care when arriving in The Wash from the north-east.

Banks in approaches to King's Lynn
King's Lynn lies in the south-east corner of The Wash and can be approached by various channels through the extensive sandbanks of the inner part of The Wash. It is important to use the latest version of Admiralty chart 1200 when navigating in this area.

Seal Sand and Daseley's Sand form the largest expanse of drying banks in the approaches to King's Lynn, with drying heights up to 4.5 metres. The buoyed Teetotal Channel, which can be entered above half-flood, leads west of Seal Sand and then curves west and south of Daseley's Sand. You pick up the outer marks of the Lynn Cut south of Pandora Sand, where the West Stones N-cardinal beacon is left 100 metres to the west. An alternative route, within 2 hours of high water, lies through Cork Hole east of Styleman's Middle and then east of Pandora

Sand to reach West Stones N-cardinal beacon from the north-east.

Approaches to the River Nene
The River Nene is approached by the Wisbech Channel, normally above half-flood. First make for Bar Flat E-cardinal buoy and then head south-west to pick up No 1 green buoy at the entrance to the Wisbech Channel. Thereafter the channel passes west of the sandbank known as Outer Westmark Knock and is well marked right up to the entrance to Wisbech Cut.

The approaches to Boston
Boston lies in the south-west corner of The Wash and is approached via Lower Road inside Roger Sand. Boston Deep leads into Lower Road from the north-east, inside Long Sand, and provides the normal coasting route between Skegness and Boston. You can also enter Lower Road from the main expanse of The Wash via the buoyed Freeman Channel, which leads close past the north edge of Roger Sand. To approach Freeman Channel from The Wash, you first need to pick up Boston Roads red-and-white fairway buoy.

Long Sand
This long drying bank lies on the west side of The Wash, with drying heights up to 2.7 metres. About 5 miles long by 1 mile wide, Long Sand has no buoys guarding its seaward edge, so take care when approaching The Wash from the north-east. A direct line between North Well red-and-white fairway buoy and Roaring Middle red-and-white light-float leads safely into The Wash a good mile clear of Long Sand. The buoyed channel known as Boston Deep leads inside Long Sand and provides the normal coasting route between Skegness and Boston.

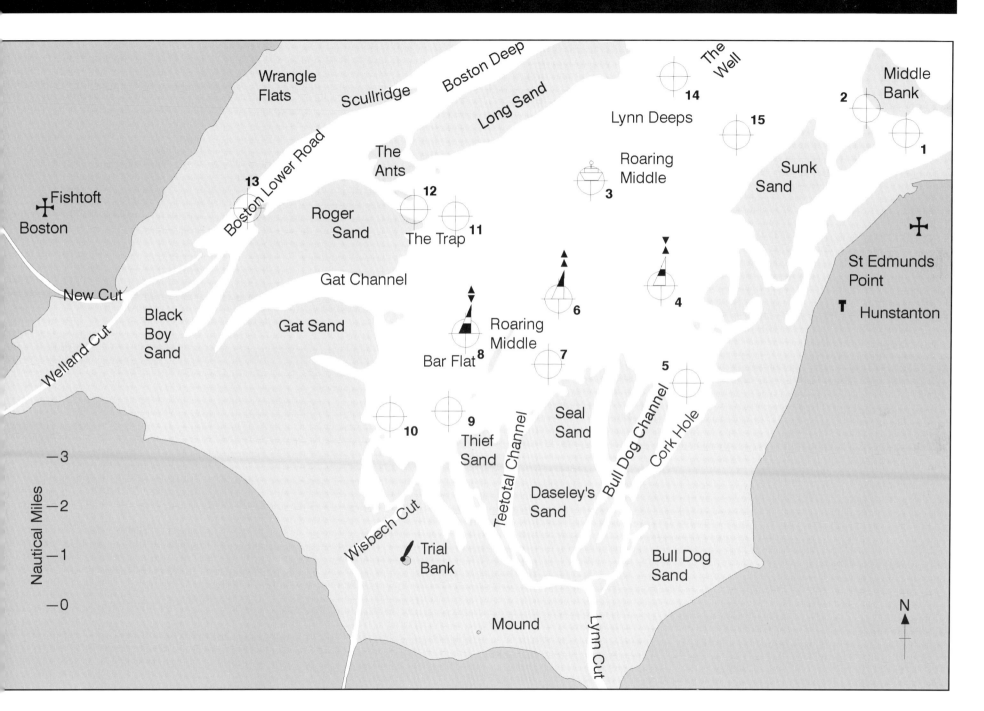

Wrangle Flats

Scullridge

Boston Deep

The Well

Long Sand

Lynn Deeps

Middle Bank

2

1

14

15

Sunk Sand

The Ants

Boston Lower Road

13

Roaring Middle

3

Fishtoft

Boston

Roger Sand

12

11

The Trap

St Edmunds Point

Hunstanton

New Cut

Gat Channel

6

4

Black Boy Sand

Gat Sand

Roaring Middle

Bar Flat **8**

7

Welland Cut

5

10

9

Thief Sand

Teetotal Channel

Seal Sand

Bull Dog Channel

Cork Hole

−3

−2

Nautical Miles

−1

Wisbech Cut

Trial Bank

Daseley's Sand

Bull Dog Sand

−0

Mound

Lynn Cut

N

WP No	Waypoint name and position	Latitude	Longitude
30–1	Scott Patch, ¾ M SE of Scott Patch E-card buoy	53°10.58'N	00°37.38'E
30–2	Inner Dowsing SW, 1.2 M due W of S Inner Dowsing bell buoy	53°12.10'N	00°31.78'E
30–3	Ingoldmells offing, 3.4 M due E of Ingoldmells church tower	53°11.62'N	00°25.75'E
30–4	North Docking N-card buoy, actual position	53°14.80'N	00°41.60'E
30–5	North Docking west, ¾ M west of N Docking N-card buoy	53°14.80'N	00°40.35'E
30–6	North Docking east, ¾ M east of N Docking N-card buoy	53°14.80'N	00°42.85'E
30–7	West Ridge clearing, ¾ M west of West Ridge W-card buoy	53°19.04'N	00°43.31'E
30–8	Inner Dowsing NE, 1 M due E of Inner Dowsing light float	53°19.50'N	00°35.66'E
30–9	Chapel Point clearing, 5 M due E of Huttoft church tower	53°15.78'N	00°24.35'E
30–10	Inner Dowsing west, 5.6 M due W of Inner Dowsing light-float	53°19.50'N	00°24.62'E

Datum OSGB 36 The waypoint latitudes and longitudes in this table refer to Ordnance Survey of Great Britain (1936) Datum

North Ridge

The West Ridge W-cardinal buoy guards the west end of a long narrow bank known as North Ridge, which extends north-westwards from the Dudgeon Shoal. North Ridge and the Dudgeon Shoal have sufficient depths for boats to pass over in quiet weather, but both these shoals cause steep over-falls in a strong weather-going tide. When on passage directly between Cromer and the River Humber, boats should stick to the wide buoyed channel between Docking Shoal and Race Bank.

COASTAL DANGERS
Refer to Admiralty charts 108 and 1190

Inner Dowsing

The narrow Inner Dowsing bank runs parallel with the Lincolnshire coast about 8 miles offshore. The north end is marked by the Inner Dowsing light float and the south end by the South Inner Dowsing S-cardinal bell buoy. The shallowest part of the Inner Dowsing bank lies towards the south end and has only 1.2 metres depth at LAT, but most of the bank has patches with between 3 and 5 metres depth.

Overfalls are likely across the whole length of Inner Dowsing during a weather-going tide, but the most agitated area is usually across some comparatively deep patches (about 6½ metres LAT) off the north-west tip of the narrow part of the bank. The sea breaks steeply across Inner Dowsing in heavy onshore weather.

Docking Shoal

The wide Docking Shoal forms the point of an extensive triangle of shallows stretching north from the north coast of Norfolk for about 16 miles. The north tip of this triangle is marked by the North Docking N-cardinal buoy and the shallowest parts of the Docking Shoal lie a couple of miles south-east of Scott Patch E-cardinal buoy, where depths vary between 3½ and 4½ metres. Boats can cross this shoal safely in quiet weather, but should stick to the main buoyed channels in fresh or strong conditions.

Race Bank

The North Race green bell buoy marks the north-west corner of the Race Bank, which runs NW–SE about 2 miles north-east of the north-easterly edge of the Docking Shoal. Depths over the Race Bank are mostly greater than 5 or 6 metres, but a long 2½ metre patch lies from 5½–8 miles south-east of the North Race green bell buoy.

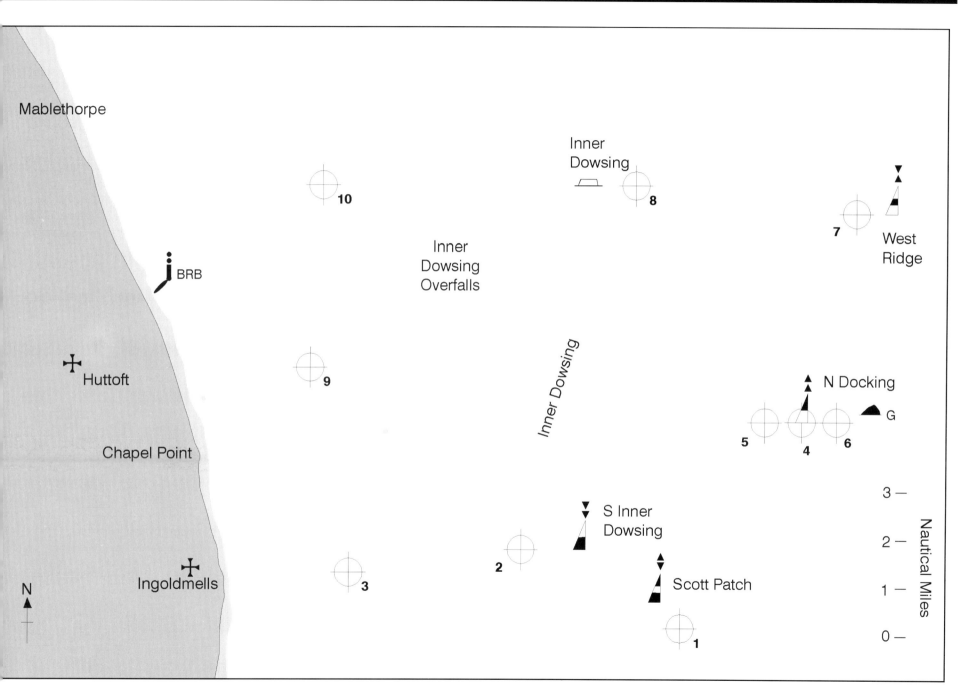

Mablethorpe

Inner
Dowsing

10

Inner
Dowsing
Overfalls

8

7   West
Ridge

BRB

Inner Dowsing

Huttoft

9

N Docking

G

Chapel Point

5   4   6

3 —

S Inner
Dowsing

2 —

Nautical Miles

2

Ingoldmells

Scott Patch

1 —

N

3

0 —

1

WP No	Waypoint name and position	Latitude	Longitude
31–1	Inner Dowsing west, 5.6 M due W of Inner Dowsing light float	53°19.50'N	00°24.62'E
31–2	Protector west clearing, 1½ M due W of the Protector red buoy	53°24.83'N	00°22.72'E
31–3	Rosse Spit, 7.4 M 051°T from North Somercotes church tower	53°31.01'N	00°18.10'E
31–4	Haile Sand clearing, 8 M 055°T from Marshchapel church tower	53°32.62'N	00°13.95'E
31–5	Humber red-and-white fairway buoy, actual position	53°36.71'N	00°21.70'E
31–6	New Sand Hole, 13 M due E of Grimsby Royal Dock tower	53°34.97'N	00°17.76'E
31–7	Spurn outer, 3 ca SE of Spurn E-card light float	53°33.31'N	00°14.69'E
31–8	Chequer No 3 clearing, 3 ca due S of S-card buoy	53°32.77'N	00°10.72'E
31–9	Bull Sand south, 6 ca due S of Bull Sand Fort	53°33.09'N	00°04.15'E
31–10	Bull Sand west, ½ M due W of Bull Sand Fort	53°33.69'N	00°03.30'E
31–11	Spurn Head SW clearing, 6 ca SW of Spurn Head pilot station	53°34.06'N	00°06.10'E

Datum OSGB 36 The waypoint latitudes and longitudes in this table refer to Ordnance Survey of Great Britain (1936) Datum

COASTAL DANGERS
Refer to Admiralty charts 107, 109 and 1190

Coastal shoals opposite Theddlethorpe
In the south approaches to the River Humber, opposite Mablethorpe and Theddlethorpe, shallow coastal banks extend up to 1 mile off the long beach, with LAT depths down to ½ metre or less. Care must be taken, therefore, not to stray too far inshore, especially as you draw north of Theddlethorpe.

Protector Overfalls
These two narrow banks, each less than 1 mile long, lie just over 6 miles offshore opposite Theddlethorpe gas terminal. The least depth over Protector Overfalls is 2.7 metres at LAT and the banks are guarded on their seaward side by the Protector red buoy.

Rosse Spit
North of Theddlethorpe, in the south approaches to the River Humber, the coastal shoals begin to curve seawards to form a long sandspit shoal – Rosse Spit – that extends almost 5 miles offshore to the Rosse Spit red buoy. Depths over the inner part of this spit, where the shoals start to turn seawards, are less than ½ metre in parts. The outer part of the spit has depths between 2 and 4 metres.

Not only are these shoals potentially dangerous in themselves, but they are also used as a firing practice area by the Donna Nook firing range. Use of this range is indicated by the display of red flags or red lights, but in any case boats should keep well offshore to pass outside Danger Zone No 4 yellow buoy, Danger Zone No 3 yellow buoy and then Rosse Spit red buoy. From here you head north-west to pass outside Haile Sand red buoy before entering the river.

Haile Sand Flat
Haile Sand and Haile Sand Flat lie 2 miles west and north-west of Rosse Spit, an extensive area of coastal shoals stretching up to 5 miles offshore from Donna Nook to the Haile Sand red buoy. The inner part of Haile Sand dries up to 2½ metres and this drying area extends 2 miles seaward from the firing range. Beyond the drying sands, Haile Sand Flats have depths ranging from 0.2 metres inshore to 4.3 metres out near the red buoy. Boats approaching the River Humber from the south should steer to pass seaward of Haile Sand red buoy before following the main channel buoys into the estuary.

Spurn Head
The narrow, rather eerie sandspit of Spurn Head curves south-west to form the east arm of the entrance to the River Humber. A long string of shoals with drying patches, known as The Binks, extends for more than 3 miles east of Spurn Head marked at the seaward end by the Outer Binks E-cardinal buoy and the South Binks yellow buoy. These buoys are left clear to the north as you approach the estuary from the east.

Banks in the River Humber entrance
Bull Sand and its fort lie right in the middle of the Humber entrance, guarded on either side by buoys. The Bull Channel leads north-east of Bull Sand and the Haile Channel passes to the south-west. The Hawke Channel runs close under Spurn Head and then curves round the north-east side of the estuary to pass north of Middle Shoal. The Hawke Channel then runs directly into the Sunk Channel.

On the south-west side of the estuary, Clee Ness Sand juts well out into the river as far as the Clee Ness light float, where the Haile Channel joins the Bull Channel.

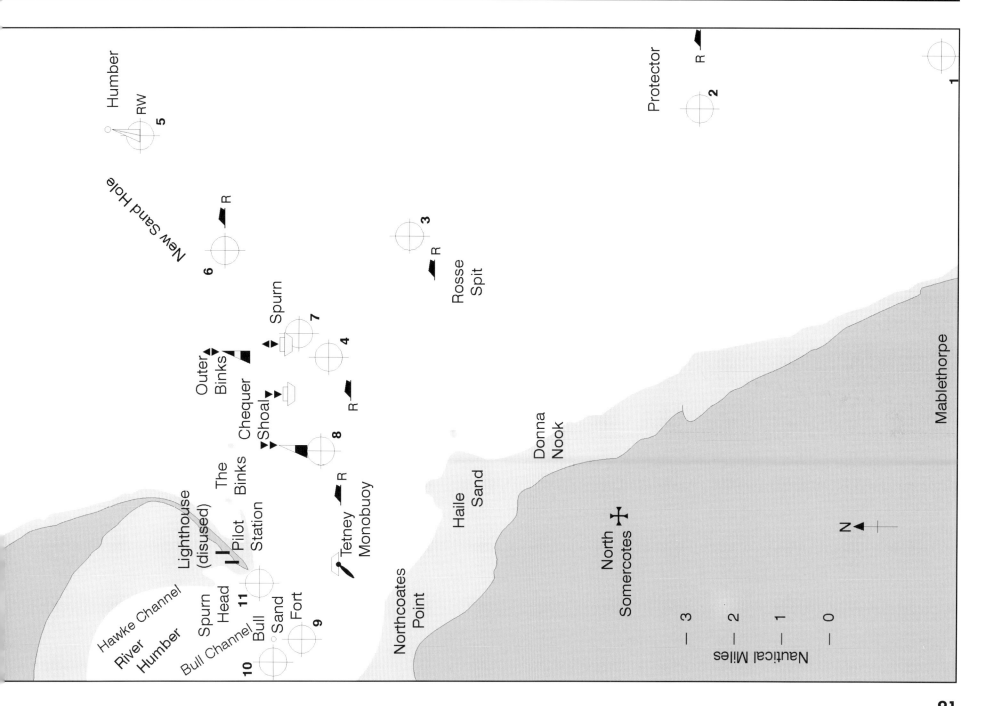

Humber
RW
5

New Sand Hole

R
6

Protector
R
2

R
3

Rosse
Spit

Spurn
7

Outer
Binks

Chequer
Shoal
4

R
8

The
Binks

Pilot
Station

Lighthouse
(disused)

Tetney
Monobuoy
R

Northcoates
Point

Haile
Sand

Donna
Nook

Hawke Channel
River Humber
Spurn
Head
11

Bull
Channel
Bull
Sand
Fort
9

10

North
Somercotes

Mablethorpe

Nautical Miles

3

2

1

0

N

1

Calais and Cap Gris-Nez

WP No	Waypoint name and position	Latitude	Longitude
32–1	ZC2 yellow buoy off Cap Gris-Nez, actual position	50°53.50'N	01°30.98'E
32–2	Cap Gris-Nez inner, 1½ M NW of lighthouse	50°53.14'N	01°33.40'E
32–3	La Barrière outer, ¼ M NW of Abbeville W-card buoy	50°56.05'N	01°37.34'E
32–4	La Barrière inner, 4.4 M 047°T from Cap Gris-Nez lighthouse	50°55.67'N	01°39.00'E
32–5	Les Quénocs clearing, 2 ca NW of CA3 green buoy	50°56.97'N	01°41.00'E
32–6	CA4 W-card buoy, actual position	50°58.94'N	01°45.19'E
32–7	Calais CA6 red approach buoy, actual position	50°58.30'N	01°45.70'E
32–8	Calais CA10 red buoy, actual position	50°58.59'N	01°50.00'E
32–9	Calais entrance, midway between outer pierheads	50°58.37'N	01°50.52'E
32–10	Ruytingen SW green buoy, actual position	51°04.98'N	01°46.87'E
32–11	Dyck red buoy, actual position	51°02.96'N	01°57.87'E

Datum OSGB 36 The waypoint latitudes and longitudes in this table refer to Ordnance Survey of Great Britain (1936) Datum

COASTAL DANGERS
Refer to Admiralty charts 323 and 1892

Ridens de la Rade
This narrow bank runs WSW–ENE off Calais, forming a partial natural breakwater up to 1 mile offshore. The shallowest depths are about 0.8 metres at LAT ½ mile seaward of Calais break-waters, with a wider, more shoal area further east over 1 mile off the hoverport.

In reasonably quiet weather, with sufficient rise of tide, it is safe for boats to cut across Ridens de la Rade, especially when leaving Calais near high water. However, the bank is dangerous in fresh to strong onshore winds, or in fresh north-easterlies or south-westerlies when the tide is weather-going.

Ferry traffic
More than natural coastal dangers, the greatest threat to craft in the Dover Strait is posed by the almost continuous and rapid movement of cross-Channel ferries. The Strait is one of the busiest seaways in the world, with shipping movements monitored by the Channel Navigation Information Service run by Dover Coastguard and the French 'CROSSMA' station at Cap Gris-Nez.

Shipping lanes
It is a legal requirement that you cross the Dover Strait shipping lanes at right-angles, regardless of what the tide happens to be doing. Low-powered vessels and sailing yachts should not make allowance for the tidal stream while crossing if, by so doing, they will not have a heading nearly at right-angles to the traffic flow.

For most boats, therefore, the enforced strategy will be one of dashing across the 10 mile wide shipping lanes as quickly as possible while keeping careful track of the effect of the tide. Because of the powerful streams in the Dover Strait — up to 3½–4 knots at top of springs — it is best to time your departure so that the overall effect of the tide works in your favour.

Cap Blanc-Nez
About 6 miles WSW of Calais entrance, various shoal patches lie up to 1½ miles seaward of Cap Blanc-Nez, a prominent rise in the cliffs some 130 metres high. Le Rouge Riden bank has a minimum depth of 1.3 metres, and a shallow wreck, with only 0.2 metres over it, lies only about ¼ mile inside CA3 (Les Quénocs) green buoy. Boats should stay outside a line between this buoy and Cap Gris-Nez, to avoid La Barrière shoals and Banc à la Ligne.

Banc à la Ligne
The shallow Banc à la Ligne extends within a couple of miles north-east of Cap Gris-Nez, with depths in parts only just above datum. Boats making between Cap Gris-Nez and Calais need to stay outside CA1 green buoy and CA3 (Les Quénocs) green buoy.

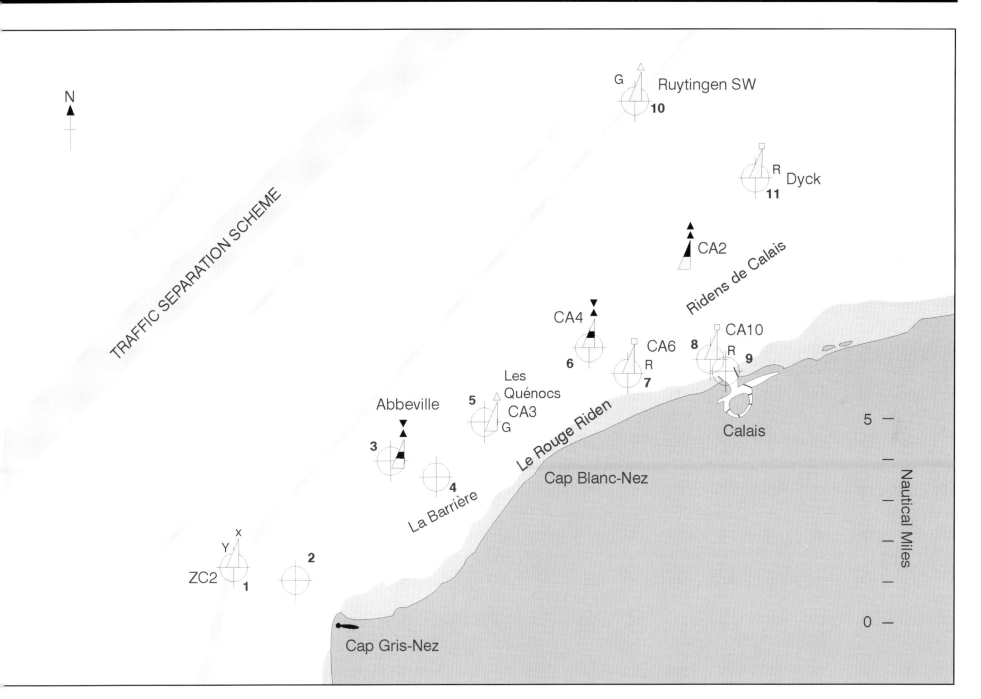

N

TRAFFIC SEPARATION SCHEME

G Ruytingen SW
10

R Dyck
11

CA2

Ridens de Calais

CA4

CA10

CA6
8
R
9

Les
Quénocs
CA3
5
G

R
7

Abbeville

6

3

Le Rouge Riden

4

La Barrière

Cap Blanc-Nez

Calais

5

Nautical Miles

X
Y
ZC2
1

2

Cap Gris-Nez

0

WP No	Waypoint name and position	Latitude	Longitude
33–1	Calais CA10 red buoy, actual position	50°58.59'N	01°50.00'E
33–2	Calais entrance, midway between outer pierheads	50°58.37'N	01°50.52'E
33–3	Ridens de la Rade, 1 M due N of Calais west pierhead	50°59.30'N	01°50.48'E
33–4	Ridens de la Rade offing, 2 M due N of Calais west pierhead	51°00.30'N	01°50.48'E
33–5	Dyck red buoy, actual position	51°02.96'N	01°57.87'E
33–6	RCE green buoy, actual position	51°02.40'N	01°53.23'E
33–7	DKA red-and-white fairway buoy, actual position	51°02.52'N	01°57.08'E
33–8	DW5, 1 ca due S of DW5 green buoy	51°02.10'N	02°01.01'E
33–9	DW9, 1 ca due S of DW9 green buoy	51°02.56'N	02°04.10'E
33–10	Gravelines entrance, 2 ca NW of Gravelines W p/head outer bn	51°01.13'N	02°05.32'E
33–11	DW8, 1 ca due N of DW8 red buoy	51°02.88'N	02°02.67'E
33–12	DW10, 1 ca due N of DW10 red buoy	51°03.08'N	02°04.22'E
33–13	Haut-Fond de Gravelines, 3 ca due W of W-card buoy	51°04.10'N	02°04.65'E

Datum OSGB 36 The waypoint latitudes and longitudes in this table refer to Ordnance Survey of Great Britain (1936) Datum

COASTAL DANGERS

Refer to Admiralty charts 323 and 1352

Ridens de la Rade

This long bank runs WSW–ENE off Calais, forming a partial natural breakwater up to 1 mile offshore. The least depth opposite Calais is about 0.8 metres, ½ mile off the entrance. A wider, shallower area lies further east over 1 mile off the hoverport.

In reasonably quiet weather, with sufficient rise of tide, it is safe for boats to cut across Ridens de la Rade, especially when leaving Calais near high water. However, the bank is dangerous in fresh to strong onshore winds, or in fresh north-easterlies or south-westerlies when the tide is weather-going.

Ferry traffic

Keep well clear of cross-Channel ferries in the long approaches to Calais. Boats must look out for themselves and avoid becoming caught in any close-quarters incidents.

Coastal shoals east of Calais

Just east of Calais and Ridens de la Rade, coastal shoals extend almost 1½ miles offshore, with depths almost to datum and a few drying patches. When you leave Calais bound east along the coast, head NNW to cross Ridens de la Rade immediately, if it is safe to do so. Strike offshore to within 1 mile of CA2 N-cardinal buoy before turning east to follow the coast.

Wide drying sands extend up to 1 mile offshore east of the Walde lighthouse, which itself stands 6 cables offshore on drying sand. These banks are littered with wrecks and you should keep well off until almost opposite the two long piers of Gravelines harbour.

Shipping in the Dunkerque approach channel

Take great care to avoid large ships using the long approach channel to Dunkerque. This channel follows the coast between 4 and 2 miles offshore from the Dyck red buoy eastwards via DKA red-and-white fairway buoy and along the buoyed dredged channel towards Dunkerque Port Ouest. Boats coasting between Calais and Gravelines or Dunkerque would normally keep inshore of this buoyed channel, safely out of the way of ships.

East Dyck Bank

The long Dyck Occidental shoal runs parallel to the coast some 3–4 miles offshore between the Dyck red buoy at the west end and the Dyck Est E-cardinal buoy at the east end. There is plenty of depth for boats to cross this bank in reasonably quiet weather although steep seas will start to build up along its length in sustained fresh onshore weather. Normal seamanship and circumspection must be applied to all the offshore banks along this coast. It will be safe to cross many of them in calm to moderate conditions, but the situation changes as the seas start to build.

Haut-Fond de Gravelines

This narrow shoal lies about 3 miles offshore between Gravelines and Dunkerque Port Ouest, just north of where the deep-water approach channel starts to turn south-east towards the entrance to Port Ouest. Depths over the bank vary between 4 and 9 metres, but a large area of wreckage, parts of which have only 1.9 metres depth at LAT, lurks between ½ and 1 mile east of the Haut-Fond de Gravelines W-cardinal buoy. This danger zone should be given a wide berth, although most yachts would normally stay inside the shipping channel if coasting between Calais and, say, Dunkerque or Oostende.

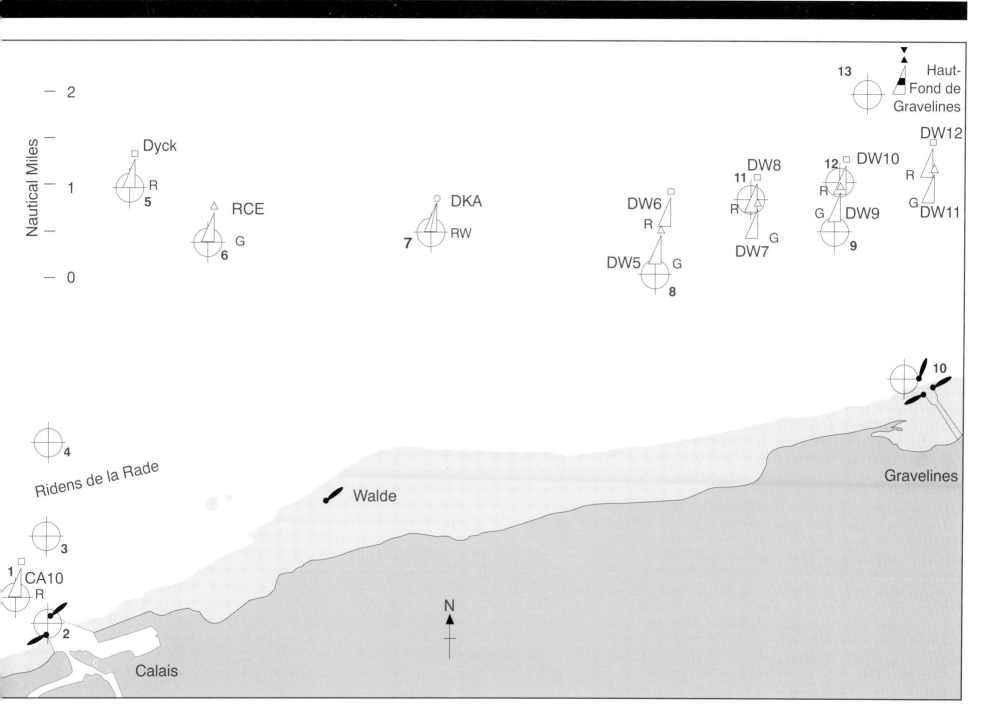

2

1

Nautical Miles

Dyck

R

5

RCE

G

6

DKA

RW

7

DW6

R

DW5 G

8

DW8

11

R

DW7 G

12 DW10

R

G DW9

9

DW12

R

G DW11

13

Haut-
Fond de
Gravelines

10

Gravelines

4

Ridens de la Rade

Walde

3

1 CA10

R

2

N

Calais

95

Gravelines to Dunkerque

WP No	Waypoint name and position	Latitude	Longitude
34–1	Gravelines entrance, 2 ca NW of Gravelines W p/head outer bn	51°01.13'N	02°05.32'E
34–2	DW11, 1 ca due S of DW11 green buoy	51°02.83'N	02°05.85'E
34–3	DW12, 1 ca due N of DW12 red buoy	51°03.34'N	02°05.65'E
34–4	DW13, 1 ca due S of DW13 green buoy	51°03.01'N	02°07.18'E
34–5	DW14, 1 ca due N of DW14 red buoy	51°03.51'N	02°07.22'E
34–6	Haut-Fond de Gravelines NW, ¾ M due N of W-card buoy	51°04.85'N	02°05.11'E
34–7	Haut-Fond de Gravelines E, 1½ M N of Port Ouest E pierhead	51°04.19'N	02°09.87'E
34–8	Dyck East E-card buoy, actual position	51°05.70'N	02°05.70'E
34–9	Passe de l'Ouest inner, midway DW16 red and DKB W-card	51°03.18'N	02°09.20'E
34–10	Rade de Dunkerque, 4½ ca 350°T from Dunkerque E pierhead	51°04.08'N	02°21.17'E
34–11	Dunkerque entrance, 1 ca 060°T from Dunkerque W pierhead	51°03.73'N	02°21.19'E
34–12	Banc du Snouw north, 4.6 M 057°T from Port Ouest E pierhead	51°05.19'N	02°16.02'E
34–13	Banc Breedt west, 4½ M 040°T from Port Ouest E pierhead	51°06.12'N	02°14.48'E
34–14	Chenal Intermediaire, 3.6 M 073°T from Port Ouest E pierhead	51°03.74'N	02°15.33'E
34–15	Banc Braek NE, 1.2 M 350°T from Dunkerque E pierhead	51°04.82'N	02°20.96'E

Datum ED 50 The waypoint latitudes and longitudes in this table refer to European Datum (1950).

COASTAL DANGERS
Refer to Admiralty charts 323 and 1350

Shipping in the Dunkerque approach channel
Take great care to avoid large ships using the long approach channel to Dunkerque. This channel follows the coast between 4 and 2 miles offshore from the Dunkerque LANBY eastwards via DKA red-and-white fairway buoy and along the buoyed dredged channel towards Dunkerque Port Ouest.

Boats coasting between Calais and Gravelines or Dunkerque would normally keep inshore of this buoyed channel as far as Dunkerque Port Ouest, safely out of the way of monster ships.

Off Dunkerque Port Ouest, most of the larger ships will be coming in and out of the huge Avant-Port Ouest, but some will be following the buoyed Passe de l'Ouest and Chenal Intermediaire which lead close along the coast to Dunkerque Port Est. Most small boats and yachts will also follow this route if coasting between Calais and Dunkerque or Oostende.

Haut-Fond de Gravelines
This narrow shoal lies 3 miles offshore between Gravelines and Dunkerque Port Ouest, just north of where the deep-water approach channel starts to turn south-east towards the entrance to Port Ouest. Depths over the bank vary between 4 and 9 metres, but a large area of wreckage, parts of which have only 1.9 metres depth at LAT, lurks between ½ and 1 mile east of the Haut-Fond de Gravelines W-cardinal buoy. This danger zone should be given a wide berth, although most boats would normally stay inside the shipping channel if coasting between Calais and, say, Dunkerque or Oostende.

Banc Breedt
This extensive shoal lies 2½–3 miles offshore between Dunkerque Port Ouest and the older harbour at Dunkerque where the town and yacht marinas are situated. Least depths over this west end of Banc Breedt are about 1 metre.

There would normally be no need for boats to be in this area at all unless, for any reason, you were approaching Dunkerque directly from the Thames Estuary, or perhaps leaving Dunkerque near high water in quiet weather with a view to crossing the offshore banks and heading directly for Ramsgate or the Thames Estuary.

Banc du Snouw
This narrow bank lies between Banc Breedt and the coast, with a least depth of 2 metres. Banc du Snouw is guarded on its south side only, by the red buoys of the shipping channel that leads between Dunkerque Port Ouest and Port Est.

Banc Braek
This shallow bank lies just ¾ mile offshore opposite the approaches to Dunkerque Port Est. The shallowest parts of Banc Braek have less than ½ metre depth at LAT. Banc Braek is marked only on its south side, by the red channel buoys of the Rade de Dunkerque.

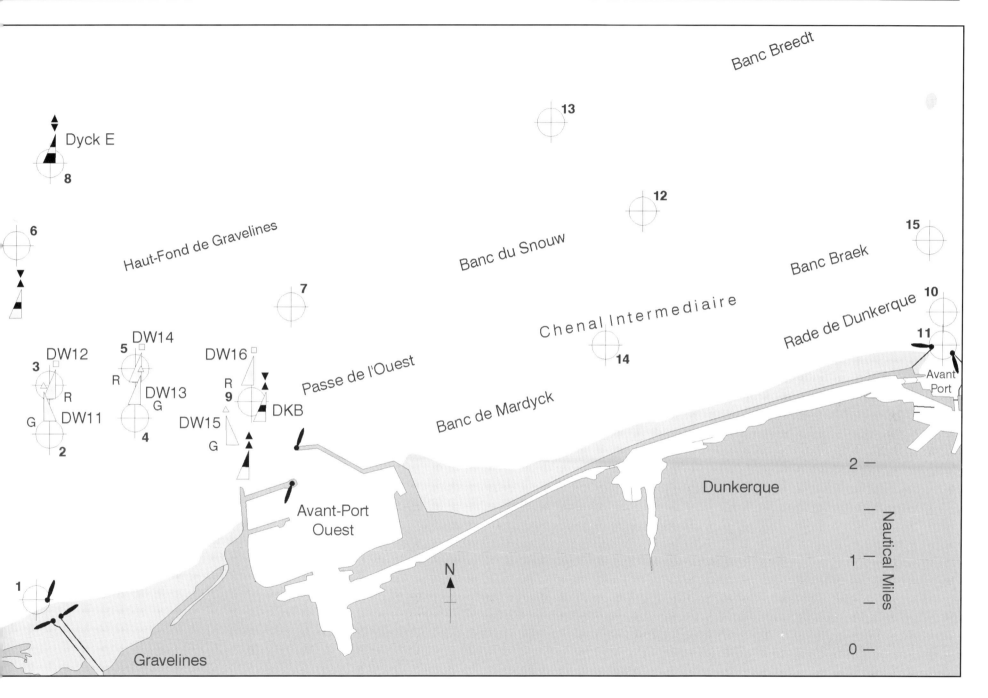

Dyck E

8

6

13

12

15

Banc Breedt

Haut-Fond de Gravelines

Banc du Snouw

Banc Braek

7

Chenal Intermediaire

Rade de Dunkerque

10

11

Avant Port

DW14

DW12

5

DW16

Passe de l'Ouest

3

R

R

DW13

R

DKB

14

G

DW11

G

9

DW15

4

2

G

Banc de Mardyck

Avant-Port
Ouest

N

Dunkerque

2 —

1 —

Nautical Miles

0 —

1

Gravelines

East approaches to Dunkerque

WP No	Waypoint name and position	Latitude	Longitude
35–1	Rade de Dunkerque, 4½ ca 350°T from Dunkerque E pierhead	51°04.08'N	02°21.17'E
35–2	Dunkerque entrance, 1 ca 060°T from Dunkerque W pierhead	51°03.73'N	02°21.19'E
35–3	Banc Braek NE, 1.2 M 350°T from Dunkerque E pierhead	51°04.82'N	02°20.96'E
35–4	Passe de l'Est, 1½ ca due S of E4 red buoy	51°04.48'N	02°24.60'E
35–5	Passe de Zuydcoote SW, E7 green buoy, actual position	51°05.23'N	02°28.60'E
35–6	Passe de Zuydcoote NE, 2 ca NW of E11 green buoy	51°07.44'N	02°30.50'E
35–7	Westdiep west, ½ M due N of Trapegeer green buoy	51°08.97'N	02°34.44'E
35–8	Nieuwpoort bank W-card buoy, actual position	51°10.20'N	02°36.17'E
35–9	Westdiep east, 2 M 304°T from Nieuwpoort west pierhead light	51°10.53'N	02°40.42'E
35–10	Noordpas SW, 4 ca NW of Nieuwpoort bank W-card buoy	51°10.50'N	02°35.70'E

Datum ED 50 The waypoint latitudes and longitudes in this table refer to European Datum (1950).

COASTAL DANGERS
Refer to Admiralty charts 1350, 1872 and 1873

Banc Braek
This shallow bank lies just ¾ mile offshore opposite the approaches to Dunkerque Port Est. The shallowest parts of Banc Braek have less than ½ metre depth at LAT. Banc Braek is marked only on its south side, by the red channel buoys of the Rade de Dunkerque.

Banc Smal
This long narrow bank extends for about 13 miles ENE from just north of Dunkerque entrance, diverging slightly from the shore as it trends east. Depths are well under 1 metre at the shallow south-west end near Dunkerque, with several patches either drying at LAT or almost awash. Boats coasting between Dunkerque and Oostende normally pass safely south of Banc Smal via the Passe de l'Est and the Passe de Zuydcoote.

Banc Hills
This shallow bank lies just south of the west end of Banc Smal, with some drying patches on its south side. Banc Hills is marked on its south side by the red channel buoys of the Dunkerque Passe de l'Est.

Trapegeer and Broers Bank
These two banks lie a mile or two east of the Passe de Zuydcoote, which dog-legs between Dunkerque Passe de l'Est and the Westdiep. Trapegeer has a least depth of 1.3 metres, but Broers Bank is much shallower, with depths generally well under 1 metre and a couple of small drying patches. A wreck with only 1.2 metres over it lies off the north-west tip of Broers Bank, marked by a N-cardinal buoy. The north-east edge of Trapegeer bank is guarded by the Trapegeer green buoy.

Den Oever
This shallow coastal shoal area has depths between 2½ and 4 metres, but there is a wreck almost awash guarded by a N-cardinal buoy and another wreck with 1.6 metres over it guarded by N-cardinal and S-cardinal buoys.

Nieuwpoort Bank
The long narrow Nieuwpoort Bank has depths between 3 and 4½ metres and is normally left either close to the north by boats coasting through the Westdiep or to the south if they are using the Noordpas.

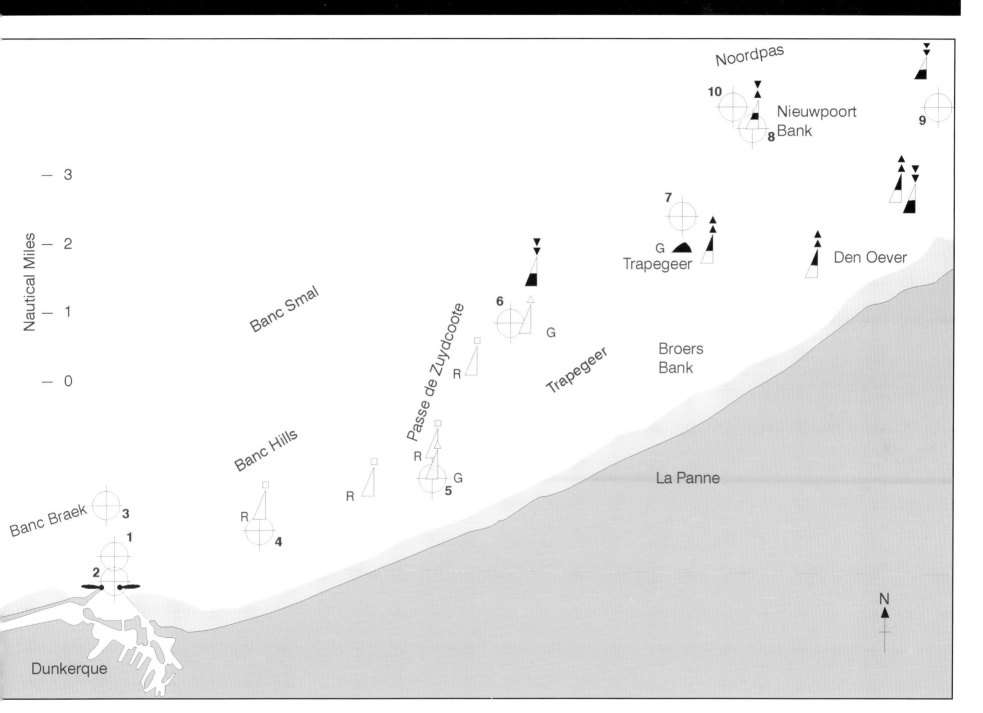

Noordpas

10

Nieuwpoort
8 Bank

9

3

2

7

1

G
Trapegeer

Den Oever

Banc Smal

Nautical Miles

6

Passe de Zuydcoote

G

R

Trapegeer

Broers
Bank

0

Banc Hills

R

R

R

G

La Panne

5

Banc Braek 3

R

1

4

2

N

Dunkerque

■■■ Nieuwpoort to Oostende ■■

WP No	Waypoint name and position	Latitude	Longitude
36–1	Noordpas SW, 4 ca NW of Nieuwpoort bank W-card buoy	51°10.50'N	02°35.70'E
36–2	Nieuwpoort bank W-card buoy, actual position	51°10.20'N	02°36.17'E
36–3	Westdiep east, 2 M 304°T from Nieuwpoort W pierhead light	51°10.53'N	02°40.42'E
36–4	Noordpas NE, 4.6 M 342°T from Nieuwpoort W pierhead	51°13.79'N	02°40.84'E
36–5	Banc Smal NE, D1 E-card buoy, actual position	51°14.00'N	02°38.67'E
36–6	Negenvaam SW, 1.6 M NW from Middelkerke Zuid red buoy	51°15.94'N	02°40.17'E
36–7	Middelkerke Zuid red buoy, actual position	51°14.78'N	02°41.97'E
36–8	Oostendebank west W-card buoy, actual position	51°16.25'N	02°44.83'E
36–9	NE Channel west, 8 ca 310°T from Weststroombank red buoy	51°11.90'N	02°42.12'E
36–10	NE Channel east, 3.2 M 338°T from Middelkerke church spire	51°14.18'N	02°47.43'E
36–11	Weststroombank SW, 2 ca SE of Weststroombank red buoy	51°11.24'N	02°43.33'E
36–12	Stroom bank south, 2 ca SE of Zuidstroombank red buoy	51°12.18'N	02°47.69'E
36–13	Grote Rede, 3 ca due N of Buitenstroombank N-card buoy	51°15.52'N	02°51.79'E
36–14	Oostende approach, ½ M 300°T from Oostende W pierhead	51°14.62'N	02°54.40'E
36–15	Oostende entrance, midway between the outer pierhead lights	51°14.40'N	02°55.17'E
36–16	Nieuwpoort entrance, 150 m due N of W pierhead light	51°09.48'N	02°43.08'E

Datum ED 50 The waypoint latitudes and longitudes in this table refer to European Datum (1950).

COASTAL DANGERS
Refer to Admiralty charts 1872 and 1873

Den Oever
This shallow coastal shoal area has depths between 2½ and 4 metres, but there is a wreck almost awash guarded by a N-cardinal buoy and another wreck with 1.6 metres over it guarded by N-cardinal and S-cardinal buoys.

Nieuwpoort Bank
The long narrow Nieuwpoort Bank has depths between 3 and 4½ metres and is normally left either close to the north by boats coasting through the Westdiep or to the south if they are using the Noordpas.

Stroombank
The Stroombank lies between 1 and 1½ miles offshore just west of the entrance to Oostende. It is marked at its east end by Binnenstroombank E-cardinal buoy and off its south-west edge by the Weststroombank and Zuidstroombank red buoys. Boats coasting between Dunkerque and Oostende would normally pass through Westdiep and then cut inside the Stroombank, arriving near Binnenstroombank E-cardinal buoy just off Oostende entrance.

Offshore banks
The whole of this stretch of coast is peppered with offshore banks between 5 and 15 miles from the coast, mostly running NE–SW and lying more or less parallel to each other. Closest inshore are the Oostendebank, Middelkerke Bank and Kwinte Bank. These outer shoals generally have enough depth of water for yachts to cross over them in quiet or moderate weather, but you need to exercise caution when wind and sea start to increase. There are wide channels between most of these banks, shown clearly on Admiralty chart 1873.

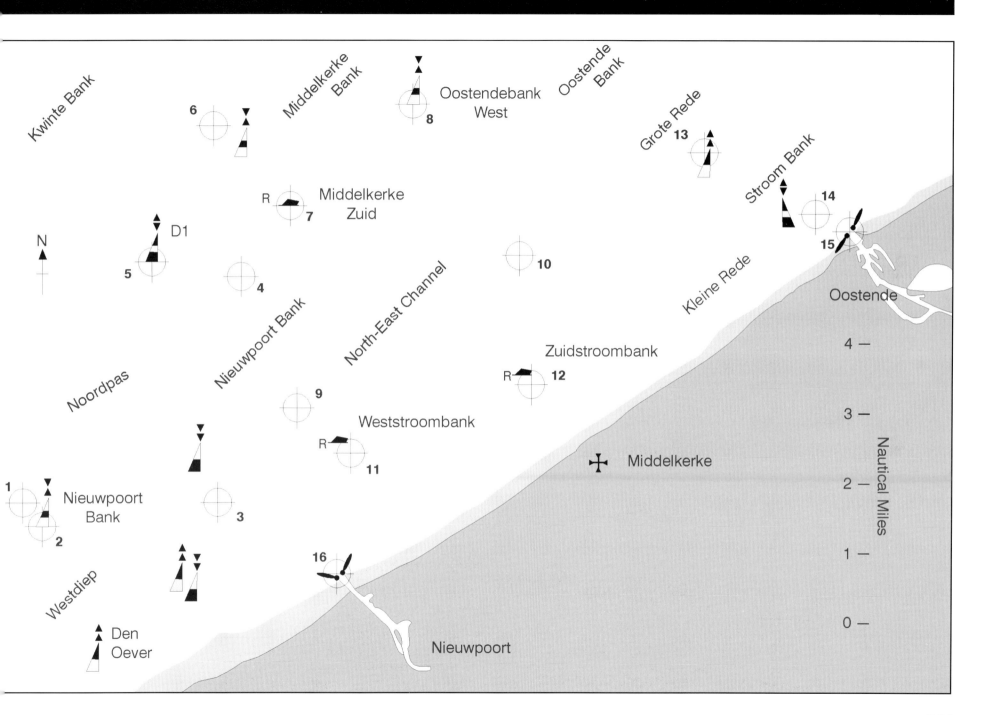

Kwinte Bank

Middelkerke Bank

Oostende Bank

6

Oostendebank
West

8

Grote Rede

13

Stroom Bank

R **7** Middelkerke
Zuid

D1

14

N

5

4

15

Kleine Rede

10

Oostende

North-East Channel

Nieuwpoort Bank

4 —

Zuidstroombank

R **12**

Noordpas

9

3 —

Weststroombank

R **11**

Middelkerke

2 —

Nautical Miles

1

Nieuwpoort
Bank

3

2

1 —

16

Westdiep

0 —

Den
Oever

Nieuwpoort

Oostende to Zeebrugge

WP No	Waypoint name and position	Latitude	Longitude
37–1	Oostende approach, ½ M 300°T from Oostende W pierhead	51°14.62'N	02°54.40'E
37–2	Oostende entrance, midway between the outer pierhead lights	51°14.40'N	02°55.17'E
37–3	Wenduine Bank west, 2 ca due west of W-card buoy	51°17.29'N	02°52.50'E
37–4	Oostendebank N-cardinal buoy, actual position	51°21.25'N	02°53.00'E
37–5	A1 red-and-white fairway buoy, actual position	51°22.42'N	02°53.40'E
37–6	A1 *bis* red-and-white fairway buoy, actual position	51°21.74'N	02°58.10'E
37–7	Wielingen W, midway SW Wandelaar red/Wenduine Bk green	51°21.77'N	03°01.85'E
37–8	A2 red-and-white fairway buoy, actual position	51°22.48'N	03°07.14'E
37–9	Zeebrugge approach, mid Zand green/Wielingen Zand W-card	51°22.57'N	03°10.41'E
37–10	Zeebrugge entrance, midway Zeebrugge outer pierhead lights	51°21.80'N	03°11.58'E
37–11	Grote Rede east, 4.3 M 028°T from Oostende east pierhead	51°18.27'N	02°58.47'E
37–12	Wenduine Bank east, 2 ca due S of red buoy	51°18.68'N	03°01.71'E
37–13	Blankenberge approach, ½ M 320°T from west pierhead	51°19.34'N	03°06.00'E
37–14	Blankenberge entrance, midway Blankenberge pierheads	51°18.95'N	03°06.58'E
37–15	MOW 1 north, 2 ca due N of MOW 1 light tower	51°21.90'N	03°07.18'E
37–16	MOW 1 south, 6 ca due S of MOW 1 light tower	51°21.10'N	03°07.18'E

Datum ED 50 The waypoint latitudes and longitudes in this table refer to European Datum (1950)

Boats coasting close inshore past Zeebrugge should be aware of the potentially strong tidal stream surging past the long breakwaters and across the harbour entrance. Do not put yourself into a position where you could be carried on to one of the Zeebrugge breakwaters by a strong tide.

COASTAL DANGERS
Refer to Admiralty charts 1872, 1873 and 1874

Wenduinebank
This narrow coastal bank curves out from the coast just west of Zeebrugge and tails off in a south-westerly direction parallel to the shore. Depths are mostly between 3½ and 4½ metres and there is plenty of water for boats to cross. However, the bank does kick up some steep overfalls on a weather-going spring tide, so should be avoided if possible in these conditions.

Nautica Ena wreck
A wreck with only 1.9 metres over it at LAT lies 1 mile north-west of the south-west tip of the Wenduinebank, marked on its seaward side by a N-cardinal buoy. Various other buoyed wrecks lie north of the Wenduinebank, but the *Nautica Ena* is the shallowest and should be given a wide berth.

Zeebrugge harbour entrance
Large ships use Zeebrugge harbour and small boats and yachts should keep well clear of all shipping in the deep-water approach channels.

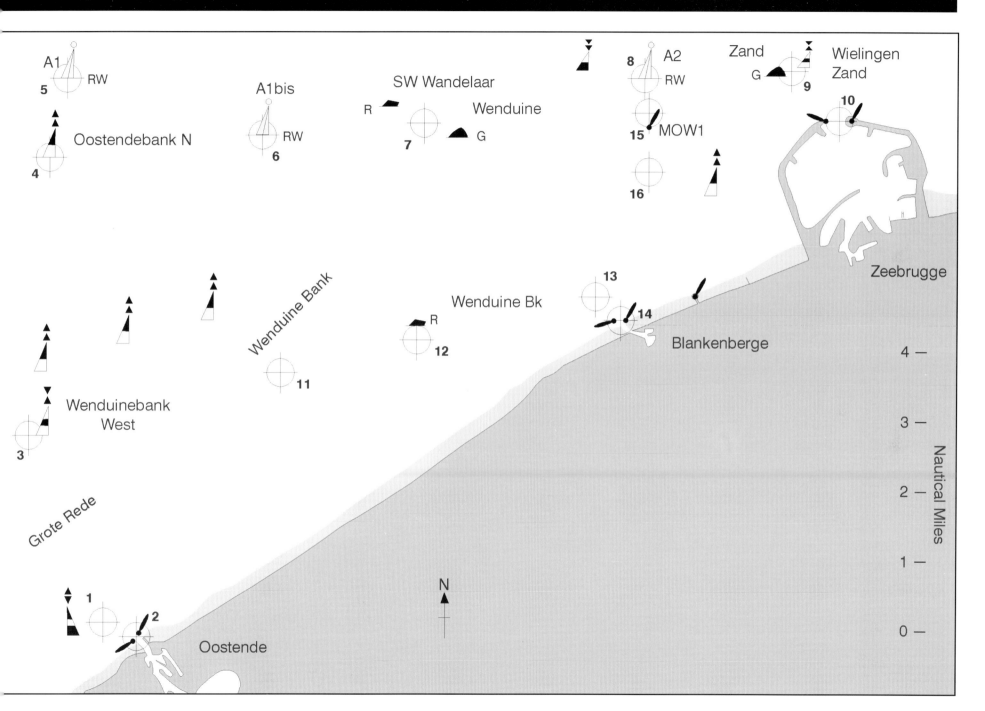

A1
RW
5

Oostendebank N

4

A1bis
RW
6

SW Wandelaar
R
Wenduine
7 G

8
A2
RW

15 MOW1

16

Zand
G
9
Wielingen
Zand

10

Wenduine Bank

13

Wenduine Bk
R
12

14

Blankenberge

Zeebrugge

11

Wenduinebank
West

3

Grote Rede

N

1

2

Oostende

4 —
3 —
2 —
1 —
0 —

Nautical Miles

WP No	Waypoint name and position	Latitude	Longitude
38–1	A1 red-and-white fairway buoy, actual position	51°22.42'N	02°53.40'E
38–2	A2 red-and-white fairway buoy, actual position	51°22.48'N	03°07.14'E
38–3	Zeebrugge approach, mid Zand green/Wielingen Zand W-card	51°22.57'N	03°10.41'E
38–4	Akkaert Middle E-card buoy, actual position	51°24.24'N	02°53.59'E
38–5	Goote Bank E-card buoy, actual position	51°27.00'N	02°52.80'E
38–6	SW Thornton red-and-white fairway buoy, actual position	51°31.00'N	02°51.00'E
38–7	DL2, ½ M due S of DL2 red buoy	51°31.05'N	03°13.00'E
38–8	Akkaert NE E-card buoy, actual position	51°27.33'N	02°59.42'E
38–9	Scheur outer, Scheur 3 N-card whistle buoy, actual position	51°24.35'N	03°03.00'E
38–10	Scheur channel west, midway Sch 5 green and Sch 6 red buoys	51°24.00'N	03°06.00'E

Datum ED 50 The waypoint latitudes and longitudes in this table refer to European Datum (1950)

COASTAL DANGERS

Refer to Admiralty chart 1874

Shipping in the Westerschelde approaches

Traffic can be heavy in the approaches to the Westerschelde, with ships and barges of all types and sizes bound to and from Vlissingen or Antwerp. Boats should stay just outside the main shipping channels wherever possible, keeping just the 'wrong' side of the buoys wherever the depth allows.

Particular care should be taken at night or in poor visibility, when the possible danger from shipping is the most significant hazard for boats in the approaches to the Westerschelde.

Vlakte van de Raan shoal

The Raan shoal lies right in the middle of the Westerschelde estuary, tailing away westwards to the Vlakte van de Raan. The Vlakte van de Raan and the Droogte van Schooneveld have least depths between 3 and 4½ metres and boats can cross safely if necessary in quiet or moderate weather. However, steep seas can soon build up over all the Westerschelde banks when the wind increases, especially if a strong north-westerly is blowing against an ebb tide. In these conditions boats should keep to the main deep-water channels.

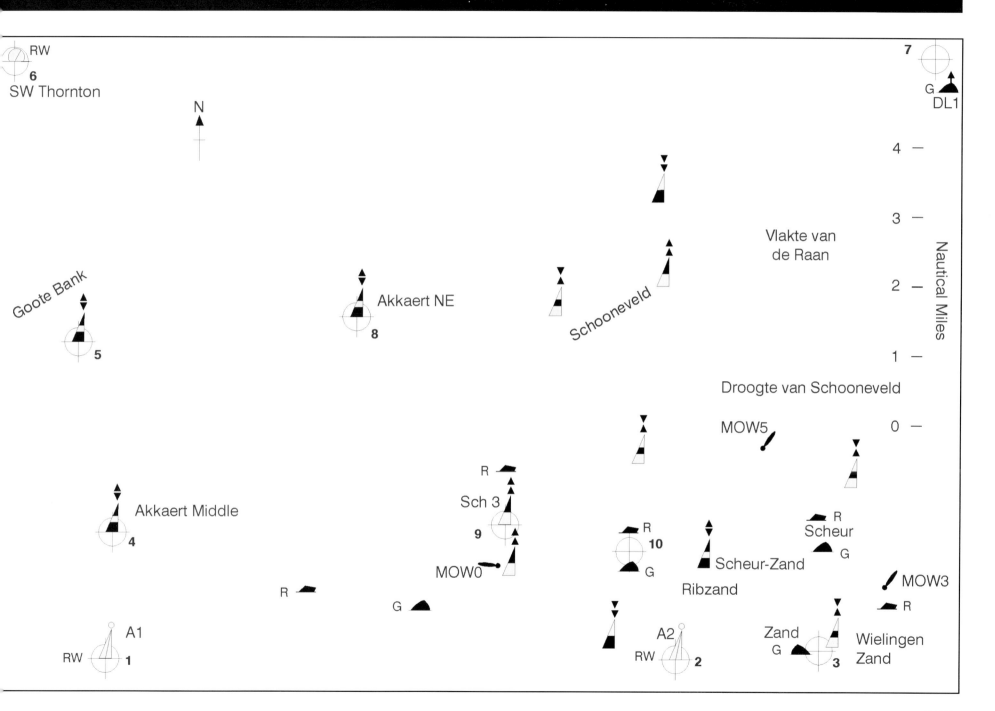

WP No	Waypoint name and position	Latitude	Longitude
39–1	Westpit red-and-white fairway buoy, actual position	51°33.70'N	03°10.00'E
39–2	Deurloo red-and-white fairway buoy, actual position	51°32.00'N	03°10.00'E
39–3	Oostgat 'OG1' green buoy, actual position	51°36.20'N	03°20.00'E
39–4	Kaloo 'KL' red-and-white fairway buoy, actual position	51°35.60'N	03°23.31'E
39–5	Oostgat 'OG' red-and-white fairway buoy, actual position	51°33.62'N	03°25.19'E
39–6	Westkapelle, 8½ ca 256°T from Westkapelle lighthouse	51°31.60'N	03°25.59'E
39–7	DL2, ½ M due S of DL2 red buoy	51°31.05'N	03°13.00'E
39–8	DL4, 3 ca due S of DL4 red buoy	51°30.78'N	03°16.11'E
39–9	DL6, 1½ ca due S of DL6 red buoy	51°30.45'N	03°19.21'E
39–10	Deurloo inner, 1.9 M 223°T from Westkapelle lighthouse	51°30.41'N	03°24.83'E

Datum ED 50 The waypoint latitudes and longitudes in this table refer to European Datum (1950)

COASTAL DANGERS
Refer to Admiralty chart 1874

Rassen shoal
This 2 mile wide shoal lies opposite Westkapelle, the far west tip of Walcheren, and is left to the west if you come in through the Kaloo and the Oostgat, or left to the north if you come through the Deurloo channel. The east edge of the Rassen shoal dries to 0.7 metres and you should take particular care when approaching this corner of Walcheren in poor visibility, especially with an onshore wind.

Spleet shoal
The long narrow Spleet shoal lies parallel to the west side of Walcheren opposite the east edge of the Raan. Least depths over the Spleet are less than 1 metre in parts, and the shoal is guarded on its east side by the green buoys of the inner part of the Deurloo channel. If you enter the Westerschelde by the Deurloo, the Spleet is left fairly close to the west. In quiet weather, you can pass between the Raan and the Spleet by following the green buoys that lead between DL-GvW N-cardinal buoy and Trawl S-cardinal buoy.

Bankje van Zoutelande
This long narrow bank lies close off the west coast of Walcheren, on the seaward side of the Oostgat channel. Depths are less than 1 metre over much of the Bankje van Zoutelande, with one or two drying patches. The bank is guarded on its east (landward) side by the green channel buoys of the Oostgat.

Shipping in the Westerschelde approaches
Traffic can be heavy in the approaches to the Westerschelde, with ships and barges of all types and sizes bound to and from Vlissingen or Antwerp. The Oostgat channel is surprisingly busy, with an almost continuous stream of traffic close along the west coast of Walcheren. Particular care should be taken at night or in poor visibility, when the possible danger from shipping is the most significant hazard for boats in the approaches to the Westerschelde.

Raan shoal
The Raan shoal lies right in the middle of the Westerschelde estuary, tailing away westwards to the Vlakte van de Raan. Most of the Raan has least depths between 2½ and 4 metres, but a nasty patch on the south side – the Walvischstaart – only has just over 1 metre at LAT. Although boats can cross most of the Raan safely if necessary in quiet weather, steep seas can soon build up over all the Westerschelde banks when the wind increases, especially if a strong north-westerly is blowing against an ebb tide. In these conditions boats should keep to the main deep-water channels.

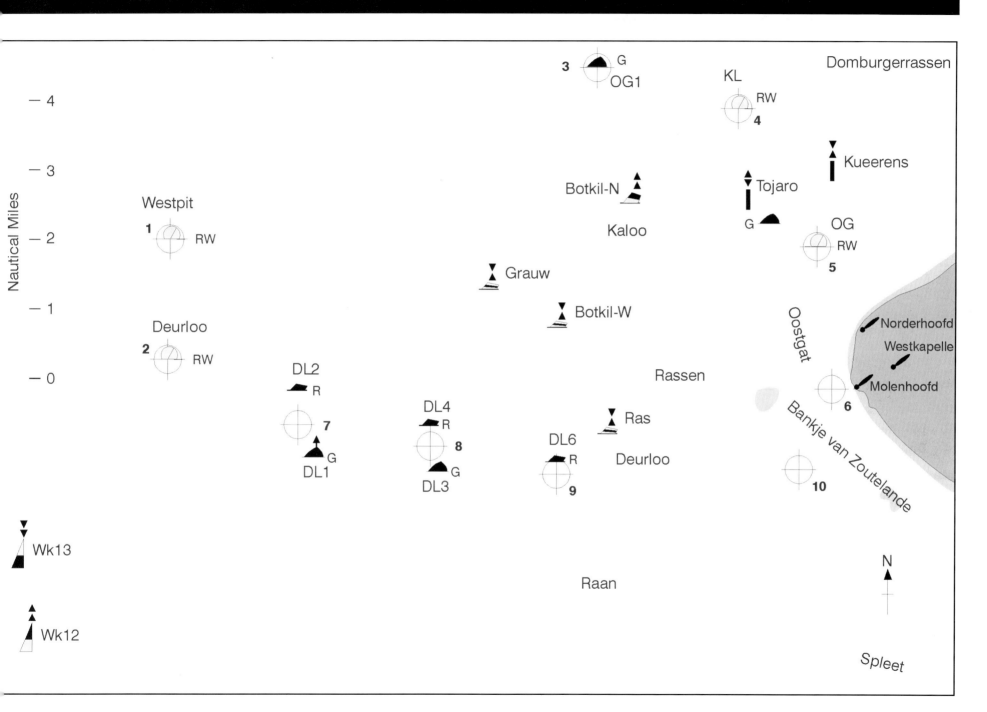

▪ Approaches to Vlissingen (Flushing) ▪

WP No	Waypoint name and position	Latitude	Longitude
40–1	Scheur middle, midway Sch 9 green and Sch 10 red buoys	51°24.68'N	03°15.07'E
40–2	Scheur channel east, 2 ca due S of W2 red buoy	51°24.44'N	03°21.57'E
40–3	Nieuwe Sluis, 1 M 316°T from Nieuwe Sluis lighthouse	51°25.19'N	03°30.27'E
40–4	DL6, 1½ ca due S of DL6 red buoy	51°30.45'N	03°19.21'E
40–5	Deurloo inner, 1.9 M 223°T from Westkapelle lighthouse	51°30.41'N	03°24.83'E
40–6	Spleet inner, 3 ca NE of Trawl S-card buoy	51°26.53'N	03°28.62'E
40–7	Westerschelde inner, midway Songa green and W10 red buoys	51°25.56'N	03°33.39'E
40–8	Schaar van Spijkerplaat, 1½ M 045°T from Breskens W p/head	51°25.14'N	03°35.86'E
40–9	Breskens NW approach, 3 ca N of Breskens Ferry Hr W p/head	51°24.71'N	03°33.18'E
40–10	Breskens entrance, 1 ca N of Breskens W breakwater head	51°24.18'N	03°34.14'E
40–11	Vlissingen W approach, 8 ca due E of W12 red buoy	51°26.18'N	03°34.66'E
40–12	Vlissingen S approach, 3½ ca S of Vlissingen W pierhead light	51°26.08'N	03°36.13'E
40–13	Vlissingen entrance, 100 m due E of Vlissingen W pierhead light	51°26.43'N	03°36.22'E

Datum ED 50 The waypoint latitudes and longitudes in this table refer to European Datum (1950)

COASTAL DANGERS
Refer to Admiralty charts 120 and 1874

Raan shoal
The Raan shoal lies right in the middle of the Westerschelde estuary, tailing away westwards to the Vlakte van de Raan. Most of the Raan has least depths between 2½ and 4 metres, but a nasty patch on the south side – the Walvischstaart – only has just over 1 metre at LAT. Although boats can cross most of the Raan safely if necessary in quiet weather, steep seas can soon build up over all the Westerschelde banks when the wind increases, especially if a strong north-westerly is blowing against an ebb tide. In these conditions boats should keep to the main deep-water channels.

Spleet shoal
The long narrow Spleet shoal lies parallel to the west side of Walcheren opposite the east edge of the Raan. Least depths over the Spleet are less than 1 metre in parts and the shoal is guarded on its east side by the green buoys of the inner part of the Deurloo channel. If you enter the Westerschelde by the Deurloo, the Spleet is left fairly close to the west. In quiet weather, you can pass between the Raan and the Spleet by following the green buoys that lead between DL-GvW N-cardinal buoy and Trawl S-cardinal buoy.

Bankje van Zoutelande
This long narrow bank lies close off the west coast of Walcheren, on the seaward side of the Oostgat channel. Depths are less than 1 metre over much of the Bankje van Zoutelande, with one or two

drying patches. The bank is guarded on its east (landward) side by the green channel buoys of the Oostgat.

Shipping in the Westerschelde approaches
Traffic can be heavy in the approaches to the Westerschelde, with ships and barges of all types and sizes bound to and from Vlissingen or Antwerp. The Oostgat channel is surprisingly busy, with an almost continuous stream of traffic close along the west coast of Walcheren. Particular care should be taken at night or in poor visibility, when the possible danger from shipping is the most significant hazard for boats in the approaches to the Westerschelde.

Boats approaching the Westerschelde by the main Scheur channel should stay just outside the buoyed fairway where possible, keeping just the 'wrong' side of the buoys wherever the depth allows.

Nolleplaat shoal
This shallow bank lies a couple of miles west of the entrance to Vlissingen. It is left well clear to the north if you enter the Westerschelde by the main Scheur channel, but close to the south-west if you come in through the Oostgat and follow the buoys close along the Walcheren shore.

The Nolleplaat is about 2½ miles long from east to west, and about ¾ mile from north to south at its widest part. Depths over the Nolleplaat are generally less than 1½ metres and a couple of patches dry. Particular care must be taken when you are leaving the Westerschelde via the Oostgat, because the south-east entrance to this channel lies very close to the Vlissingen seafront, just inside the Nolleplaat.

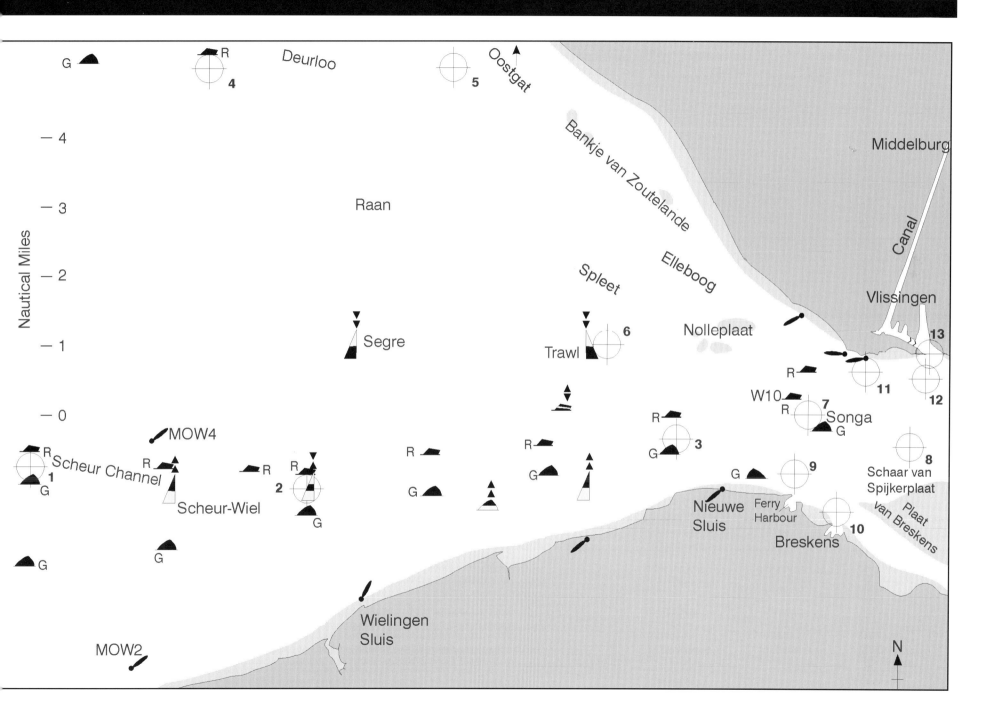

G R Deurloo Oostgat
4 5

— 4 Middelburg

Raan

— 3

Bankje van Zoutelande

Nautical Miles

Elleboog

— 2 Spleet

Nolleplaat Vlissingen

— 1 Segre 6
Trawl 13

R
W10 11
R 7 12
— 0 Songa
R 3 G
MOW4 R
R G 8
Scheur Channel R R 2
R G 9 Schaar van
1 Scheur-Wiel G G G Spijkerplaat
G G Nieuwe Ferry
Sluis Harbour 10 Plaat
G Breskens van Breskens

G

Wielingen
Sluis

N
MOW2

109

WP No	Waypoint name and position	Latitude	Longitude
41–1	Magne N-card buoy, actual position	51°39.20'N	03°19.80'E
41–2	Kaloo 'KL' red-and-white fairway buoy, actual position	51°35.60'N	03°23.31'E
41–3	Oostgat 'OG' red-and-white fairway buoy, actual position	51°33.62'N	03°25.19'E
41–4	Oostgat 'OG1' outer green buoy, actual position	51°36.20'N	03°20.00'E
41–5	Botkil-North N-card buoy, actual position	51°34.24'N	03°20.80'E
41–6	ZBJ W-card buoy, actual position	51°38.60'N	03°23.90'E
41–7	Oosterschelde Westgat outer, midway WG1 and WG2 buoys	51°38.30'N	03°26.30'E
41–8	Oosterschelde Westgat middle, 2 ca S of WG4 light beacon	51°38.47'N	03°28.88'E
41–9	Oosterschelde Westgat inner, 2 ca S of WG–GB S-card buoy	51°39.58'N	03°32.76'E
41–10	DR1, 2 ca due N of DR1 green buoy	51°35.24'N	03°26.25'E
41–11	DR3, 2 ca due N of DR3 green buoy	51°35.45'N	03°28.27'E
41–12	DR5, 2 ca due N of DR5 green buoy	51°35.78'N	03°30.30'E
41–13	Roompot outer, 3½ M 320°T from Oostkapelle church tower	51°36.67'N	03°29.52'E
41–14	Roompot west, midway R1 green buoy and R4 red buoy	51°36.20'N	03°32.00'E
41–15	Roompot middle, 2½ M 027°T from Oostkapelle church tower	51°36.23'N	03°35.00'E
41–16	Oude Roompot N entrance, 1 ca due E of OR2 red buoy	51°39.52'N	03°33.96'E

Datum ED 50 The waypoint latitudes and longitudes in this table refer to European Datum (1950)

COASTAL DANGERS
Refer to Admiralty charts 110 and 1874

Steenbanken
This long narrow shoal lies about 7 miles off the north coast of Walcheren and runs more or less NE–SW for nearly 8 miles, although the shallowest part of the Steenbanken, the north-eastern half, is only about 4 miles long. This north-east end, and the deeper part to the south-west, are both marked by their own cardinal buoys.

Minimum soundings over the bank are just over 4 metres, so there is plenty of depth for boats to cross in quiet weather. However, the Steenbanken rises quickly from depths of around 25 metres on its seaward side, so steep seas can build up and break over the bank in sustained fresh to strong north-westerly weather. In this case boats should aim to cross the Steenbanken at its deeper, south-westerly end, to the west of 'MSB–W' west-cardinal buoy and 'MSB–O' east-cardinal buoy. From here, in relatively clear water, you can set a course for the outer buoys of either the Westgat or the Roompot channels to reach the Oosterschelde storm-surge barrier and the lock at Noordland.

Alternatively, if making for the Oostgat entrance channel into the Westerschelde, you can head south-east to pick up the Kaloo red-and-white fairway buoy and then the Oostgat 'OG' red-and-white fairway buoy, both of which lie on the line of the Westkapelle leading lights.

Coastal shoals off Walcheren
The north shore of Walcheren is fringed with coastal shoals with depths of 2½ metres or less. The shallowest parts are towards the east end of this north coast, where the buoyed Roompot channel converges with the long line of low cliffs and featureless dunes as it runs east towards the south end of the massive Oosterschelde storm-surge barrier.

Remember that this north Walcheren coast is an exposed lee shore in north-westerly weather, and you should be particularly careful to identify all buoys accurately when navigating in this area, especially if making a direct landfall from England

Hompels shoals
The broad Hompels shoals lie in the immediate seaward approaches to the Oosterschelde storm-surge barrier. The Roompot channel cuts south of the Hompels, while the Westgat and Oude Roompot skirt north and east of these shoals.

The shallowest parts of the Hompels dry and much of the shoals have less than ½ metre over them, so it is important to pick up either the outer Westgat buoys or the outer Roompot buoys before getting too close to the Hompels. Note that, between the Westgat and the Roompot, the Hompels shoals are unguarded on their west side for about 2½ miles, a potential risk in poor visibility if you stray into this area.

Shipping approaching the Oostgat
Large ships are continually using the Oostgat channel, which leads close along the south-west shore of Walcheren into the Westerschelde estuary opposite Vlissingen. Boats should take care to stay clear of large and often fast-moving ships approaching or leaving the Oostgat, especially in poor visibility.

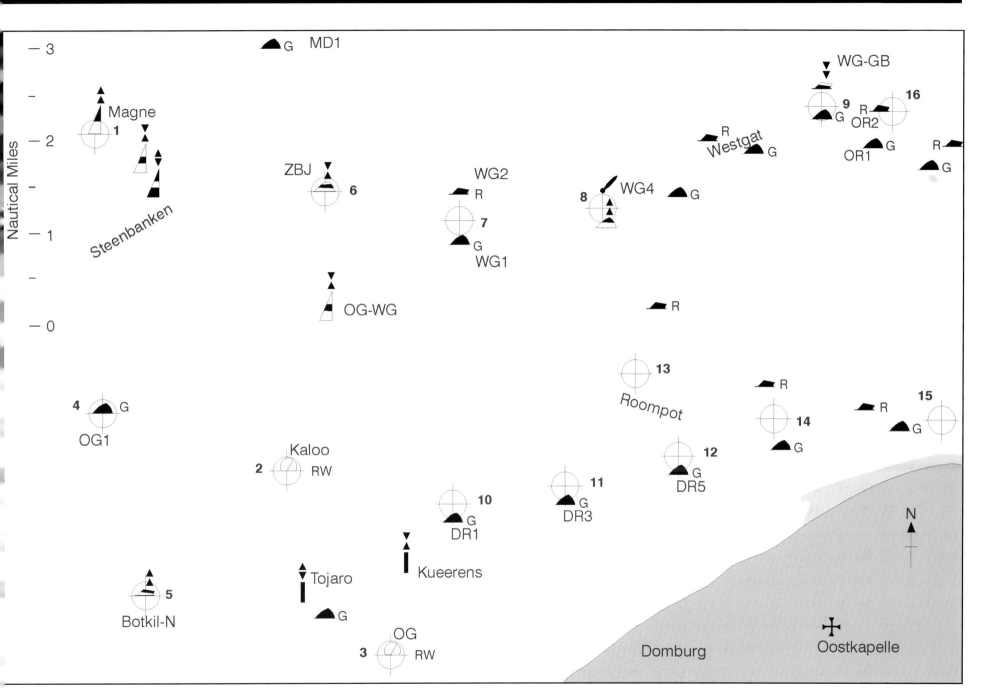

WP No	Waypoint name and position	Latitude	Longitude
42–1	Oosterschelde Westgat middle, 2 ca S of WG4 light beacon	51°38.47'N	03°28.88'E
42–2	Oosterschelde Westgat inner, 2 ca S of WG–GB S-card buoy	51°39.58'N	03°32.76'E
42–3	Oude Roompot outer, midway OR5 green and OR6 red buoys	51°38.74'N	03°36.02'E
42–4	Oude Roompot inner, midway OR11 green and OR12 red buoys	51°37.17'N	03°38.91'E
42–5	Noordland approach, 300 m 221°T from Buitenhaven N p/head Lt	51°37.23'N	03°40.00'E
42–6	DR3, 2 ca due N of DR3 green buoy	51°35.45'N	03°28.27'E
42–7	DR5, 2 ca due N of DR5 green buoy	51°35.78'N	03°30.30'E
42–8	Roompot outer, 3½ M 320°T from Oostkapelle church tower	51°36.67'N	03°29.52'E
42–9	Roompot west, midway R1 green buoy and R4 red buoy	51°36.20'N	03°32.00'E
42–10	Roompot middle, 2½ M 027°T from Oostkapelle church tower	51°36.23'N	03°35.00'E
42–11	Roompot east, midway R9 green buoy and R12 red buoy	51°36.22'N	03°38.37'E
42–12	'OR' E-card buoy, actual position	51°36.46'N	03°39.04'E
42–13	Geul van de Banjaard middle, 1 ca due E of GB5 green buoy	51°41.82'N	03°33.34'E
42–14	Geul van de Banjaard inner, 1 ca due E of GB7 green buoy	51°40.50'N	03°33.96'E
42–15	Oude Roompot N entrance, 1 ca due E of OR2 red buoy	51°39.52'N	03°33.96'E

Datum ED 50 The waypoint latitudes and longitudes in this table refer to European Datum (1950)

COASTAL DANGERS
Refer to Admiralty chart 110

The Banjaard shoals
These broad offshore shoals lie from 6–9 miles seaward of the Oosterschelde storm-surge barrier, with minimum depths of less than 1 metre and large areas with depths less than 2½ metres. The Westgat cuts south of the Banjaard shoals and Geul van de Banjaard runs along their east side, but the seaward edge of the Banjaard is marked only by 'NBJ' and 'MBJ' west-cardinal buoys, which are well spaced. Care must therefore be taken if approaching the vicinity of the Banjaard from seaward.

Hompels shoals
The broad Hompels shoals lie in the immediate seaward approaches to the Oosterschelde storm-surge barrier. The Roompot channel cuts south of the Hompels, while the Westgat and Oude Roompot skirt north and east of these shoals. The shallowest parts of the Hompels dry and much of the shoals have less than ½ metre over them, so it is important to pick up either the outer Westgat buoys or the outer Roompot buoys before getting too close to the Hompels. Note that, between the Westgat and the Roompot, the Hompels shoals are unguarded on their west side for about 2½ miles, a potential risk in poor visibility if you stray into this area.

Coastal shoals off Walcheren
The north shore of Walcheren is fringed with coastal shoals with depths of 2½ metres or less. The shallowest parts are towards the east end of the north coast, where the buoyed Roompot channel converges with a long line of low cliffs and featureless dunes as it runs east towards the south end of the massive Oosterschelde storm-surge barrier.

Remember that this north Walcheren coast is an exposed lee shore in north-westerly weather, and you should be particularly careful to identify all buoys accurately when navigating in this area, especially if making a direct landfall from England.

Noordland shoals
A long tongue of progressively deepening shoals extends north-westward from Noordland, the main 'island' between the north and south sections of the Oosterschelde barrier. These shoals are caused by the tidal stream 'shadow' effect of Noordland, and are likely to become steadily shallower over the years. The present depths are down to less than ½ metre nearly 2 miles seaward of Noordland.

The Noordland shoals are effectively marked on their south-west side by the red buoys of the Oude Roompot channel. Boats should not venture anywhere near the north side of the shoals, which is a dangerous area fronting the north, impassable section of the storm-surge barrier.

Strong currents near the storm-surge barrier
Boats entering the Oosterschelde do so through the large sea-lock – the Roompotsluis – at the east end of the Buitenhaven on Noordland.

Approaching the Oosterschelde from the west or north-west, the usual way to reach Noordland is through the Roompot channel, the east end of which passes just over 1 mile from the storm-surge barrier, through which the tide normally flows with great ferocity. The whole area for 1 mile seaward of the barrier is cordoned off by a line of nine west-cardinal buoys, which you should never stray inside. From the east end of the Roompot, you skirt outside this line of buoys to reach the Buitenhaven and the Roompotsluis.

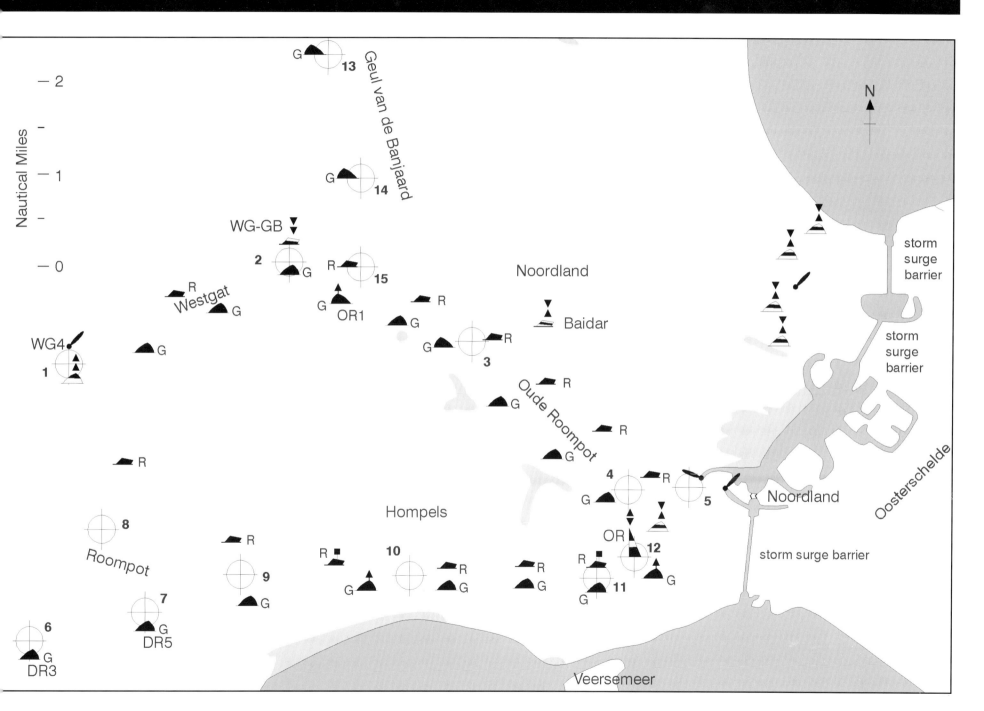

WP No	Waypoint name and position	Latitude	Longitude
43–1	'MD3' green buoy, actual position	51°42.77'N	03°27.08'E
43–2	'SD4' red buoy, actual position	51°47.70'N	03°26.30'E
43–3	'MN' N-card buoy, actual position	51°47.70'N	03°30.00'E
43–4	Ooster north clearing, 2 ca NW of Ooster W-card buoy	51°48.09'N	03°41.14'E
43–5	'BG2' beacon, 2 ca NW of BG2 light beacon	51°46.26'N	03°36.89'E
43–6	Banjaard approach, midway GB1 green and GB2 red buoys	51°44.13'N	03°33.17'E
43–7	Geul van de Banjaard outer, midway GB3 green and GB4 red buoys	51°43.04'N	03°32.79'E
43–8	Geul van de Banjaard middle, 1 ca due E of GB5 green buoy	51°41.82'N	03°33.34'E

Datum ED 50 The waypoint latitudes and longitudes in this table refer to European Datum (1950)

COASTAL DANGERS

Refer to Admiralty chart 110

The Banjaard shoals

These broad offshore shoals lie 6–9 miles seaward of the Oosterschelde storm-surge barrier, with minimum depths of less than 1 metre and large areas with depths less than 2½ metres. The Westgat cuts south of the Banjaard shoals while the Geul van de Banjaard runs along their east side, but the seaward edge of the Banjaard is marked only by 'NBJ' and 'MBJ' west-cardinal buoys, which are well spaced. Care must therefore be exercised if approaching the vicinity of the Banjaard from seaward.

Geul van de Banjaard is a narrow buoyed channel which leads through the east side of the Banjaard shoals towards the inner buoys of the Westgat and the outer buoys of the Oude Roompot channels. Narrow shoals with barely 2 metres depth lie close each side of Geul van de Banjaard, so be sure to stay midway between the buoys as you come through.

Coastal shoals off West Schouwen

An extensive area of coastal shoals extends westwards from the west shore of Schouwen, parts of which dry and much have well under 1 metre depth at LAT. This whole shoal area is roughly rectangular, stretching 4 miles west from Schouwen and about 3½ miles from north to south.

The seaward edges of these shoals are marked only by the red channel buoys of Geul van de Banjaard, so take care to pick up and identify these buoys when approaching the Oosterschelde estuary from the north or north-east. This whole coastal zone from Schouwen out to beyond the Banjaard is not a healthy place to be in strong onshore winds.

A useful (and rather rare) distinctive landmark on this coast is the West Schouwen lighthouse, nearly 60 metres high, which has red and white diagonal stripes like a helter-skelter.

Kous shoals

A long triangle of shoals, the deepest part of which is known as the Kous, extends westwards from the west coast of Goeree and the stark engineering of the Brouwersdam, a massive sea-defence wall which has no lock through into the Grevelingen Meer. Parts of the shoals north and south of the Kous dry and large areas have less than 1 metre depth at LAT. The bleak character of this stretch of coast is somehow accentuated when you notice the Refuge harbour on the chart, located towards the north end of the Brouwersdam. The Refuge harbour lies opposite a slightly deeper cut through the Kous shoals and is reached, if necessary, by first finding the Kous yellow buoy, over 4 miles west of the harbour entrance (the buoy lies just off this waypoint chart to the east).

In normal circumstances, boats should avoid getting too close to this austere stretch of coast between Schouwen and Goeree, keeping well offshore in the buoyed channels or beyond the coastal shoals.

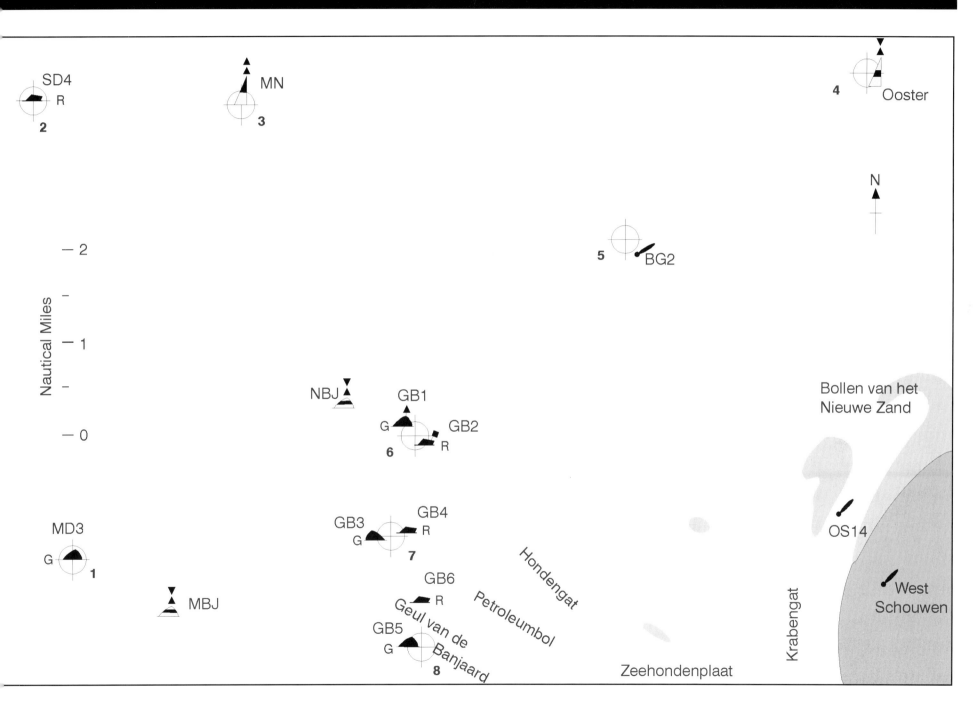

SD4
R
2

MN
3

4
Ooster

N

5 BG2

Nautical Miles

— 2

— 1

NBJ
GB1

GB2

— 0
G
6
R

Bollen van het
Nieuwe Zand

GB4
GB3
R
G
7

OS14

MD3
G
1

MBJ

GB6
R

Hondengat

Petroleumbol

West
Schouwen

GB5
G
8

Geul van de
Banjaard

Krabengat

Zeehondenplaat

WP No	Waypoint name and position	Latitude	Longitude
44–1	Ooster north clearing, 2 ca NW of Ooster W-card buoy	51°48.09'N	03°41.14'E
44–2	Stelle Hoek, 2 ca NW of Stelle Hoek W-card buoy	51°49.68'N	03°45.65'E
44–3	Slijkgat 'SG' red-and-white fairway buoy, actual position	51°52.00'N	03°51.50'E
44–4	Slijkgat entrance, 2.3 M 289°T from Kwade Hoek lighthouse	51°51.00'N	03°55.58'E
44–5	'Hinder', 2 ca NW of Hinder W-card buoy	51°54.74'N	03°55.28'E
44–6	*Adriana* inshore WP, 6.7 M 251°T from Maasvlakte light	51°56.14'N	03°50.66'E
44–7	Goeree east, 1½ M due E of Goeree light platform	51°55.55'N	03°42.60'E

Datum ED 50 The waypoint latitudes and longitudes in this table refer to European Datum (1950)

COASTAL DANGERS

Refer to Admiralty chart 110 or the Dutch chart 1801.6

Kous shoals

A long triangle of shoals, the deepest part of which is known as the Kous, extends westwards from the west coast of Goeree and the stark engineering of the Brouwersdam, a massive sea-defence dyke which has no lock through into the Grevelingen Meer. The most northerly and largest drying part of these shoals extends for up to 3½ miles W and WSW of Westhoofd lighthouse, a tall red tower, nearly 60 metres high, on the north-west corner of Goeree. This drying spur, nearly 3 miles long, is guarded on its seaward side by Stelle Hoek west-cardinal buoy.

Ribben and Hinderplaat

The approaches to Stellendam and Haringvliet are partly sheltered from seaward by a long sandy shoal, called the Ribben, which juts out from the north side of the estuary for over 2 miles to form a partial natural breakwater. A small part of this sandbank, known as the Hinderplaat, is above water all the time and effectively forms the north promontory of the outer approaches to Stellendam.

To the south and SSE of the Ribben and Hinderplaat, the middle part of the estuary is very shallow, with two sizeable drying patches and LAT depths generally below 1½ metres. Therefore, when approaching Stellendam, it is important to pick up the outer buoys of the Slijkgat and follow the buoyed channel east along the north coast of Goeree and then round the corner towards the Buitenhaven.

At the south-east end of the Buitenhaven is the sea lock into Haringvliet, from where it is not far inland to the large and fascinating yacht harbour at Hellevoetsluis.

Dangerous currents near the Haringvlietsluizen

The Haringvlietdam has sluices which can be opened to allow either free passage of seawater into Haringvliet or to allow a build-up of river water from the Rhine and Maas to escape into the sea. In either case, locally strong currents can be experienced in the immediate approaches to Stellendam, so it is important to stay well clear to seaward of the four yellow buoys that cordon off the sluices through the Haringvlietdam. When sluicing operations are in progress, red lights are shown on the Haringvlietdam.

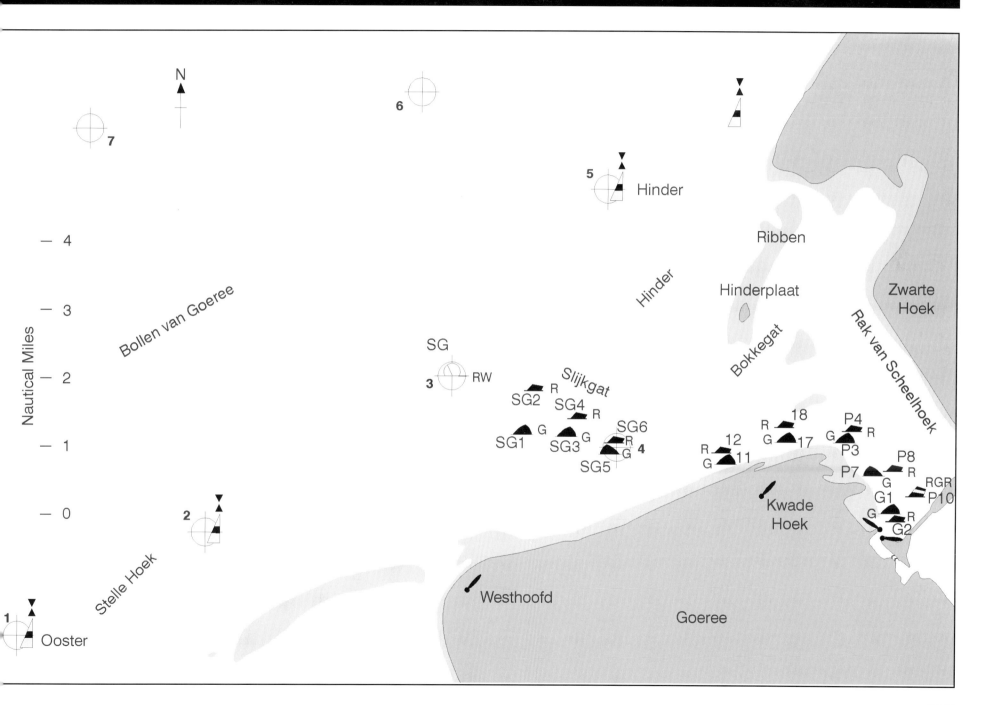

N

7

6

5 Hinder

Ribben

4

Hinder

Hinderplaat

Zwarte
Hoek

3

Bollen van Goeree

SG

Rak van Scheelhoek

2

3 RW

Slijkgat

Bokkegat

SG2 R
SG4 R

18 P4
R G R

12 R G 17 P3

SG6

SG1 G SG3 G R 4
G

R G 11

P8
P7 R
G RGR

P10

SG5

Kwade
Hoek

G1
G R
G2

2

0

Westhoofd

Goeree

Stelle Hoek

1

Ooster

Nautical Miles

WP No	Waypoint name and position	Latitude	Longitude
45–1	MW5 green buoy, actual position	51°58.40'N	03°46.60'E
45–2	*Adriana* inshore WP, 6.7 M 251°T from Maasvlakte light	51°56.14'N	03°50.66'E
45–3	'Hinder', 2 ca NW of Hinder W-card buoy	51°54.74'N	03°55.28'E
45–4	MV W-card buoy, actual position	51°57.50'N	03°58.52'E
45–5	MV outer, ½ M due W of MV W-card buoy	51°57.50'N	03°57.70'E
45–6	MVN N-card buoy, actual position	51°59.64'N	04°00.31'E
45–7	MVN outer, ½ M due W of MVN W-card buoy	51°59.64'N	03°59.50'E
45–8	Maas entrance, midway between outer pierhead lights	51°59.52'N	04°02.79'E
45–9	Indusbank N-card buoy, actual position	52°02.93'N	04°03.66'E
45–10	Maasgeul 'MO' red-and-white fairway buoy, actual position	52°01.00'N	03°58.14'E
45–11	Maas Center 'MC' red-and-white fairway buoy, actual position	52°01.18'N	03°53.56'E
45–12	Eurogeul 'E15' yellow buoy, actual position	52°00.96'N	03°48.86'E

Datum ED 50 The waypoint latitudes and longitudes in this table refer to European Datum (1950)

COASTAL DANGERS

Refer to Admiralty charts 122 and 132 and Dutch charts 1801.6 and 1801.7

Shipping approaching Hoek van Holland

The Dutch coastline to the north and south of the famous Hook of Holland is low, flat and largely devoid of natural features, although you can hardly miss the massive industrial towers, tanks, cranes and containers a little way inland at Europoort. There are no significant offshore or coastal hazards along this stretch of coast and the principal danger for boats comes from the intense volume of shipping entering and leaving Europoort and the River Maas at all hours of the day and night, in any weather.

Strictly speaking, it would be best and safest if no boats were to enter or leave the Dutch inland waterways at Hoek van Holland, but this vast commercial dockland is completely fascinating to anyone who follows the European economy, and who appreciates commercial shipping and the sheer scale of tonnage flowing through this most modern of ports. As a general rule, it is important to appreciate that yachts are very small fry in these commercial comings and goings and skippers should do everything possible to avoid all ships entering, leaving or manoeuvring in the Maas or the approaches to the Maas.

Approaching the Maas — VHF procedure

Boats approaching Hoek van Holland from well offshore should call 'Maas Approach' on VHF Ch 01, giving the name and type of boat, current position and destination, and then follow the traffic instructions and VHF working channels given to them. Craft coasting towards Hoek van Holland close inshore should call 'Maas entrance' on VHF Ch 03 and follow the same procedure.

Crossing the Maasgeul

Boats coasting past Hoek van Holland and wishing to cross the Maas approach channel (the Maasgeul) should call 'Maas entrance' on VHF Ch 03, giving their current position, course and intentions and asking for traffic instructions. You should then standby on Ch 03. The general procedure is to cross the approach channel under power at right-angles on a course of 030°T/210°T just seaward of a line joining the 'MV' west-cardinal buoy (about 2½ miles south of the approach channel) and 'MVN' north-cardinal buoy (on the south edge of the Maasgeul channel).

When following this procedure, watch out for shipping entering or leaving the Maas (and remember that most large ships will be moving considerably faster than you are) and take account of the potentially strong tidal streams across the entrance.

Sea conditions off Hoek van Holland

The seas in the approach to Hoek van Holland can be extremely steep and unpleasant in, for example, a brisk south-westerly wind against the outpouring ebb. You should also avoid approaching and entering the Maas in strong north-westerlies, when a heavy swell can build up over a period of time. The seas can be steep off the Hook in strong north-easterlies against a north-going stream, or strong south-westerlies against a south-going stream.

Other things being equal, the best time to enter the Maas is during the last hour before high water but of course that also tends to be the time when shipping movements are heaviest.

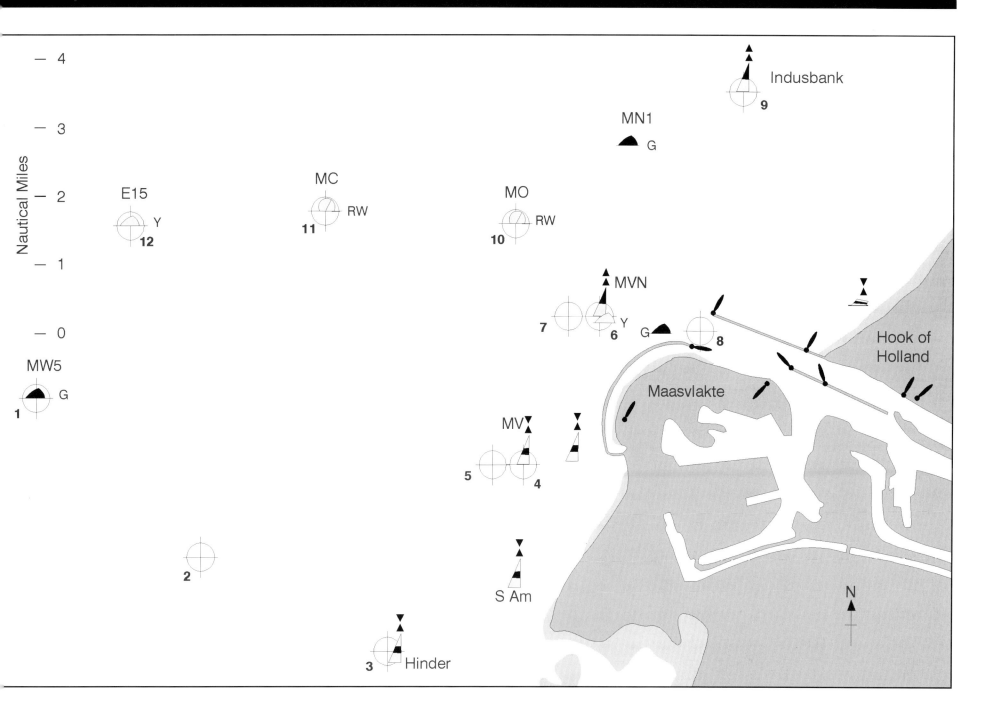

Nautical Miles

— 4

— 3

— 2

— 1

— 0

Indusbank

9

MN1

G

MC

RW

11

E15

Y

12

MO

RW

10

MVN

Y

7

6

G

8

MW5

G

1

Maasvlakte

Hook of Holland

MV

5

4

2

S Am

N

Hinder

3

WP No	Waypoint name and position	Latitude	Longitude
46–1	Goeree north, 1½ M due N of Goeree light platform	51°57.05'N	03°40.17'E
46–2	Goeree east, 1½ M due E of Goeree light platform	51°55.55'N	03°42.60'E
46–3	MW5 green buoy, actual position	51°58.40'N	03°46.60'E
46–4	Adriana inshore WP, 6.7 M 251°T from Maasvlakte light	51°56.14'N	03°50.66'E
46–5	Eurogeul 'E11' yellow buoy, actual position	52°00.22'N	03°39.58'E
46–6	Eurogeul 'E13' yellow buoy, actual position	52°00.60'N	03°44.22'E
46–7	Eurogeul 'E15' yellow buoy, actual position	52°00.96'N	03°48.86'E
46–8	Maas Center 'MC' red-and-white fairway buoy, actual position	52°01.18'N	03°53.56'E
46–9	MW6 red buoy, actual position	52°04.93'N	03°45.23'E
46–10	MN2 red buoy, actual position	52°05.78'N	03°51.00'E
46–11	MN3 green buoy, actual position	52°04.58'N	03°58.88'E
46–12	Scheveningen approach, 1.9 M 321°T from main lighthouse	52°07.77'N	04°14.24'E
46–13	Scheveningen entrance, between pierhead lights on leading line	52°06.28'N	04°15.34'E
46–14	Noordwijk aan Zee offing, 2 M 300°T from main lighthouse	52°16.00'N	04°23.38'E
46–15	Noordwijk yellow offshore buoy, actual position	52°17.00'N	04°17.00'E
46–16	A-NE yellow approach buoy, actual position	52°28.00'N	03°48.70'E
46–17	IJ1 yellow approach buoy, actual position	52°29.66'N	04°04.23'E
46–18	IJ3 yellow approach buoy, actual position	52°29.79'N	04°12.10'E
46–19	IJ5 yellow approach buoy, actual position	52°29.36'N	04°15.98'E
46–20	IJ7 yellow approach buoy, actual position	52°28.95'N	04°19.90'E
46–21	IJM red-and-white fairway buoy, actual position	52°28.48'N	04°23.80'E
46–22	IJmuiden entrance, between outer pierhead lights on leading line	52°28.00'N	04°32.37'E
46–23	Egmond aan Zee offing, 2 M due W of Egmond lighthouse	52°37.19'N	04°34.02'E
46–24	Petten offing, 2½ M due W of Petten church tower	52°46.10'N	04°35.76'E
46–25	Vinca-G west clearing, 1½ M W of Vinca-G W-card buoy	52°45.96'N	04°10.06'E
46–26	Vinca-G east clearing, 1½ M E of Vinca-G E-card buoy	52°45.97'N	04°15.62'E

principal danger for boats comes from the intense volume of shipping entering and leaving Europoort and the River Maas at all hours of the day and night, in any weather.

Approaching the Maas — VHF procedure

Boats approaching Hoek van Holland from well offshore should call 'Maas Approach' on VHF Ch 01, giving the name and type of boat, current position and destination, and then follow the traffic instructions and VHF working channels given to them. Craft coasting towards Hoek van Holland close inshore should call 'Maas entrance' on VHF Ch 03 and follow the same procedure.

Crossing the Maasgeul

Boats coasting past Hoek van Holland and wishing to cross the Maas approach channel (the Maasgeul) should call 'Maas entrance' on VHF Ch 03, give their current position, course and intentions and ask for traffic instructions. You should then standby on Ch 03. The general procedure is to cross the approach channel under power at right-angles on a course of 030ГТ/210ГТ, just seaward of a line joining the 'MV' west-cardinal buoy (about 2½ miles south of the approach channel) and 'MVN' north-cardinal buoy (on the south edge of the Maasgeul channel)

COASTAL DANGERS
Refer to Admiralty charts 122, 124 and 2322 and Dutch charts 1801.6 and 1801.7

Shipping approaching Hoek van Holland

The Dutch coastline to the north and south of the famous Hook of Holland is low, flat and largely devoid of natural features, although you can hardly miss the massive industrial towers, tanks, cranes and containers a little way inland at Europoort. There are no significant offshore or coastal hazards along this stretch of coast and the

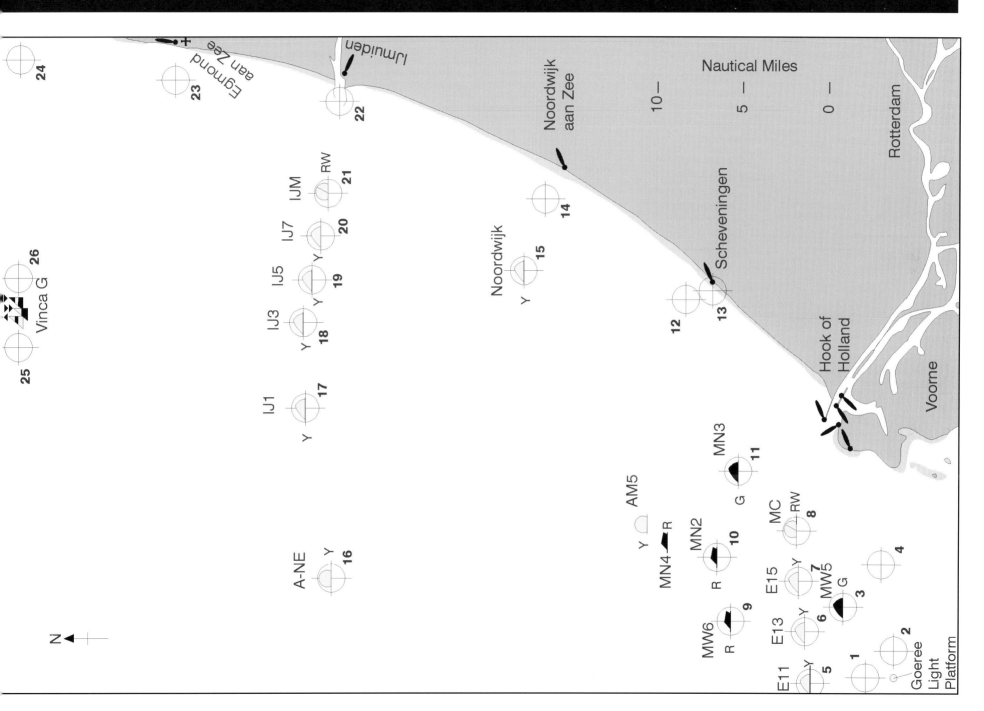

Nautical Miles

10 — 5 — 0 —

Rotterdam

Voorne

Hook of Holland

Scheveningen

Noordwijk aan Zee

IJmuiden

Egmond aan Zee

24

23

22

Noordwijk

Vinca G

26

25

A-NE

IJ1

IJ3

IJ5

IJ7

IJM

RW

21

20

19

18

17

16

15

14

13

12

11

10

9

8

7

6

5

4

3

2

1

MN3

MN2

MN4

AM5

MW6

MW5

MC

E15

E13

E11

Goeree
Light
Platform

N

121

WP No	Waypoint name and position	Latitude	Longitude
46–1	Goeree north, 1½ M due N of Goeree light platform	51°57.05'N	03°40.17'E
46–2	Goeree east, 1½ M due E of Goeree light platform	51°55.55'N	03°42.60'E
46–3	MW5 green buoy, actual position	51°58.40'N	03°46.60'E
46–4	*Adriana* inshore WP, 6.7 M 251°T from Maasvlakte light	51°56.14'N	03°50.66'E
46–5	Eurogeul 'E11' yellow buoy, actual position	52°00.22'N	03°39.58'E
46–6	Eurogeul 'E13' yellow buoy, actual position	52°00.60'N	03°44.22'E
46–7	Eurogeul 'E15' yellow buoy, actual position	52°00.96'N	03°48.86'E
46–8	Maas Center 'MC' red-and-white fairway buoy, actual position	52°01.18'N	03°53.56'E
46–9	MW6 red buoy, actual position	52°04.93'N	03°45.23'E
46–10	MN2 red buoy, actual position	52°05.78'N	03°51.00'E
46–11	MN3 green buoy, actual position	52°04.58'N	03°58.88'E
46–12	Scheveningen approach, 1.9 M 321°T from main lighthouse	52°07.77'N	04°14.24'E
46–13	Scheveningen entrance, between pierhead lights on leading line	52°06.28'N	04°15.34'E
46–14	Noordwijk aan Zee offing, 2 M 300°T from main lighthouse	52°16.00'N	04°23.38'E
46–15	Noordwijk yellow offshore buoy, actual position	52°17.00'N	04°17.00'E
46–16	A-NE yellow approach buoy, actual position	52°28.00'N	03°48.70'E
46–17	IJ1 yellow approach buoy, actual position	52°29.66'N	04°04.23'E
46–18	IJ3 yellow approach buoy, actual position	52°29.79'N	04°12.10'E
46–19	IJ5 yellow approach buoy, actual position	52°29.36'N	04°15.98'E
46–20	IJ7 yellow approach buoy, actual position	52°28.95'N	04°19.90'E
46–21	IJM red-and-white fairway buoy, actual position	52°28.48'N	04°23.80'E
46–22	IJmuiden entrance, between outer pierhead lights on leading line	52°28.00'N	04°32.37'E
46–23	Egmond aan Zee offing, 2 M due W of Egmond lighthouse	52°37.19'N	04°34.02'E
46–24	Petten offing, 2½ M due W of Petten church tower	52°46.10'N	04°35.76'E
46–25	Vinca-G west clearing, 1½ M W of Vinca-G W-card buoy	52°45.96'N	04°10.06'E
46–26	Vinca-G east clearing, 1½ M E of Vinca-G E-card buoy	52°45.97'N	04°15.62'E

Datum ED 50 The waypoint latitudes and longitudes in this table refer to European Datum (1950)

Gas rigs north of IJmuiden

Large gas rigs operate in the shallow coastal waters north of IJmuiden and should always be given a wide berth. Their areas of operation are often marked by cardinal buoys, which may not always appear on even the latest Admiralty charts

Seas off Hoek van Holland and IJmuiden

The seas in the approaches to Hoek van Holland can be steep and unpleasant in a brisk south-westerly wind against an outpouring ebb. You should also try to avoid approaching and entering either the Maas or the Noordzee Kanaal in strong north-westerlies, when a heavy swell can build up offshore over a period of time. The seas can be steep off the Hook and IJmuiden in strong north-easterlies against a north-going stream, or strong south-westerlies against a south-going stream.

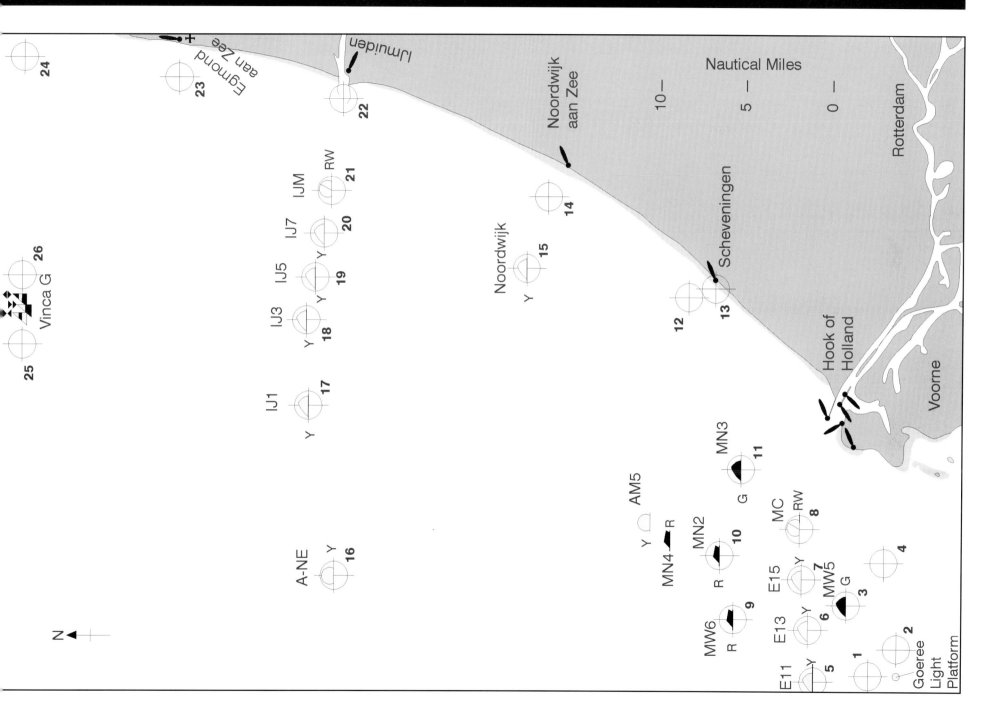

Nautical Miles

10 —
5 —
0 —

Rotterdam

IJmuiden

Egmond
aan Zee

Noordwijk
aan Zee

Noordwijk

Scheveningen

Hook of
Holland

Voorne

Vinca G

N

Goeree
Light
Platform

24
23
22
21 RW
     IJM
20 IJ7
19 Y IJ5
18 Y IJ3
17 IJ1 Y
26
25
15 Y
14
13
12
16 Y A-NE
AM5 Y
MN3 G 11
MN4 R MN2
10 R
8 RW MC
7 Y MW5
9 R MW6
6 Y E15 G 3
5 Y E13 E11
1
2
4

123

WP No	Waypoint name and position	Latitude	Longitude
47–1	Petten offing, 2½ M due W of Petten church tower	52°46.10'N	04°35.76'E
47–2	Pettemer Polder offing, 3 M due W of power station N chimney	52°47.40'N	04°35.60'E
47–3	Schulpengat 'SG' red-and-white fairway buoy, actual position	52°52.95'N	04°38.00'E
47–4	WR13 W-card buoy, actual position	52°53.92'N	04°33.32'E
47–5	ZH S-card buoy, actual position	52°54.70'N	04°34.83'E
47–6	MR W-card buoy, actual position	52°56.81'N	04°33.90'E
47–7	Noorderhaaks 'NH' N-card buoy, actual position	53°00.29'N	04°35.46'E
47–8	Molengat 'MG' N-card buoy, actual position	53°03.69'N	04°39.38'E

Datum ED 50 The waypoint latitudes and longitudes in this table refer to European Datum (1950)

COASTAL DANGERS

Refer to Admiralty charts 2322 and 191

Pettemer Polder

Just over 10 miles south of Den Helder, among the low dunes of the North Sea coast, the nuclear power station near Petten has two tall chimneys, 45 metres high. Opposite the chimneys, an underwater cooling pipeline extends offshore for nearly 2 miles, marked at its seaward end by a yellow buoy and the Petten west-cardinal buoy. Not far inside these buoys is a small shoal patch with 4.3 metres over it. It is advisable to pass outside these buoys and give the whole area of the power station a wide berth.

Zuider Haaks

The south approach channel to Zeegat van Texel and Den Helder leads inside a broad area of shoals, the southern end of which is known as the Zuider Haaks. The shallowest part of the Zuider Haaks has 1.3 metres depth at LAT, although most of the bank has more than 2½ metres and can be crossed safely by boats in quiet weather.

However, the Zuider Haaks become dangerous in heavy onshore weather, when steep seas break over them. Then it is important to keep to the Schulpengat buoyed channel into Zeegat van Texel, first picking up Verkenningston red-and-white fairway buoy which lies 3 miles west of Grote Kaap lighthouse. The Schulpengat leaves Zuider Haaks to the west and these shoals provide a partial natural breakwater for the approaches to Zeegat van Texel.

Fransche Bankje

Fransche Bankje is a patchy shifting shoal ½ mile east (inshore) of Verkenningston fairway buoy, with depths mostly between 2½ and 4½ metres. Boats can safely sail over the bank in quiet weather, but seas break over the shallowest parts in heavy onshore weather, when you must stick to the Schulpengat buoyed channel and leave the shoals clear to the east.

Bollen van Kijkduin

A mile or so north of Fransche Bankje, also on the inshore side of the buoyed Schulpengat, the

Bollen van Kijkduin shoal has a least depth of 1.7 metres and is left clear to the east (inshore) as you pass S3, S5 and S7 green buoys.

Noorderhaaks

The low, sandy, above-water (just about) island known as Noorderhaaks lies just opposite the Marsdiep, the mile-wide channel between Den Helder and the south end of Texel. Broad areas of drying sand fringe the above-water part of Noorderhaaks and shallow shoal areas extend well out to the west and north. The seaward edges of Noorderhaaks are guarded by 'MR' west-cardinal buoy and 'NH' north-cardinal buoy, while the southern, inshore edge is guarded by the red buoys of the Schulpengat.

On the north side of Noorderhaaks, a roughly triangular shoal stretches north for 3 miles, with least depths of under ½ metre up to 1 mile north of Noorderhaaks, and a 1½ metre patch about 1¼ miles north of Noorderhaaks. These shoals are left close to the west by the narrow buoyed channel known as Molengat, which leads close along the south-west edge of Texel and provides a useful route into Marsdiep from the north.

Ferries in Marsdiep

Watch out for the fast-moving ferries that shuttle across Marsdiep between Den Helder and Texel.

Strong tides in the Marsdiep

The tides run strongly through the narrow gap between Texel and Den Helder, reaching 3½–4 knots near the middle of a spring ebb, so it is always best to time your entry or exit for a fair or slack stream. A fresh wind over the tide kicks up short steep seas in the Marsdiep, especially a south-westerly blowing in from seaward over the ebb.

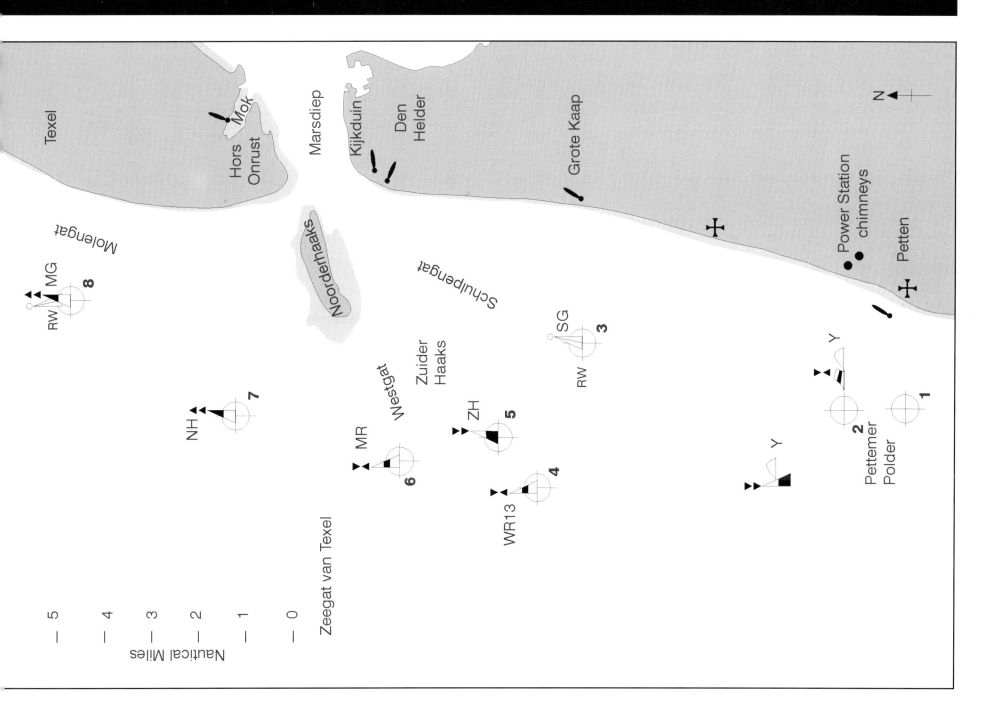

WP No	Waypoint name and position	Latitude	Longitude
48–1	Schulpengat 'SG' red-and-white fairway buoy, actual position	52°52.95'N	04°38.00'E
48–2	Schulpengat SW, between S3 and S4 buoys on leading line	52°54.58'N	04°39.30'E
48–3	Breewijd SW, 1.53 M at 250°T from Huisduinen lighthouse	52°56.68'N	04°41.00'E
48–4	Breewijd NE, 8½ ca 015°T from Kijkduin lighthouse	52°58.18'N	04°44.00'E
48–5	Molengat S, between MG13 and MG14 buoys on leading line	52°59.27'N	04°42.48'E
48–6	Noorderhaaks E, between MG15 and MG16 buoys on leading line	52°58.88'N	04°42.97'E

Datum ED 50 The waypoint latitudes and longitudes in this table refer to European Datum (1950)

COASTAL DANGERS
Refer to Admiralty chart 191

Zuider Haaks
The south approach channel to Zeegat van Texel and Den Helder leads inside a broad area of shoals, the southern end of which is known as the Zuider Haaks. The shallowest part of the Zuider Haaks has 1.3 metres depth at LAT, although most of the bank has more than 2½ metres and can safely be crossed by boats in quiet weather.

However, the Zuider Haaks become dangerous in heavy onshore weather, when steep seas break over them. Then it is important to keep to the Schulpengat buoyed channel into Zeegat van Texel, first picking up Verkenningston red-and-white fairway buoy which lies 3 miles west of Grote Kaap lighthouse. The Schulpengat leaves Zuider Haaks to the west and these shoals provide a partial natural breakwater for the approaches to Zeegat van Texel.

Fransche Bankje
Fransche Bankje is a patchy shifting shoal ½ mile east (inshore) of Verkenningston fairway buoy, with depths mostly between 2½ and 4½ metres.

Boats can safely sail over the bank in quiet weather, but seas break over the shallowest parts in heavy onshore weather, when you must stick to the Schulpengat buoyed channel and leave the shoals clear to the east.

Bollen van Kijkduin
A mile or so north of Fransche Bankje, also on the inshore side of the buoyed Schulpengat, the Bollen van Kijkduin shoal has a least depth of 1.7 metres and is left clear to the east (inshore) as you pass S3, S5 and S7 green buoys.

Noorderhaaks
The low, sandy, above-water (just about) island known as Noorderhaaks lies just opposite the Marsdiep, the mile-wide channel between Den Helder and the south end of Texel. Broad areas of drying sand fringe the above-water part of Noorderhaaks and shallow shoal areas extend well out to the west and north. The seaward edges of Noorderhaaks are guarded by 'MR' west-cardinal buoy and 'NH' north-cardinal buoy, while the southern, inshore edge is guarded by the red buoys of the Schulpengat.

On the north side of Noorderhaaks, a roughly triangular shoal stretches north for 3 miles, with least depths of under ½ metre up to 1 mile north of Noorderhaaks, and a 1½ metre patch about 1½ miles north of Noorderhaaks. These shoals are left close to the west by the narrow buoyed channel known as Molengat, which leads close along the south-west edge of Texel and provides a useful route into Marsdiep from the north.

Strong tides in the Marsdiep
The tides run strongly through the narrow gap between Texel and Den Helder, reaching 3½–4 knots near the middle of a spring ebb, so it is always best to time your entry or exit for a fair or slack stream. A fresh wind over the tide kicks up short steep seas in the Marsdiep, especially a south-westerly blowing in from seaward over the ebb.

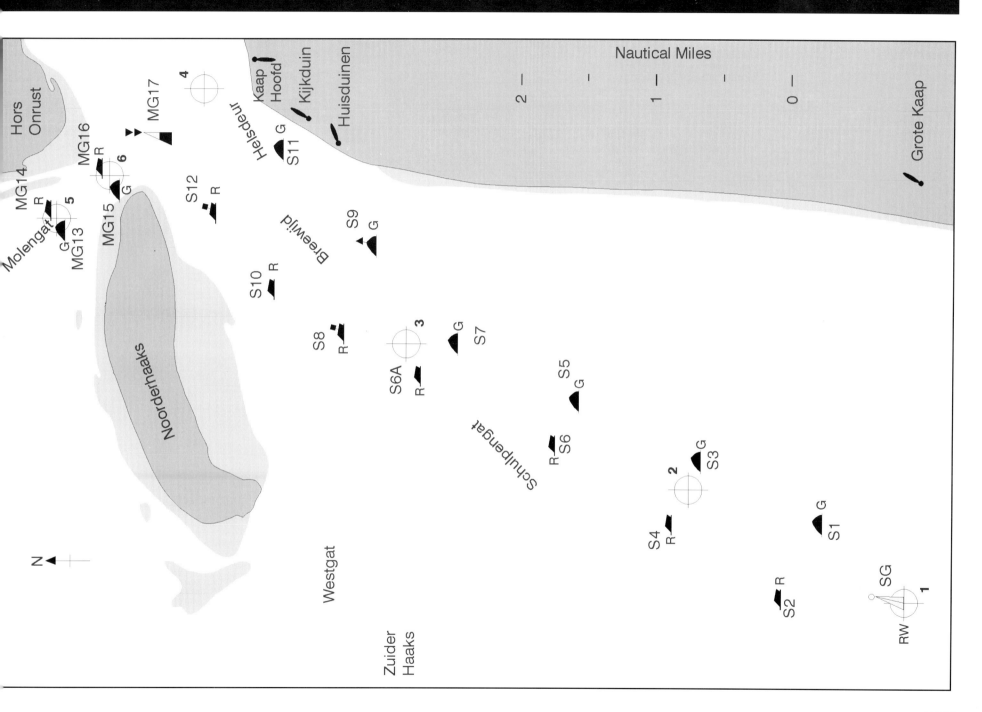

Nautical Miles

Hors
Onrust

Kaap
Hoofd

Kijkduin

Huisduinen

Grote Kaap

MG17

4

Helsdeur

MG16

R

MG14

MG15

G

S11

S12

R

R

6

MG13

G

5

R

Molengat

G

Breewild

S9

G

S10

R

S8

R

Noorderhaaks

3

S7

G

S6A

R

S5

G

Schulpengat

S6

R

S3

G

2

S4

R

S1

G

Westgat

S2

R

SG

Zuider
Haaks

RW

1

N

Zeegat van Texel and approaches to Den Helder

WP No	Waypoint name and position	Latitude	Longitude
49–1	Breewijd SW, 1.53 M at 250°T from Huisduinen lighthouse	52°56.68'N	04°41.00'E
49–2	Breewijd NE, 8½ ca 015°T from Kijkduin lighthouse	52°58.18'N	04°44.00'E
49–3	Marsdiep, 1.7 M at 047°T from Kijkduin lighthouse	52°58.52'N	04°45.70'E
49–4	Den Helder N outer, 1.9 M 011°T from front leading light	52°59.28'N	04°47.74'E
49–5	Den Helder N inner, 1 M 011°T from front leading light	52°58.41'N	04°47.48'E
49–6	Den Helder entrance, ¾ M 011°T from front leading light	52°58.16'N	04°47.38'E
49–7	Texelstroom SW, 2¼ M due E of Schilbolsnol lighthouse	53°00.55'N	04°49.50'E
49–8	Noorderhaaks E, between MG15 and MG16 buoys on leading line	52°58.88'N	04°42.97'E
49–9	Molengat S, between MG13 and MG14 buoys on leading line	52°59.27'N	04°42.48'E
49–10	Molengat inner, 2.45 M 265°T from Schilbolsnol lighthouse	53°00.34'N	04°41.72'E

Datum ED 50 The waypoint latitudes and longitudes in this table refer to European Datum (1950)

COASTAL DANGERS
Refer to Admiralty chart 191

Schulpengat channel
The Schulpengat is the main, southern approach channel to Zeegat van Texel and Den Helder. The well-buoyed fairway leads inside a broad area of shoals, the southern end of which is known as the Zuider Haaks. The shallowest part of Zuider Haaks has 1.3 metres depth at LAT, although most of the bank has more than 2½ metres and can safely be crossed by boats in quiet weather.

However, the Zuider Haaks become dangerous in heavy onshore weather, when steep seas break over them. Then it is important to keep to the Schulpengat buoyed channel into Zeegat van Texel, first picking up Verkenningston red-and-white fairway buoy which lies 3 miles west of Grote Kaap lighthouse. The Schulpengat leaves Zuider Haaks to the west and these shoals provide a partial natural breakwater for the approaches to Zeegat van Texel.

Noorderhaaks
The low, sandy, above-water (just about) island known as Noorderhaaks lies just opposite the Marsdiep, the mile-wide channel between Den Helder and the south end of Texel. Broad areas of drying sand fringe the above-water part of Noorderhaaks and shallow shoal areas extend well out to the west and north. The seaward edges of Noorderhaaks are guarded by 'MR' west-cardinal buoy and 'NH' north-cardinal buoy, while the southern, inshore edge is guarded by the red buoys of the Schulpengat.

On the north side of Noorderhaaks, a roughly triangular shoal stretches north for 3 miles, with least depths of under ½ metre up to 1 mile north of Noorderhaaks, and a 1½ metre patch about 1½ miles north of Noorderhaaks. These shoals are left close to the west by the narrow buoyed channel known as Molengat, which leads close along the south-west edge of Texel and provides a useful route into Marsdiep from the north.

Strong tides in the Marsdiep
The tides run strongly through the narrow gap between Texel and Den Helder, reaching 3½–4 knots near the middle of a spring ebb, so it is always best to time your entry or exit for a fair or slack stream. A fresh wind over the tide kicks up short steep seas in the Marsdiep, especially a south-westerly blowing in from seaward over the ebb.

Ferries in Marsdiep
Watch out for the fast-moving ferries that shuttle across Marsdiep between Den Helder and Texel.

Shoals east of Den Helder
To the east of Den Helder, inside Zeegat van Texel, a vast area of drying sands and shallow channels – the Balgzand – fills most of the 8-mile wide bight between Den Helder and Den Oever. The north edge of these sands is marked by the green buoys of the Malzwin channel which leads ENE towards Den Oever from near Den Helder harbour entrance.

128

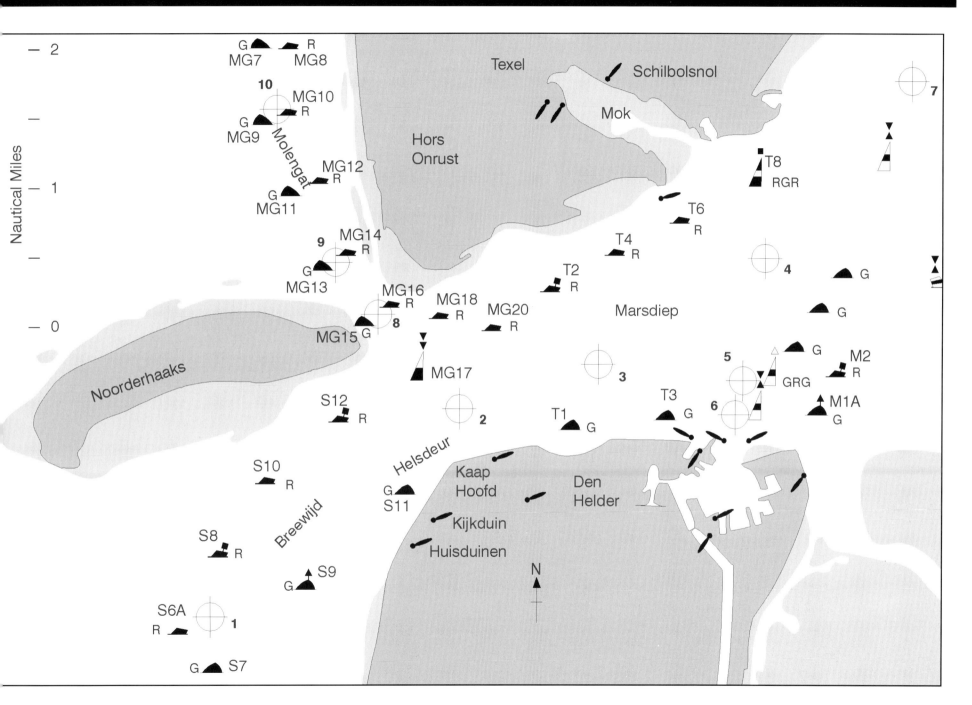

G MG7   R MG8

Texel

Schilbolsnol

10

MG10
R

G
MG9

Molengat

Mok

Hors
Onrust

T8

RGR

MG12
R

G
MG11

R

T6
R

MG14
R

9

T4
R

G
MG13

T2
R

Marsdiep

MG16
R

MG18
R

MG20
R

4

G

MG15 G

8

G

T3

5

G

G

GRG

M2
R

MG17

3

M1A
G

S12
R

2

T1
G

6

S10
R

Helsdeur

Kaap
Hoofd

Den
Helder

G
S11

S8
R

Breewijd

Kijkduin

Huisduinen

N

S9
G

S6A
R   1

G S7

Noorderhaaks

Nautical Miles

— 2

— 1

— 0

129

WP No	Waypoint name and position	Latitude	Longitude
50–1	Molengat 'MG' red-and-white fairway buoy, actual position	53°03.95'N	04°39.47'E
50–2	Molengat N-card buoy, actual position	53°03.69'N	04°39.38'E
50–3	Molengat outer, 2.12 M 290°T from Den Hoorn N leading light	53°02.39'N	04°41.82'E
50–4	Molengat inner, 2.45 M 265°T from Schilbolsnol lighthouse	53°00.34'N	04°41.72'E
50–5	Molengat S, between MG13 and MG14 buoys on leading line	52°59.27'N	04°42.48'E
50–6	Noorderhaaks E, between MG15 and MG16 buoys on leading line	52°58.88'N	04°42.97'E
50–7	Marsdiep, 1.7 M at 047°T from Kijkduin lighthouse	52°58.52'N	04°45.70'E
50–8	Breewijd NE, 8½ ca 015°T from Kijkduin lighthouse	52°58.18'N	04°44.00'E

Datum ED 50 The waypoint latitudes and longitudes in this table refer to European Datum (1950)

COASTAL DANGERS

Refer to Admiralty chart 191

Noorderhaaks

The low, sandy, above-water (just about) island known as Noorderhaaks lies just opposite the Marsdiep, the mile-wide channel between Den Helder and the south end of Texel. Broad areas of drying sand fringe the above-water part of Noorderhaaks and shallow shoal areas extend well out to the west and north. The seaward edges of Noorderhaaks are guarded by 'MR' west-cardinal buoy and 'NH' north-cardinal buoy, while the southern, inshore edge is guarded by the red buoys of the Schulpengat.

On the north side of Noorderhaaks, a roughly triangular shoal stretches north for 3 miles, with least depths of under ½ metre up to 1 mile north of Noorderhaaks, and a 1½ metre patch about 1½ miles north of Noorderhaaks. These shoals are left close to the west by the narrow buoyed channel known as Molengat, which leads close along the south-west edge of Texel and provides a useful route into Marsdiep from the north.

Strong tides in the Marsdiep

The tides run strongly through the narrow gap between Texel and Den Helder, reaching 3½–4 knots near the middle of a spring ebb, so it is always best to time your entry or exit for a fair or slack stream. A fresh wind over the tide kicks up short steep seas in the Marsdiep, especially a south-westerly blowing in from seaward over the ebb.

Molengat in heavy weather

In strong sustained winds from between north and west, the building onshore swell makes Molengat a dangerous entrance, when the steep seas breaking over the northern shoals of Noorderhaaks extend across the narrow buoyed channel. In these conditions, Molengat is also close to a dangerous lee shore, with the south-west coast of Texel only ½ mile to the east.

In any heavy onshore weather, you should enter Zeegat van Texel by the main southern channel, the much wider Schulpengat, which becomes progressively sheltered as you draw north under the lee of the partial natural break-water provided by the above-water part of Noorderhaaks.

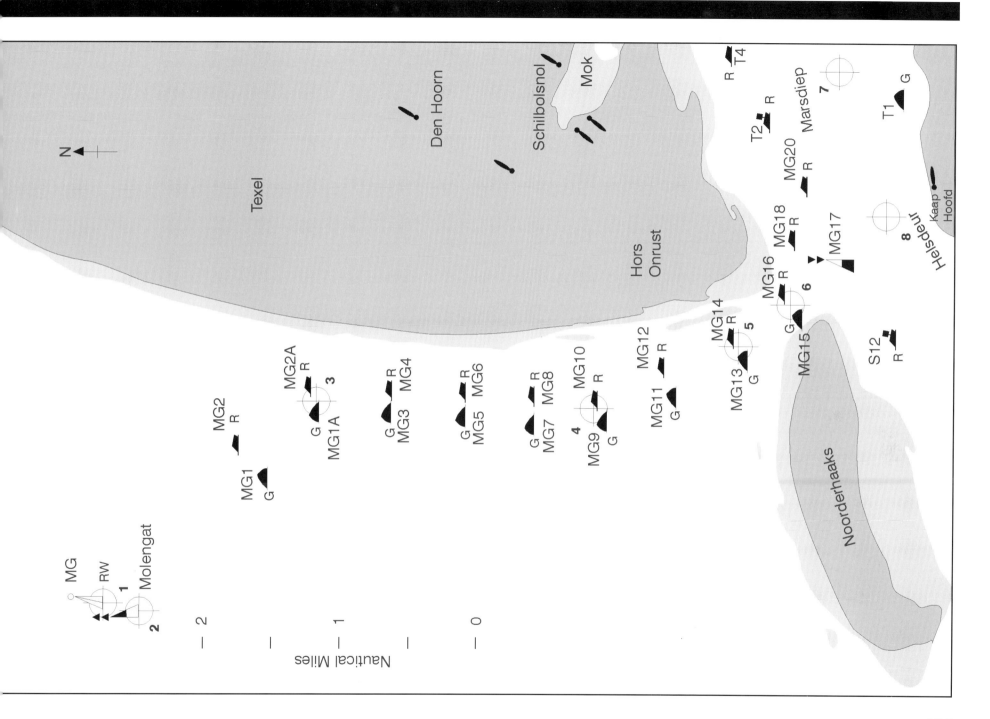

N

Texel

Den Hoorn

Schilbolsnol

Mok

Hors
Onrust

Noorderhaaks

Helsdeur

Kaap
Hoofd

Marsdiep

R
T4

T2
R

MG20
R

MG18
R

MG17

MG16
R
G

6

MG15

S12
R

T1
G

7

8

MG14
R
5

MG13
G

MG12
R

MG11
G

MG10
R
4
MG9
G

MG8
R
MG7
G

MG6
R
MG5
G

MG4
R
MG3
G

MG2A
R
3
MG1A
G

MG2
R

MG1
G

MG
RW
1
Molengat
2

Nautical Miles

2

1

0

Den Helder to Den Oever

WP No	Waypoint name and position	Latitude	Longitude
51–1	Den Helder N outer, 1.9 M 011°T from front leading light	52°59.28'N	04°47.74'E
51–2	Den Helder N inner, 1 M 011°T from front leading light	52°58.41'N	04°47.48'E
51–3	Den Helder entrance, ¾ M 011°T from front leading light	52°58.16'N	04°47.38'E
51–4	Texelstroom SW, 2¼ M due E of Schilbolsnol lighthouse	53°00.55'N	04°49.50'E
51–5	Texelstroom middle, 7 ca 120°T from Oudeschild N pierhead	53°02.07'N	04°52.43'E
51–6	Oudeschild approach, midway T14 red and OS1 red-and-green bys	53°02.33'N	04°51.67'E
51–7	Gat van de Stier, 2 ca due S of KLZ-D yellow buoy	52°59.68'N	04°49.73'E
51–8	Malzwin SW, midway M5 green and M6 red buoys	52°58.50'N	04°50.09'E
51–9	Malzwin middle, midway M11 green and M12 green-and-red bys	52°59.18'N	04°51.81'E
51–10	Malzwin NE, midway M15 green and M18 red buoys	52°59.59'N	04°53.56'E
51–11	LW red-and-white fairway buoy, actual position	52°59.57'N	04°55.99'E
51–12	Wierbalg approach, midway W1 green and W2 green-red-green bys	52°59.00'N	04°56.86'E

Datum ED 50 The waypoint latitudes and longitudes in this table refer to European Datum (1950)

COASTAL DANGERS

Refer to Admiralty chart 191 and Dutch chart 1811.3

Strong tides in the Marsdiep

The tides run strongly through the narrow gap between Texel and Den Helder, reaching 3½–4 knots near the middle of a spring ebb, so it is always best to time your entry or exit for a fair or slack stream. A fresh wind over the tide kicks up short steep seas in the Marsdiep, especially a south-westerly blowing in from seaward over the ebb.

Ferries in Marsdiep

Watch out for the fast-moving ferries that shuttle across Marsdiep between Den Helder and Texel.

Balgzand

To the east of Den Helder, inside Zeegat van Texel, a vast area of drying sands and shallow channels – the Balgzand – fills most of the 8-mile-wide bight between Den Helder and Den Oever. The north edge of these sands is marked by the green buoys of the Malzwin channel which trends ENE from Den Helder harbour entrance and round the top of Balgzand towards the buoyed channels leading to Den Oever. At the south-east end of the Voorhaven at Den Oever is the sea-lock through the Afsluitdijk into the IJsselmeer.

Breehorn

The Breehorn sands lie to the west of Den Oever and have least depths mostly well under 1 metre. The north edge of Breehorn is marked by the green buoys of the narrow Wierbalg channel, which is the main buoyed route to and from Den Oever.

Lutjeswaard

This extensive area of shoals lies between Texel and the outer dam of the IJsselmeer, the massive Afsluitdijk. The central part of Lutjeswaard dries to about ½ metre, but a shallow buoyed channel leads across the west end from north to south, providing a short cut near HW between Oudeschild harbour on Texel and the buoyed channels leading towards Den Oever.

The far west tip of Lutjeswaard dries to 0.7 metres and is guarded by the main green buoys of Texelstroom.

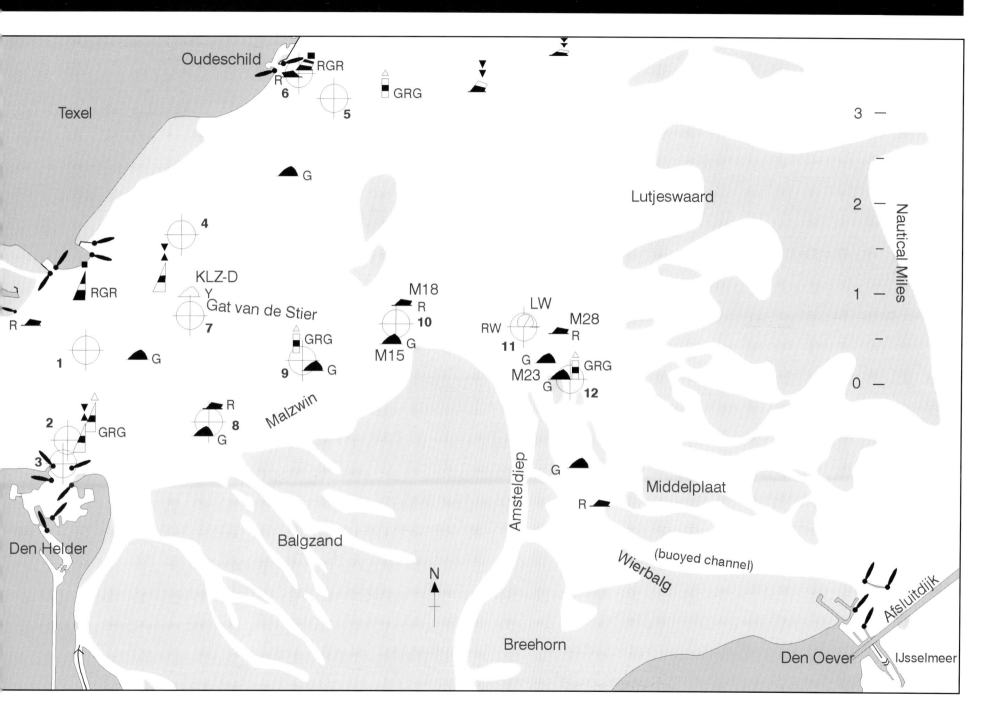

Oudeschild

Texel

RGR

R
6

GRG

5

G

Lutjeswaard

3 —

—

2 —

Nautical Miles

4

RGR

R

KLZ-D
Y

Gat van de Stier

7

1 —

M18
R
10

G

M15

LW

M28
R

RW

11

G

M23

G

GRG

12

—

0 —

GRG

1

G

9

G
G

R
8

G

2

GRG

3

R

Malzwin

Amsteldiep

G

Middelplaat

R

Den Helder

Balgzand

Wierbalg

(buoyed channel)

N

Breehorn

Afsluitdijk

Den Oever   IJsselmeer

133

WP No	Waypoint name and position	Latitude	Longitude
52–1	MR west clearing, ½ M W of MR W-card buoy	52°56.82'N	04°33.05'E
52–2	NH west clearing, ½ M W of Noorderhaaks N-card buoy	53°00.29'N	04°34.61'E
52–3	Verkenningston MG west clearing, ½ M W of fairway buoy	53°03.96'N	04°38.62'E
52–4	EG west clearing, ½ M W of Eierlandsche Gat W-card buoy	53°13.38'N	04°46.33'E
52–5	Baden west clearing, ½ M W of Baden W-card buoy	53°13.61'N	04°40.30'E
52–6	VL1 green shipping lane buoy, actual position	53°11.00'N	04°35.40'E
52–7	VL3 green shipping lane buoy, actual position	53°17.00'N	04°39.70'E
52–8	VL5 green shipping lane buoy, actual position	53°22.90'N	04°44.00'E
52–9	VL7 green shipping lane buoy, actual position	53°25.52'N	04°54.00'E
52–10	VL9 green shipping lane buoy, actual position	53°28.15'N	05°03.96'E
52–11	Stortemelk 'SM' red-and-white fairway buoy, actual position	53°19.06'N	04°55.73'E
52–12	TG west clearing, ½ M NW of TG W-card buoy	53°24.59'N	05°01.80'E
52–13	Stolzenfels west clearing, ½ M NW of W-card buoy	53°26.58'N	05°09.17'E

Datum ED 50 The waypoint latitudes and longitudes in this table refer to European Datum (1950)

COASTAL DANGERS

Refer to Admiralty charts 112, 191 and 2593 and Dutch chart 1811

Molengat in heavy weather

In strong sustained winds from between north and west, the building onshore swell makes Molengat a dangerous entrance to Zeegat van Texel, when the steep seas breaking over the northern shoals of Noorderhaaks extend across the narrow buoyed channel. In these conditions, Molengat also runs close to a dangerous lee shore, with the south-west coast of Texel only ½ mile to the east.

In any heavy onshore weather, you should enter Zeegat van Texel by the main southern channel, the much wider Schulpengat, which becomes progressively sheltered as you draw north under the lee of the partial natural break-water provided by the above-water part of Noorderhaaks.

Eierlandsche Gat

No waypoints have been given for this shallow shifting channel between Texel and Vlieland, which is only passable by strangers in calm weather with no onshore swell. To enter Eierlandsche Gat you must have the latest version of the Dutch Hydrografische Kaart No 1811 and approach 1 hour before local high water. Dedicated Frisian Island sand-hoppers can find some quiet anchorages behind Vlieland, but keep an eye on the weather.

Zeegat van Terschelling

This well-buoyed channel through the gap between the north-east end of Vlieland and the south-west end of Terschelling is used regularly in the summer by large numbers of local boats. The outer 'Stortemelk' red-and-white fairway buoy lies 5 miles WNW from Oost Vlieland lighthouse and it is important to find and positively identify this buoy before proceeding any further inshore.

Just over 1 mile east of the 'Stortemelk' fairway buoy you leave 'ZS Bank' north-cardinal buoy close to the south before following the 4-mile trail of reds and greens eastwards towards the north tip of Vlieland. In common with all the *zeegat* channels between the Frisian Islands, you should not attempt to enter or leave Zeegat van Terschelling in strong onshore winds or when a heavy onshore swell is running.

Terschelling Sands

A dangerous area of shoals extends 5 miles west from the south-west end of Terschelling island. Parts of these shoals dry and much of the area has less than 1 metre depth at LAT. In any fresh onshore weather, these sands are a seething mass of breakers and great care must be taken, particularly if coasting outside Terschelling, to stay well seaward of the cardinal buoys which guard these dangers – Terschellinger Gronden 'TG' west-cardinal buoy and Stolzenfels west-cardinal wreck buoy.

The buoyed channel through Zeegat van Terschelling leads a good 1½ miles south of Terschelling Sands and it is important to find and positively identify the 'Stortemelk' fairway buoy when approaching this channel from seaward.

Offshore shipping lanes

The coastal shipping lanes lie between 8 and 12 miles seaward of Texel, Vlieland and Terschelling. Boats cruising the Frisian Islands will normally stay inshore of these lanes during daylight, but care must be taken to keep clear of shipping if you are standing further offshore, perhaps for a night passage.

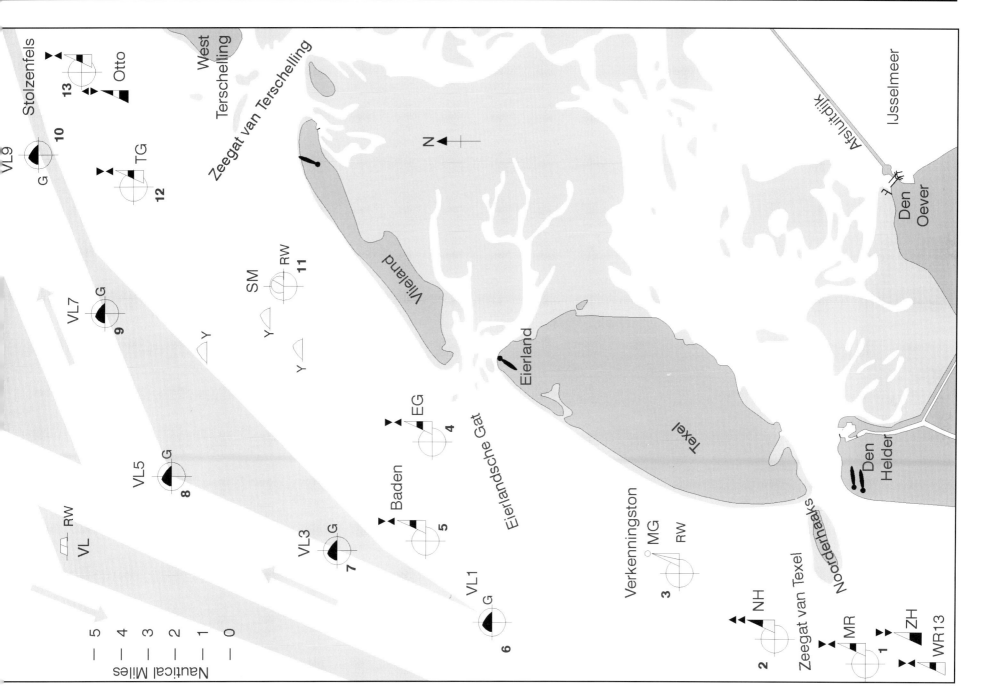

Nautical Miles

135

WP No	Waypoint name and position	Latitude	Longitude
53–1	Stortemelk 'SM' red-and-white fairway buoy, actual position	53°19.06'N	04°55.73'E
53–2	ZS Bank outer, 1 ca N of Zuider Stortemelk N-card buoy	53°19.02'N	04°57.94'E
53–3	ZS Bank inner, 1 M due N of Oost Vlieland lighthouse	53°18.80'N	05°03.60'E
53–4	Vlieland NE, 1½ ca due N of ZS13 / VS2 green-and-red buoy	53°18.88'N	05°05.84'E
53–5	Stortemelk inner, midway ZS15 green and ZS18 red buoys	53°19.17'N	05°07.02'E
53–6	Schuitengat outer approach, 1½ ca SE of ZS20 red buoy	53°19.65'N	05°08.58'E
53–7	Richel N clearing, 2 ca due N of VL1 green buoy	53°19.17'N	05°08.81'E
53–8	VL7 green shipping lane buoy, actual position	53°25.52'N	04°54.00'E
53–9	TG W clearing, ½ M NW of TG W-card buoy	53°24.59'N	05°01.80'E

Datum ED 50 The waypoint latitudes and longitudes in this table refer to European Datum (1950)

COASTAL DANGERS

Refer to Admiralty chart 112 and Dutch chart 1811

Stortemelk channel

This well-buoyed channel through the gap between the north-east end of Vlieland and the south-west end of Terschelling is used regularly in the summer by large numbers of local boats. The outer 'Stortemelk' red-and-white fairway buoy lies 5 miles WNW from Oost Vlieland lighthouse and it is important to find and positively identify this buoy before proceeding any further inshore.

Just over 1 mile east of the 'Stortemelk' fairway buoy you leave 'ZS Bank' north-cardinal buoy close to the south before following the 4-mile trail of reds and greens eastwards towards the north tip of Vlieland. In common with all the *zeegat* channels between the Frisian Islands, you should not attempt to enter or leave Zeegat van Terschelling in strong onshore winds or when a heavy onshore swell is running.

The channel buoys are lit and it is quite feasible to enter or leave Zeegat van Terschelling at night in quiet weather or offshore winds.

Terschelling Sands

A dangerous area of shoals extends 5 miles west from the south-west end of Terschelling island. Parts of these shoals dry and much of the area has less than 1 metre depth at LAT. In any fresh onshore weather, these sands are a seething mass of breakers and great care must be taken, particularly if coasting outside Terschelling, to stay well seaward of the cardinal buoys which guard these dangers – Terschellinger Gronden 'TG' west-cardinal buoy and Stolzenfels west-cardinal wreck buoy.

The Stortemelk buoyed channel through Zeegat van Terschelling leads a good 1½ miles south of Terschelling Sands and it is important to find and positively identify the 'SM' fairway buoy when approaching this channel from seaward.

Offshore shipping lanes

The coastal shipping lanes lie 8–12 miles seaward of Vlieland and Terschelling. Boats cruising the Frisian Islands will normally stay inshore of these lanes during daylight, but care must be taken to keep clear of shipping in the lanes if you are either approaching this coast from seaward or passing it well offshore, perhaps at night.

Fast ferries off West Terschelling

Regular fast ferries run between West Terschelling harbour and Harlingen on the mainland, so watch out for their movements if you are either passing through Zeegat van Terschelling *en route* for Harlingen or else entering or leaving West Terschelling harbour.

The narrow buoyed fairway approaching West Terschelling – the Schuitengat – is often packed with yachts and sailing barges in high summer, and the ferries come through this channel quite briskly, leaving a heavy wash.

Buoys obscured by yachts

In high summer, especially at weekends, the channels behind Terschelling and Vlieland are full of yachts, sailing barges and motor boats of every conceivable type, cruising about in all directions. You obviously need to keep a careful watch when passing through this *mêlée*, but one particular hazard is the risk of a critical channel buoy being obscured by a yacht or the large sail of a traditional barge.

Follow the Dutch chart 1811 carefully and do not jump to hasty conclusions just because an expected buoy does not immediately appear – it may be lurking behind someone's massive gaff mainsail. Carefully setting your own GPS waypoints to pick up particular channel buoys can be extremely useful, so long as you are using the latest version of chart 1811.

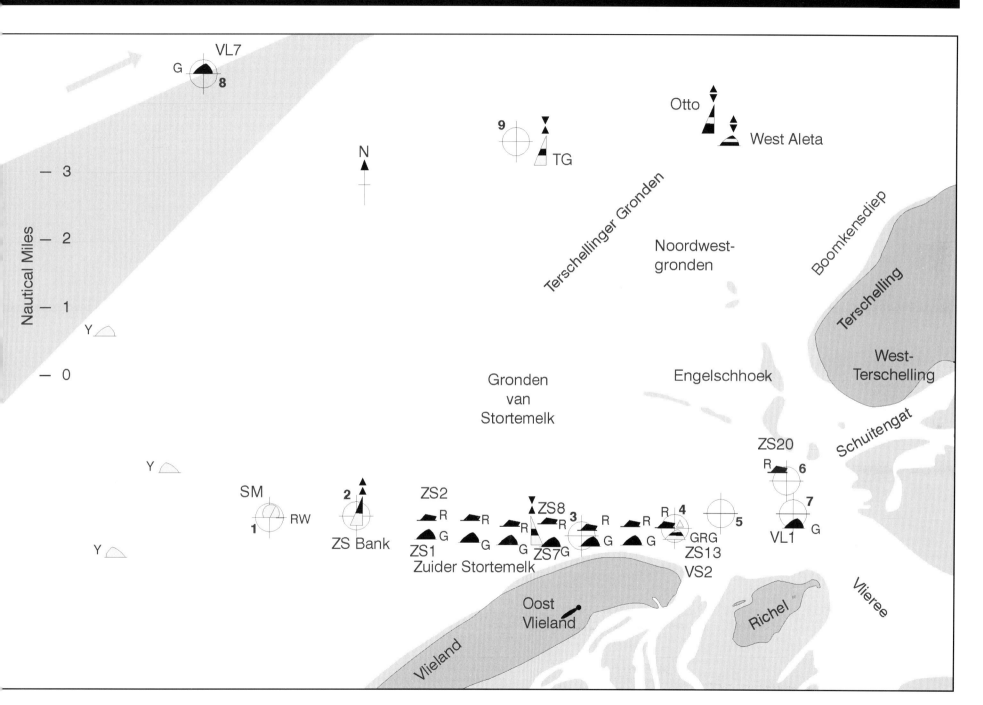

WP No	Waypoint name and position	Latitude	Longitude
54–1	ZS Bank inner, 1 M due N of Oost Vlieland lighthouse	53°18.80'N	05°03.60'E
54–2	Vlieland NE, 1½ ca due N of ZS13 / VS2 green-and-red buoy	53°18.88'N	05°05.84'E
54–3	Stortemelk inner, midway ZS15 green and ZS18 red buoys	53°19.17'N	05°07.02'E
54–4	Richel N clearing, 2 ca due N of VL1 green buoy	53°19.17'N	05°08.81'E
54–5	Schuitengat outer approach, 1½ ca SE of ZS20 red buoy	53°19.65'N	05°08.58'E
54–6	Schuitengat entrance, 3 M 231°T from Brandaris lighthouse	53°19.79'N	05°08.99'E
54–7	Terschelling harbour entrance, 70 m SE of W breakwater head	53°21.28'N	05°13.21'E
54–8	Richel NE, midway VL5 green buoy and VL6 red buoy	53°18.75'N	05°10.05'E
54–9	WM1 W-card buoy, actual position	53°17.36'N	05°11.32'E
54–10	Vliestroom entrance, 3 ca due W of WM1 W-card buoy	53°17.36'N	05°10.80'E
54–11	Blauwe Slenk NW, actual position of BS1-IN2-card buoy	53°15.30'N	05°10.13'E
54–12	West Meep entrance, midway WM2 red and WM3 green buoys	53°17.60'N	05°12.46'E
54–13	WM9 / ZM2 green-and-red buoy, actual position	53°17.97'N	05°14.55'E

Datum ED 50 The waypoint latitudes and longitudes in this table refer to European Datum (1950)

COASTAL DANGERS

Refer to Admiralty chart 112 and Dutch chart 1811

Schuitengat

This narrow buoyed channel leading to West Terschelling harbour is particularly constricted at its outer (south-west) end, where shoals and drying sandbanks press in on either side. The narrowest part of the Schuitengat is the first mile, between the outer 'SG1' west-cardinal buoy and 'SG7' green buoy. The drying sands are closest to the north side of these narrows, and towards high water, if you are pressed for room, there is scope to slip just the wrong side of the buoys on the south side.

Fast ferries off West Terschelling

Regular fast ferries run between West Terschelling harbour and Harlingen on the mainland, so watch out for their movements if you are either passing through Zeegat van Terschelling *en route* for Harlingen or else entering or leaving West Terschelling harbour.

The narrow buoyed fairway approaching West Terschelling – the Schuitengat – is often packed with yachts and sailing barges in high summer, and the ferries come through this channel quite briskly, leaving a heavy wash.

Buoys obscured by yachts

In high summer, especially at weekends, the channels behind Terschelling and Vlieland are full of yachts, sailing barges and motor boats of every conceivable type, cruising about in all directions. You obviously need to keep a careful watch when passing through this *mêlée*, but one particular hazard is the risk of a critical channel buoy being obscured by a yacht or the large sail of a traditional barge.

Follow the Dutch chart 1811 carefully and do not jump to hasty conclusions just because an expected buoy does not immediately appear – it may be lurking behind someone's massive gaff mainsail. Carefully setting your own GPS waypoints to pick up particular channel buoys can be extremely useful, so long as you are using the latest version of chart 1811.

Strong tides in the Vliestroom

The tidal streams run briskly through the Vliestroom and through the gap between Vlieland and Terschelling. Spring rates can reach 3–3½ knots during the strongest part of the ebb, when even a moderate wind over the tide will kick up short steep seas down off Richel island, and in the outer approaches to West Terschelling and Vlieland harbours.

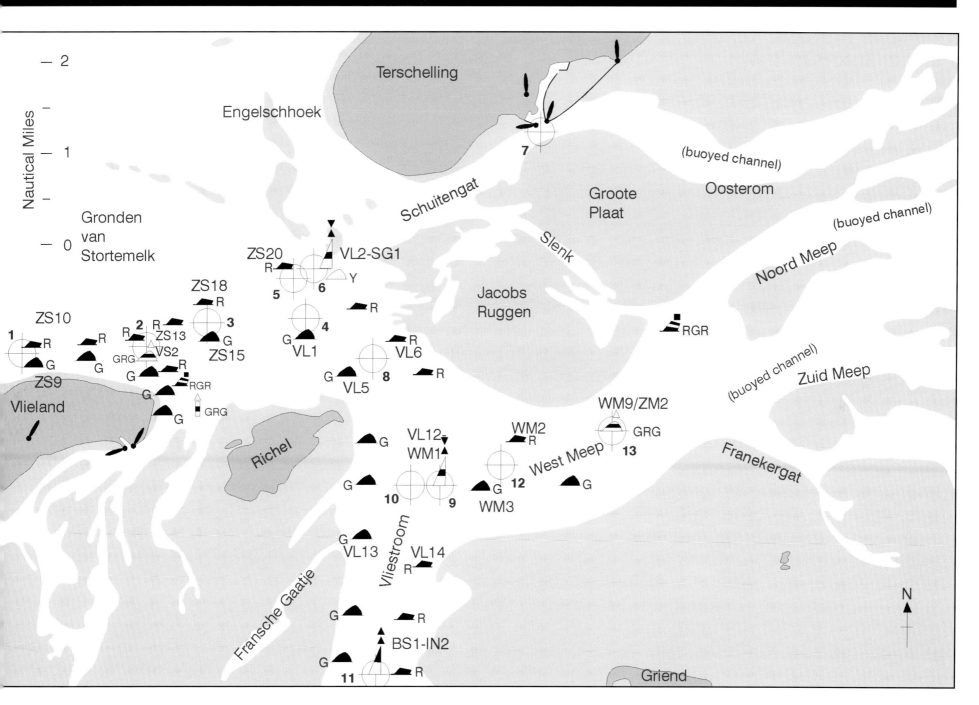

Terschelling

Engelschhoek

Nautical Miles

— 2

— 1

— 0

Gronden
van
Stortemelk

7

(buoyed channel)

Groote
Plaat

Oosterom

(buoyed channel)

Schuitengat

Slenk

Noord Meep

ZS20
R

VL2-SG1

5   6   Y

Jacobs
Ruggen

ZS18
R

R   3

G

R

VL1
G   4

R
VL6

RGR

(buoyed channel)

Zuid Meep

ZS10

R   2   R
R   ZS13
GRG   VS2
G   R
G   RGR
G   GRG

1
R

G

ZS9

Vlieland

ZS15

R   8
VL5
G

R

WM9/ZM2
GRG

13

West Meep

Franekergat

Richel

G

VL12
WM1
WM2
R

G   G
10   9
WM3

12
G

VL13
G

Vliestroom

VL14
R

G   R

Fransche Gaatje

BS1-IN2

G   R
11

Griend

N

139

Waddenzee approaches to Harlingen

WP No	Waypoint name and position	Latitude	Longitude
55–1	Blauwe Slenk NW, actual position of BS1-IN2-card buoy	53°15.30'N	05°10.13'E
55–2	Blauwe Slenk west, 1 ca due S of BS8 red buoy	53°14.14'N	05°11.55'E
55–3	Blauwe Slenk middle, midway BS11 green and BS12 red buoys	53°13.85'N	05°13.09'E
55–4	BS15 green buoy, actual position	53°13.73'N	05°15.10'E
55–5	Blauwe Slenk east, midway BS19 green and BS20 red buoys	53°13.48'N	05°17.10'E
55–6	BS29 green buoy, actual position	53°11.68'N	05°19.04'E
55–7	Harlingen entrance, 50 m due N of west pierhead light	53°10.64'N	05°24.24'E

Datum ED 50 The waypoint latitudes and longitudes in this table refer to European Datum (1950)

COASTAL DANGERS
Refer to Admiralty chart 112 and Dutch charts 1811.4 and 1811.5

Fast ferries between Harlingen and Terschelling
Regular fast ferries run between West Terschelling harbour and Harlingen on the mainland, so watch out for their movements if you are using the main buoyed channels between these two harbours – the Blauwe Slenk and Vliestroom channels.

Sailing barges and fishing boats
This area is well known for its traditional old sailing barges, many of them sizeable ships, which gather in the local harbours each night and cruise the channels inside the Frisian Islands by day. These barges make a spectacular sight, especially when sailing in a fleet, but you have to be careful about picking a safe route past buoys and barges together. A steady nerve is often required when perhaps 20 boats are converging on a critical buoy in a sluicing tide, but there always seems room for everyone at the last moment.

A good many fishing boats also work the shallow waters of the Waddenzee, and you will see the traditional local boats motoring out with their trawl nets raised high on derrick booms, like giant bat-wings. These boats will trawl placidly for a while, sometimes in more or less straight lines but often changing course, then they will suddenly lift up their trawls and shoot off to a different fishing ground. Watch out for these erratic movements.

Buoys obscured by yachts
In high summer, especially at weekends, all the channels between Terschelling and Harlingen are full of yachts, sailing barges and motor boats of every conceivable type, cruising about in all directions. You obviously need to keep a careful watch when passing through this *mêlée*, but one particular hazard is the risk of a critical channel buoy being obscured by a yacht or the large sail of a traditional barge.

Follow the Dutch chart 1811 carefully and do not jump to hasty conclusions just because an expected buoy does not immediately appear – it may be lurking behind someone's massive gaff mainsail. Carefully setting your own GPS waypoints to pick up particular channel buoys can be extremely useful, so long as you are using the latest version of chart 1811.

Strong tides in the Blauwe Slenk
The tidal streams run briskly through the Blauwe Slenk channel and the junction with the Vliestroom. Spring rates here can reach 2½–3 knots during the strongest part of the ebb, when even a moderate wind over the tide will kick up short steep seas in the wide southern reaches of the Vliestroom.

Pollendam training wall
In the final east approaches to Harlingen there is a long training wall, the Pollendam, which is normally left to the north, ie to port as you approach Harlingen from the direction of Terschelling. This training wall is well marked by red beacons and is not easy to miss, but you'll often see local boats sailing on the 'wrong' (north) side of it. This is perfectly feasible for strangers using the Dutch chart 1811.5 and the traffic is usually less congested on the north side of the Pollendam, but of course you have to make up your mind about your route at either end – there is no changing sides half-way along.

Cross-current off Harlingen pierheads
The tidal streams can be strong off Harlingen harbour entrance, especially during the third and fourth hours of the ebb, so watch out for cross-currents as you enter or leave Harlingen and do not cut the pierheads too close.

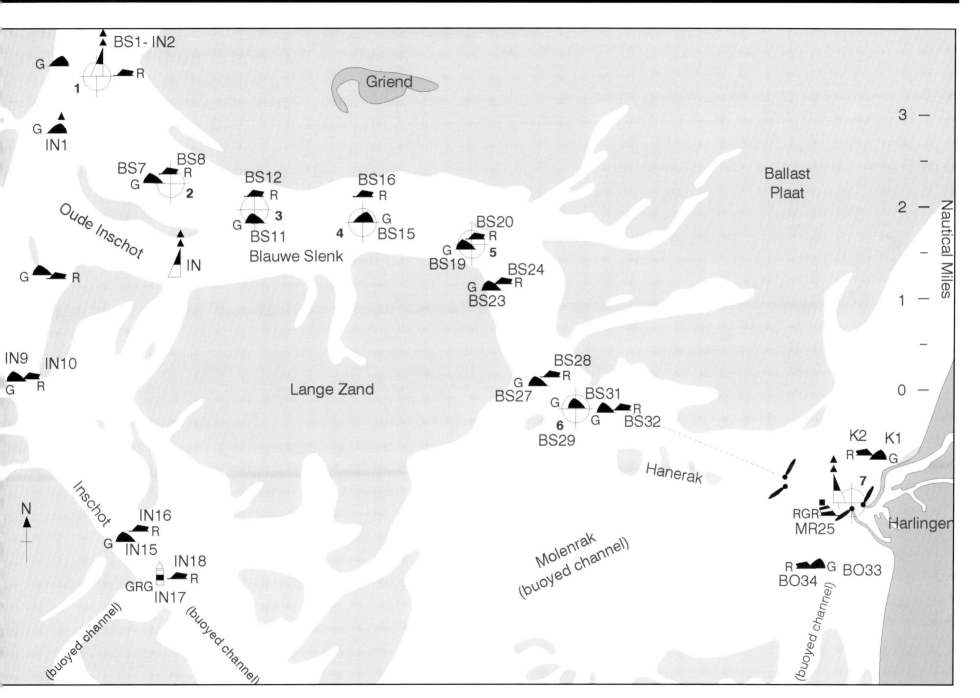

Griend

Ballast
Plaat

BS1- IN2

G   R

1

IN1
G

BS7   BS8
G   R

2

BS12
R

3

BS11
BS16
R

BS20
R

G

Blauwe Slenk

IN

G   R

IN9   IN10

G   R

Lange Zand

BS28
R

G

BS27   BS31
G   R

6

G   BS32
BS29

Oude Inschot

4

G   BS15

BS19   5

BS24
R

G

BS23

Hanerak

K2   K1
R   G

7

RGR
MR25

Harlingen

Inschot

N

IN16
R

G

IN15

IN18
R

GRG

IN17

Molenrak
(buoyed channel)

R   G   BO33

BO34

(buoyed channel)

(buoyed channel)

(buoyed channel)

Nautical Miles

3 —

—

2 —

—

1 —

—

0 —

WP No	Waypoint name and position	Latitude	Longitude
56–1	TG west clearing, ½ M NW of TG W-card buoy	53°24.59'N	05°01.80'E
56–2	Stolzenfels west clearing, ½ M NW of W-card buoy	53°26.58'N	05°09.17'E
56–3	VL9 green shipping lane buoy, actual position	53°28.15'N	05°03.96'E
56–4	TE1 green shipping lane buoy, actual position	53°30.00'N	05°13.60'E
56–5	TS north clearing, ½ M due N of TS N-card buoy	53°28.71'N	05°21.61'E
56–6	Ameland Westgat 'WA' fairway buoy, actual position	53°27.70'N	05°24.60'E
56–7	TE3 green shipping lane buoy, actual position	53°31.87'N	05°23.15'E
56–8	Bornrif north clearing, ½ M due N of 'BR' N-card buoy	53°31.20'N	05°33.60'E
56–9	Ameland N clearing, ½ M due N of 'AM' N-card buoy	53°31.50'N	05°44.80'E
56–10	TE5 green shipping lane buoy, actual position	53°33.70'N	05°32.66'E
56–11	TE7 green shipping lane buoy, actual position	53°35.57'N	05°42.25'E
56–12	TE9 green shipping lane buoy, actual position	53°37.41'N	05°51.80'E

Datum ED 50 The waypoint latitudes and longitudes in this table refer to European Datum (1950)

COASTAL DANGERS

Refer to Admiralty chart 2593 and Dutch charts 1811 and 1812

Stortemelk channel

This well-buoyed channel leads through the gap between the north-east end of Vlieland and the south-west end of Terschelling and is used regularly in the summer by large numbers of local craft. The outer 'Stortemelk' red-and-white fairway buoy lies 5 miles WNW from Oost Vlieland lighthouse and it is important to find and positively identify this buoy before proceeding any further inshore.

Terschelling Sands

A dangerous area of shoals extends 5 miles west from the south-west end of Terschelling island. Parts of these shoals dry and much of the area has less than 1 metre depth at LAT. In any fresh onshore weather, these sands are a seething mass of breakers and great care must be taken, particularly if coasting outside Terschelling, to stay well seaward of the cardinal buoys which guard these dangers – Terschellinger Gronden 'TG' west-cardinal buoy and Stolzenfels west-cardinal wreck buoy.

Offshore shipping lanes

The coastal shipping lanes lie 8–12 miles seaward of Terschelling and Ameland. Boats cruising the Frisian islands will normally stay inshore of these lanes during daylight, but care must be taken to keep clear of shipping in the lanes if you are either approaching this coast from seaward or passing it well offshore, perhaps at night.

Danger from onshore winds

Skippers of boats cruising fairly close inshore along the Frisian Islands should always keep a careful eye on the weather. Although in quiet summer conditions this is a fascinating and rewarding cruising area, the long low line of the Frisians, with their off-lying sandbanks and tricky *zeegat* entrances, are not to be trifled with in fresh onshore winds, when a building swell can soon make the *zeegats* dangerous to pass.

If strong onshore winds are forecast, make sure you are tucked up in a safe harbour before they arrive. Precarious though they sometimes look on the chart, most of the small yacht harbours on the inner shores of the Frisian Islands are quite snug in rough weather, so long as you reach them in good time.

Zeegat van Ameland

No waypoints are given for this rather tricky *zeegat*, where a shallow bar curves seawards between the east end of Terschelling and the west end of Ameland. Strangers should only approach Zeegat van Ameland in quiet weather without any swell. If you do go in, try to time your entrance for about 1½ hours before local HW.

The Westgat buoyed channel leads in from the west and it is important to pick up and positively identify 'WA' red-and-white fairway buoy before proceeding any further inshore. At the east end of the Westgat, near 'WA8' red buoy, you cross the inner part of the bar into the deeper water of Borndiep, which skirts the west end of Ameland. Once behind the island you can pick up the line of red buoys for the Molengat, a narrow channel which follows the south coast of Ameland towards the shallow harbour at Nes.

Nes harbour has less than 1 metre depth at low springs and is only suitable for boats that can sit on the bottom safely, but you'll find quite a snug deep-water anchorage just 1 mile west of Nes in the Brandgat. This is a very sheltered spot in north-westerlies and a good place to ride out a blow from that direction, provided you get there when things are still quiet.

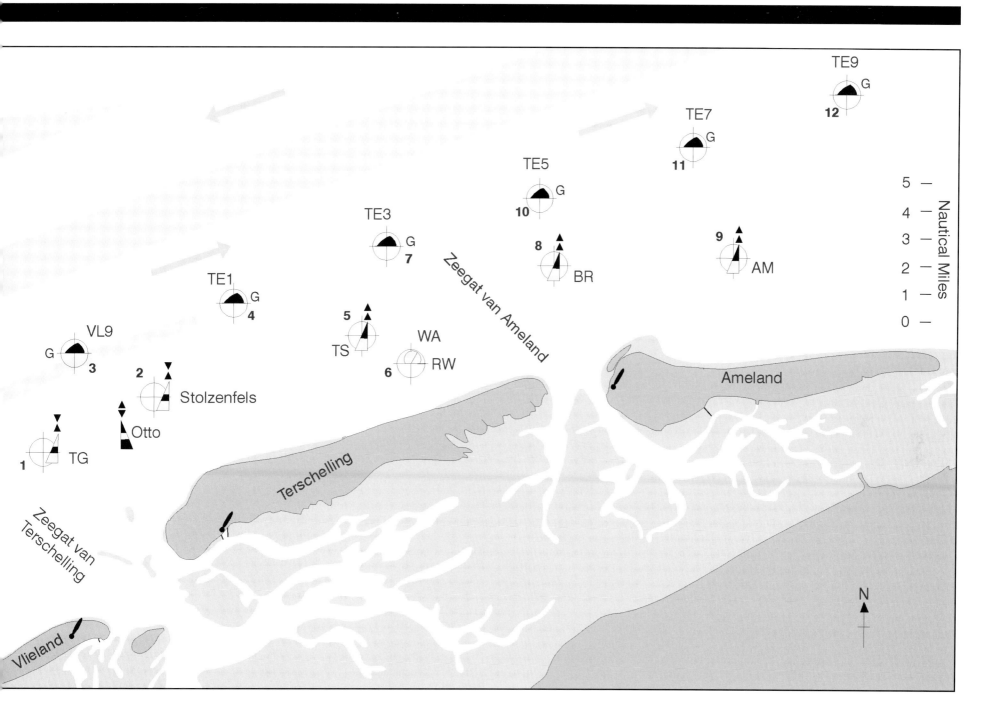

Ameland to Borkum

WP No	Waypoint name and position	Latitude	Longitude
57–1	TE11 green shipping lane buoy, actual position	53°39.25'N	06°01.40'E
57–2	Riffgat red-and-white fairway buoy, actual position	53°39.00'N	06°27.15'E
57–3	Westereems fairway buoys, actual position	53°36.97'N	06°19.48'E
57–4	Riffgat inner, 2 ca SW of Westereems No 10 red buoy	53°36.86'N	06°30.92'E
57–5	Borkum NW, 1 ca due N of Westereems No 11 green buoy	53°36.70'N	06°33.24'E
57–6	Borkum W, 1.3 M W of Borkum Kleiner lighthouse	53°34.77'N	06°37.90'E
57–7	Hubertgat fairway buoys, actual position	53°34.90'N	06°14.30'E
57–8	Huibertgat entrance, 12½ M W of Borkum Kleiner lighthouse	53°34.77'N	06°19.01'E
57–9	'WRG' (Wierumer Gronden) N-card buoy, actual position	53°32.90'N	06°03.32'E
57–10	'WG' fairway, 2.9 M 351°T from Schiermonnikoog lighthouse	53°32.14'N	06°08.20'E

Datum ED 50 The waypoint latitudes and longitudes in this table refer to European Datum (1950)

COASTAL DANGERS

Refer to Admiralty charts 2593 and 3509 and Dutch charts 1811 and 1812

Danger from onshore winds

Skippers of boats cruising fairly close inshore along the Frisian islands should always keep a careful eye on the weather. Although in quiet summer conditions this is a fascinating and rewarding cruising area, the long low line of the Frisians, with their off-lying sandbanks and tricky *zeegat* entrances, are not to be trifled with in fresh onshore winds, when a building swell can soon make the *zeegats* dangerous to pass.

If strong onshore winds are forecast, make sure you are tucked up in a safe harbour before they arrive. Precarious though they sometimes look on the chart, most of the small yacht harbours on the inner shores of the Frisian Islands are quite snug in rough weather, so long as you reach them in good time.

Zeegat van Ameland

No waypoints are given for this rather tricky *zeegat*, where a shallow bar curves seawards between the east end of Terschelling and the west end of Ameland. Strangers should only approach Zeegat van Ameland in quiet weather without any swell. If you do go in, try to time your entrance for about 1½ hours before local HW.

The Westgat buoyed channel leads in from the west and it is important to pick up and positively identify 'WA' red-and-white fairway buoy before proceeding further inshore. At the east end of the Westgat, near 'WA8' red buoy, you cross the inner part of the bar into the deeper water of Borndiep, which skirts the west end of Ameland. Once behind the island you can pick up the line of red buoys for the Molengat, a narrow channel which follows the south coast of Ameland towards the shallow harbour at Nes.

Nes harbour has less than 1 metre depth at low springs and is only suitable for boats that can sit on the bottom safely, but you'll find quite a snug

deep-water anchorage just 1 mile west of Nes in the Brandgat. This is a very sheltered spot in north-westerlies and a good place to ride out a blow from that direction, provided you get in there when things are still quiet.

Offshore shipping lanes

The coastal shipping lanes lie 8–12 miles seaward of Terschelling and Ameland. Boats cruising the Frisian Islands will normally stay inshore of these lanes during daylight, but care must be taken to keep clear of shipping in the lanes if you are either approaching this coast from seaward or passing it well offshore, perhaps at night.

Shoals north of Borkum

The seaward approaches to the Eems estuary are fringed by several wide shoals which extend up to 5 miles north and north-west of Borkum. Particular care is needed if approaching Borkum and the Eems from the east, when you have to keep safely seaward of these shoals until the way is clear to drop south into the Westereems, normally in the vicinity of the Riffgat buoys. For these outer approaches, it is important to follow the latest version of the Dutch Hydrografische Kaart No 1812.

Strong tides in the Eems estuary

Tidal streams can be strong in the Eems estuary, so it is important to time your arrival or departure accordingly. Rates in the Randzelgat, just west of Borkum, can reach 3 knots at springs, so a wind over tide soon kicks up nasty steep seas, especially in the reaches below Eemshaven. Perhaps the most unpleasant mix is a brisk north-westerly over a strong ebb, so try to avoid this situation if possible.

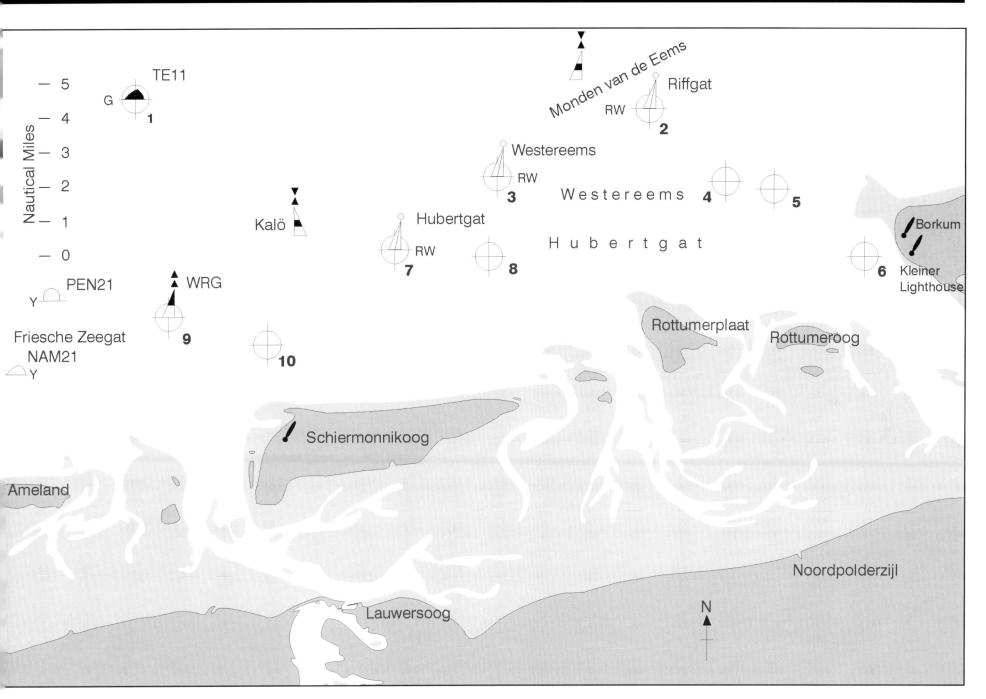

Nautical Miles

— 5
— 4
— 3
— 2
— 1
— 0

TE11

G **1**

Monden van de Eems

Riffgat

RW **2**

Westereems

RW **3**

W e s t e r e e m s **4** **5**

Kalö

Hubertgat

RW **7**

H u b e r t g a t

8

Borkum

6 Kleiner Lighthouse

PEN21

Y

WRG

9

10

Rottumerplaat

Rottumeroog

Friesche Zeegat

NAM21

Y

Schiermonnikoog

Ameland

Noordpolderzijl

Lauwersoog

N

Outer approaches to Schiermonnikoog and Lauwersoog

WP No	Waypoint name and position	Latitude	Longitude
58–1	'WRG' (Wierumer Gronden) N-card buoy, actual position	53°32.90'N	06°03.32'E
58–2	'WG' fairway, 2.9 M 351°T from Schiermonnikoog lighthouse	53°32.14'N	06°08.20'E
58–3	Westgat inner, 2.1 M due W from Schiermonnikoog lighthouse	53°29.25'N	06°05.27'E
58–4	Engelsmanplaat NE, 9 ca 037°T from north point beacon	53°28.16'N	06°04.47'E
58–5	Engelsmanplaat east, 4½ ca due E from north point beacon	53°27.43'N	06°04.30'E
58–6	Hubertgat fairway buoys, actual position	53°34.90'N	06°14.30'E
58–7	Huibertgat entrance, 12½ M W of Borkum Kleiner lighthouse	53°34.77'N	06°19.01'E

Datum ED 50 The waypoint latitudes and longitudes in this table refer to European Datum (1950)

COASTAL DANGERS
Refer to Admiralty chart 2593 and Dutch charts 1812.3 and 1812.8

Entrance to Plaatgat
Although the *zeegat* entrance channels between Ameland and Schiermonnikoog are shallow and prone to shifting, they provide a well-trodden route for boats entering or leaving the Dutch canal system at Lauwersoog. Just inside the entrance to Lauwersoog harbour, a sea-lock leads into the Lauwersmeer, from where you can join the fascinating canals that run right along the Dutch Friesland coast between Delfzijl, on the River Eems, and Harlingen on the Waddenzee. The Plaatgat channel is most commonly used by boats on passage between Lauwersoog and Norderney, the first substantial yacht harbour (after Borkum) along the German Frisian islands.

Approaching the Plaatgat, normally from the east, you must first find and positively identify 'WG' red-and-white fairway buoy, which lies about 3 miles just west of north from the tall lighthouse on the west end of Schiermonnikoog. From 'WG' fairway buoy steer SSW to pick up the first pair of red and green buoys, and then it is a simple matter to follow the channel past the west end of Schiermonnikoog and just east of the low, rather eerie looking island known as Engelsmanplaat. From here the Zoutkamperlaag turns ESE towards Lauwersoog harbour, which is easy to enter at any time. If arriving late, boats can moor in the outer harbour overnight, before clearing Customs next day and then passing through the lock into the Lauwersmeer.

Sea conditions in the Plaatgat
The shallowest part of the Plaatgat is between the first and fourth pairs of reds and greens, where depths range from about 3½–4½ metres at low springs. Close to the west, as you come through this shallow section, is the shallowest part of the bar, with less than ½ metre over it at low springs. The sea breaks heavily over this area in fresh onshore winds or during a heavy residual north-westerly swell. To the east are the drying sands that extend 1 mile out from the west end of Schiermonnikoog.

Careful judgement must be exercised about whether conditions are quiet enough for approaching the Plaatgat channel. Coming along the coast from the west, you have to pass the entrance any way and can form a pretty accurate impression of the likely sea state over the bar. If things look too boisterous, you can always press on to Borkum. Coming from the east, however, you need to make a decision about the Plaatgat before passing the Riffgat and the relatively straightforward bolt-hole approach to Borkum.

Entry at night
Although the 'WG' fairway and alternate pairs of red and green buoys are lit, it is generally not a good idea to approach the Plaatgat entrance channel at night, unless you are certain of your position offshore and conditions are quiet. The approaches to Borkum, on the other hand, are relatively safe and straightforward at night.

The west entrance
A narrow entrance leads in from the west, cutting just south of the outer bar and just north of another wide shoal with only ½ metre over it at low springs. This entrance is marked by yellow buoys, which are moved quite frequently to take account of changes in the channel. Keep very close south of these yellow buoys, which are unlit. The west entrance is only suitable in calm conditions when you are certain of your position off the east end of Ameland. If in doubt, pass well outside the bar, make for the 'WG' fairway buoy and enter by the Plaatgat, as above.

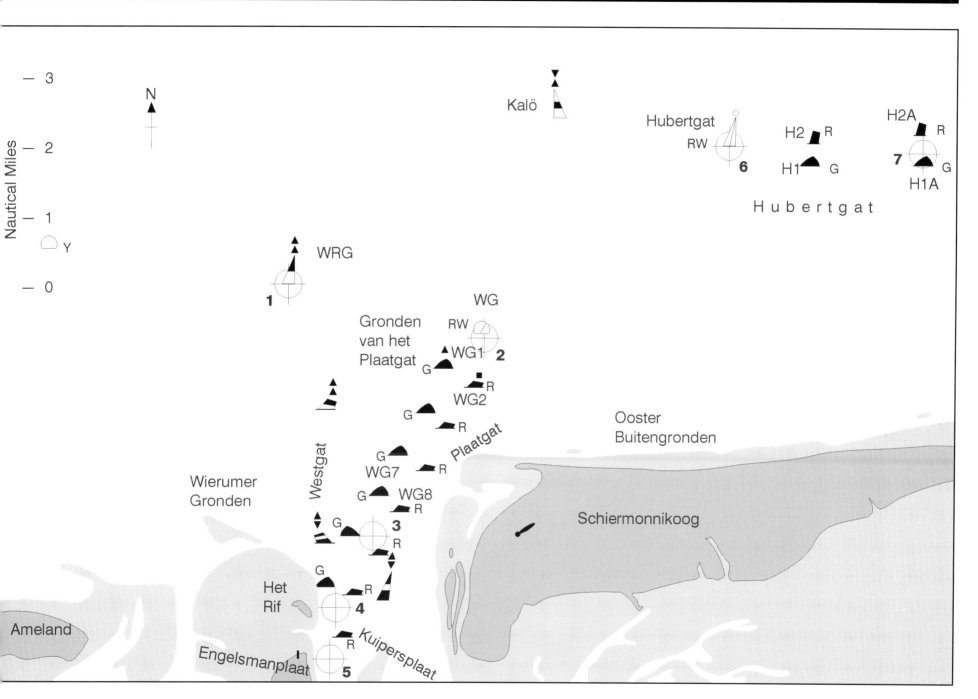

Nautical Miles

3

N

2

1

Y

0

Kalö

Hubertgat
RW
6

H2 R

H1 G

H2A R

7

H1A G

Hubertgat

WRG

1

WG
RW
2

Gronden
van het
Plaatgat

WG1
G

WG2
R

G

R

G
WG7
R

Plaatgat

Ooster
Buitengronden

Westgat

Wierumer
Gronden

G WG8
R

G

3

R

G

R

Het
Rif

G

R 4

Schiermonnikoog

Ameland

R 5
Engelsmanplaat

Kuipersplaat

WP No	Waypoint name and position	Latitude	Longitude
59–1	Engelsmanplaat NE, 9 ca 037°T from north point beacon	53°28.16'N	06°04.47'E
59–2	Engelsmanplaat east, 4½ ca due E from north point beacon	53°27.43'N	06°04.30'E
59–3	Zoutkamperlaag NW, 3.48 M 219°T from Schiermonnikoog L/H	53°26.55'N	06°05.20'E
59–4	Zoutkamperlaag SE, 3.41M 178°T from Schiermonnikoog L/H	53°25.83'N	06°09.04'E
59–5	Lauwersoog N approach, 2.7 ca N of Lauwersoog W pierhead	53°25.00'N	06°12.07'E
59–6	Lauwersoog entrance, midway between outer pierhead lights	53°24.72'N	06°12.10'E

Datum ED 50 The waypoint latitudes and longitudes in this table refer to European Datum (1950)

COASTAL DANGERS
Refer to Dutch chart 1812.3

Entrance to Plaatgat
Although the *zeegat* entrance channels between Ameland and Schiermonnikoog are shallow and prone to shifting, they provide a well-trodden route for boats entering or leaving the Dutch canal system at Lauwersoog. Just inside the entrance to Lauwersoog harbour, a sea-lock leads into the Lauwersmeer, from where you can join the fascinating canals that run right along the Dutch Friesland coast between Delfzijl, on the River Eems, and Harlingen on the Waddenzee. The Plaatgat channel is most commonly used by boats on passage between Lauwersoog and Norderney, the first substantial yacht harbour (after Borkum) along the German Frisian Islands.

Approaching the Plaatgat, normally from the east, you must first find and positively identify 'WG' red-and-white fairway buoy, which lies about 3 miles just west of north from the tall lighthouse on the west end of Schiermonnikoog. From 'WG' fairway buoy steer SSW to pick up the first pair of red and green buoys, and then it is a simple matter to follow the channel past the west end of Schiermonnikoog and just east of the low, rather eerie looking island known as Engelsmanplaat. From here the Zoutkamperlaag turns ESE towards Lauwersoog harbour, which is easy to enter at any time. If arriving late, boats can moor in the outer harbour overnight, before clearing Customs next day and then passing through the lock into the Lauwersmeer.

Sea conditions in the Plaatgat
The shallowest part of the Plaatgat is between the first and fourth pairs of reds and greens, where depths range from about 3½–4½ metres at low springs. Close to the west, as you come through this shallow section, is the shallowest part of the bar, with less than ½ metre over it at low springs. The sea breaks heavily over this area in fresh onshore winds or during a heavy residual northwesterly swell. To the east are the drying sands that extend 1 mile out from the west end of Schiermonnikoog.

Careful judgement must be exercised about whether conditions are quiet enough for approaching the Plaatgat channel. Coming along the coast from the west, you have to pass the entrance any way and can form a pretty accurate impression of the likely sea state over the bar. If things look too boisterous, you can always press on to Borkum. Coming from the east, however, you need to make a decision about the Plaatgat before passing the Riffgat and the relatively straightforward bolt-hole approach to Borkum.

Entry at night
Although the 'WG' fairway and alternate pairs of red and green buoys are lit, it is generally not a good idea to approach the Plaatgat entrance channel at night, unless you are certain of your position offshore and conditions are quiet. The approaches to Borkum, on the other hand, are relatively safe and straightforward at night.

The west entrance
A narrow entrance leads in from the west, cutting just south of the outer bar and just north of another wide shoal with only ½ metre over it at low springs. This entrance is marked by yellow buoys, which are moved quite frequently to take account of changes in the channel. Keep very close south of these yellow buoys, which are unlit. The west entrance is only suitable in calm conditions when you are certain of your position off the east end of Ameland. If in doubt, pass well outside the bar, make for the 'WG' fairway buoy and enter by the Plaatgat, as above.

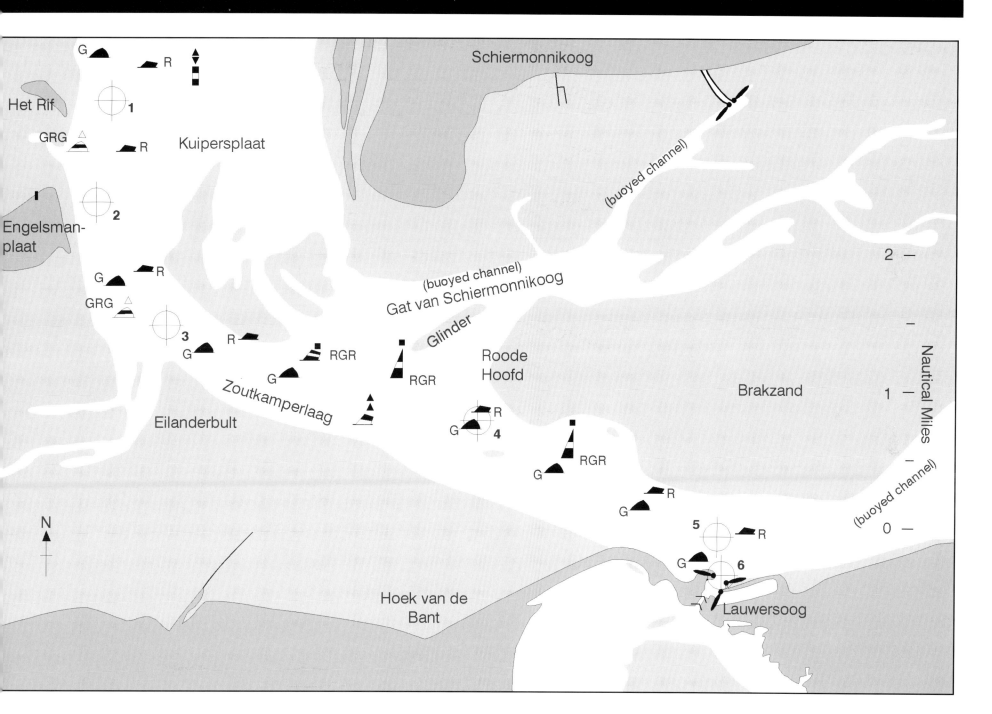

Het Rif

G ◢ R ▱ ⬦

GRG △ R ▱

⊕ 1

Engelsman-plaat

⊕ 2

Kuipersplaat

Schiermonnikoog

(buoyed channel)

G ◣ R ▱

GRG △

⊕ 3 R ▱

G ◣

Zoutkamperlaag

G ◣ RGR

RGR

(buoyed channel)
Gat van Schiermonnikoog

Glinder

Roode
Hoofd

Brakzand

Eilanderbult

▲

G ◣ ⊕ R ▱
      4

G ◣ RGR

G ◣ R ▱

5 ⊕ R ▱

G ◣ ⊕ 6

Hoek van de
Bant

Lauwersoog

N

2 —

1 —

0 —

Nautical Miles

(buoyed channel)

West approaches to Borkum

WP No	Waypoint name and position	Latitude	Longitude
60–1	Riffgat red-and-white fairway buoy, actual position	53°39.00'N	06°27.15'E
60–2	Westereems fairway buoys, actual position	53°36.97'N	06°19.48'E
60–3	Riffgat inner, 2 ca SW of Westereems No 10 red buoy	53°36.86'N	06°30.92'E
60–4	Borkum NW, 1 ca due N of Westereems No 11 green buoy	53°36.70'N	06°33.24'E
60–5	Borkum W, 1.3 M W of Borkum Kleiner lighthouse	53°34.77'N	06°37.90'E
60–6	Huibertgat entrance, 12½ M W of Borkum Kleiner lighthouse	53°34.77'N	06°19.01'E
60–7	Huibertgat middle, 8 M W of Borkum Kleiner lighthouse	53°34.77'N	06°26.61'E
60–8	Huibertgat inner, 3.9 M W of Borkum Kleiner lighthouse	53°34.77'N	06°33.50'E
60–9	Horsborn Plaat, 2.31 M 254°T from Borkum Kleiner lighthouse	53°34.13'N	06°36.34'E

Datum ED 50 The waypoint latitudes and longitudes in this table refer to European Datum (1950)

COASTAL DANGERS
Refer to Admiralty chart 3509 and Dutch chart 1812

Danger from onshore winds
Skippers of boats cruising fairly close inshore along the Frisian Islands should always keep a careful eye on the weather. Although in quiet summer conditions this is a fascinating and rewarding cruising area, the long low line of the Frisians, with their off-lying sandbanks and tricky entrances, are not to be trifled with in fresh onshore winds, when a building swell can soon make the *zeegats* dangerous to pass.

The Eems is a wide deep estuary, used by large ships and well buoyed, but the entrance and lower reaches can still be unpleasant in strong winds from anywhere between west through north to about north-east, especially when the tide is weather-going. If strong onshore winds are forecast when you are cruising this coast, try to make sure you are tucked up in a safe harbour before they arrive.

Shipping in the approaches to the Eems
Large ships go in and out of the Eems at all hours and in practically any weather, so keep well clear of them in the buoyed channels. Wherever possible, in the open reaches of the estuary, try to keep just the 'wrong' side of channel buoys to leave the fairways clear for shipping.

Shoals north of Borkum
The seaward approaches to the Eems estuary are fringed by several wide shoals that extend up to 5 miles north and north-west of Borkum. Particular care is needed if approaching Borkum and the Eems from the east, when you have to keep safely seaward of these shoals until the way is clear to drop south into the Westereems, normally near the Riffgat buoys. For these outer approaches, it is important to follow the latest version of the Dutch Hydrografische Kaart No 1812.

Ballonplate
This long, mid-channel shoal separates the wide buoyed entrance of the Westereems and the narrower buoyed channel known as Huibertgat. The Westereems lies north of the Ballonplate and Huibertgat lies to the south. The least depth over Ballonplate is generally 2½–3 metres, but there is a shallower area, ¾ mile long, at its south-east end. This shallower area, known as Hubertplate, has a least depth of only 0.3 metres very close to the north edge of the Huibertgat channel, near H12 red buoy.

Strong tides in the Eems estuary
Tidal streams can be strong in the Eems estuary, so it is important to time your arrival or departure accordingly. Rates in the Randzelgat, just west of Borkum, can reach 3 knots at springs, so a wind over tide soon kicks up nasty steep seas, especially in the reaches below Eemshaven. Perhaps the most unpleasant mix is a brisk north-westerly over a strong ebb, so try to avoid this situation if possible.

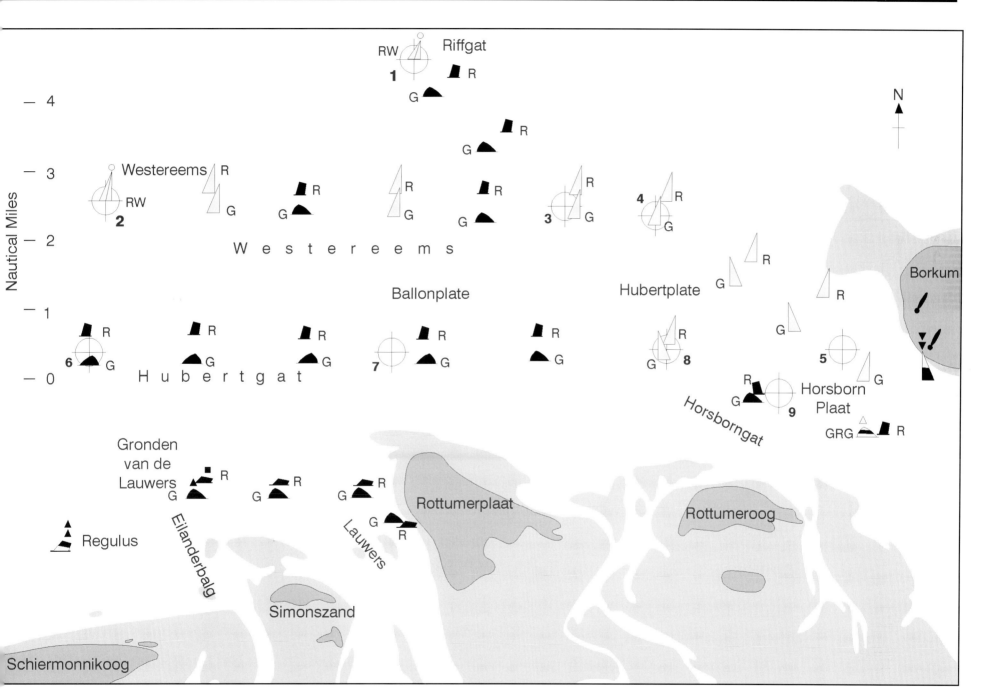

Outer approaches to Borkum and the Eems

WP No	Waypoint name and position	Latitude	Longitude
61–1	Borkumriff offshore fairway buoy, actual position	53°47.50'N	06°22.15'E
61–2	TE13 green shipping lane buoy, actual position	53°41.13'N	06°11.15'E
61–3	TG1/Ems green shipping lane buoy, actual position	53°43.41'N	06°22.38'E
61–4	TG3 green shipping lane buoy, actual position	53°44.68'N	06°31.22'E
61–5	TG5 green shipping lane buoy, actual position	53°45.92'N	06°40.04'E
61–6	TG7 green shipping lane buoy, actual position	53°47.33'N	06°49.78'E
61–7	Hubertgat fairway buoys, actual position	53°34.90'N	06°14.30'E
61–8	Huibertgat entrance, 12½ M W of Borkum Kleiner lighthouse	53°34.77'N	06°19.01'E
61–9	Westereems fairway buoys, actual position	53°36.97'N	06°19.48'E
61–10	Riffgat red-and-white fairway buoy, actual position	53°39.00'N	06°27.15'E
61–11	Riffgat inner, 2 ca SW of Westereems No 10 red buoy	53°36.86'N	06°30.92'E
61–12	Borkum NW, 1 ca due N of Westereems No 11 green buoy	53°36.70'N	06°33.24'E
61–13	Borkum W, 1.3 M W of Borkum Kleiner lighthouse	53°34.77'N	06°37.90'E
61–14	Osterems fairway buoy, actual position	53°41.92'N	06°36.20'E
61–15	Juisterriff N-card buoy, actual position	53°42.90'N	06°45.80'E
61–16	Juist N-card buoy, actual position	53°43.90'N	06°55.50'E

COASTAL DANGERS
Refer to Admiralty charts 3509 and 3761 and Dutch chart 1812

Danger from onshore winds
The Eems is a wide deep estuary, used by large ships and well buoyed, but the entrance and lower reaches can still be unpleasant in strong winds from anywhere between west through north to about north-east, especially when the tide is weather-going. If strong onshore winds are forecast when you are cruising this coast, try to make sure you are tucked up in a safe harbour before they arrive.

Strong tides in the Eems estuary
Tidal streams can be strong in the Eems estuary, so it is important to time your arrival or departure accordingly. Rates in the Randzelgat, just west of Borkum, can reach 3 knots at springs, so a wind over tide soon kicks up nasty steep seas, especially in the more exposed reaches below Eemshaven. Perhaps the most unpleasant mix is a brisk north-westerly over a strong ebb, so try to avoid this situation if possible.

Shipping in the approaches to the Eems
The coastal shipping lanes run ENE–WSW from between 10 and 15 miles off Borkum, marked on their south side by a line of green buoys. Boats cruising along this coast will normally stay inshore of these lanes during daylight, but care must be taken to keep clear of shipping in the lanes if you are either approaching Borkum and the Eems

from seaward or passing well offshore, perhaps at night.

Large ships go in and out of the Eems at all hours and in practically any weather, so keep well clear of all commercial traffic in the buoyed channels. Wherever possible, in the deep open reaches of the estuary, try to keep just the 'wrong' side of channel buoys to leave the fairways clear for shipping.

Shoals north of Borkum
The seaward approaches to the Eems are fringed by several wide shoals that extend up to 5 miles north and north-west of Borkum. Particular care is needed if approaching Borkum and the Eems from the east, when you have to keep safely seaward of these shoals until the way is clear to drop south into the Westereems, usually near the Riffgat buoys. For these outer approaches, it is important to follow the latest version of the Dutch Hydrografische Kaart No 1812.

Outer shoals west of Juist and Memmert
A broad expanse of sandy shoals, most of it drying, some mostly above-water, stretches up to 4 miles west of Juist and Memmert islands, forming the east edge of the narrow buoyed entrance of the Oostereems – now spelt 'Osterems' since we have moved into German waters. The above-water part of these shoals is the low flat dune known as Katchelot Plate, which seems barely out of reach of the sea at HW.

The Osterems route into the extensive shoal waters behind the German Frisian Islands is not much used by boats, except sometimes by those making for the small drying harbour on the south side of Juist. This shallow entrance is uneasy in any onshore swell and dangerous in heavy weather, when the sea breaks malevolently over

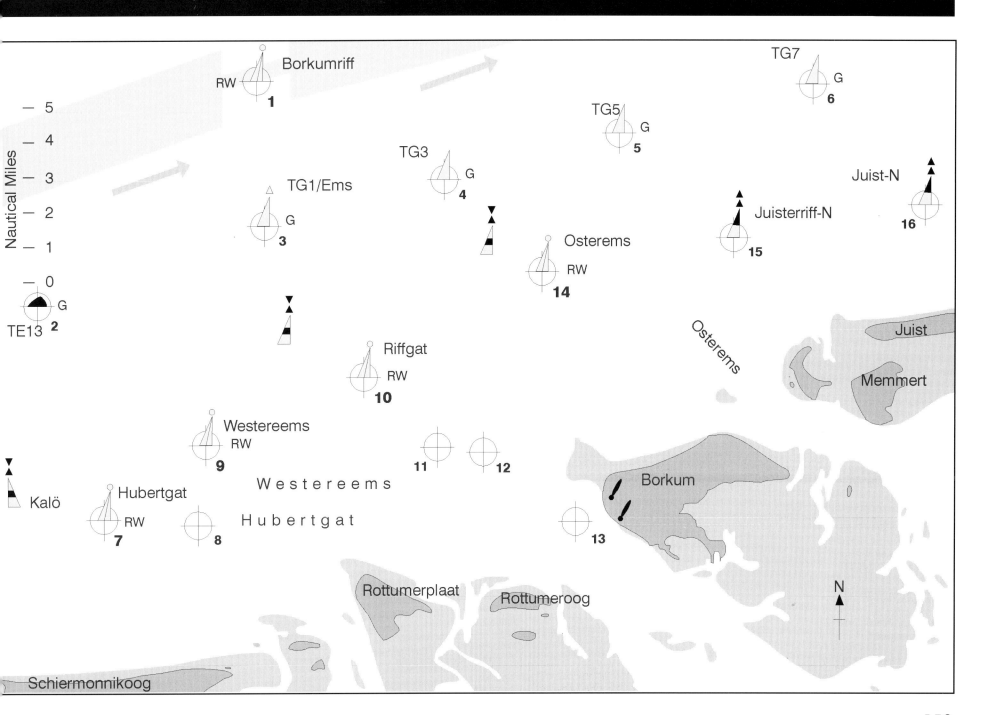

Borkumriff

RW

1

TG7

G

6

TG5

G

5

TG3

G

4

Juist-N

16

Juisterriff-N

15

TG1/Ems

G

3

Osterems

RW

14

TE13 2

G

Osterems

Juist

Memmert

Riffgat

RW

10

Westereems

RW

9

W e s t e r e e m s

11   12

Borkum

Kalö

Hubertgat

RW

7   8

H u b e r t g a t

13

Rottumerplaat

Rottumeroog

N

Schiermonnikoog

Nautical Miles

— 5

— 4

— 3

— 2

— 1

— 0

WP No	Waypoint name and position	Latitude	Longitude
61–1	Borkumriff offshore fairway buoy, actual position	53°47.50'N	06°22.15'E
61–2	TE13 green shipping lane buoy, actual position	53°41.13'N	06°11.15'E
61–3	TG1/Ems green shipping lane buoy, actual position	53°43.41'N	06°22.38'E
61–4	TG3 green shipping lane buoy, actual position	53°44.68'N	06°31.22'E
61–5	TG5 green shipping lane buoy, actual position	53°45.92'N	06°40.04'E
61–6	TG7 green shipping lane buoy, actual position	53°47.33'N	06°49.78'E
61–7	Hubertgat fairway buoys, actual position	53°34.90'N	06°14.30'E
61–8	Huibertgat entrance, 12½ M W of Borkum Kleiner lighthouse	53°34.77'N	06°19.01'E
61–9	Westereems fairway buoys, actual position	53°36.97'N	06°19.48'E
61–10	Riffgat red-and-white fairway buoy, actual position	53°39.00'N	06°27.15'E
61–11	Riffgat inner, 2 ca SW of Westereems No 10 red buoy	53°36.86'N	06°30.92'E
61–12	Borkum NW, 1 ca due N of Westereems No 11 green buoy	53°36.70'N	06°33.24'E
61–13	Borkum W, 1.3 M W of Borkum Kleiner lighthouse	53°34.77'N	06°37.90'E
61–14	Osterems fairway buoy, actual position	53°41.92'N	06°36.20'E
61–15	Juisterriff N-card buoy, actual position	53°42.90'N	06°45.80'E
61–16	Juist N-card buoy, actual position	53°43.90'N	06°55.50'E

Datum ED 50 The waypoint latitudes and longitudes in this table refer to European Datum (1950)

the banks on each side of the tenuous channel.
The key outer marks are the two Osterems red-
and-white fairway buoys, which lie about 7½ miles
NNW of the Borkum Kleiner lighthouse. From
this pair of buoys, the reds and greens marking
the Osterems channel trend ESE and then SE to
pass about 1½ miles west of Katchelot Plate.

When cruising seaward of Borkum and Juist,
these outer shoals are avoided by keeping north of
the Osterems fairway buoys and Juisterriff north-
cardinal buoy.

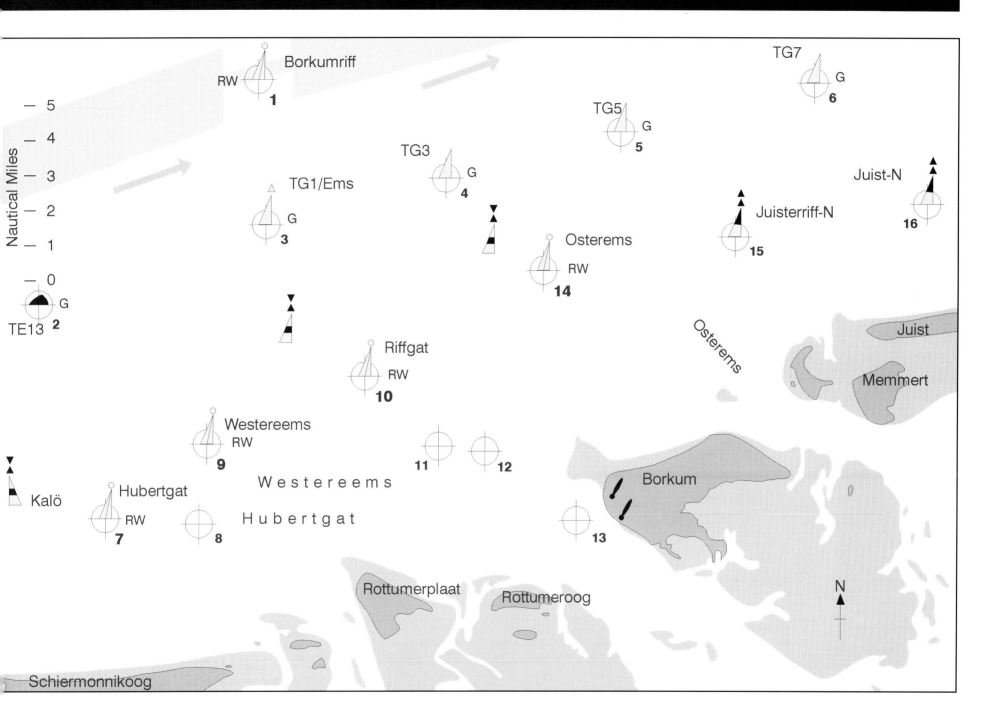

Borkumriff
RW
1

TG7
G
6

TG5
G
5

TG3
G
4

TG1/Ems
G
3

Juist-N
16

Juisterriff-N
15

Nautical Miles
— 5
— 4
— 3
— 2
— 1
— 0

Osterems
RW
14

G
TE13 **2**

Osterems

Juist

Memmert

Riffgat
RW
10

Westereems
RW
9

W e s t e r e e m s

Borkum

Kalö

Hubertgat

H u b e r t g a t

RW
7

8

11

12

13

N

Rottumerplaat

Rottumeroog

Schiermonnikoog

WP No	Waypoint name and position	Latitude	Longitude
62–1	Borkum W, 1.3 M W of Borkum Kleiner lighthouse	53°34.77'N	06°37.90'E
62–2	Horsborn Plaat, 2.31 M 254°T from Borkum Kleiner lighthouse	53°34.13'N	06°36.34'E
62–3	Huibertgat SE, 1.54 M 217°T from Borkum Kleiner lighthouse	53°33.53'N	06°38.58'E
62–4	Borkum south, 1.59 M 156°T from Borkum Kleiner lighthouse	53°33.32'N	06°41.17'E
62–5	Borkum harbour approach, 3½ ca SW of Leitdamm pierhead Lt	53°32.98'N	06°42.56'E
62–6	Borkum SE, 4.12 M 138°T from Borkum Kleiner lighthouse	53°31.69'N	06°44.75'E

Datum ED 50 The waypoint latitudes and longitudes in this table refer to European Datum (1950)

Tankers anchored downstream from Eemshaven

There is a designated tanker anchorage just south of Meeuwen Staart shoal and just north of the red channel buoys of the Oude Westereems. Keep clear of anchored ships and their cables if you are using this route, especially when the tide is strong. The powerful deck-lights of anchored tankers can be confusing at night, when it is best to use the main Westereems channel and follow the buoys carefully.

COASTAL DANGERS

Refer to Admiralty chart 3509 and Dutch chart 1812.5

Hoog Rif

A long shoal area, much of it drying, extends north-westwards from the north-west corner of Borkum for a good 2 miles. These flats are guarded by No 14 and No 16 red buoys of the Westereems channel, but care must be taken on a strong flood tide to avoid being set too close. Hoog Rif is part of a designated nature reserve and anchoring in the vicinity is prohibited between 1 May and 1 October.

Meeuwen Staart

This long, partly drying shoal lies NW–SE in mid-estuary south of Borkum, separating the main Westereems channel from the Oude Westereems. The shallowest part of Meeuwen Staart is 3½ miles long, with patches drying up to ½ metre and much of the shoal with less than ½ metre depth at low springs. Particular care must be taken at night to make sure you are following the correct buoys on their right side.

Strong onshore winds

The Eems is a wide deep estuary, used by large ships and well buoyed, but the entrance and lower reaches can still be unpleasant in strong winds from anywhere between west through north to about north-east, especially when the tide is weather-going.

Strong tides in the Eems estuary

Tidal streams can be strong in the Eems estuary, so it is important to time your arrival or departure accordingly. Rates in the Randzelgat, just west of Borkum, can reach 3 knots at springs, so a wind over tide soon kicks up nasty steep seas, especially in the more exposed reaches below Eemshaven. Perhaps the most unpleasant mix is a brisk north-westerly over a strong ebb, so try to avoid this situation if possible.

Shipping in the Eems estuary

Large ships go in and out of the Eems at all hours and in practically any weather, so keep well clear of all commercial traffic in the buoyed channels. Wherever possible, in the deep open reaches of the estuary, try to keep just the 'wrong' side of channel buoys to leave the fairways clear for shipping.

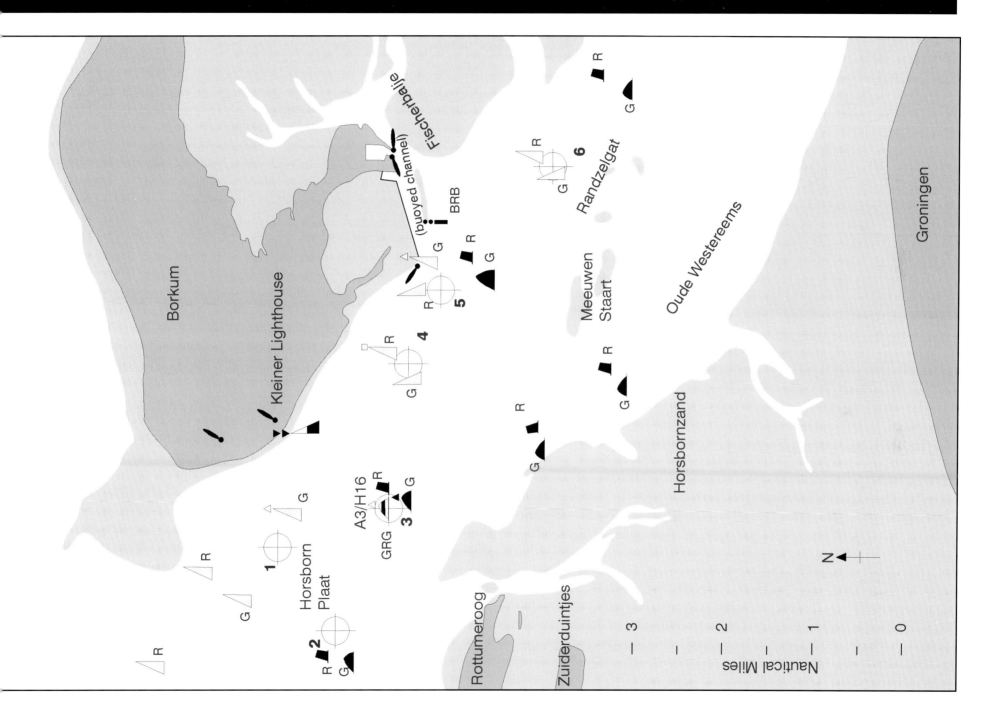

Borkum

Kleiner Lighthouse

Fischerbalje

(buoyed channel)

BRB

R

G

R

G

R

G

Meeuwen
Staart

Randzelgat

6

R

G

R

5

R

G

R

G

4

R

G

Oude Westereems

Horsbornzand

A3/H16

GRG

3

R

G

Horsborn
Plaat

1

R

G

R

2

R

G

Rottumeroog

Zuiderduintjes

Groningen

N

Nautical Miles

0

1

2

3

▪ Borkum to Eemshaven ▪

WP No	Waypoint name and position	Latitude	Longitude
63–1	Borkum south, 1.59 M 156°T from Borkum Kleiner lighthouse	53°33.32'N	06°41.17'E
63–2	Borkum harbour approach, 3½ ca SW of Leitdamm pierhead light	53°32.98'N	06°42.56'E
63–3	Borkum SE, 4.12 M 138°T from Borkum Kleiner lighthouse	53°31.69'N	06°44.75'E
63–4	Randzelgat SE, midway No 26 red buoy and No 27 green buoy	53°30.38'N	06°47.76'E
63–5	Eemshaven north, 1.12 M due N of Eemshaven W pierhead light	53°28.90'N	06°50.15'E
63–6	Doekegat, 0.95 M due E of Eemshaven W pierhead light	53°27.78'N	06°51.74'E
63–7	Oude Westereems NW, midway A6 red and A9 green buoys	53°30.99'N	06°41.00'E
63–8	Oude Westereems, midway A10 red and A11 green buoys	53°30.00'N	06°44.24'E
63–9	Oude Westereems SE, 1 ca SW of A16 red buoy	53°28.84'N	06°48.42'E

Datum ED 50 The waypoint latitudes and longitudes in this table refer to European Datum (1950)

COASTAL DANGERS
Refer to Admiralty chart 3509 and Dutch chart 1812.5

Meeuwen Staart
This long, partly drying shoal lies NW–SE in mid-estuary south of Borkum, separating the main Westereems channel from the Oude Westereems. The shallowest part of Meeuwen Staart is 3½ miles long, with patches drying up to ½ metre and much of the shoal with less than ½ metre depth at low springs. Particular care must be taken at night to make sure you are following the correct buoys on their right side.

Randzel sands
A vast expanse of drying sand and shallow channels extends south-east from Borkum to about 5 times the size of the island. Most of the eastern part of Randzel is designated a nature reserve, where it is forbidden to anchor off or land on the sands between 1 April and 1 October.

The south-west edge of Randzel is guarded by the red buoys of the Westereems channel, but the eastern fringes are more sparsely marked by the smaller buoys of the shallow Osterems.

Eemshorn Plaat
This roughly triangular mile-long shoal lies in the junction between the main Westereems channel and the much shallower Osterems, drying to about ½ metre at low springs. Half a mile south-west of Eemshorn Plaat is a longer, much narrower shoal known as Dukegat Plate, marked on each side by yellow buoys. Much of Dukegat Plate has less than 1 metre depth at low springs and a small patch near the north-west tip just dries.

Shoals through the Osterems
The shallow Osterems channel, which leads just east of Randzel between the Westereems and Memmert island, is well used by boats cruising between Delfzijl and Norderney inside Juist. Both the Osterems and the channels inside Juist should be negotiated on a rising tide, which is straightforward if you are sailing from Norderney towards Delfzijl, but more difficult to time from Delfzijl towards Norderney. In the latter case, the normal strategy is to leave Delfzijl harbour on the last of the ebb, so that the flood is well under way by the time you get down to Osterems No 42 red buoy, where the Osterems channel branches to starboard east of Randzel.

There are numerous patchy shoals through the Osterems as you pass the east fringes of Randzel, many of which dry at low springs in the north part of the buoyed channel. Carefully follow the latest version of Dutch chart 1812.5, travel slowly through the shallowest parts and watch the echo-sounder all the time.

Strong tides in the Eems estuary
Tidal streams can be strong in the Eems estuary, so it is important to time your arrival or departure accordingly. Rates in the Randzelgat, just west of Borkum, can reach 3 knots at springs, so a wind over tide soon kicks up nasty steep seas, especially in the more exposed reaches below Eemshaven. Perhaps the most unpleasant mix is a brisk north-westerly over a strong ebb, so try to avoid this situation if possible.

Shipping in the Eems estuary
Large ships go in and out of the Eems at all hours and in practically any weather, so keep well clear of all commercial traffic in the buoyed channels. Wherever possible, in the deep open reaches of the estuary, try to keep just the 'wrong' side of channel buoys to leave the fairways clear for shipping.

Tankers anchored downstream from Eemshaven
There is a designated tanker anchorage just south of Meeuwen Staart shoal and just north of the red channel buoys of the Oude Westereems. Keep clear of anchored ships and their cables, especially when the tide is strong. The powerful deck-lights of anchored tankers can be confusing at night, when it is best to use the main Westereems channel and follow the buoys carefully.

158

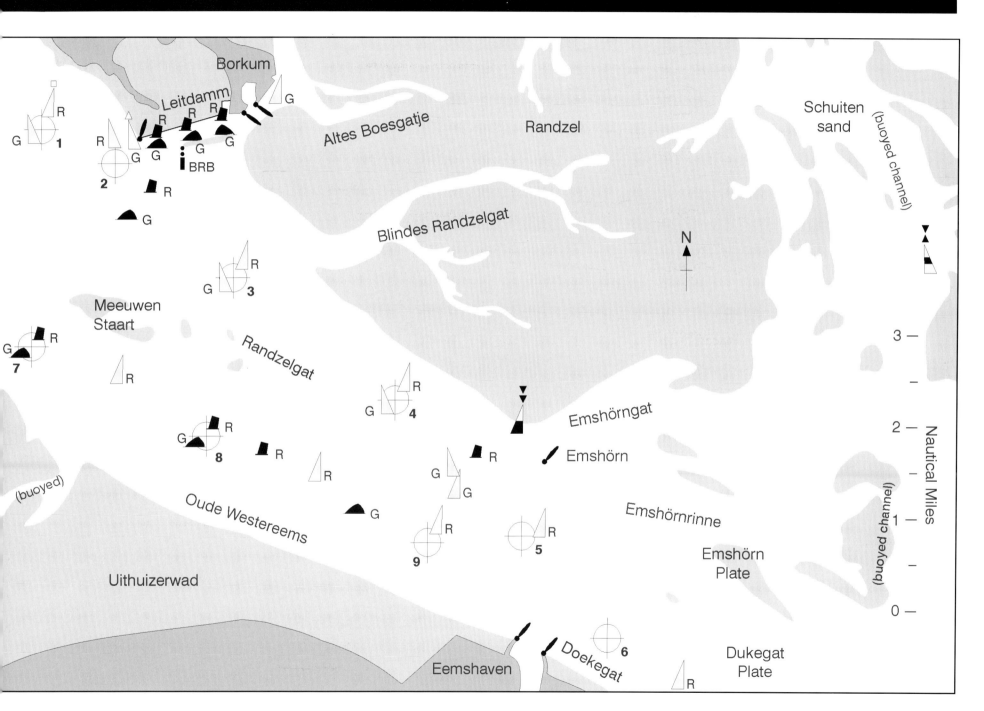

Borkum

Leitdamm

Altes Boesgatje

Randzel

Schuiten
sand

(buoyed channel)

G
R
1

R
G
G
R
R
G
G

BRB

R

G

Blindes Randzelgat

N

R
G
3

Meeuwen
Staart

Randzelgat

3

R

R
G
7

R

R
G
4

Emshörngat

Emshörn

2

Nautical Miles

R
G
8

R

G

R

Emshörnrinne

R
G

(buoyed)

Oude Westereems

G

G
G

1

R

R
9

R
5

Emshörn
Plate

(buoyed channel)

Uithuizerwad

0

Eemshaven

Doekegat

6

Dukegat
Plate

R

WP No	Waypoint name and position	Latitude	Longitude
64–1	Doekegat, 0.95 M due E of Eemshaven W pierhead light	53°27.78'N	06°51.74'E
64–2	Eems red buoy No 34, ½ ca NE of buoy	53°27.29'N	06°53.22'E
64–3	Eems red buoy No 36, ½ ca NE of buoy	53°26.20'N	06°55.22'E
64–4	Eems red buoy No 38, ½ ca NE of buoy	53°25.29'N	06°56.19'E
64–5	Eems red buoy No 40, ½ ca NE of buoy	53°24.42'N	06°57.11'E
64–6	Eems green buoy No 35, ½ ca SW of buoy	53°27.04'N	06°52.82'E
64–7	Eems green buoy No 37, ½ ca SW of buoy	53°26.02'N	06°54.89'E
64–8	Eems green buoy No 39, ½ ca SW of buoy	53°25.11'N	06°55.84'E
64–9	Eems green buoy No 41, ½ ca SW of buoy	53°24.27'N	06°56.71'E
64–10	Osterems south, 3½ M 307°T from Campen lighthouse	53°26.49'N	06°56.34'E

Datum ED 50 The waypoint latitudes and longitudes in this table refer to European Datum (1950)

COASTAL DANGERS

Refer to Admiralty chart 3509, 3510 and Dutch chart 1812

Eemshorn Plaat

This roughly triangular mile-long shoal lies in the junction between the main Westereems channel and the much shallower Osterems, drying to about ½ metre at low springs.

Dukegat Plate

Half a mile south-west of Eemshorn Plaat is a longer, much narrower shoal known as Dukegat Plate, marked on each side by yellow buoys. Much of Dukegat Plate has less than 1 metre depth at low springs and a small patch near the north-west tip just dries.

Shoals through the Osterems

The shallow Osterems channel, which leads just east of Randzel between the Westereems and Memmert island, is well used by boats cruising between Delfzijl and Norderney inside Juist. Both the Osterems and the channels inside Juist should be negotiated on a rising tide, which is straightforward if you are sailing from Norderney towards Delfzijl, but more difficult to time from Delfzijl towards Norderney. In the latter case, the normal strategy is to leave Delfzijl harbour on the last of the ebb, so that the flood is well under way by the time you get down to Osterems No 42 red buoy, where the Osterems channel branches to starboard east of Randzel.

There are numerous patchy shoals through the Osterems as you pass the east fringes of Randzel, many of which dry at low springs in the north part of the buoyed channel. Carefully follow the latest version of Dutch chart 1812.5, travel slowly through the shallowest parts and watch the echo-sounder all the time.

Strong tides in the Eems estuary

Tidal streams can be strong in the Eems estuary, so it is important to time your arrival or departure accordingly. Rates in the Randzelgat, just west of Borkum, can reach 3 knots at springs, so a wind over tide soon kicks up nasty steep seas, especially in the more exposed reaches opposite and below Eemshaven. Perhaps the most unpleasant mix is a brisk north-westerly over a strong ebb, so try to avoid this situation if possible.

Shipping off Eemshaven

Large ships go in and out of Eemshaven at all hours, so keep well clear of all commercial traffic in the estuary. Wherever possible, in the deepest open reaches of the Eems, try to keep just the 'wrong' side of channel buoys to leave the fairways clear for shipping.

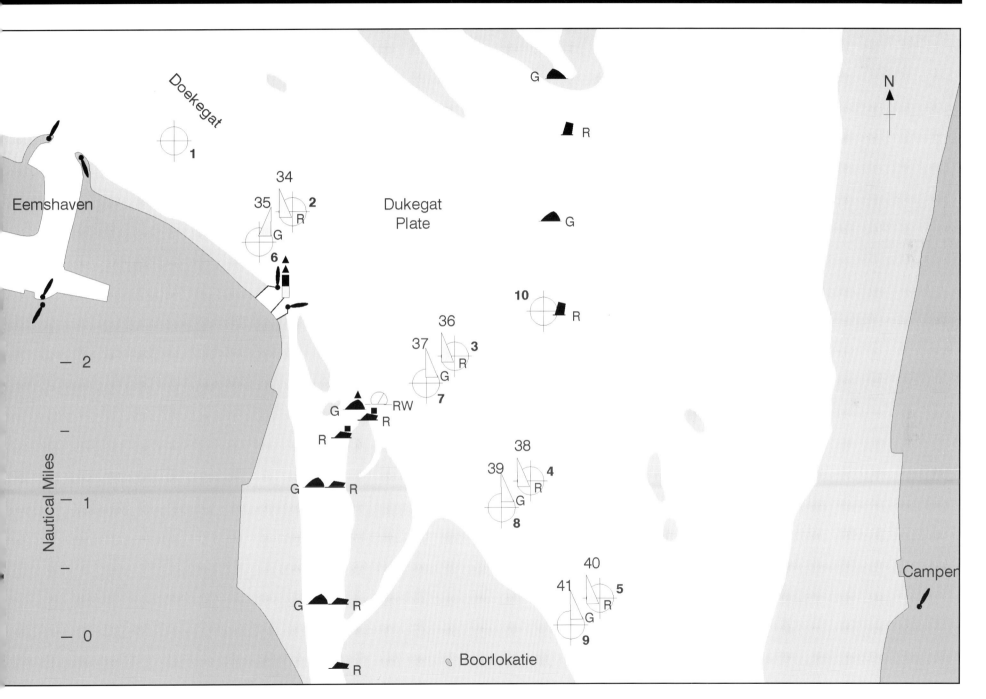

Doekegat

N

G

R

⊕ 1

34

35   2

R

Eemshaven

G

6

Dukegat
Plate

G

10   R

36

37   3

R

2   G

7

RW

G

R

R

R

38

39   4

R

1   G   R

G   R

8

40

41   5

R

G   9

Camper

0

R

Boorlokatie

WP No	Waypoint name and position	Latitude	Longitude
65–1	Eems red buoy No 38, ½ ca NE of buoy	53°25.29'N	06°56.19'E
65–2	Eems red buoy No 40, ½ ca NE of buoy	53°24.42'N	06°57.11'E
65–3	Eems red buoy No 42, ½ ca NE of buoy	53°23.28'N	06°57.98'E
65–4	Eems red buoy No 44, ½ ca NE of buoy	53°22.15'N	06°58.84'E
65–5	Eems red buoy No 46, ½ ca E of buoy	53°21.00'N	06°59.67'E
65–6	Eems red buoy No 48, ½ ca E of buoy	53°20.07'N	07°00.01'E
65–7	Eems red buoy No 50, ½ ca NE of buoy	53°19.68'N	07°00.59'E
65–8	Eems green buoy No 39, ½ ca SW of buoy	53°25.11'N	06°55.84'E
65–9	Eems green buoy No 41, ½ ca SW of buoy	53°24.27'N	06°56.71'E
65–10	Eems green buoy No 43, ½ ca SW of buoy	53°23.13'N	06°57.57'E
65–11	Eems green buoy No 45, ½ ca SW of buoy	53°22.00'N	06°58.45'E
65–12	Eems green buoy No 47, ½ ca W of buoy	53°21.00'N	06°59.26'E
65–13	Eems green buoy No 49, ½ ca W of buoy	53°20.02'N	06°59.67'E
65–14	Eems green buoy No 51, ½ ca SW of buoy	53°19.51'N	07°00.31'E
65–15	Delfzijl entrance, midway between pierhead lights	53°19.02'N	07°00.52'E

Datum ED 50 The waypoint latitudes and longitudes in this table refer to European Datum (1950)

COASTAL DANGERS

Refer to Admiralty chart 3510 and Dutch chart 1812

Hond Paap

Much of the west side of the River Eems from just above Eemshaven to Delfzijl harbour entrance is occupied by the expansive drying shoal known as Hond Paap, which is 2 miles wide and nearly 7 miles long. Drying heights range from ½ metre to just over 2 metres. The main channel buoys lead well clear to the east of Hond Paap and a shallow, very narrow buoyed cut leads around the west side, close to the low Groningen shore.

Strong tides in the River Eems

The tides can be strong in the Eems estuary, so it is important to carry a fair stream whenever possible. A fresh wind over the tide will set up a steep chop in this section of the river, the most unpleasant conditions being caused by a brisk northerly or north-westerly over a strong ebb.

With the strong river tides in mind, do not pass too close to the channel buoys, because there is always a risk of being swept onto them. By the same token, watch out for cross-current when entering Delfzijl and do not cut the pierheads too close.

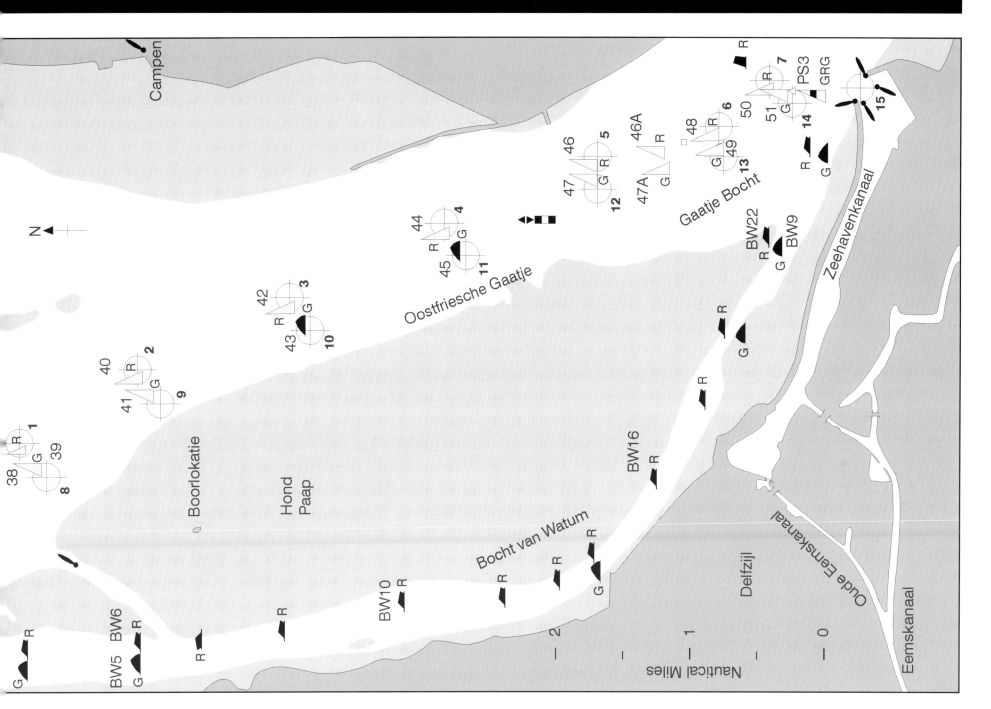

Campen

N

Boorlokatie

Hond
Paap

Oostfriesche Gaatje

Gaatje Bocht

Bocht van Watum

Zeehavenkanaal

Oude Eemskanaal

Eemskanaal

Delfzijl

38 R 1
G 39
8

40 R 2
G 9
41

42 R 3
G 10
43

44 R 4
R G 11
45

46 R 5
47 G 12

47A R
G 48
46A

R 6
G 13
49

50 R 7
51 G 14
PS3 GRG

R 15

R
G

BW22 R
G BW9

R
G

R

R
BW16

R

R
BW10 R

R

R
G

BW5 BW6
G R

G R

Nautical Miles
0 1 2

WP No	Waypoint name and position	Latitude	Longitude
66–1	Borkum NW, 1 ca due N of Westereems No 11 green buoy	53°36.70'N	06°33.24'E
66–2	Borkum W, 1.3 M W of Borkum Kleiner lighthouse	53°34.77'N	06°37.90'E
66–3	Huibertgat inner, 3.9 M W of Borkum Kleiner lighthouse	53°34.77'N	06°33.50'E
66–4	Horsborn Plaat, 2.31 M 254°T from Borkum Kleiner lighthouse	53°34.13'N	06°36.34'E
66–5	Huibertgat SE, 1.54 M 217°T from Borkum Kleiner lighthouse	53°33.53'N	06°38.58'E
66–6	Osterems fairway buoy, actual position	53°41.92'N	06°36.20'E
66–7	Osterems outer, 6¾ M 348°T from Borkum Kleiner lighthouse	53°41.39'N	06°37.85'E
66–8	Memmert west, F16 green-red-green buoy, actual position	53°37.79'N	06°48.52'E
66–9	Memmertbalje, midway M1 green buoy and M4 red buoy	53°37.13'N	06°54.52'E
66–10	Memmert SE, midway O13 green buoy and O18 red buoy	53°36.10'N	06°54.68'E

Datum ED 50 The waypoint latitudes and longitudes in this table refer to European Datum (1950)

COASTAL DANGERS

Refer to Admiralty chart 3509 and Dutch chart 1812

Shoals north of Borkum

The seaward approaches to the Eems are fringed by several wide shoals that extend up to 5 miles north and north-west of Borkum. Particular care is needed if approaching Borkum and the Eems from the east, when you have to keep safely seaward of these shoals until the way is clear to drop south into the Westereems, usually near the Riffgat buoys. For these outer approaches, it is important to follow the latest version of the Dutch Hydrografische Kaart No 1812.

Hoog Rif

A long shoal area, much of it drying, extends north-westwards from the north-west corner of Borkum for a good 2 miles. These flats are guarded by No 14 and No 16 red buoys of the Westereems channel, but care must be taken on a strong flood tide to avoid being set too close.

Hoog Rif is part of a designated nature reserve and anchoring in the vicinity is prohibited between 1 May and 1 October.

Outer shoals west of Juist and Memmert

A broad expanse of sandy shoals, most of it drying, some mostly above-water, stretches up to 4 miles west of Juist and Memmert islands, forming the east edge of the narrow buoyed entrance of the Oostereems – now spelt 'Osterems' since we have moved into German waters. The above-water part of these shoals is the low flat dune known as Katchelot Plate, which seems barely out of reach of the sea at HW.

The Osterems route into the extensive shoal waters behind the German Frisian Islands is not much used by boats, except sometimes by those making for the small drying harbour on the south side of Juist. This shallow entrance is uneasy in any onshore swell and dangerous in heavy weather, when the sea breaks malevolently over the banks on each side of the tenuous channel.

The key outer marks are the two Osterems red-and-white fairway buoys, which lie about 7½ miles NNW of the Borkum Kleiner lighthouse. From this pair of buoys, the reds and greens marking the Osterems channel trend ESE and then SE to pass about 1½ miles west of Katchelot Plate.

When cruising seaward of Borkum and Juist, these outer shoals are avoided by keeping north of the Osterems fairway buoys and Juisterriff north-cardinal buoy.

Shoals through the Osterems east of Randzel

The inner part of the shallow Osterems channel, which leads just east of Randzel between the Westereems and Memmert island, is well used by boats cruising between Delfzijl and Norderney inside Juist. Both the Osterems and the channels inside Juist should be negotiated on a rising tide, which is straightforward if you are sailing from Norderney towards Delfzijl, but more difficult to time from Delfzijl towards Norderney. In the latter case, the normal strategy is to leave Delfzijl harbour on the last of the ebb, so that the flood is well under way by the time you get down to Osterems No 42 red buoy, where the Osterems channel branches to starboard east of Randzel.

There are numerous patchy shoals through the Osterems as you pass the east fringes of Randzel, many of which dry at low springs in the north part of the buoyed channel. Carefully follow the latest version of Dutch chart 1812.5, travel slowly through the shallowest parts, and watch the echo-sounder all the time.

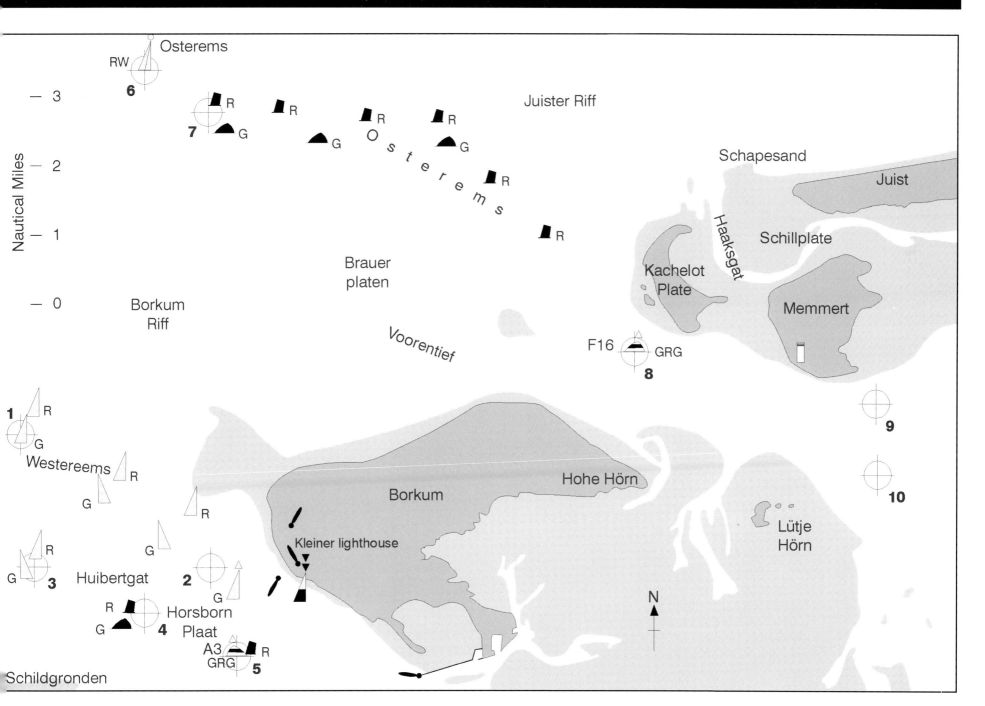

Osterems

RW

6

7 R

R R R

G R R

G G

O s t e r e m s

R

R

Juister Riff

Schapesand

Juist

Schillplate

Haaksgat

Kachelot
Plate

Memmert

Brauer
platen

Borkum
Riff

Voorentief

F16 GRG

8

9

1 R

G

Westereems R

G

R

G

R

G

G

3

Huibertgat

2

G

R

G

4

Horsborn
Plaat

A3 R

GRG

5

Schildgronden

Kleiner lighthouse

Borkum

Hohe Hörn

Lütje
Hörn

N

10

Nautical Miles

— 3

— 2

— 1

— 0

WP No	Waypoint name and position	Latitude	Longitude
67–1	TG9 green shipping lane buoy, actual position	53°48.45'N	06°57.83'E
67–2	Juist N-card buoy, actual position	53°43.90'N	06°55.50'E
67–3	Schluchter red-and-white fairway buoy, actual position	53°44.73'N	07°04.22'E
67–4	Schluchter S1 green outer buoy, actual position	53°43.27'N	07°05.36'E
67–5	Dovetief fairway, 3.55 M 323°T from Norderney main light	53°45.43'N	07°10.27'E
67–6	Dovetief D4 red buoy, actual position	53°44.53'N	07°09.90'E

Datum ED 50 The waypoint latitudes and longitudes in this table refer to European Datum (1950)

COASTAL DANGERS

Refer to Admiralty chart 3761, Dutch chart 1812 and German chart 89

Danger from onshore winds

Skippers of boats cruising fairly close inshore along the Frisian Islands should always keep a careful eye on the weather. Although in quiet summer conditions this is a fascinating and rewarding cruising area, the long low line of the Frisians, with their off-lying sandbanks and tricky entrances, are not to be trifled with in fresh onshore winds, when a building swell can soon make the *seegats* dangerous to pass.

Although the Norderneyer Seegat is much used during the summer by boats bound for and leaving the popular yacht harbour on the south side of Norderney island, its very popularity can sometimes mean that one assumes the approach channels to be safe in practically any conditions. This is far from true and the seaward approaches to Norderneyer Seegat should be treated with as much respect as the least frequently used channels between less popular islands. In freshening onshore winds and building swell, if you are in any doubt, do not take any risks.

Offshore shipping lanes

The Terschelling to German Bight shipping lanes lie from 7–15 miles seaward of Juist and Norderney, marked on their south side by a long line of green buoys. Yachts cruising the Frisian Islands will normally stay inshore of these lanes during daylight, following the line of cardinal and fairway buoys between 2 and 3 miles north of the islands. However, care must be taken to keep clear of shipping in the lanes if you are either approaching this coast from seaward or passing it well offshore, perhaps at night.

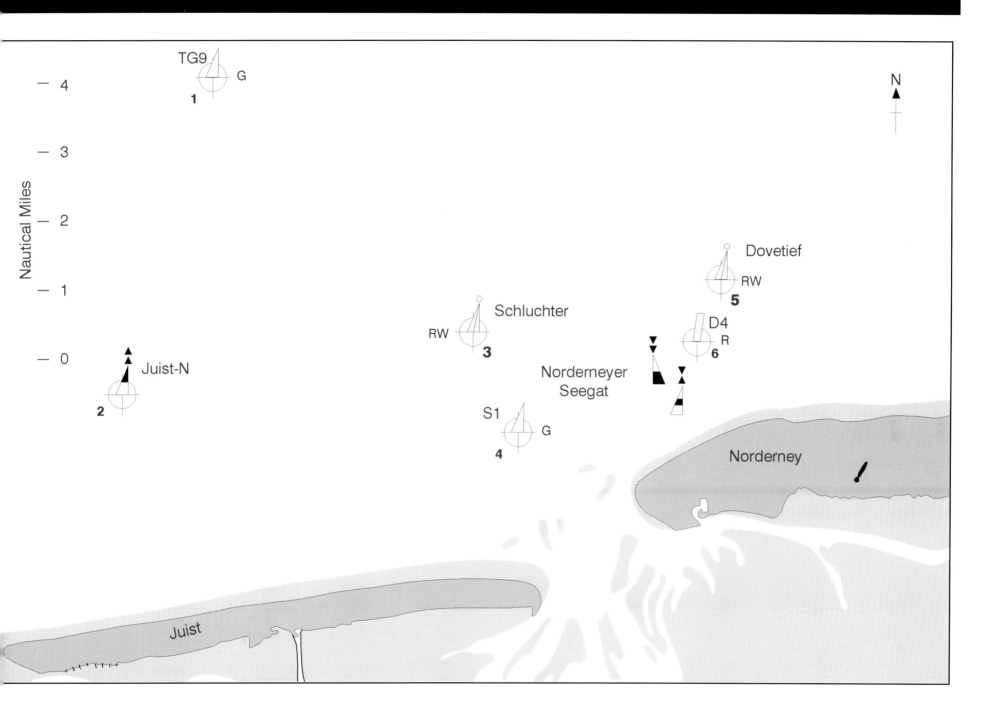

Nautical Miles

— 4

— 3

— 2

— 1

— 0

TG9 G

1

N

Dovetief
RW
5

Schluchter
RW
3

D4
R
6

Juist-N

2

Norderneyer
Seegat

S1 G

4

Norderney

Juist

Approaches to Norderneyer Seegat

WP No	Waypoint name and position	Latitude	Longitude
68–1	Schluchter red-and-white fairway buoy, actual position	53°44.73'N	07°04.22'E
68–2	Schluchter S1 green outer buoy, actual position	53°43.27'N	07°05.36'E
68–3	Dovetief fairway, 3.55 M 323°T from Norderney main light	53°45.43'N	07°10.27'E
68–4	Dovetief D4 red buoy, actual position	53°44.53'N	07°09.90'E
68–5	Norderney N outer, 3.4 M 276°T from Norderney lighthouse	53°42.95'N	07°08.16'E
68–6	Dovetief D16 red buoy, actual position	53°42.50'N	07°08.02'E
68–7	Norddeich approach, 40 m due W of Norddeich E pierhead light	53°38.79'N	07°08.93'E

Datum ED 50 The waypoint latitudes and longitudes in this table refer to European Datum (1950)

COASTAL DANGERS

Refer to Admiralty chart 3761, Dutch chart 1812 and German chart 89

Danger from onshore winds

Skippers of boats cruising close inshore along the German Frisian Islands should always keep a careful eye on the weather. Although in quiet summer conditions this is a fascinating and rewarding cruising area, the long low line of the Frisians, with their off-lying sandbanks and tricky entrances, are not to be trifled with in fresh onshore winds, when a building swell can soon make the *seegats* dangerous to pass.

Norderneyer Seegat

Although the Norderneyer Seegat is much used during the summer by boats bound for and leaving the popular yacht harbour on the south side of Norderney island, its very popularity can sometimes mean that one assumes the approach channels to be safe in practically any conditions. This is far from true and the seaward approaches to Norderneyer Seegat should be treated with as much respect as the least frequently used channels

between less popular islands. In freshening onshore winds and building swell, if you are in any doubt, do not take any risks.

Ferries approaching and leaving Norderney

Watch out for fast ferries on the move as you approach or leave Norderney harbour. The ferry pier is immediately on the port hand as you come in through the pierheads, and there's not much room to manoeuvre in the narrow entrance channel.

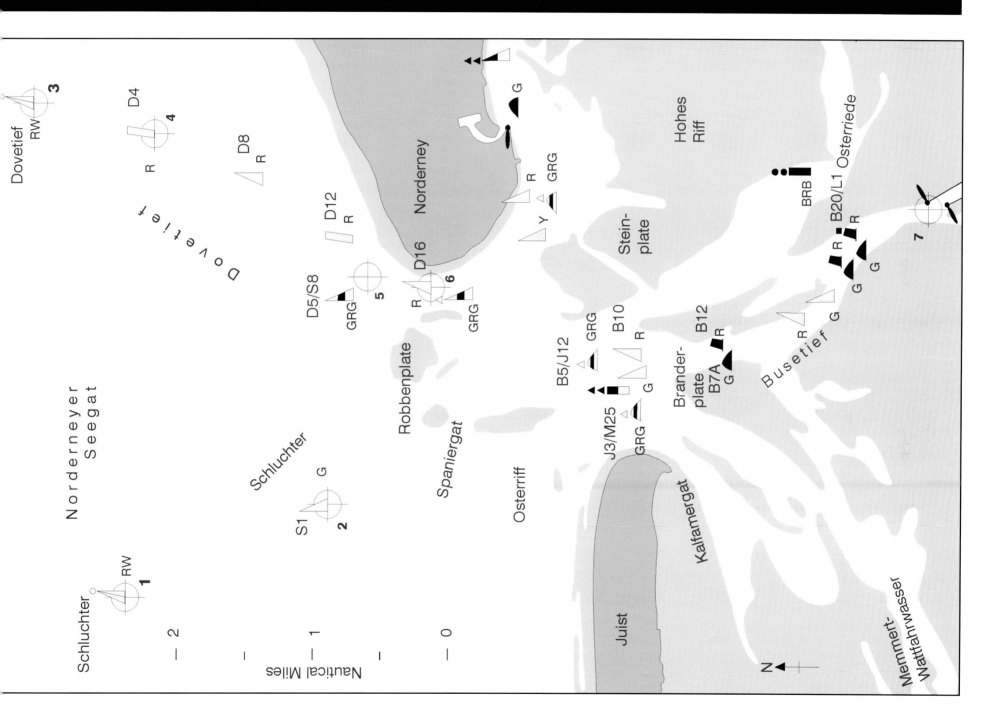

Norderney to Spiekeroog

WP No	Waypoint name and position	Latitude	Longitude
69–1	Dovetief fairway, 3.55 M 323°T from Norderney main light	53°45.43'N	07°10.27'E
69–2	Norderney N-cardinal buoy, actual position	53°46.10'N	07°17.20'E
69–3	Accumer Ee approach, 3.2 M 310°T from Langeoog church	53°46.88'N	07°24.88'E
69–4	Otzumer Balje approach, 5.9 M 056°T from Langeoog church	53°48.10'N	07°37.29'E
69–5	TG11 green shipping lane buoy, actual position	53°49.68'N	07°06.65'E
69–6	TG13 green shipping lane buoy, actual position	53°50.93'N	07°15.52'E
69–7	TG15 green shipping lane buoy, actual position	53°52.24'N	07°24.35'E
69–8	TG17/Weser 1 green shipping lane buoy, actual position	53°53.48'N	07°33.22'E
69–9	Weser 1a green shipping lane buoy, actual position	53°52.97'N	07°38.62'E

Datum ED 50 The waypoint latitudes and longitudes in this table refer to European Datum (1950)

COASTAL DANGERS

Refer to Admiralty charts 1875 and 3761 and German chart 89

Offshore shipping lanes

The Terschelling to German Bight shipping lanes lie from 7–15 miles seaward of Norderney and Langeoog, marked on their south side by a long line of green buoys. Boats cruising the German Frisian Islands will normally stay inshore of these lanes during daylight, following the line of cardinal and fairway buoys between 2 and 3 miles north of the islands. However, care must be taken to keep clear of shipping in the lanes if you are either approaching this coast from seaward or passing it well offshore, perhaps at night.

Danger from onshore winds

Skippers of yachts cruising close inshore along the German Frisian Islands should always keep a careful eye on the weather. Although in quiet summer conditions this is a fascinating and rewarding cruising area, the long low line of the Frisians, with their off-lying sandbanks and tricky entrances, are not to be trifled with in fresh onshore winds, when a building swell can make the *seegats* dangerous to pass.

Norderneyer Seegat

Although the Norderneyer Seegat is much used during the summer by boats heading for or leaving the popular yacht harbour on the south side of Norderney island, its very popularity can sometimes mean that one assumes the approach channels to be safe in practically any conditions. This is far from true and the seaward approaches to Norderneyer Seegat should be treated with as much respect as the least frequently used channels between less popular islands. In freshening onshore winds and building swell, if you are in any doubt, do not take any risks.

Wichter Ee

This shallow *seegat* between Norderney and Baltrum is not recommended even in quiet weather, since the shifting channel is unmarked and parts of the outer banks dry. The best way to visit Baltrum harbour, which is small and shallow but doesn't entirely dry, is by following the shallow channel inside Norderney about 1½ hours before HW. This narrow sheltered route, known as the Norderneyer Wattfahrwasser, is marked mostly by red spar buoys except across the shallowest part of the watershed, where you follow a short stretch of port-hand withies.

Accumer Ee

No waypoints are given for this rather delicate *seegat* between Baltrum and Langeoog, since the outer part of the channel is prone to shifting and silting. In quiet weather, however, with no onshore swell, the Accumer Ee is a feasible entrance channel for vessels of moderate draught. The best time to approach is about 1½ hours before local HW. Once south of the outer banks, there is plenty of depth in the main channel behind Langeoog and in the approaches to the yacht harbour, where the pontoon berths have depths between 1.8 and 2.2 metres.

Approaches to Spiekeroog

The *seegat* between Langeoog and Spiekeroog is similar to Norderneyer Seegat, with two outer channels – Westerbalje and Otzumer Balje. The approaches are rather gloomily cluttered with wrecks, marked by various cardinal buoys. The outer mark is the Otzumer Balje red-and-white fairway buoy, which lies about 3 miles north-west of the most seaward church spire at the west end of Spiekeroog.

Like the other *seegats*, neither the Westerbalje or Otzumer Balje should be used unless conditions are quiet. Aim to approach about 1½ hours before local HW. The pontoons in Spiekeroog harbour dry out to soft mud, but most boats sit happily upright in the ooze (be careful not to fall in!).

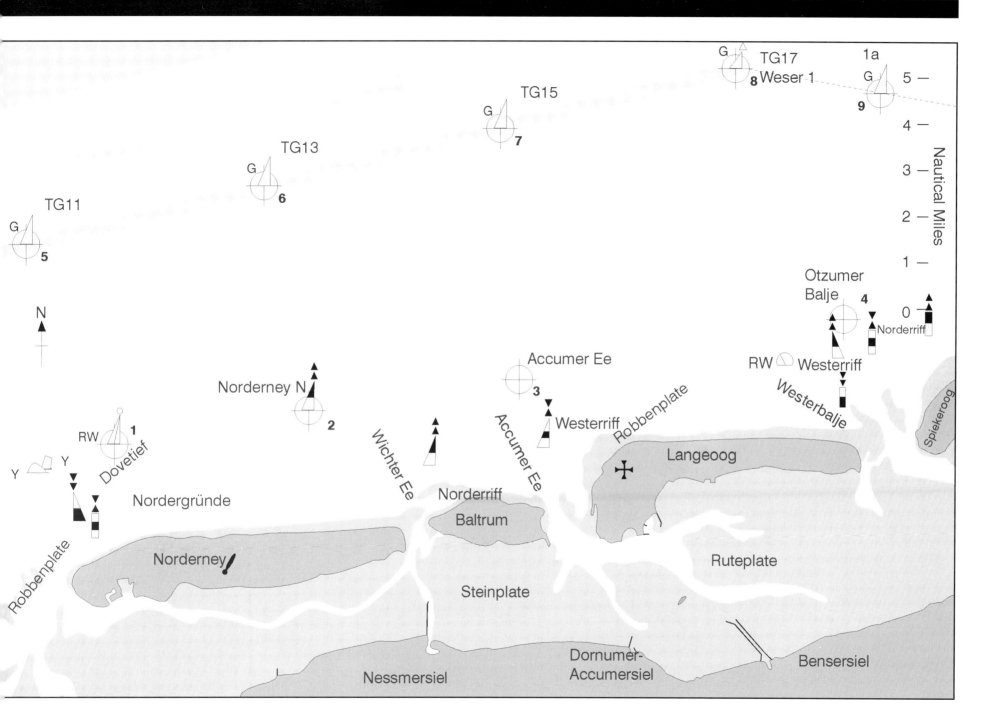

TG17

TG15

TG13

TG11

Nautical Miles

Weser 1

1a

Otzumer
Balje

Norderriff

RW   Westerriff

Westerbalje

N

Accumer Ee

Norderney N

Robbenplate

Langeoog

RW   Dovetief

Y   Y

Westerriff

Wichter Ee

Accumer Ee

Spiekeroog

Y

Nordergründe

Norderriff

Baltrum

Ruteplate

Robbenplate

Norderney

Steinplate

Nessmersiel

Dornumer-
Accumersiel

Bensersiel

WP No	Waypoint name and position	Latitude	Longitude
70–1	Otzumer Balje approach, 5.9 M 056°T from Langeoog church	53°48.10'N	07°37.29'E
70–2	Harle fairway, 2.3 M 320°T from Wangerooge main lighthouse	53°49.23'N	07°49.01'E
70–3	Weser 1a green shipping lane buoy, actual position	53°52.97'N	07°38.62'E
70–4	Weser 1b/Jade 1 green buoy, actual position	53°52.45'N	07°44.11'E
70–5	Jade 2 green-red-green buoy, actual position	53°52.12'N	07°47.36'E
70–6	Wangerooger Fahrwasser, 3 M N of Wangerooge lighthouse	53°50.46'N	07°51.50'E
70–7	TG19/Weser 2 green shipping lane buoy, actual position	53°55.08'N	07°44.73'E
70–8	Weser 2a red buoy, actual position	53°53.63'N	07°46.00'E
70–9	Weser 4 red buoy, actual position	53°53.39'N	07°47.86'E
70–10	Weser 4a red buoy, actual position	53°52.50'N	07°53.67'E
70–11	Weser 3a / Neue Weser Reede green buoy, actual position	53°51.50'N	07°53.30'E
70–12	Neue Weser outer, 2.6 M E of Neue Weser Reede green buoy	53°51.50'N	07°57.72'E
70–13	Schlüsseltonne red-and-white fairway buoy, actual position	53°56.30'N	07°54.90'E
70–14	Alte Weser outer, 6½ M 300°T from Alte Weser lighthouse	53°55.10'N	07°58.16'E
70–15	Jade–Weser red-and-white fairway buoy, actual position	53°58.32'N	07°38.86'E
70–16	SZ-N separation zone N-card buoy, actual position	54°00.98'N	07°43.10'E

Datum ED 50 The waypoint latitudes and longitudes in this table refer to European Datum (1950)

COASTAL DANGERS

Refer to Admiralty charts 1875, 3761 and German chart 89

Jade-Weser shipping junction

About 12 miles north of the west end of Spiekeroog island, the 'Terschelling–German Bight' shipping lanes (which run ENE–WSW) meet the 'Jade Approach' shipping lanes (which run NNW–SSE). The junction between these two separation schemes is marked by the Jade-Weser red-and-white fairway buoy, which is fitted with a Racon beacon (identification 'T'). This buoy is an important 'crossroads' mark for shipping.

Boats cruising the German Frisian Islands will normally stay inshore of both these sets of lanes during daylight, following the line of cardinal and fairway buoys between 2 and 3 miles north of the Islands. However, care must be taken to keep clear of shipping in the lanes if you are either approaching this coast from seaward or passing it well offshore, perhaps at night.

Boats cruising from the Frisian Islands towards the Elbe will at some stage cross the inshore end of the 'Jade Approach' shipping lanes while making for the southern edge of the Elbe approach channel. Care must be taken to cross these approach lanes more or less at right-angles. Where possible, boats cruising from the German Frisian Islands towards the Elbe should stay south of the east-going shipping travelling from the Terschelling–German Bight lanes towards the Elbe approach channel.

Approaches to Spiekeroog

The *seegat* between Langeoog and Spiekeroog is similar to Norderneyer Seegat, with two outer channels – Westerbalje and Otzumer Balje. The approaches are rather gloomily cluttered with wrecks, marked by various cardinal buoys. The outer mark is the Otzumer Balje red-and-white fairway buoy, which lies about 3 miles north-west of the most seaward church spire at the west end of Spiekeroog.

Like the other *seegats*, neither the Westerbalje or Otzumer Balje should be used unless conditions are quiet. Aim to approach about 1½ hours before local HW. The pontoons in Spiekeroog harbour dry out to soft mud, but most boats sit happily upright in the ooze (be careful not to fall in!).

Approaches to Wangerooge

The Harle channel between Spiekeroog and Wangerooge has similar characteristics to the other *seegats* between the German Frisian Islands. The Harle should only be approached in quiet weather in the absence of swell.

The important outer mark is the Harle red-and-white fairway buoy, which lies just under 2½ miles north-west of the 60-metre high red light-tower (with two white bands) that stands on the west end of Wangerooge. From Harle fairway buoy the entrance channel trends south between the outer shoals and across a shallow bar.

Once Wangerooge lighthouse bears due east, the depths start to increase and you enter the relatively deep inner channel, the Dove Harle, which leads round to Wangerooge harbour. The boat haven is fairly shallow and some pontoons only have about 0.6 metres depth at low water springs, but Wangerooge is an intriguing island and well worth visiting if you don't mind settling on the bottom near low tide.

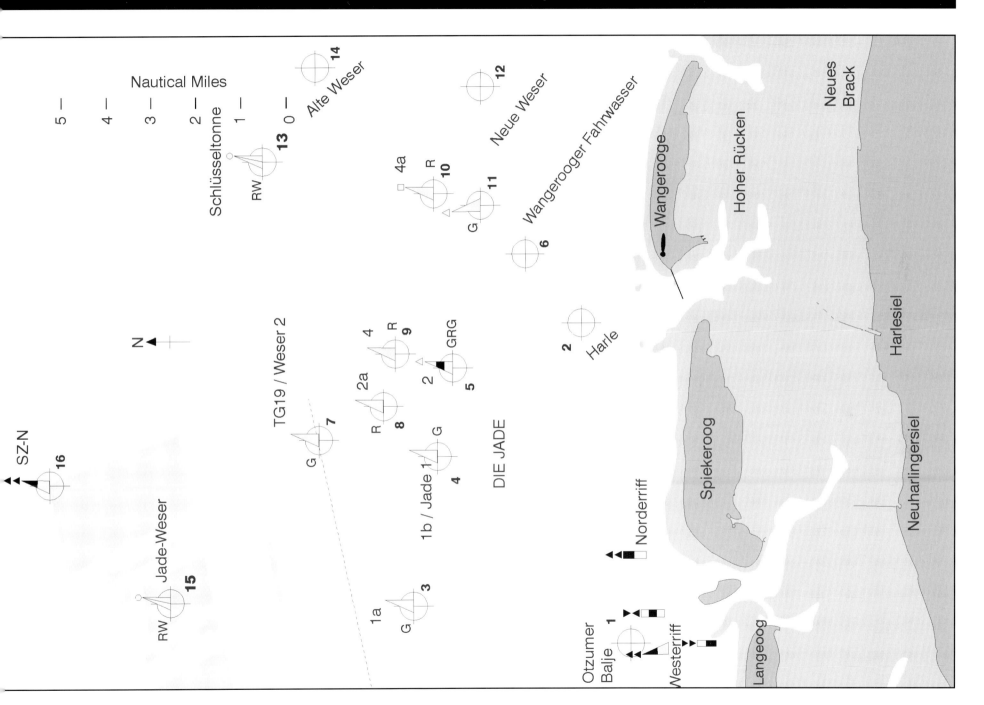

Nautical Miles

5 — 4 — 3 — 2 — 1 — 0 —

Schlüsseltonne

RW **13**

Alte Weser **14**

Neue Weser **12**

4a

R **10**

11

G

6

Wangerooger Fahrwasser

Wangerooge

Hoher Rücken

Neues Brack

TG19 / Weser 2

4

R **9**

GRG

2 **5**

2a

R **8**

1b / Jade 1

G **4**

DIE JADE

2 Harle

Harlesiel

Neuharlingersiel

SZ-N

16

N

G **7**

1a

G **3**

Jade-Weser

RW **15**

Norderriff

Spiekeroog

Otzumer Balje **1**

Westerriff

Langeoog

Outer approaches to Helgoland

WP No	Waypoint name and position	Latitude	Longitude
71–1	E1 red-and-white fairway buoy, actual position	54°10.84'N	07°33.00'E
71–2	E2 red-and-white fairway buoy, actual position	54°07.24'N	07°43.85'E
71–3	E3 red-and-white fairway buoy, actual position	54°03.61'N	07°54.70'E
71–4	Sellebrunn W-card buoy, actual position	54°14.48'N	07°49.82'E
71–5	Nathurn N-card buoy, actual position	54°13.40'N	07°49.00'E
71–6	Helgoland W-card buoy, actual position	54°10.70'N	07°48.26'E
71–7	Helgoland E-card buoy, actual position	54°09.00'N	07°53.56'E
71–8	Düne S-card buoy, actual position	54°09.57'N	07°56.04'E
71–9	Helgoland S inner, 2.8 ca 130°T from Südmole light on L/line	54°10.10'N	07°54.38'E
71–10	Helgoland entrance, midway Vorhafen outer pierhead lights	54°10.32'N	07°54.02'E
71–11	Düne E-card buoy, actual position	54°10.90'N	07°56.18'E
71–12	Düne N-card buoy, actual position	54°13.50'N	07°56.00'E
71–13	Steingrund E-card buoy, actual position	54°14.00'N	08°05.50'E
71–14	Aussenelbe Reede-2 yellow anchorage buoy, actual position	54°03.50'N	08°06.97'E

Datum ED 50 The waypoint latitudes and longitudes in this table refer to European Datum (1950)

COASTAL DANGERS
Refer to Admiralty charts 126 and 1875

Tidal streams around Helgoland
Tides can be strong around Helgoland, especially at springs in the south-west approaches. You can also find local streams setting in unexpected directions. Be careful approaching Helgoland in poor visibility, even when using GPS, when the 'cross-track error' display may suddenly indicate a significant local cross-tide. Be prepared to make bold course alterations if necessary to stay on track for the final approach to a critical buoy. Radar can be useful in helping to locate and identify the various outer buoys. The high north part of Helgoland shows up well on radar.

Shoals around Dune
The small island of Düne, close east of Helgoland, has long extensive shoals on its north-west side, stretching for almost 3 miles out towards Sellebrunn west-cardinal buoy. These dangerous shoals, some almost awash at low springs, have only one buoy – Düne north-cardinal – guarding their east edge. Take care to avoid these shoals if approaching Düne island from the east in poor visibility, perhaps from the direction of the Eider river.

Shoals also extend south of Düne for just under 1 mile, parts of which have less than 2 metres depth at low springs. Although these southern banks are not quite so shallow as those north of the island, they are still dangerous in any significant sea or swell. The west edge of these southern shoals is guarded by three green buoys, which are left to starboard as you approach Helgoland harbour from the south.

Dangers north-west of Helgoland
A broad shoal area, called Nathurn Brunn, extends immediately north-west of Helgoland for about 1 mile. Minimum depths over Nathurn Brunn range from ½–1 metre at low springs. A long breakwater – the Nordmole – some of which is partially submerged, extends north-west for 6½ cables from the north-west tip of Helgoland, effectively forming the western edge of Nathurn Brunn. There are also some shoals within about 3 cables of the west side of the breakwater, with minimum depths of less than 1 metre. Boats would not normally be near this area except if approaching Helgoland from almost due west, but you should be careful to avoid being set towards the Nordmole and the north-west tip of Nathurn Brunn in poor visibility.

Cruise ships approaching Helgoland
Helgoland is a popular destination for German cruise ships, which bring hundreds of day tourists out from the mainland for tax-free shopping. Large launches shuttle these tourists ashore from the anchorage between Helgoland and Düne. Boats approaching or leaving Helgoland should keep a close eye on the movements of cruise ships, which should not be obstructed when manoeuvring in any of the narrow buoyed channels.

Heavy weather in German Bight
This corner of the North Sea is extremely inhospitable in heavy weather, especially in prolonged strong winds from the west or north-west. Helgoland, despite its rather austere atmosphere and surrounding shoals, is actually quite straightforward to approach from the south and should always be kept in mind as a possible port of refuge if heavy weather threatens. The harbour itself, once you are inside, is secure in all conditions, and Helgoland is arguably the safest of all the German North Sea harbours to approach in deteriorating weather.

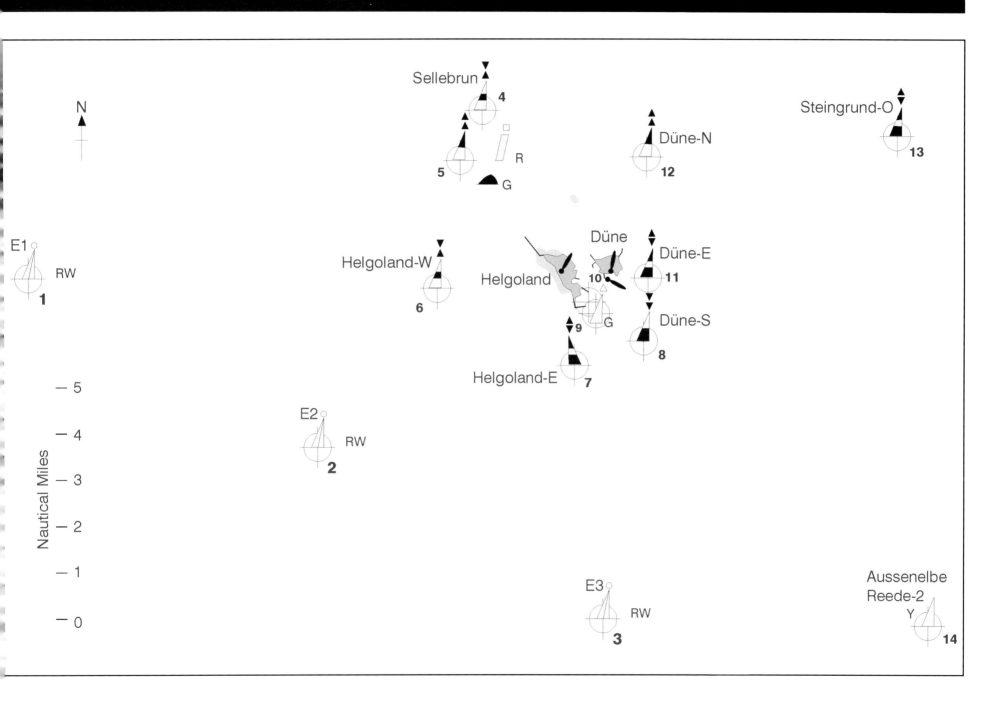

N

Sellebrun
4
5
R
G

Düne-N
12

Steingrund-O
13

E1
RW
1

Helgoland-W
6

Düne
Helgoland
10
G
9

Düne-E
11

Düne-S
8

Helgoland-E
7

— 5

E2
RW
2

— 4

— 3

— 2

Nautical Miles

— 1

E3
RW
3

Aussenelbe
Reede-2
Y
14

— 0

WP No	Waypoint name and position	Latitude	Longitude
72–1	E3 red-and-white fairway buoy, actual position	54°03.61'N	07°54.70'E
72–2	Aussenelbe Reede-2 yellow anchorage buoy, actual position	54°03.50'N	08°06.97'E
72–3	Aussenelbe Reede-4 yellow anchorage buoy, actual position	54°03.51'N	08°10.00'E
72–4	Aussenelbe Reede-1 yellow anchorage buoy, actual position	54°01.83'N	08°06.97'E
72–5	SZ-N separation zone N-card buoy, actual position	54°00.98'N	07°43.10'E
72–6	Elbe outward, 1 M due N of the Elbe light float	54°01.00'N	08°06.60'E
72–7	Elbe light float, actual position	54°00.00'N	08°06.60'E
72–8	Elbe inward, 1 M due S of the Elbe light float	53°59.00'N	08°06.60'E
72–9	Westertill-N, 3 ca NW of Westertill N-card buoy	53°58.40'N	08°06.43'E
72–10	Scharhörnriff-W, 3 ca NW of Scharhörnriff W-card buoy	53°58.77'N	08°08.45'E
72–11	Jade-Weser red-and-white fairway buoy, actual position	53°58.32'N	07°38.86'E
72–12	Schlüsseltonne red-and-white fairway buoy, actual position	53°56.30'N	07°54.90'E
72–13	TG19/Weser 2 green shipping channel buoy, actual position	53°55.08'N	07°44.73'E
72–14	Weser 1a green buoy, actual position	53°52.97'N	07°38.62'E
72–15	Weser 1b/Jade 1 green buoy, actual position	53°52.45'N	07°44.11'E
72–16	Jade 2 green-red-green buoy, actual position	53°52.12'N	07°47.36'E
72–17	Weser 2a red buoy, actual position	53°53.63'N	07°46.00'E
72–18	Weser 4 red buoy, actual position	53°53.39'N	07°47.86'E
72–19	Weser 4a red buoy, actual position	53°52.50'N	07°53.67'E
72–20	Weser 3a/Neue Weser Reede green buoy, actual position	53°51.50'N	07°53.30'E
72–21	Neue Weser outer, 2.6 M E of Neue Weser Reede green buoy	53°51.50'N	07°57.72'E
72–22	Norder Gründe north clearing, 3 ca due N of N-card buoy	53°57.10'N	08°00.18'E
72–23	Alte Weser outer, 6½ M 300°T from Alte Weser lighthouse	53°55.10'N	07°58.16'E
72–24	Alte Weser middle, 3½ M 300°T from Alte Weser lighthouse	53°53.60'N	08°02.57'E
72–25	Alte Weser inner, 1 M 300°T from Alte Weser lighthouse	53°52.34'N	08°06.25'E

Datum ED 50 The waypoint latitudes and longitudes in this table refer to European Datum (1950)

COASTAL DANGERS

Refer to Admiralty charts 1875, 3368 and 3761 and German chart 89

Jade-Weser shipping junction

About 12 miles north of Spiekeroog island, the 'Terschelling–German Bight' shipping lanes meet the 'Jade Approach' lanes. The junction between these two separation schemes is marked by the Jade-Weser red-and-white fairway buoy, which is fitted with a Racon beacon (identification 'T'). This buoy is an important 'crossroads' for shipping.

Boats cruising the German Frisian Islands usually stay inshore of these lanes by day, following the line of cardinal and fairway buoys 2–3 miles north of the islands. However, take care to keep clear of shipping in the lanes if you are either approaching this coast from seaward or passing well offshore, perhaps at night.

Boats cruising from the Frisian Islands towards the Elbe will at some stage cross the inshore end of the 'Jade Approach' shipping lanes while making for the southern edge of the Elbe approach channel. Take care to cross these lanes more or less at right-angles. Where possible, boats cruising from the Frisian Islands towards the Elbe should stay south of the east-going shipping travelling in the same direction from the Terschelling–German Bight lanes.

Jade approaches

The 'Jade Approach' shipping lanes close the coast in a south-south-easterly direction from the Jade-Weser fairway buoy, along the fixed white sector of Wangerooge lighthouse. Just over 5 miles from the lighthouse, abreast 'Jade 2' green-red-green buoy, the shipping channel turns more easterly to converge with the north shore of Wangerooge and enter the Jade ¾ mile north-east of Minsener-Oog island. Boats cruising from the German Frisian Islands towards the Elbe will cross these lanes more or less at right-angles and should watch out for shipping entering or leaving the Jade.

Elbe approaches

Most boats approaching the Elbe arrive along the coast a few miles north of the German Frisian Islands, cross the 'Jade Approach' shipping lanes more or less at right-angles and should then make for Schlüsseltonne red-and-white fairway buoy at the mouth of the Alte Weser. This line of approach will keep you just south of the main Terschelling–German Bight shipping lanes and you can then head towards Westertill north-cardinal buoy to stay on the southern edge of the Elbe approach channel.

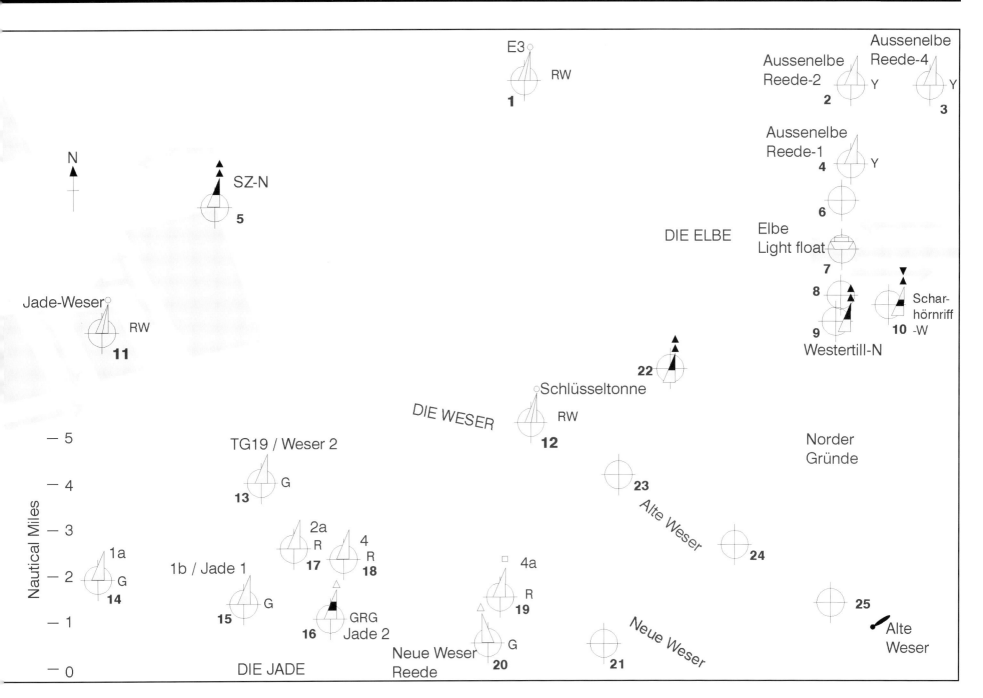

E3 ○
RW
1

Aussenelbe
Reede-2
2 Y

Aussenelbe
Reede-4
3 Y

Aussenelbe
Reede-1
4 Y

6

DIE ELBE

Elbe
Light float
7

8

Schar-
hörnriff
10 -W

9

Westertill-N

N

SZ-N
5

Jade-Weser ○
RW
11

22

○ Schlüsseltonne
RW
DIE WESER
12

Norder
Gründe

Nautical Miles

— 5

— 4

— 3

— 2

— 1

— 0

TG19 / Weser 2
G
13

23

Alte Weser

24

1a
G
14

1b / Jade 1

2a
R
17

4
R
18

4a

R
19

25

Alte
Weser

G
15

GRG
Jade 2
16

Neue Weser
Reede

G
20

Neue Weser

21

DIE JADE

177

WP No	Waypoint name and position	Latitude	Longitude
73–1	Alte Weser outer, 6½ M 300°T from Alte Weser lighthouse	53°55.10'N	07°58.16'E
73–2	Alte Weser middle, 3½ M 300°T from Alte Weser lighthouse	53°53.60'N	08°02.57'E
73–3	Alte Weser inner, 1 M 300°T from Alte Weser lighthouse	53°52.34'N	08°06.25'E
73–4	Alte Weser light, 4½ ca due W of Alte Weser lighthouse	53°51.84'N	08°06.96'E
73–5	Weser 4a red buoy, actual position	53°52.50'N	07°53.67'E
73–6	Weser 3a / Neue Weser Reede green buoy, actual position	53°51.50'N	07°53.30'E
73–7	Neue Weser outer, 2.6 M E of Neue Weser Reede green buoy	53°51.50'N	07°57.72'E
73–8	Roter Grund turning, 3.8 M 258°T from Alte Weser lighthouse	53°51.06'N	08°01.39'E
73–9	Neue Weser inner, 2.7 M 188°T from Alte Weser lighthouse	53°49.15'N	08°07.08'E
73–10	Mellumplate E, 2.7 M due E of Mellumplate lighthouse	53°46.34'N	08°10.20'E
73–11	Fahrwasser middle, 7.9 M 252°T from Alte Weser lighthouse	53°49.39'N	07°54.92'E
73–12	Blaue Balje, 6.35 M 236°T from Alte Weser lighthouse	53°48.29'N	07°58.77'E
73–13	Oldoogrinne north, 2.1 M 293°T from Mellumplate lighthouse	53°47.15'N	08°02.38'E
73–14	Mellumplate west, 1.8 M due W of Mellumplate lighthouse	53°46.34'N	08°02.59'E

Datum ED 50 The waypoint latitudes and longitudes in this table refer to European Datum (1950)

COASTAL DANGERS
Refer to Admiralty charts 1875 and 3368

Wangerooger Fahrwasser
The channel approaching the mouth of the Jade leads in from the WNW, converging gradually with the north coast of Wangerooge before swinging south into the estuary opposite the low island known as Minsener-Oog.

This buoyed approach channel – the Wangerooger Fahrwasser – passes south of a long shoal called Strand-plate which has least depths mostly between 3 and 4 metres except for a small 1.9 metre patch on its south-east edge. On the landward side of the channel is the broad shoal area that extends north from Wangerooge for just under 1 mile, with least depths ranging from just awash to about 4 metres.

The Wangerooger Fahrwasser is a straightforward shipping channel, with pairs of large lateral buoys at intervals of about 1¼ miles. However the fairway is relatively narrow and, when ships are about, boats should keep just the wrong side of the red or green buoys where depths allow, to leave the way clear for commercial traffic constrained by draught.

Mellumplate
On the east side of the entrance to the Jade, a long drying sandbank – called Mellumplate – stretches north from Alte Mellum island for over 4 miles. Beyond the north end of the drying area, a shallow bank continues to curve round to the north-west for a further 3 miles, with least depths between ½ metre and about 4 metres. These outer shoals are known as Oldoog-plate and Mittel-plate, and they lie just south of the buoyed Neue Weser channel.

A narrow secondary channel – the Mittelrinne – leads between the Neue Weser and the Jade, passing between Mittel-plate and Strand-plate and marked by a line of red buoys only. The Mittelrinne channel is quite straightforward for boats in quiet weather and can be useful if you are coming out of the Jade bound for the Elbe.

Roter Sand and Roter Grund
A narrow fork of shoals extends north-westwards from near Alte Weser light-tower for about 5 miles, effectively separating the outer reaches of the Alte Weser and the Neue Weser. There is plenty of depth over most of these shoals, which are well buoyed on their north and south sides and only become significant as dangers in heavy weather. However, care must be taken if you are approaching the Weser estuary in poor visibility, when you need to be certain that you are either safely in the Neue Weser channel or the Alte Weser, not somewhere in between.

Danger in strong onshore winds
The wide outer estuaries of the Weser and the Jade, with their long fingers of shoals and banks stretching out to the north-west, present a dangerous prospect in strong onshore winds. In this context, sustained north-westerlies of, say, force 5–6 will build up a nasty onshore swell that breaks and seethes over the estuary shoals and makes careful pilotage at once more vital and more difficult. Great care must be taken in all the wide German estuaries in strong onshore weather – if in doubt, stay in harbour and enjoy the bracing sea air from a safe distance.

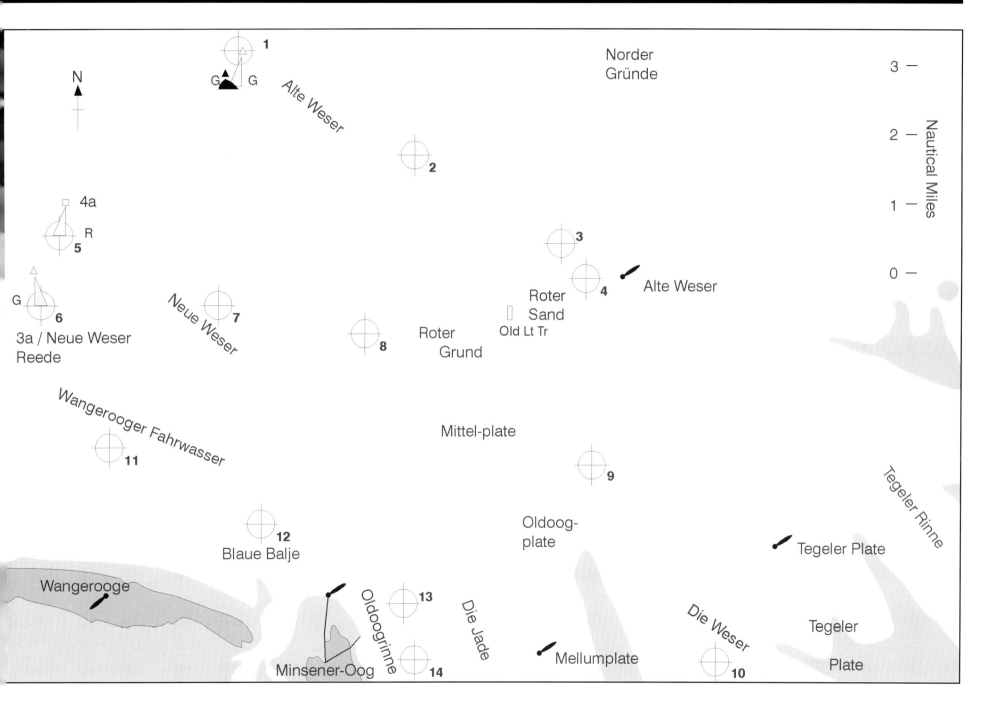

N

1

G G

Alte Weser

Norder
Gründe

3 —

2 —

2

Nautical Miles

1 —

4a

R

5

0 —

3

4

Alte Weser

G

6

Neue Weser

7

Roter
Sand
Old Lt Tr

3a / Neue Weser
Reede

8

Roter
Grund

Wangerooger Fahrwasser

11

Mittel-plate

9

Oldoog-
plate

12

Blaue Balje

Tegeler Rinne

Tegeler Plate

Wangerooge

13

Oldoogrinne

Die Jade

Die Weser

Tegeler

14

Minsener-Oog

Mellumplate

10

Plate

Die Jade to Wilhelmshaven

WP No	Waypoint name and position	Latitude	Longitude
74–1	Oldoogrinne north, 2.1 M 293°T from Mellumplate lighthouse	53°47.15'N	08°02.38'E
74–2	Mellumplate west, 1.8 M due W of Mellumplate lighthouse	53°46.34'N	08°02.59'E
74–3	Kilometre 22, 2.45 M 290°T from Hooksielplate light tower	53°41.04'N	08°05.12'E
74–4	Hooksiel approach, 1.8 M 235°T from Hooksielplate light tower	53°39.17'N	08°06.51'E
74–5	Hooksiel entrance, 1½ ca 071°T from Hooksiel S pierhead	53°38.68'N	08°05.51'E
74–6	Kilometre 15, 2¼ M 186°T from Hooksielplate light tower	53°37.96'N	08°08.57'E
74–7	Kilometre 10, 1.7 M 059°T from Voslapp S L/light	53°35.81'N	08°10.37'E
74–8	Nassauhafen N approach, 2 M 282°T from Eckwarden S L/light	53°31.73'N	08°10.74'E
74–9	Nassauhafen entrance, 4½ ca 103°T from lock radar tower	53°30.89'N	08°09.50'E

Datum ED 50 The waypoint latitudes and longitudes in this table refer to European Datum (1950)

COASTAL DANGERS

Refer to Admiralty charts 3368 and 3369

Wangerooger Fahrwasser

This long buoyed channel approaching the Jade leads in from the WNW, converging gradually with the north coast of Wangerooge before swinging south into the estuary opposite the low island of Minsener-Oog. The Fahrwasser passes south of a long shoal called Strand-plate, which has least depths mostly between 3 and 4 metres except for a 1.9 metre patch on its south-east edge. On the landward side, shoals extend north from Wangerooge for just under 1 mile, with least depths from just awash to 4 metres.

The Wangerooger Fahrwasser is a straightforward shipping channel, with pairs of large lateral buoys at intervals of about 1¼ miles. However the fairway is relatively narrow and, when ships are about, boats should keep just the wrong side of the red or green buoys where depths allow, to leave the way clear for commercial traffic constrained by draught.

Mellumplate

On the east side of the entrance to the Jade, a long drying sandbank – called Mellumplate – stretches north from Alte Mellum island for over 4 miles. Beyond the north end of the drying area, a shallow bank continues to curve round to the north-west for a further 3 miles, with least depths between ½ metre and about 4 metres. These outer shoals are known as Oldoog-plate and Mittel-plate, and they lie just south of the buoyed Neue Weser channel.

Shipping in the Jade

Wilhelmshaven is a large commercial and naval port, with extensive docks and massive tanker piers serving the Voslapper oil refinery. Yachts are small fry here and should watch out for shipping movements on all sides. When approaching the Jade you should listen on VHF Ch 63 for any traffic control instructions, switching to VHF Ch 20 south of buoys 33/34.

Tidal streams in the Jade

The tidal streams can be quite strong in the Jade, up to about 2½ knots at springs, so do not cut too close to buoys, jetties or other obstructions. Also take account of the tide when manoeuvring to avoid ships or to approach locks.

Approaching Hooksiel yacht basin

Hooksiel is the largest yacht haven on the North Sea coast of Germany and is entered from the Jade just south of buoys No 37 and 38. A large tanker pier juts out into the channel just south of Hooksiel entrance, so watch out for shipping movements and take account of the tidal stream when approaching Hooksiel pierheads. Green buoy H3 leads up to Hooksiel entrance, where you pass into the Vorhafen to wait for the lock into the yacht basin.

Approaching Nassauhafen Marina

The tidal marina in the Nassauhafen, at the south end of the Wilhelmshaven waterfront, is a convenient berth for a short stay and fairly handy for the city centre. The approach is straightforward, so long as you keep well over towards the Wilhelmshaven shore after passing the wide Neuer Vorhafen entrance, steering to leave No 56 red buoy well to port.

Danger in strong onshore winds

The wide outer estuaries of the Weser and the Jade, with their long fingers of shoals and banks stretching out to the north-west, present a dangerous prospect in strong onshore winds. In this context, sustained north-westerlies of, say, force 5–6 will build up a nasty onshore swell that breaks and seethes over the estuary shoals and makes careful pilotage at once more vital and more difficult. Great care must be taken in all the wide German estuaries in strong onshore weather – if in doubt, stay in harbour and enjoy the bracing sea air from a safe distance.

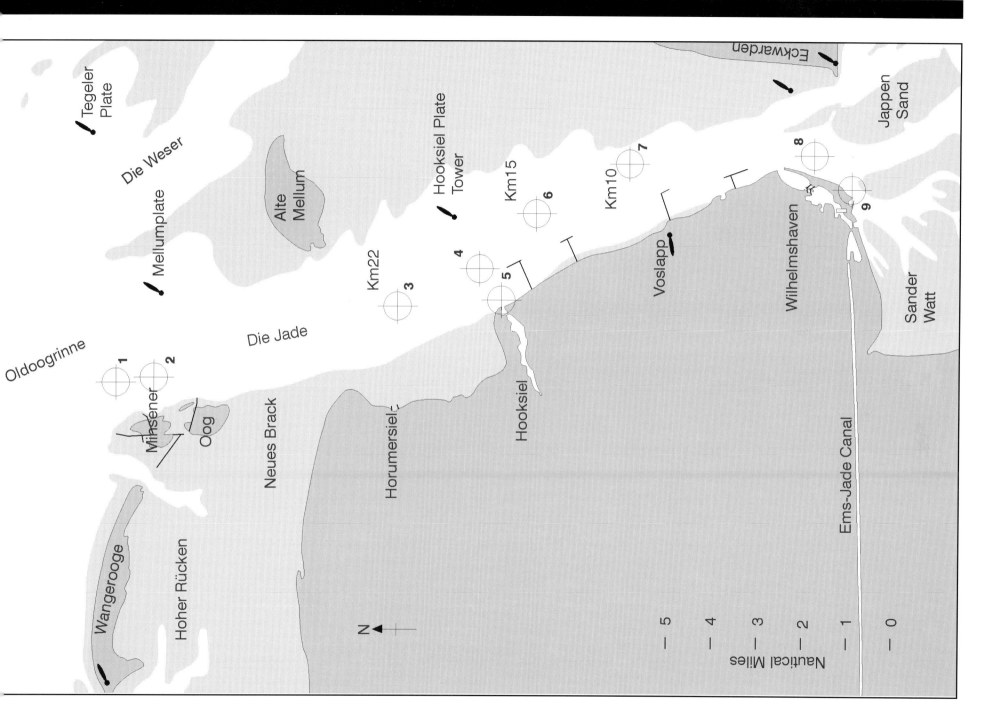

WP No	Waypoint name and position	Latitude	Longitude
75–1	Aussenelbe Reede-2 yellow anchorage buoy, actual position	54°03.50'N	08°06.97'E
75–2	Aussenelbe Reede-4 yellow anchorage buoy, actual position	54°03.51'N	08°10.00'E
75–3	Aussenelbe Reede-1 yellow anchorage buoy, actual position	54°01.83'N	08°06.97'E
75–4	Aussenelbe Reede-3 red buoy, actual position	54°01.64'N	08°13.59'E
75–5	Elbe No 4 red buoy, actual position	54°01.15'N	08°16.23'E
75–6	Norderelbe fairway, 3.8 M 330°T from Grosser Vogelsand Tr	54°03.10'N	08°25.50'E
75–7	Elbe outward, 1 M due N of the Elbe light float	54°01.00'N	08°06.60'E
75–8	Elbe light float, actual position	54°00.00'N	08°06.60'E
75–9	Elbe inward, 1 M due S of the Elbe light float	53°59.00'N	08°06.60'E
75–10	Westertill-N, 3 ca NW of Westertill N-card buoy	53°58.40'N	08°06.43'E
75–11	Scharhörnriff-W, 3 ca NW of Scharhörnriff W-card buoy	53°58.77'N	08°08.45'E
75–12	Scharhörnriff-N, 1 ca due N of Scharhörnriff N-card buoy	53°59.10'N	08°11.25'E
75–13	Elbe No 1, 1 ca due N of Elbe No 1 green buoy,	53°59.36'N	08°13.29'E
75–14	Elbe No 5, 1½ ca due N of 'A' green-white-green tower	53°59.26'N	08°19.00'E
75–15	Elbe No 9, 1½ ca due N of 'B' green-white-green tower	53°58.87'N	08°24.00'E
75–16	Elbe No 13, 1½ ca due N of 'C' green-white-green tower	53°58.40'N	08°28.15'E
75–17	Elbe No 6, 1½ ca due S of 'Z' red-white-red tower	54°00.70'N	08°18.97'E
75–18	Elbe No 10, 1½ ca due S of 'Y' red-white-red tower	53°59.91'N	08°24.37'E
75–19	Grosser Vogelsand outer, 8 ca due S of light tower	53°59.00'N	08°28.70'E
75–20	Grosser Vogelsand inner, ½ M due S of light tower	53°59.30'N	08°28.70'E

Datum ED 50 The waypoint latitudes and longitudes in this table refer to European Datum (1950)

COASTAL DANGERS

Refer to Admiralty charts 1875 and 3261

Elbe approaches

Most boats approaching the Elbe from the North Sea arrive by following the German coast a few miles north of the Frisian Islands, crossing the 'Jade Approach' shipping lanes more or less at right-angles and then heading towards Schlüsseltonne red-and-white fairway buoy off the mouth of the Alte Weser.

This line of approach will keep you just south of the main Terschelling–German Bight shipping lanes. From the Schlüsseltonne buoy you can aim towards Westertill north-cardinal buoy, keeping clear of the main flow of ships by following the southern edge of the Elbe approach channel. You would thus arrive in the outer estuary at a position about 1½ miles south of the Elbe light float.

Norder Grunde

This wide shoal area extends north-west for almost 9 miles from Grosser Knechtsand, effectively forming the north edge of the Alte Weser channel. Least depths over Norder Gründe range from less than 1 metre to about 2 metres even well offshore, so this is not an area to stray into by accident. The sea breaks over Norder Gründe in heavy onshore weather. The seaward edge of the shoals is effectively guarded by the Schlüsseltonne red-and-white fairway buoy, the Nordergründe north-cardinal buoy and the Westertill north-cardinal buoy.

Scharhörn Riff

This wide shoal extends seawards from Scharhörn island to form the southern boundary of the Elbe approaches. The west edge of Scharhörn Riff is guarded by Westertill north-cardinal buoy, Scharhörnriff west-cardinal buoy and Scharhörnriff north-cardinal buoy. The north edge is guarded by the green buoys and green-and-white towers of the Elbe entrance channel. Least depths over Scharhörn Riff vary from 1½ to 3½ metres and the sea breaks heavily over these shoals in strong onshore winds.

Shipping in the Elbe approaches

Shipping can be heavy in the outer approaches to the Elbe. As a general rule, boats should keep just the 'wrong' side of the main channel buoys wherever possible, to leave the way clear for commercial traffic which might itself be involved in overtaking.

Effect of fresh onshore winds

The fast-flowing Elbe is not particularly hospitable and short steep seas quickly build up when even a moderate wind is blowing against the tide. The most notoriously grim conditions in the Elbe occur when a fresh westerly or north-westerly is blowing against a spring ebb, a particularly nasty combination for boats trying to leave the Elbe from Cuxhaven. In any event, you should certainly not try to leave the Elbe in any strong onshore winds. Arriving is generally a slightly easier proposition, so long as you know exactly where you are.

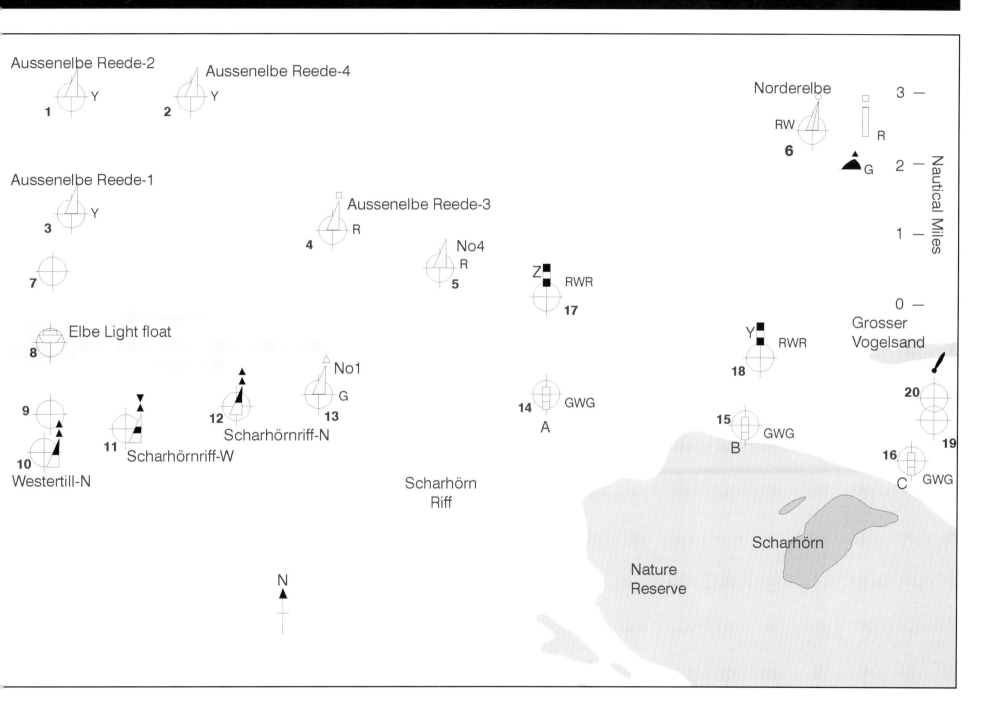

Aussenelbe Reede-2

Aussenelbe Reede-4

Norderelbe

1   Y

2   Y

RW

6

3 — Nautical Miles

R

2 —

G

Aussenelbe Reede-1

3   Y

Aussenelbe Reede-3

4   R

No4

5   R

1 —

Z

RWR

17

7

0 —

Grosser
Vogelsand

Elbe Light float

8

Y

RWR

18

20

No1

9

13   G

12

14   GWG

A

15

GWG

19

11

Scharhörnriff-N

B

16

10

Scharhörnriff-W

C   GWG

Westertill-N

Scharhörn
Riff

Scharhörn

N

Nature
Reserve

WP No	Waypoint name and position	Latitude	Longitude
76–1	Elbe No 9, 1½ ca due N of 'B' green-white-green tower	53°58.87'N	08°24.00'E
76–2	Elbe No 13, 1½ ca due N of 'C' green-white-green tower	53°58.40'N	08°28.15'E
76–3	Elbe No 19, 1½ ca due N of 'E' green-white-green tower	53°57.85'N	08°34.40'E
76–4	Elbe No 25, 2½ ca due N of 'F' green-white-green tower	53°56.81'N	08°38.27'E
76–5	Elbe No 29, 4 ca 073°T from kilometre mark 3	53°55.00'N	08°40.42'E
76–6	Cuxhaven N approach, 4 ca due N of Cuxhaven lighthouse	53°52.77'N	08°42.57'E
76–7	Cuxhaven S approach, 4 ca 107°T from Cuxhaven lighthouse	53°52.24'N	08°43.22'E
76–8	Cuxhaven entrance, midway between the Jachthafen pierheads	53°52.48'N	08°42.56'E
76–9	Elbe No 32a, ¾ M 010°T from Cuxhaven lighthouse	53°53.11'N	08°42.79'E
76–10	Elbe No 28, 4 ca due W of Tide Gauge	53°56.29'N	08°40.35'E
76–11	Elbe No 26, ¾ ca SW of 'W' red-white-red tower	53°57.31'N	08°39.50'E
76–12	Elbe No 24, 5.9 M 058°T from Neuwerk lighthouse	53°58.08'N	08°38.33'E
76–13	Elbe No 20, ½ ca SW of 'X' red-white-red tower	53°59.28'N	08°34.78'E
76–14	Grosser Vogelsand inner, ½ M due S of light tower	53°59.30'N	08°28.70'E
76–15	Elbe No 10, 1½ ca due S of 'Y' red-white-red tower	53°59.91'N	08°24.37'E
76–16	Elbe NL12, 1 ca due N of NL12 E-card buoy	53°57.72'N	08°37.57'E
76–17	Elbe NL8, 1 ca due N of NL8 S-card buoy	53°58.29'N	08°34.59'E
76–18	Elbe NL4, 1 ca due N of NL4 S-card buoy	53°58.61'N	08°31.10'E
76–19	Grosser Vogelsand outer, 8 ca due S of light tower	53°59.00'N	08°28.70'E

Datum ED 50 The waypoint latitudes and longitudes in this table refer to European Datum (1950)

COASTAL DANGERS

Refer to Admiralty chart 3261

Elbe approaches

Most boats approaching the Elbe arrive by following the German coast a few miles north of the Frisian Islands, crossing the 'Jade Approach' shipping lanes more or less at right-angles and then heading towards Schlüsseltonne red-and-white fairway buoy off the mouth of the Alte Weser. From the Schlüsseltonne buoy you can aim towards Westertill N-cardinal buoy, keeping clear of the main flow of ships by following the southern edge of the Elbe approach channel.

Scharhörn Riff

This wide shoal extends seawards from Scharhörn to form the southern boundary of the Elbe entrance. The west edge of Scharhörn Riff is guarded by Westertill N-cardinal buoy, Scharhörnriff W-cardinal and Scharhörnriff N-cardinal. The north edge is guarded by the green buoys and towers of the Elbe channel. Least depths over Scharhörn Riff vary from 1½–3½ metres and the sea breaks heavily over these shoals in strong onshore winds.

Shipping in the Elbe approaches

Shipping can be heavy in the outer approaches to the Elbe. As a rule, boats should keep just the 'wrong' side of the main channel buoys wherever possible. This leaves the way clear for commercial traffic, which might itself be involved in overtaking.

Effect of fresh onshore winds

In the fast-flowing Elbe, short steep seas quickly build up when even a moderate wind is blowing against the tide. The worst conditions in the Elbe occur in a fresh westerly or north-westerly against a spring ebb, a nasty combination for boats trying to leave the river from Cuxhaven. You should certainly not try to leave the Elbe in any strong onshore winds. Arriving is generally a slightly easier proposition, so long as you know exactly where you are.

Strong tides in the Elbe

Although the tides near the Elbe light-float only reach about 2 knots at springs, the streams increase within the constrained channel between Scharhörn and Grosser Vogelsand. A spring ebb can exceed 3 knots just north of Scharhörn. Further upstream off Cuxhaven, a spring ebb can touch 4 knots, which explains the dramatic effect of even a moderate breeze against the tide. Do not underestimate the effect of any weather-going stream in the Elbe.

Approaching Cuxhaven

Because of the strong streams in the Elbe, take great care when approaching and turning into Cuxhaven Yacht Club Marina (just upstream from the ferry harbour). Yachts should begin their turn and approach while some distance up-tide of the marina entrance. This caution is particularly relevant if you are coming downstream from the Kiel Canal lock at Brunsbüttel, when you might well be arriving off Cuxhaven during the strongest part of the ebb.

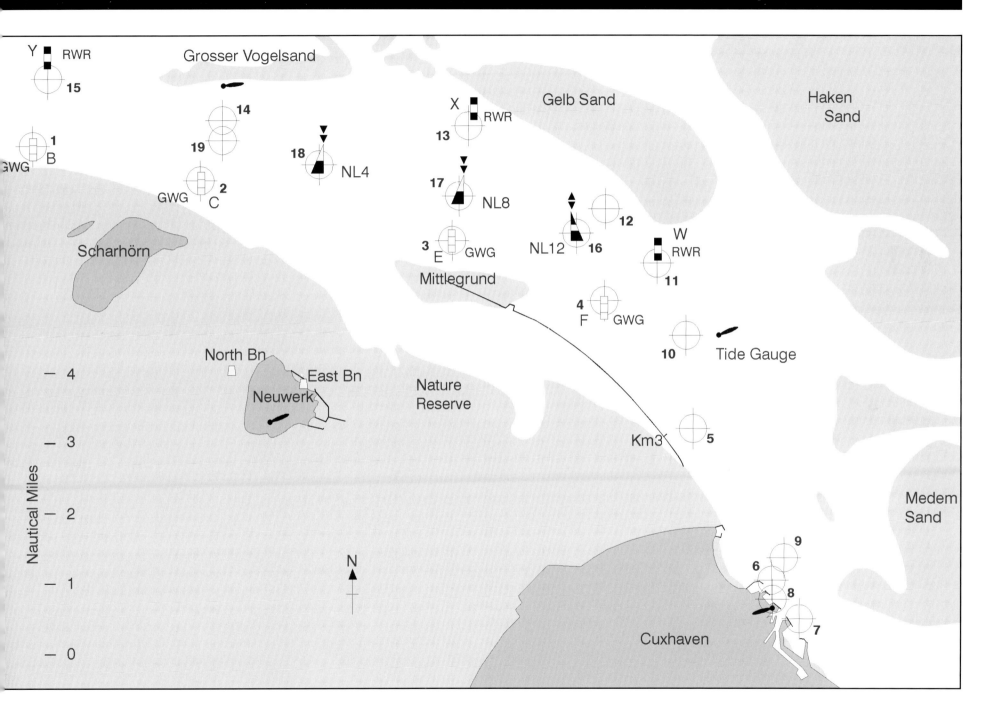

Y ■ RWR

15

Grosser Vogelsand

Gelb Sand

Haken Sand

14

X ■ RWR

13

1

B

GWG

19

18 NL4

17 NL8

2

GWG C

12

3 E GWG

NL12 16

W RWR

11

Scharhörn

Mittlegrund

4 F GWG

North Bn

10 Tide Gauge

East Bn

Neuwerk

Nature Reserve

Km3

5

— 4

— 3

Nautical Miles

Medem Sand

— 2

9

— 1

N

6

8

— 0

7

Cuxhaven

WP No	Waypoint name and position	Latitude	Longitude
77–1	Falsches Tief outer, 4.35 M 025°T from Grosser Vogelsand tower	54°03.71'N	08°31.85'E
77–2	Norderelbe fairway, 3.8 M 330°T from Grosser Vogelsand tower	54°03.10'N	08°25.50'E
77–3	Norderelbe entrance, 3¼ M 338°T from Grosser Vogelsand tower	54°02.79'N	08°26.66'E
77–4	Norderelbe middle, 2.35 M 019°T from Grosser Vogelsand tower	54°02.00'N	08°30.00'E
77–5	Norderelbe inner, 3.95 M 073°T from Grosser Vogelsand tower	54°00.94'N	08°35.11'E
77–6	Luechterloch north, 2.3 M 054°T from Grosser Vogelsand tower	54°01.14'N	08°31.88'E
77–7	Luechterloch south, 2.45 M 093°T from Grosser Vogelsand tower	53°59.67'N	08°32.88'E

Datum ED 50 The waypoint latitudes and longitudes in this table refer to European Datum (1950)

COASTAL DANGERS
Refer to Admiralty chart 3261

Norderelbe channel
This secondary buoyed channel runs parallel to the main Elbe approach channel about 3 miles to the north. The Norderelbe leads north of Grosser Vogelsand and Gelb-Sand, joining the main estuary either via the Luechterloch, opposite Elbe red buoy No 18, or opposite Elbe 'W' red-white-red tower via a narrow buoyed cut known as Zehnerloch, which skirts the south-east edge of Gelb-Sand.

The Norderelbe is not often used by boats, but can be a handy route in quiet weather if you are cruising between, say, Cuxhaven and the North Frisian Islands, or Cuxhaven and the Eider river. With GPS making navigation easier along these coasts, the Norderelbe can also provide an interesting route into the estuary if you are arriving from Helgoland.

However, only approach the Norderelbe in reasonably quiet weather or in offshore winds. With a moderate north-westerly astern, you are much safer coming into the Elbe by the main channel.

Grosser Vogelsand
This extensive wide shoal forms the north boundary of the main Elbe channel and the south boundary of the Norderelbe. The south-east fringes dry to about 1 metre. The large Grosser Vogelsand light-tower (red with white bands) has a distinctive helicopter platform and stands near the south drying edge of the shoals, more or less opposite Scharhörn.

The seaward 5 miles of Grosser Vogelsand, west of 'Y' red-white-red tower, mostly have least depths between 3 and 8 metres, but there are various wrecks on the shoals, one of which has a swept depth of only 2.7 metres. If you are heading north from the Elbe, you can cross the outer tongue of Grosser Vogelsand in quiet weather with some rise of tide, but do not try this short cut with any onshore swell running.

Luechterloch channel
This narrow buoyed channel cuts more or less north–south between the Norderelbe and the main Elbe channel. The south end of the Luechterloch joins the Elbe opposite red buoy No 18, about 1 mile west of 'X' red-white-red tower.

Strangers should only use the Norderelbe and the Luechterloch in quiet weather in the absence of onshore swell. In fresh onshore winds, the sea breaks heavily on the shoals immediately east and west of the Luechterloch, and rough water usually extends into the Luechterloch itself.

Falsches Tief
This relatively minor channel cuts into the outer Elbe estuary a couple of miles north of the Norderelbe, but is generally only used by local boats. Two tongues of shallow sandbanks extend WNW on each side of Falsches Tief and the fairway is marked by red buoys only. However, in quiet settled weather, if you are arriving from the North Frisian Islands or from Helgoland, Falsches Tief can provide an interesting sand-dodging route into the Elbe for those who enjoy threading shallow enigmatic channels.

Shipping in the Elbe approaches
Shipping can be heavy in the outer approaches to the Elbe. As a rule, boats should keep the 'wrong' side of the main channel buoys wherever possible. This leaves the way clear for commercial traffic.

Effect of fresh onshore winds
In the fast-flowing Elbe, short steep seas quickly build up when even a moderate wind is blowing against the tide. The worst conditions in the Elbe occur in a fresh westerly or north-westerly against a spring ebb, a nasty combination for boats trying to leave the river from Cuxhaven.

Although streams are less fierce in the Norderelbe, strangers should only use this route to or from the Elbe in quiet weather or offshore winds. In sustained onshore winds, the sea breaks heavily over Grosser Vogelsand, making the Norderelbe and the Luechterloch a potentially dangerous route.

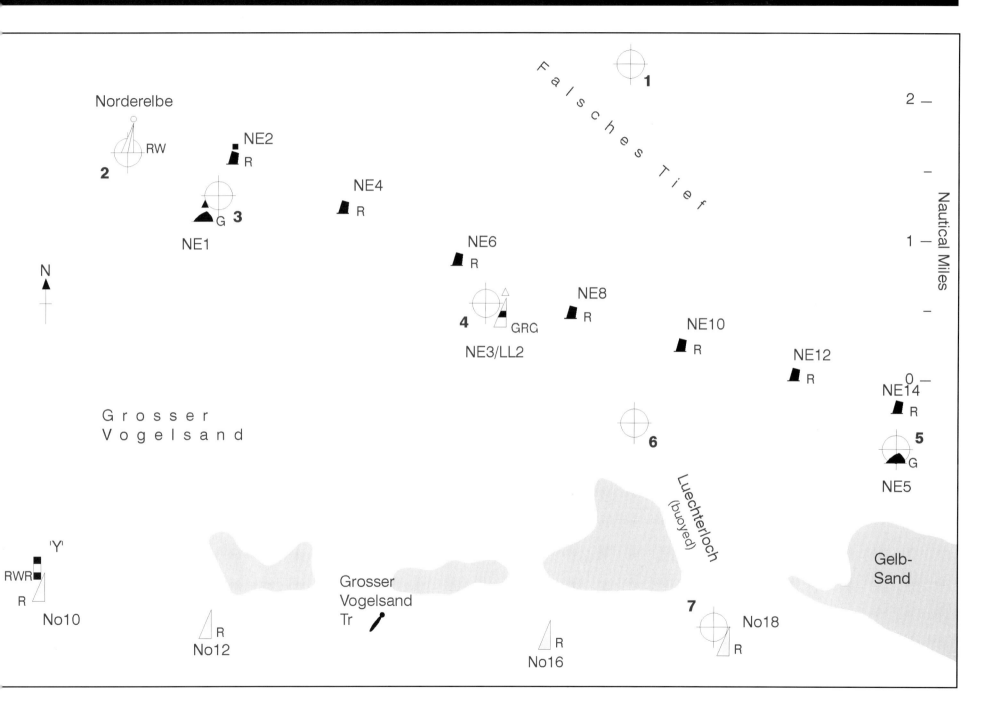

Norderelbe

RW

2

NE2
R

NE1

G 3

NE4
R

NE6
R

NE3/LL2

4

GRG

NE8
R

NE10
R

NE12
R

NE14
R

NE5

G 5

Falsches Tief

1

2 —

Nautical Miles

1 —

0 —

N

Grosser
Vogelsand

'Y'

RWR

R

No10

R

No12

Grosser
Vogelsand
Tr

6

Luechterloch
(buoyed)

No16
R

7

No18
R

Gelb-
Sand

Norderelbe – Buschsand to Zehnerloch

WP No	Waypoint name and position	Latitude	Longitude
78–1	Falsches Tief inner, 3.5 M due N of Elbe RWR tower 'W'	54°00.87'N	08°39.60'E
78–2	Norderelbe inner, 3.95 M 073°T from Grosser Vogelsand tower	54°00.94'N	08°35.11'E
78–3	Buschsand 20 buoy, 2.65 M 058°T from Elbe RWR tower 'X'	54°00.70'N	08°38.65'E
78–4	NE7 green buoy, 3.3 M 072°T from Elbe RWR tower 'X'	54°00.32'N	08°40.15'E
78–5	Grossputengat, 3.75 M 088°T from Elbe RWR tower 'X'	53°59.44'N	08°41.21'E
78–6	Zehnerloch east, 1.4 M 046°T from Elbe RWR tower 'W'	53°58.34'N	08°41.30'E
78–7	NE 30 red buoy, ¾ M 046°T from Elbe RWR tower 'W'	53°57.90'N	08°40.51'E
78–8	Zehnerloch west, 3.5 ca due N of Elbe RWR tower 'W'	53°57.72'N	08°39.60'E
78–9	Elbe No 20, ½ ca SW of 'X' red-white-red tower	53°59.28'N	08°34.78'E
78–10	Elbe No 24, 5.9 M 058°T from Neuwerk lighthouse	53°58.08'N	08°38.33'E
78–11	Elbe No 26, ¾ ca SW of 'W' red-white-red tower	53°57.31'N	08°39.50'E
78–12	Elbe NL12, 1 ca due N of NL12 E-card buoy	53°57.72'N	08°37.57'E
78–13	Elbe No 25, 2½ ca due N of 'F' green-white-green tower	53°56.81'N	08°38.27'E

Datum ED 50 The waypoint latitudes and longitudes in this table refer to European Datum (1950)

COASTAL DANGERS
Refer to Admiralty chart 3261

Norderelbe channel
The secondary buoyed channel known as the Norderelbe runs parallel to the main Elbe approach channel about 3 miles to the north. The Norderelbe leads north of Grosser Vogelsand and Gelb-Sand, joining the main estuary opposite 'W' red-white-red tower via a narrow buoyed cut known as Zehnerloch, which skirts the south-east edge of Gelb-Sand.

The Norderelbe channel is not often used by boats, but can be a handy route in quiet weather if you are cruising between, say, Cuxhaven and the North Frisian Islands, or Cuxhaven and the Eider river. With GPS making navigation easier along these coasts, the Norderelbe can also provide an interesting and quieter route into the estuary if you are arriving from Helgoland. However, you should only approach the Norderelbe channel in reasonably quiet weather or in offshore winds. With a moderate north-westerly astern, you are safer coming into the Elbe by the main channel.

Gelb-Sand
This extensive drying bank, over 4 miles long by 1 mile wide, lies to the east of Grosser Vogelsand, forming the continuation of the north boundary of the main Elbe channel and the south boundary of the Norderelbe. Drying heights range from just under 1 metre to over 2 metres. Gelb-Sand is well guarded on its south side by the buoys and towers of the Elbe channel, but rather more sparely on its north edge by the smaller buoys of the Norderelbe. The narrow Zehnerloch channel curves round the south-east edge of Gelb-Sand, providing the best cut between the Norderelbe and Elbe.

Falsches Tief
This relatively minor channel cuts into the outer Elbe estuary a couple of miles north of the Norderelbe, but is generally only used by local boats. Two tongues of shallow sandbanks extend WNW on each side of Falsches Tief and the fairway is marked by red buoys only. However, in quiet settled weather, if you are arriving from the North Frisian Islands or Helgoland, Falsches Tief can provide an interesting sand-dodging route into the Elbe for those who enjoy threading shallow, rather enigmatic channels.

Shipping in the Elbe approaches
Shipping can be heavy in the outer approaches to the Elbe. As a rule, boats should keep just the 'wrong' side of the main channel buoys wherever possible.

Effect of fresh onshore winds
In the fast-flowing Elbe, short steep seas quickly build up when even a moderate wind is blowing against the tide. The worst conditions in the Elbe occur in a fresh westerly or north-westerly against a spring ebb, a nasty combination for boats trying to leave the river from Cuxhaven. You should certainly not try to leave the Elbe in any strong onshore winds.

Strong tides in the Elbe
Although the tides near the Elbe light float only reach about 2 knots at springs, the streams increase within the constrained channel between Scharhörn and Grosser Vogelsand. A spring ebb can exceed 3 knots just north of Scharhörn. Further upstream off Cuxhaven, a spring ebb can touch 4 knots, which explains the dramatic effect of even a moderate breeze against the tide. Do not underestimate the effect of any weather-going stream in the Elbe.

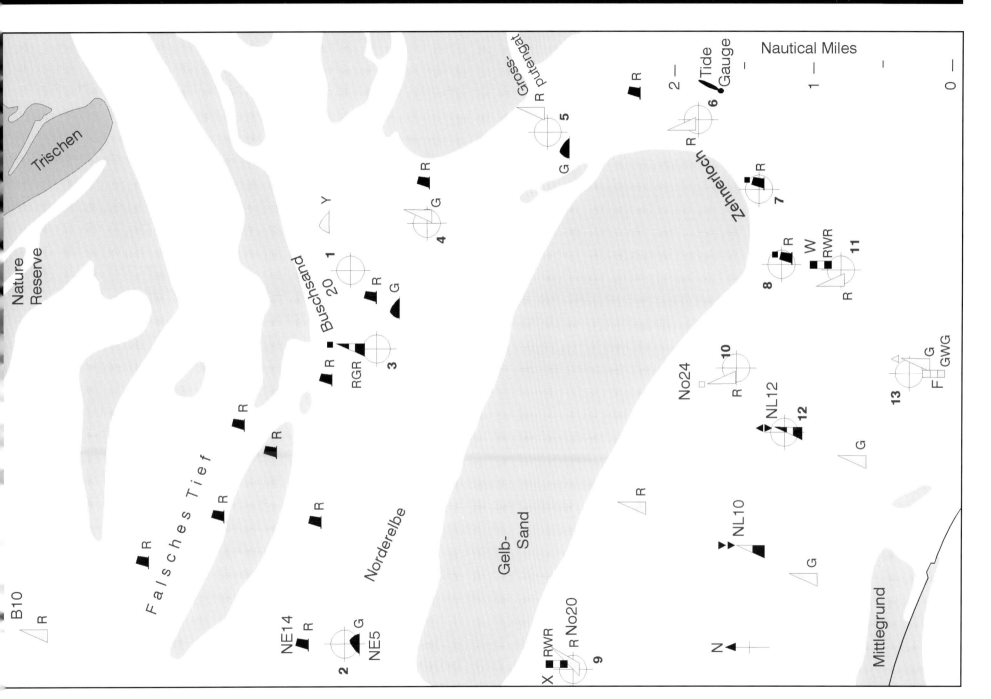

Nautical Miles

189

WP No	Waypoint name and position	Latitude	Longitude
79–1	Süderhever outer, midway No 1 green and No 2 red buoys	54°17.86'N	08°25.20'E
79–2	Eider red-and-white fairway buoy	54°14.59'N	08°27.68'E
79–3	Eider outer, midway No 1/3 green and No 2/4 red buoys	54°14.44'N	08°29.72'E
79–4	Norderpiep red-and-white fairway buoy, actual position	54°11.45'N	08°28.51'E
79–5	Norderpiep outer, midway NP1 green and NP2 red buoys	54°11.26'N	08°29.97'E
79–6	Süderpiep red-and-white fairway whistle buoy, actual position	54°05.95'N	08°22.05'E
79–7	Süderpiep outer, midway SP1 green and SP2 red buoys	54°05.95'N	08°27.40'E

Datum ED 50 The waypoint latitudes and longitudes in this table refer to European Datum (1950)

COASTAL DANGERS

Refer to Admiralty charts 1875 and 3767 and German chart 3013 (sheet 13)

Rochelsteert

About 2 miles north of the outer approaches to the River Eider, a long finger of shallow water – the Rochelsteert – juts out seawards for almost 6 miles, with least depths between 2 and 5 metres. In quiet weather, boats can safely cross the outer part of Rochelsteert, but in freshening onshore winds steep seas build up over these shoals. The seaward end of Rochelsteert is marked by Süderhever No 1 green buoy, which is left to starboard as you enter the Süderhever channel that cuts north of Rochelsteert.

Eider river approaches

The Eider river provides an interesting route across Schleswig-Holstein to the Baltic, joining the Nord-Ostsee Kanal about 20 miles north of Brunsbüttel at Gieselau. You enter the Eider through a lock at the Eider flood-control barrier – the Eidersperrwerk. Because this barrier normally allows the tide to ebb and flow, the Eider effectively remains tidal for about 16 miles up to the lock at Nordfeld.

The seaward approaches to the Eidersperrwerk lead through a long buoyed channel between drying sandbanks. The outer mark is the Eider red-and-white fairway buoy, and it is nearly 15 miles from this buoy to the Eidersperrwerk lock. The outer estuary is open to the west, but is partly protected from the north by the low shore of Eiderstedt. To the south, several other shallow inlets cut through the coastal shoals to small harbours on the Dithmarschen shore.

In many ways, the Eider river provides a more relaxing route through to the Baltic than the busy, fast-flowing Elbe, yet it still requires caution in onshore winds. There is a shallow bar 2 miles inshore from the fairway buoy, with a least depth of about 3½ metres. With the wind from anywhere between north-west through west to south-west, strangers should not approach the Eider estuary in conditions stronger than force 4. In force 5–6 onshore winds, the sea can start breaking over the bar and the outer banks each side of the channel. Then this whole coastline becomes distinctly inhospitable and you should wait for things to ease.

Norderpiep

This narrow buoyed channel leads inshore between Blauortsand and Tertiussand to the sheltered harbour at Büsum. The outer mark is Norderpiep red-and-white fairway buoy, which lies 3 miles south of the Eider fairway buoy. You can reckon about 14 miles from Norderpiep fairway buoy to Büsum.

Like the Eider approaches, Norderpiep has a shallow bar and is open to onshore winds from between north-west through west to south-west. Strangers should not approach this channel in onshore weather stronger than force 4. In fresh or strong onshore winds, seas start to break over the bar and over the outer banks each side of the buoyed fairway.

Süderpiep

The Süderpiep channel cuts south of Tertiussand to Büsum harbour, and is generally wider and deeper than Norderpiep. Süderpiep red-and-white fairway buoy lies about 11 miles north-east of the Elbe light float and 9 miles SSW of the Eider fairway buoy.

Süderpiep fairway is also the outer mark for Falsches Tief, a minor channel cutting into the Elbe estuary a couple of miles north of the Norderelbe. Two tongues of shallow banks extend WNW on each side of Falsches Tief, which is marked by red buoys only.

Approaches to Büsum harbour

Whether you arrive off Büsum via Norderpiep or Süderpiep, bear in mind that a strong cross-tide runs off the harbour entrance near half-flood or half-ebb. Once through the outer pierheads, there is a waiting area for the lock which leads through into the sheltered wet basin.

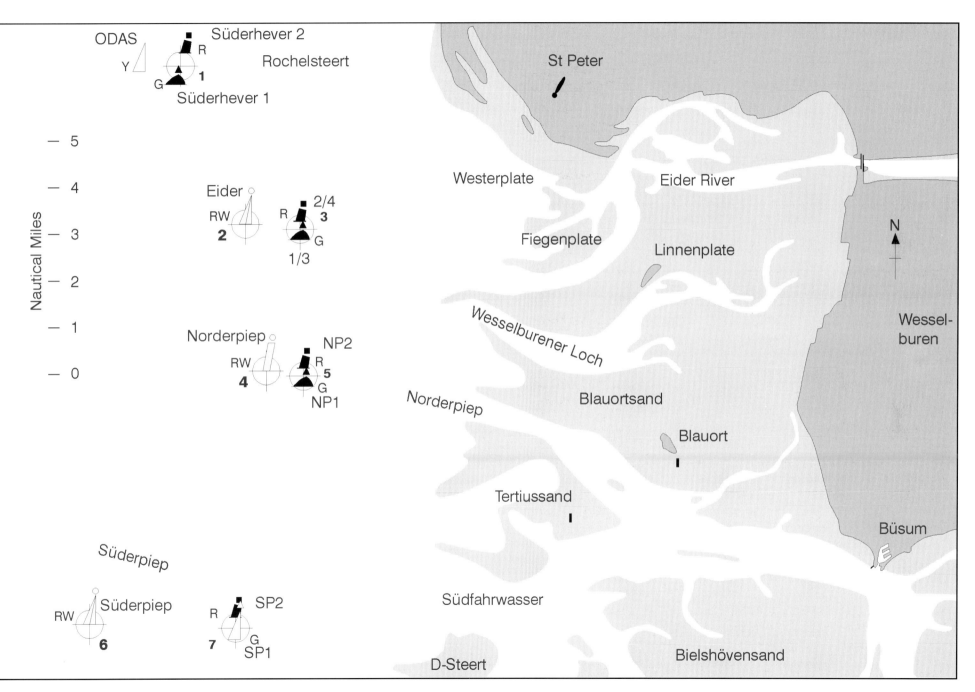

ODAS
Y

Süderhever 2
R
G
1
Süderhever 1
Rochelsteert

Eider
RW
2
R
G
2/4
3
1/3

Norderpiep
RW
4
R
G
NP2
5
NP1

Süderpiep
Süderpiep
RW
6
R
G
SP2
7
SP1

St Peter

Westerplate

Eider River

Fiegenplate

Linnenplate

N

Wessel-
buren

Wesselburener Loch

Norderpiep

Blauortsand

Blauort

Tertiussand

Südfahrwasser

Büsum

D-Steert

Bielshövensand

Nautical Miles

— 5

— 4

— 3

— 2

— 1

— 0

Approaches to Norderpiep and Süderpiep

WP No	Waypoint name and position	Latitude	Longitude
80–1	Norderpiep red-and-white fairway buoy, actual position	54°11.45'N	08°28.51'E
80–2	Norderpiep outer, midway NP1 green and NP2 red buoys	54°11.26'N	08°29.97'E
80–3	Norderpiep entrance, midway NP5 green and NP6 red buoys	54°10.85'N	08°33.34'E
80–4	Norderpiep inner, midway NP11 green and NP12 red buoys	54°10.23'N	08°38.38'E
80–5	Bezeichnet, midway NP13 green and NP14 red buoys	54°09.83'N	08°40.25'E
80–6	Blauort south, midway NP17 green and NP18 red buoys	54°08.51'N	08°43.75'E
80–7	Süderpiep red-and-white fairway whistle buoy, actual position	54°05.95'N	08°22.05'E
80–8	Süderpiep outer, midway SP1 green and SP2 red buoys	54°05.95'N	08°27.40'E

Datum ED 50 The waypoint latitudes and longitudes in this table refer to European Datum (1950)

COASTAL DANGERS

Refer to Admiralty charts 1875 and 3767 and German chart 3013 (sheet 13)

Norderpiep

This narrow buoyed channel leads inshore between Blauortsand and Tertiussand to the sheltered harbour at Büsum. The outer mark is Norderpiep red-and-white fairway buoy, which lies 3 miles south of the Eider fairway buoy. You can reckon about 14 miles from Norderpiep fairway buoy to Büsum harbour entrance.

Like the Eider approaches, Norderpiep has a shallow bar and is open to onshore winds from between north-west through west to south-west. Strangers should not approach this channel in onshore weather stronger than force 4. In fresh or strong onshore winds, seas start to break over the bar and over the outer banks each side of the buoyed fairway.

Blauortsand

This extensive area of drying sand extends seawards from the low coast north of Büsum for a good 7 miles, with drying heights ranging from just awash to just over 3 metres. The highest tip of Blauortsand forms a small sandy islet – Blauort – with an exposed height of less than 2 metres. The Norderpiep buoyed channel cuts past the southwest edge of Blauortsand and joins Süderpiep about 1½ miles south of Blauort.

Tertiussand

This 3-mile-wide expanse of drying sand lies between Norderpiep and Süderpiep, with drying heights mostly between 1 and 2 metres. The seaward edges of Tertiussand are unmarked between the Norderpiep and Süderpiep fairway buoys, so it is important to pick up one or other of these buoys when approaching this stretch of coast.

Tertiussand is a 'Zone 1' nature reserve, and no landing or anchoring is allowed around the sands between 1 May and 1 October.

Süderpiep

The Süderpiep channel cuts south of Tertiussand to Büsum harbour, and is generally wider and deeper than Norderpiep. Süderpiep red-and-white fairway buoy lies about 11 miles north-east of the Elbe light float and 9 miles SSW of the Eider fairway buoy.

Süderpiep fairway buoy is also the outer mark for Falsches Tief, a relatively minor channel cutting into the outer Elbe estuary a couple of miles north of the Norderelbe. Two tongues of shallow sandbanks extend WNW on each side of Falsches Tief and the fairway is marked by red buoys only. Falsches Tief is generally only used by local boats, but in quiet settled weather, if you are arriving from the North Frisian Islands or Helgoland, it can provide an interesting sand-dodging route into the Elbe for those who enjoy threading shallow, rather enigmatic channels.

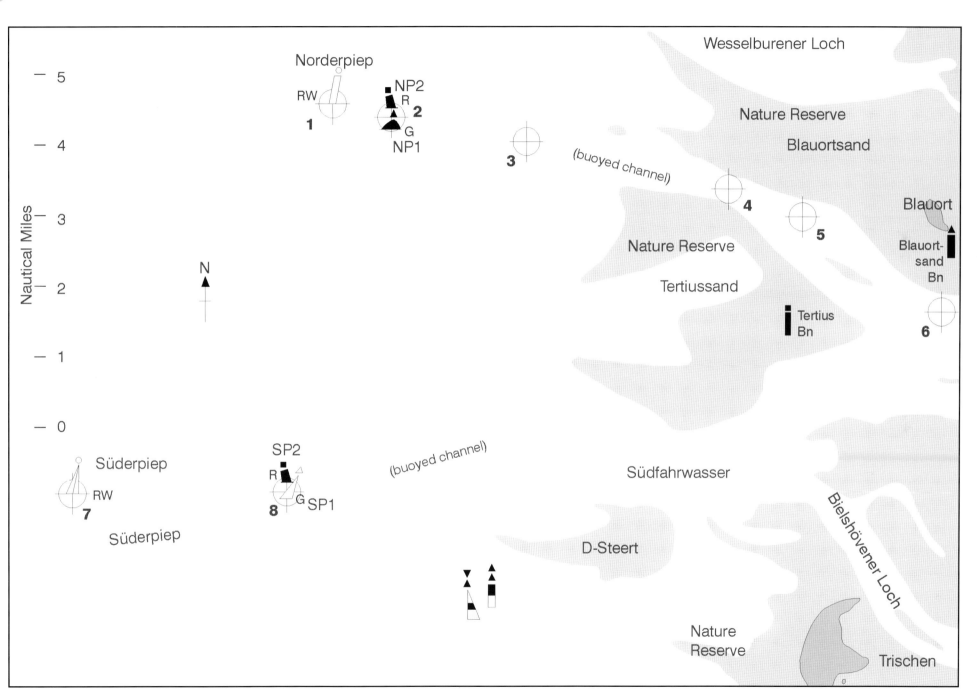

Nautical Miles

Wesselburener Loch

Norderpiep

5

NP2
RW
R 2
1
G
NP1

3
(buoyed channel)

Nature Reserve
Blauortsand

4

Blauort
5
Blauort-
sand
Bn

4

3

N

Nature Reserve

Tertiussand

Tertius
Bn

6

2

1

0

SP2
R
SP1
G
8 SP1

(buoyed channel)

Südfahrwasser

Süderpiep
RW
7

Süderpiep

D-Steert

Bielshövener Loch

Nature
Reserve

Trischen

193

WP No	Waypoint name and position	Latitude	Longitude
81–1	Eider red-and-white fairway buoy, actual position	54°14.59'N	08°27.68'E
81–2	Eider outer, midway No 1/3 green and No 2/4 red buoys	54°14.44'N	08°29.72'E
81–3	Eider entrance, midway No 9 green and No 10 red buoys	54°13.64'N	08°34.92'E
81–4	Eider inner, midway No 15 green and No 16 red buoys	54°13.28'N	08°38.93'E

Datum ED 50 The waypoint latitudes and longitudes in this table refer to European Datum (1950)

COASTAL DANGERS

Refer to Admiralty chart 3767 and German chart 3013 (sheet 13)

Rochelsteert

About 2 miles north of the outer approaches to the River Eider, a long finger of shallow water – the Rochelsteert – juts out seawards for almost 6 miles, with least depths between 2 and 5 metres. In quiet weather, boats can safely cross the outer part of Rochelsteert, but in freshening onshore winds steep seas build up over these shoals. The seaward end of Rochelsteert is marked by Süderhever No 1 green buoy, which is left to starboard as you enter the Süderhever channel that cuts north of Rochelsteert.

Eider river approaches

The Eider river provides an interesting route across Schleswig-Holstein to the Baltic, joining the Nord-Ostsee Kanal about 20 miles north of Brunsbüttel at Gieselau. You enter the Eider through a lock at the Eider flood-control barrier – the Eidersperrwerk. Because this barrier normally allows the tide to ebb and flow, the Eider effectively remains tidal for about 16 miles up to the lock at Nordfeld.

The seaward approaches to the Eidersperrwerk lead through a long buoyed channel between drying sandbanks. The outer mark is the Eider red-and-white fairway buoy, and it is nearly 15 miles from this buoy to the Eidersperrwerk lock. The outer estuary is open to the west, but is partly protected from the north by the low shore of Eiderstedt. To the south, several other shallow inlets cut through the coastal shoals to small harbours on the Dithmarschen shore.

In many ways, the Eider River provides a more relaxing route through to the Baltic than the busy, fast-flowing Elbe, yet it still requires caution in onshore winds. There is a shallow bar 2 miles inshore from the fairway buoy, with a least depth of about 3½ metres. With the wind from anywhere between north-west through west to south-west, strangers should not approach the Eider estuary in conditions stronger than force 4. In force 5–6 onshore winds, the sea can start breaking over the bar and the outer banks each side of the channel. Then this whole coastline becomes distinctly inhospitable and you should wait for things to ease.

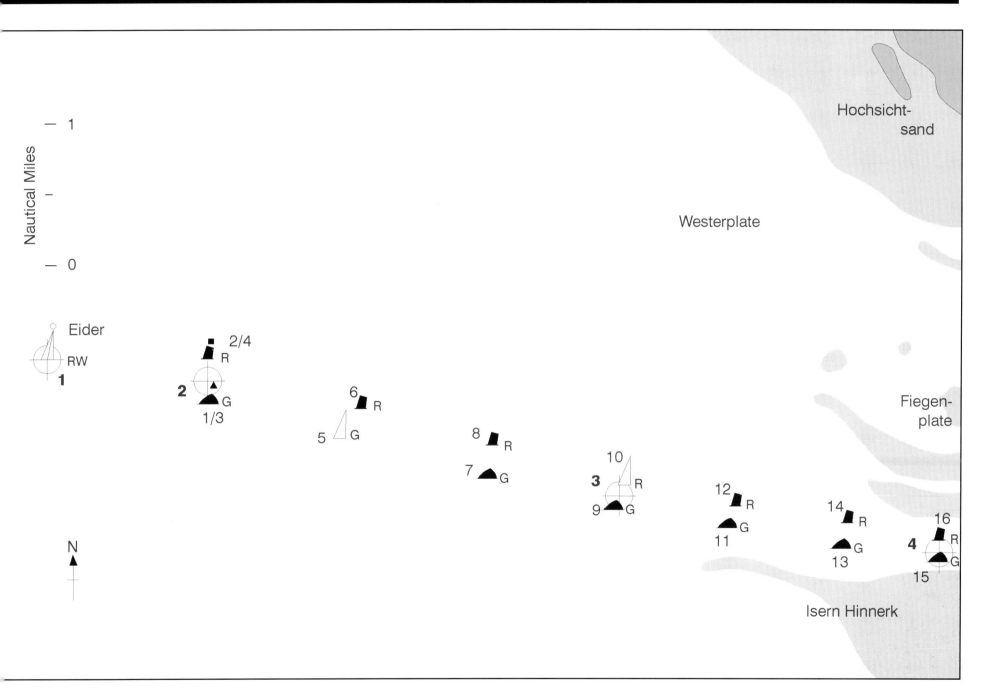

Nautical Miles

— 1

—

— 0

Hochsicht-
sand

Westerplate

Eider

RW

1

2 2/4
R

G
1/3

5 G

6 R

8 R

7 G

10
3 R

9 G

12 R

11 G

14 R

13 G

16
4 R

G
15

Fiegen-
plate

N

Isern Hinnerk

Approaches to Hever and Schmaltief

WP No	Waypoint name and position	Latitude	Longitude
82–1	Schmaltief outer, 6.1 M 265°T from Süderoogsand lighthouse	54°24.96'N	08°18.37'E
82–2	Schmaltief red-and-white fairway buoy, actual position	54°25.00'N	08°22.00'E
82–3	Schmaltief inner, 4.45 M 305°T from Süderoogsand lighthouse	54°28.07'N	08°22.51'E
82–4	Hever red-and-white fairway whistle buoy, actual position	54°20.45'N	08°18.90'E
82–5	Alte Hever 2, 1 ca SE of AH2 red buoy	54°22.82'N	08°23.20'E
82–6	Alte Hever 4, 1 ca SE of AH4 red buoy	54°23.63'N	08°26.03'E
82–7	Alte Hever 6, 1 ca SE of AH6 red buoy	54°24.15'N	08°28.09'E
82–8	Alte Hever 8, 1 ca due S of NH2 / AH8 red buoy	54°24.24'N	08°30.09'E
82–9	Hever outer, midway Hever No 1 green and No 2 red buoys	54°20.62'N	08°21.00'E
82–10	Hever middle, midway Hever No 3 green and No 4 red buoys	54°20.85'N	08°23.09'E
82–11	Hever inner, midway Hever No 7 green and No 8 red buoys	54°21.32'N	08°27.30'E
82–12	Norderhever 1, 2 ca due E of NH1 red-green-red buoy	54°22.44'N	08°31.18'E
82–13	Pellworm outer, 2.87 M 173°T from Süderoogsand lighthouse	54°22.65'N	08°29.33'E
82–14	Norderhever 5, 2.37 M 105°T from Süderoogsand lighthouse	54°24.88'N	08°32.67'E
82–15	Norderhever 4, 3.8 M 075°T from Süderoogsand lighthouse	54°26.49'N	08°35.05'E
82–16	Pellworm inner, 2 M 221°T from Pellworm front leading light	54°27.71'N	08°36.90'E
82–17	SE Pellworm, 1.5 M 112°T from Pellworm rear leading light	54°29.25'N	08°42.44'E
82–18	Süderhever outer, midway No 1 green and No 2 red buoys	54°17.87'N	08°25.20'E
82–19	Süderhever middle, midway SH3 GRG and SH8 red buoys	54°20.50'N	08°30.69'E
82–20	Süderhever inner, 3.4 M 145°T from Süderoogsand lighthouse	54°22.73'N	08°32.09'E

Datum ED 50 The waypoint latitudes and longitudes in this table refer to European Datum (1950)

COASTAL DANGERS

Refer to Admiralty chart 3767 and German chart 3013 (sheets 9 and 10)

Rochelsteert

About 2 miles north of the outer approaches to the River Eider, a long finger of shallow water – the Rochelsteert – juts out seawards for almost 6 miles, with least depths between 2 and 5 metres. In quiet weather, boats can safely cross the outer part of Rochelsteert, but in freshening onshore winds steep seas build up over these shoals. The seaward end of Rochelsteert is marked by Süderhever No 1 green buoy, which is left to starboard as you enter the Süderhever channel that cuts north of Rochelsteert.

Süderhever

The Süderhever cuts just north of Rochelsteert and then south of the Quage bank to lead into the Hever estuary between Westerheversand lighthouse and Süderoog Sand island. The outer mark for the Süderhever is *ODAS* yellow buoy, which leads you towards the gateway provided by Süderhever No 1 green buoy and Süderhever No 2 red buoy. From here the channel trends broadly north-east into the estuary.

Bear in mind that all the inlet channels along this coast require caution in onshore winds. With the wind from anywhere between north-west through west to south-west, strangers should not approach the Hever estuary in conditions stronger than force 4. In force 5–6 onshore winds, the sea can start breaking over the bars and the outer banks each side of the buoyed channels.

Hever

The main Hever channel leads north of Norderquage shoal and joins the Süderhever near red-green-red buoy No 12. The outer mark is the Hever red-and-white whistle fairway buoy, which is lit. Some of the channel buoys are also lit and the white sector of Westerheversand lighthouse leads as far as No 7 green and No 8 red buoys. The shoals each side of the Hever channel have least depths of about 1.4 metres on the north side and 1.2 metres on the south side.

Mittelhever

The old Mittelhever and Alte Hever channels are now effectively combined into a fairly deep fairway that cuts into the north side of the estuary just south of Süderoog Sand island. This fairway is marked along its northern edge only, by the 3 red buoys AH2, AH4 and AH6.

Schmaltief

This sparingly buoyed and frequently shifting channel leads towards Amrum and Föhr from the south, skirting about 2½ miles seaward of Süderoog Sand island, Norderoog Sand island and Japsand. It is important to pick up the Schmaltief red-and-white fairway buoy, which lies 4 miles just south of west from Süderoogsand lighthouse.

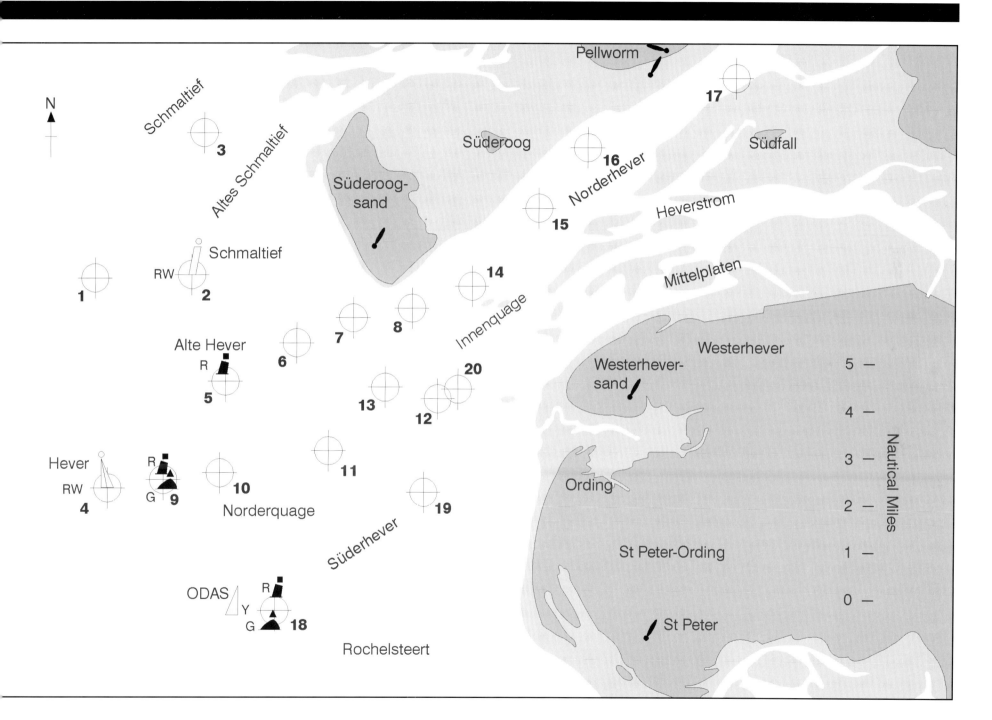

N

Schmaltief

3

Altes Schmaltief

Süderoog

Süderoog-
sand

17

16

Südfall

Norderhever

Heverstrom

15

Schmaltief

RW

2

Mittelplaten

1

14

Alte Hever

R

Innenquage

Westerhever

8

Westerhever-
sand

7

20

5

6

5 —

13

4 —

12

3 —

Hever

R

11

Ording

2 —

RW

G   9

10

Nautical Miles

4

Norderquage

19

1 —

Süderhever

St Peter-Ording

0 —

ODAS

R

Y

G   18

St Peter

Rochelsteert

Outer approaches to Rütergat, Amrum and Vortrapptief

WP No	Waypoint name and position	Latitude	Longitude
83–1	Amrumbank N-card buoy, actual position	54°45.00'N	08°07.00'E
83–2	Theeknobs W-card buoy, actual position	54°43.55'N	08°09.95'E
83–3	Holtknobsloch red-and-white fairway buoy, actual position	54°40.63'N	08°10.42'E
83–4	Holtknobsloch middle, ½ ca due S of HK4 red buoy	54°40.71'N	08°13.01'E
83–5	Amrumbank W-card buoy, actual position	54°38.00'N	07°55.00'E
83–6	Vortrapptief red-and-white fairway buoy, actual position	54°35.01'N	08°12.20'E
83–7	Amrumbank S-card buoy, actual position	54°32.00'N	08°05.00'E
83–8	Rütergat red-and-white fairway buoy, actual position	54°30.31'N	08°12.20'E

Datum ED 50 The waypoint latitudes and longitudes in this table refer to European Datum (1950)

If possible, try to arrive off the Vortrapptief fairway buoy about 2 hours before HW at Hörnum. Although the mean tidal range in this area is quite modest (2.2 metres at springs at Hörnum and 1.7 metres at neaps), it is preferable to have even an extra metre of depth over the bar near the fairway buoy, where the least depths in the channel can be down to about 3½ metres.

Avoid approaching the Vortrapptief in fresh onshore winds or in any significant onshore swell. However, if heavy weather is expected and you can enter in good time, Hörnum is a good safe harbour to tuck into and wait for conditions to improve.

COASTAL DANGERS

Refer to Admiralty chart 3767 and German chart 3013 (sheets 4, 7 and 9)

Danger in fresh onshore winds

Bear in mind that all the inlets and buoyed channels along this coast require caution in onshore winds. With the wind from anywhere between north-west through west to south-west, strangers should not approach any of the North Frisian estuaries in conditions stronger than force 4. In force 5–6 onshore winds, the sea can start breaking over the bars and the outer banks each side of the buoyed channels.

Amrum Bank

The Amrum Bank lies about 10 miles WSW of Amrum island and is marked on its north, west and south-east sides by cardinal buoys. The bank has plenty of depth for yachts to pass over it, but can produce locally steep seas during sustained spells of onshore winds.

Shoals west of Amrum

A mile or two west of Amrum island, on the seaward side of the Vortrapptief channel, a long tail of sandy shoals straggles south-west and south from the southern tip of Sylt. Parts of these banks dry and several narrow channels wind through them, although strangers making for Hörnum are advised to use the main buoyed fairway of the Vortrapptief. The minor channels are prone to shift and the buoys, where they exist, are often moved to accommodate this. It is important to use the latest edition of the German chart 3013, whose 14 large-scale sheets cover the North Frisian Islands.

The entrance mark for Vortrapptief – the Vortrapptief red-and-white fairway buoy – lies just over 11 miles SSW of Hörnum and about 5 miles south-west of Amrum. It is important to find and identify this buoy before proceeding further inshore to pick up the reds and greens of the Vortrapptief. From seaward, Amrum is fairly easy to identify, with quite high dunes in the middle and north of the island. You should also be able to pick out two windmills and the tower of Nebel church.

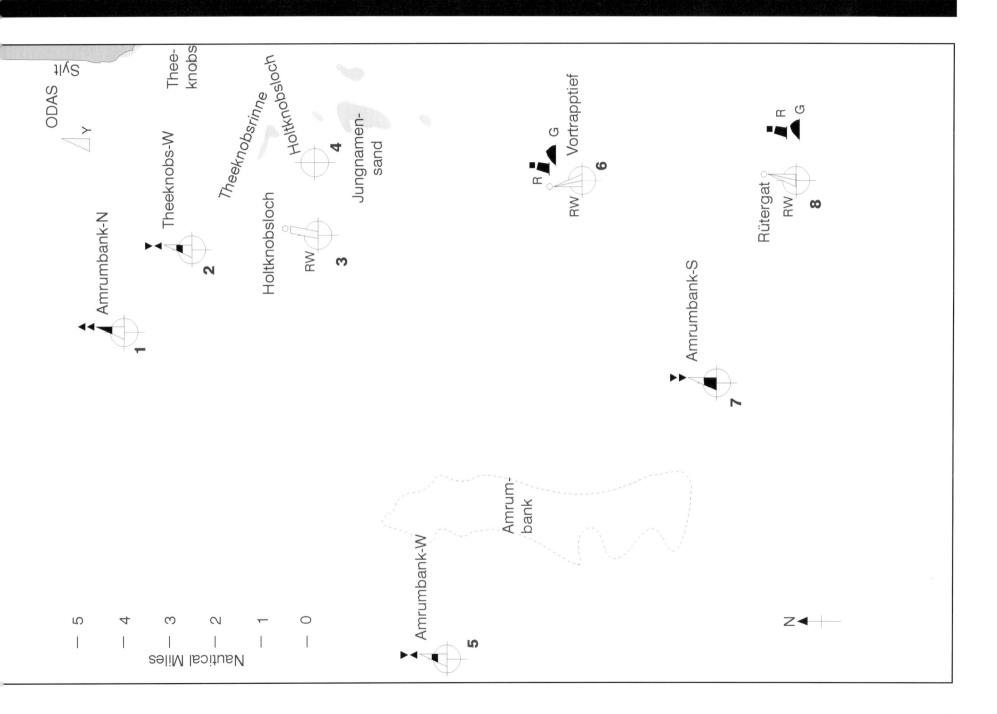

ODAS

Sylt

Amrumbank-N

Theeknobs-W

Thee-
knobs

Theeknobsrinne

Holtknobsloch

Holtknobsloch

Jungnamen-
sand

Holtknobsloch
RW

Amrumbank-W

Amrum-
bank

Amrumbank-S

Vortrapptief
R
G
RW

Rütergat
R
G
RW

1

2

3

4

5

6

7

8

5
4
3
2
1
0

Nautical Miles

N

WP No	Waypoint name and position	Latitude	Longitude
84–1	Vortrapptief red-and-white fairway buoy, actual position	54°35.01'N	08°12.20'E
84–2	Vortrapptief outer, 5.55 M 215°T from Norddorf lighthouse	54°35.64'N	08°13.12'E
84–3	Vortrapptief entrance, 3.55 M 215°T from Norddorf lighthouse	54°37.28'N	08°15.10'E
84–4	Vortrapptief inner, 1.67 M 294°T from Norddorf lighthouse	54°40.88'N	08°15.97'E
84–5	Holtknobsloch middle, ½ ca due S of HK4 red buoy	54°40.71'N	08°13.01'E
84–6	Holtknobsloch inner, midway No 14 RGR and No 13 Gn buoys	54°42.11'N	08°16.27'E
84–7	Hörnum south, midway No 18 red and No 17 GRG buoys	54°44.12'N	08°18.32'E
84–8	Rütergat red-and-white fairway buoy, actual position	54°30.31'N	08°12.20'E
84–9	Rütergat entrance, midway No 3 green and No 4 red buoys	54°30.44'N	08°15.73'E
84–10	Rütergat middle, midway No 9 green and No 10 red buoys	54°33.42'N	08°20.05'E
84–11	Rütergat inner, 2.26 M 141°T from Wriakhörn lighthouse	54°35.87'N	08°23.68'E
84–12	Amrum Hafen E approach, 1.4 M 092°T from front leading light	54°37.83'N	08°25.36'E
84–13	Amrum Hafen outer, Rütergat No 26 RGR buoy, actual position	54°37.92'N	08°24.96'E
84–14	Norderaue west, 3.31 M 080°T from Nebel lighthouse	54°39.33'N	08°27.42'E
84–15	Schmaltief outer, 6.1 M 265°T from Süderoogsand lighthouse	54°24.96'N	08°18.37'E
84–16	Schmaltief red-and-white fairway buoy, actual position	54°25.00'N	08°22.00'E
84–17	Schmaltief inner, 305°T 4.45 M from Süderoogsand lighthouse	54°28.07'N	08°22.51'E
84–18	Schmaltief north, 4.6 M 162°T from Wriakhörn lighthouse	54°33.26'N	08°23.68'E
84–19	Schmaltief ST20 red buoy, actual position	54°34.42'N	08°23.95'E
84–20	Süderaue west, 2.58 M 230°T from Nordmarsch lighthouse	54°35.94'N	08°28.46'E

Datum ED 50 The waypoint latitudes and longitudes in this table refer to European Datum (1950)

COASTAL DANGERS

Refer to Admiralty chart 3767 and German chart 3013 (sheets 4, 7 and 9)

Danger in fresh onshore winds

Bear in mind that all the inlets and buoyed channels along this coast require caution in onshore winds. With the wind from anywhere between north-west through west to south-west, strangers should not approach any of the North Frisian estuaries in conditions stronger than force 4. In force 5–6 onshore winds, the sea can start breaking over the bars and the outer banks each side of the buoyed channels.

Schmaltief

This sparingly buoyed and often shifting channel leads towards Amrum and Föhr from the south, skirting 2½ miles seaward of Süderoogsand island, Norderoogsand island and Japsand. Be sure to pick up the Schmaltief fairway buoy, which lies 4 miles just south of west from Süderoogsand lighthouse.

Rütergat

This comparatively deep and straightforward channel leads in from the south-west past the south end of Amrum and then into the Norderaue channel south of Föhr island. The outer mark for the Rütergat is the Rütergat red-and-white fairway

buoy, which lies just over 9 miles west of Norderoogsand island. From here the channel is well buoyed, leading north-east between the outer estuary shoals.

Harbours on Amrum and Föhr

Amrum harbour, on the south-east side of the island, is small and shallow, but there is a snug anchorage in the narrow fairway just north of the harbour opposite Steenodde. Further up the Norderaue, Hafen von Wyk on the south-east corner of Föhr island is a relatively large yacht harbour for this area, with least depths at the pontoons between 1.2 and 1.4 metres. Wyk has quite a good boatyard, so it is a useful refuge to make for if you need any repairs done.

Shoals west of Amrum

A mile or two west of Amrum island, on the seaward side of the Vortrapptief channel, a long tail of shoals straggles south-west and south from the tip of Sylt. Parts of these banks dry and several narrow channels wind through them, although strangers making for Hörnum are advised to use the main buoyed fairway of the Vortrapptief. The minor channels are prone to shift and the buoys, where they exist, are often moved to accommodate this. Always use the latest edition of German chart 3013, whose 14 large-scale sheets cover the North Frisian Islands.

The entrance fairway buoy for Vortrapptief lies just over 11 miles SSW of Hörnum and about 5 miles south-west of Amrum. It is important to find and identify this buoy before proceeding further inshore to pick up the reds and greens of the Vortrapptief. From seaward, Amrum is fairly easy to identify, with quite high dunes in the middle and north of the island. You should also be able to pick out two windmills and the tower of Nebel church.

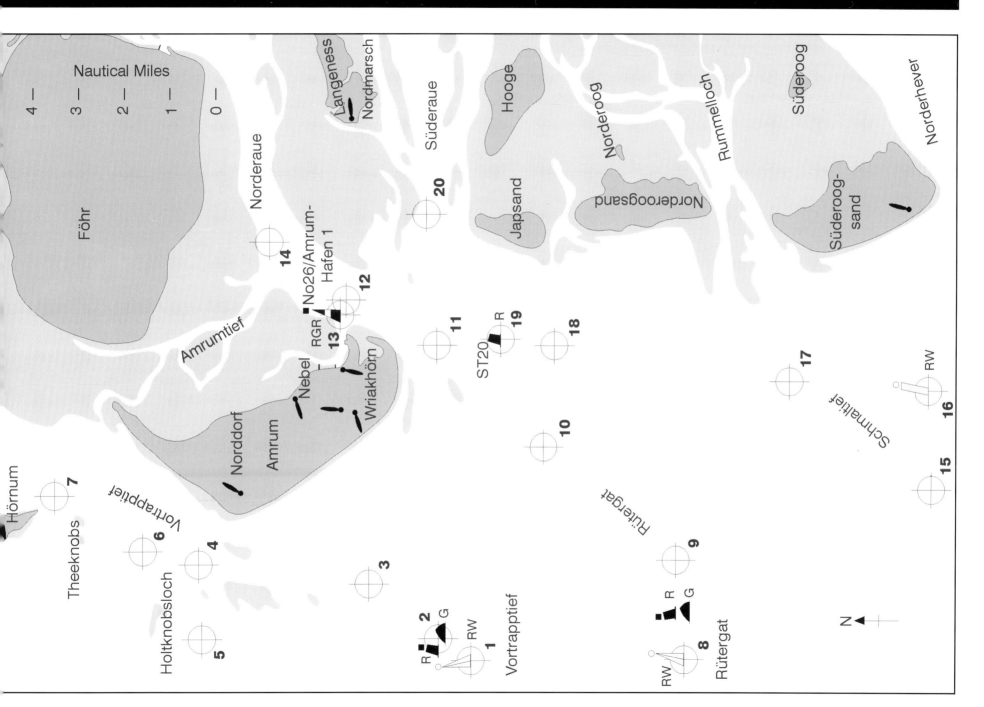

Nautical Miles

4 — 3 — 2 — 1 — 0

Föhr

Langeness

Nordmarsch

Süderaue

Hooge

Norderoog

Süderoog

Norderhever

Norderaue

No26/Amrum-Hafen 1

14

Norderoogsand

Japsand

Süderoog-sand

20

Amrumtief

12

RGR

13

11

ST20 R 19

18

Nebel

Wriakhörn

17

RW

16

Norddorf

Amrum

10

Schmaltief

Hörnum

7

15

Vortrapptief

Theeknobs

Rütergat

6

N

4

3

9

R

G

Holtknobsloch

2 G

8

RW

5

R

RW

1

Vortrapptief

Rütergat

WP No	Waypoint name and position	Latitude	Longitude
85–1	Hörnum south, midway No 18 red and No 17 GRG buoys	54°44.12'N	08°18.32'E
85–2	Hörnum harbour, 100 m 080°T from Schutzmole pierhead light	54°45.58'N	08°18.62'E
85–3	Theeknobs W-card buoy, actual position	54°43.55'N	08°09.95'E
85–4	Amrumbank N-card buoy, actual position	54°45.00'N	08°07.00'E
85–5	*ODAS* yellow buoy west of Hörnum lighthouse, actual position	54°45.65'N	08°13.80'E
85–6	*ODAS* yellow buoy west of Westerland town, actual position	54°54.54'N	08°13.39'E
85–7	*ODAS* yellow buoy west of Lister Landtief, actual position	55°02.50'N	08°17.60'E
85–8	W-card wreck buoy west of Lister Landtief, actual position	55°03.00'N	08°17.63'E
85–9	Lister Landtief red-and-white fairway buoy, actual position	55°02.64'N	08°20.94'E

Datum ED 50 The waypoint latitudes and longitudes in this table refer to European Datum (1950)

COASTAL DANGERS

Refer to Admiralty chart 3767 and German chart 3013 (sheets 3 and 4)

Danger in fresh onshore winds

Bear in mind that all the inlets and buoyed channels along this North Frisian coast require circumspection in onshore winds. With the wind from anywhere between north-west through west to south-west, strangers should avoid approaching any of the channels north or south of Sylt in conditions stronger than force 4. In force 5–6 onshore winds, the sea can start breaking heavily over the bars and the outer banks each side of the buoyed channels. In even stronger onshore conditions, this whole coastline becomes a dangerous lee shore.

Salzsand

The Salzsand shoals extend seawards for more than 3 miles from the north end of Sylt island, with least depths of ½ metre or less in parts. The sea breaks over these shoals in any significant onshore winds or swell, so be sure to keep outside the various buoys that mark the seaward edges of Salzsand. Approaching Lister Tief, the main buoyed channel leading in between Sylt and Rømø, be sure to stay west of Lister Tief red-and-white fairway buoy until you have safely reached and identified it.

Lister Landtief

In calm conditions, there is a useful short cut through Lister Landtief, a narrow buoyed channel leading close south-east of Salzsand and round the north end of Sylt. The seaward mark for this cut is the Lister Landtief red-and-white fairway buoy, which lies about 2 miles WSW of List West lighthouse. From the fairway buoy, three green buoys and two reds lead through Lister Landtief and into the main buoyed *seegat* north of Sylt.

Explosives dumping grounds

Two sizeable explosives dumping zones are shown on the Admiralty and German charts – one a couple of miles seaward of the south end of Sylt island and one a further 4 miles to the north-west. These dumping grounds are only a potential danger if you are using ground tackle and would not generally be of much concern to boats, but should be kept in mind in the unlikely event of your having to anchor offshore for any reason.

Prohibited area

About halfway along the straight west coast of Sylt island, a prohibited area is marked off by buoys, forming a rectangular corridor extending 1 mile offshore and about ½ mile north to south. This prohibited area is not shown on Admiralty chart 3767, but is marked in detail on sheet 3 of German chart 3013. For passage-making along this coast, it is usually convenient to stay just outside the *ODAS* yellow buoy, which lies 2½ miles offshore due west of the 90-metre tall radio mast in the coastal town of Westerland.

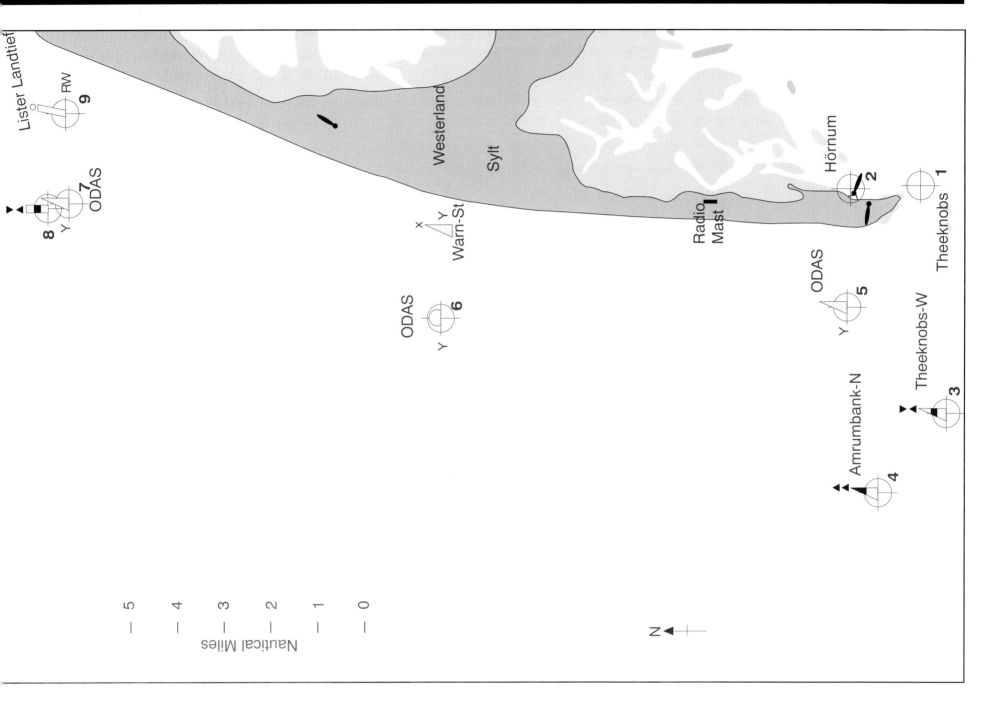

Lister Landtief
RW
9

ODAS
7

8
ODAS

Westerland

Sylt

Hörnum

Warn-St
Y
X

Radio
Mast

ODAS
6
Y

ODAS
5
Y

Amrumbank-N
4

Theeknobs-W

Theeknobs
1

2

3

Nautical Miles
5
4
3
2
1
0

N

WP No	Waypoint name and position	Latitude	Longitude
86–1	*ODAS* yellow buoy west of Lister Landtief, actual position	55°02.50'N	08°17.60'E
86–2	W-card wreck buoy west of Lister Landtief, actual position	55°03.00'N	08°17.63'E
86–3	Lister Landtief red-and-white fairway buoy, actual position	55°02.64'N	08°20.94'E
86–4	Lister Tief red-and-white fairway buoy, actual position	55°05.38'N	08°16.86'E
86–5	Lister Tief middle, 6.6 ca 004°T from List West lighthouse	55°03.89'N	08°24.24'E
86–6	Lister Tief inner, 1.1 M due E true from List Ost lighthouse	55°03.02'N	08°28.63'E
86–7	Rømø Dyb outer, midway No 1 green and No 8 red buoys	55°03.36'N	08°30.39'E
86–8	Haven von List approach, 100 m due E of red pierhead light	55°01.01'N	08°26.58'E
86–9	Røde Klit south, 10.2 M 299°T from List West lighthouse	55°08.16'N	08°08.69'E

Datum ED 50 The waypoint latitudes and longitudes in this table refer to European Datum (1950)

COASTAL DANGERS

Refer to Admiralty chart 3767 and German chart 3013 (sheets 2 and 3)

Danger in fresh onshore winds

Bear in mind that all the *seegats* and buoyed channels along the North Frisian Islands require great caution in onshore winds. With the wind from anywhere between north-west through west to south-west, strangers should avoid approaching the Lister Tief in conditions stronger than force 4. In force 5–6 onshore winds, the sea can start breaking heavily over the bars and the outer banks each side of the buoyed channels. In even stronger onshore conditions, this whole coastline soon becomes a dangerous lee shore.

Salzsand

The Salzsand shoals extend seawards for more than 3 miles from the north end of Sylt island, with least depths of ½ metre or less in parts. The sea breaks over these shoals in any significant onshore winds or swell, so be sure to keep outside the various buoys that mark the seaward edges of Salzsand. Approaching Lister Tief, which is the main buoyed channel leading in between Sylt and Rømø, be sure to stay west of Lister Tief red-and-white fairway buoy until you have safely reached and identified it.

Lister Landtief

In calm conditions, there is a useful short cut through Lister Landtief, a narrow buoyed channel leading close south-east of Salzsand and round the north end of Sylt. The seaward mark for this cut is the Lister Landtief red-and-white fairway buoy, which lies about 2 miles WSW of List West lighthouse.

Lamme-læger shoals

On the north side of the Lister Tief fairway, opposite the north end of Sylt island, a wide area of shoals extends seawards for more than 4 miles from the south-west end of Rømø (the first of the Danish North Frisian Islands). These are the Lamme-læger shoals, parts of which dry and a great deal of which has depths of less than 1 metre. The sea breaks heavily over Lamme-læger in strong westerly winds and it is important to stay in the buoyed channel as you come through Lister Tief.

Changing depths over Lister Tief bar

The seaward ends of Salzsand and Lamme-læger curve together slightly to form a partial bar across the entrance to Lister Tief. In fresh or strong onshore winds, these shoaling depths can cause the sea to break even in the buoyed channel, so strangers should only attempt to enter Lister Tief in light to moderate weather if the winds are anywhere in the west. Depths over the bar are also liable to change, so it is always as well to arrive in the entrance just before local HW if possible.

Strong tides in Lister Tief

In the narrows just north of Sylt, the tides in Lister Tief can reach 2 knots at springs, which is much stronger than the relatively weak offshore streams along this coast. A fresh onshore wind over a spring ebb will cause short steep seas in Lister Tief, although the streams are weaker and conditions much easier in the more open shallow channels – Lister Ley and Højer Dyb – to the east of the north part of Sylt.

Harbours on Sylt and Rømø

List harbour, on the north-east side of Sylt island, has two small lines of yacht pontoons on its south side. The east line has minimum depths of about 2 metres. If you can squeeze in, the harbour is obviously convenient for exploring the island, but you can find a peaceful anchorage in the shallow reaches of the Irrtief channel, a couple of miles SSW of List harbour entrance.

Rømø harbour, on the south-east side of Rømø island, is larger than List. The yacht pontoons are on the north side of the inner basin, with minimum depths of about 2 metres. Rømø is the first of the Danish North Frisian Islands, low and sandy with some dunes rising to about 17 metres and a prominent hotel near the middle of the west coast.

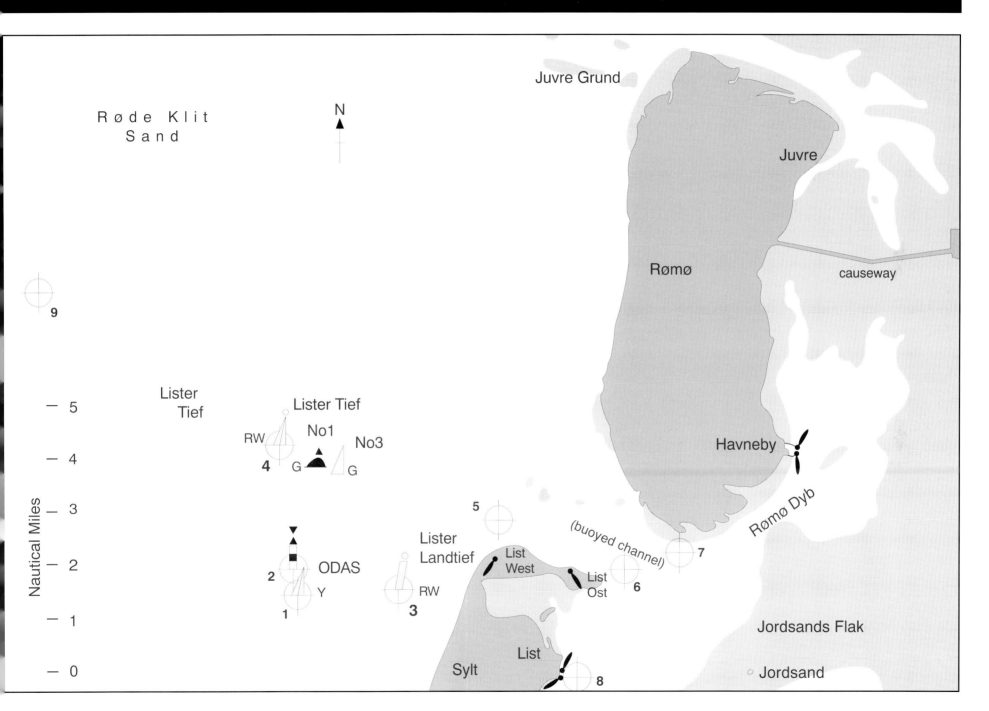

Røde Klit
Sand

Juvre Grund

N

Juvre

Rømø

causeway

Nautical Miles

— 9

Lister
Tief

Lister Tief

No1

No3

RW

4   G   G

2

ODAS

Y

1

5

Lister
Landtief

3   RW

List
West

List
Ost

(buoyed channel)

6

7

Havneby

Rømø Dyb

Jordsands Flak

List

Sylt

8

Jordsand

Approaches to Esbjerg and Fanø

WP No	Waypoint name and position	Latitude	Longitude
87–1	Juvre Dyb red-and-white fairway buoy, actual position	55°15.40'N	08°20.55'E
87–2	Juvre Dyb entrance, 1 ca due S of Juvre Dyb outer red buoy	55°14.03'N	08°23.48'E
87–3	Knudedyb red-and-white fairway buoy, actual position	55°18.97'N	08°20.18'E
87–4	Galgedyb red-and-white fairway buoy, actual position	55°20.55'N	08°24.40'E
87–5	*ODAS* yellow buoy west of Fanø, actual position	55°20.68'N	08°13.81'E
87–6	Grådyb Anduvning red-and-white fairway buoy, actual position	55°24.66'N	08°11.72'E
87–7	Grådyb outer, midway No 1 N-cardinal and No 2 red buoys	55°25.60'N	08°13.92'E
87–8	Grådyb entrance, 3½ ca NW of tide gauge, on L/line	55°26.30'N	08°15.60'E
87–9	Grådyb inner, 1 M 234°T from seaward leading light, on L/line	55°29.19'N	08°22.54'E

Datum ED 50 The waypoint latitudes and longitudes in this table refer to European Datum (1950)

COASTAL DANGERS

Refer to Admiralty charts 417 and 3768 or Danish chart 60

Danger in fresh onshore winds

Bear in mind that all the *seegats* and buoyed entrance channels along the North Frisian Islands require great caution in onshore winds. With the wind from anywhere between north-west through west to south-west, strangers should avoid making passages along this coast in conditions stronger than force 4. In force 5–6 onshore winds, the sea can start breaking heavily over the bars and over the outer banks on each side of the buoyed channels. In even stronger onshore conditions, this whole coastline soon becomes a dangerous lee shore.

Channels and shoals between Rømø and Fanø

For 8 miles between the Danish islands of Rømø and Fanø, a wide area of shoals and sandbanks presents a rather bleak and hostile front to the North Sea, which is best given a wide berth. The only feasible channel for strangers is the Knudedyb, which leads in between drying sandbanks a couple of miles south of Fanø. The outer mark is the Knudedyb red-and-white fairway buoy, from which the buoyed fairway leads east past Fanø and then turns north behind Keldsand.

The inner part of this north-running cut offers a snug sheltered anchorage just east of the drying edge of Keldsand. Use Danish chart 60 for entering Knudedyb and finding the best spot to anchor.

Approaches to Esbjerg

The main entrance channel into Esbjerg leads north-east between the north end of Fanø island and the south-east tip of the Skallingen peninsula. The main part of the channel, along the leading line, is dredged to about 10 metres, but there is relatively shallow water on either side of the channel for a good 2½ miles offshore. In any significant onshore winds or swell, it is important always to follow the channel buoys when entering Esbjerg, at the same time keeping an eye out for ships entering or leaving. The outer approaches can be rough-going in a fresh westerly or south-westerly, but entering this major port is safe in most normal conditions provided you stay in the buoyed channel.

The outer mark for Esbjerg entrance is Grådyb Anduvning red-and-white fairway buoy, which you should find and identify before turning inshore along the buoyed channel. A tide-gauge stands on the south side of the channel about 2½ miles in from the fairway buoy. Use Admiralty chart 417.

Shipping in the Esbjerg approaches

Esbjerg is a busy commercial and ferry port, so you should take great care not to impede shipping in the buoyed entrance channel and in the immediate approaches to the harbour. Also watch out for pilot launches and tugs coming and going at high speed.

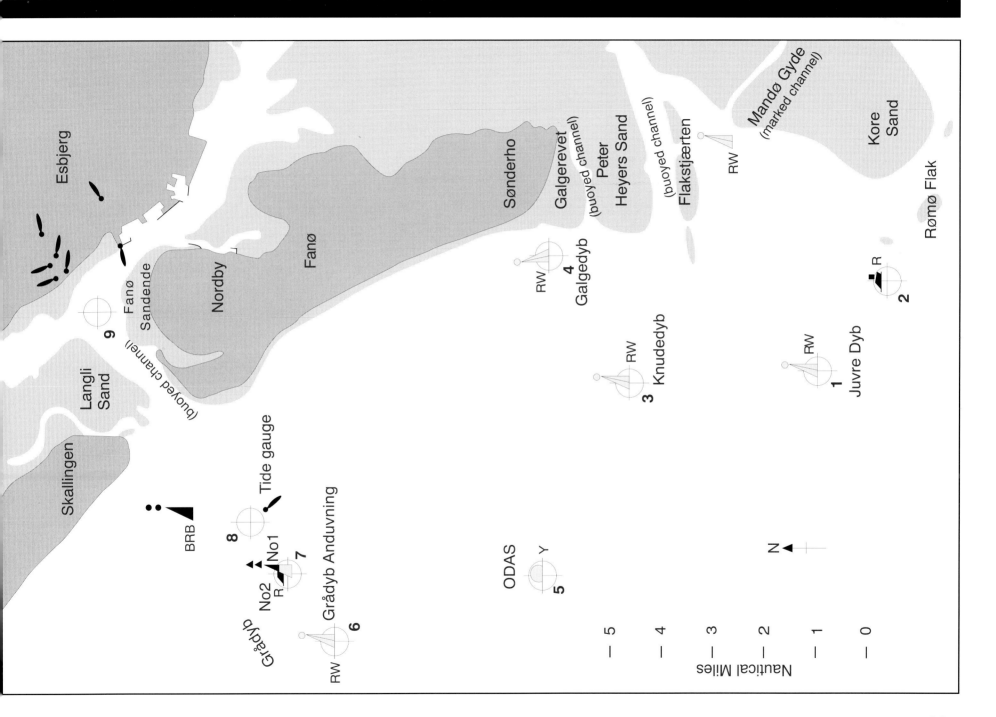

Esbjerg

Fanø Sandende

Nordby

Fanø

Sønderho

Galgerevet
(buoyed channel)

Peter Heyers Sand

(buoyed channel)
Flakstjærten

Mandø Gyde
(marked channel)

Kore Sand

Rømø Flak

Langli Sand

Skallingen

(buoyed channel)

RW **9**

Galgedyb

RW **4**

Knudedyb

RW **3**

RW

Juvre Dyb **1**

R

2

Tide gauge

BRB

8

No1

No2 R **7**

Grådyb Anduvning

Grådyb

RW **6**

ODAS

Y **5**

N

— 5

— 4

— 3

— 2

— 1

— 0

Nautical Miles

A1 buoy 102, 103, 104, 105
A1 bis buoy 102, 103
A2 buoy 102, 103, 104, 105
A3/H16 buoy 157, 165
Abbeville 92, 93
Accumer Ee 170, 171
accuracy 8–9
Admiralty charts 10, 11, 12
Adriana 116, 118, 120
Afsluitdijk 132, 133, 135
Akkaert 104, 105
Alte Hever 196, 197
Alte Mellum 178, 180, 181
Alte Weser 172, 173, 176, 177, 178, 179, 182, 184
Altes Boesgatje 159
Altes Schmaltief 197
AM buoy 142, 143
Ameland 142, 143, 144, 145, 146, 148
Amrum 196, 198, 200, 201
Amrum Hafen 200, 201
Amrumbank 198, 199, 202, 203
Amrumtief 201
A-NE buoy 120, 121, 122, 123
Ants, The 87
Antwerp 104, 106, 108
approach waypoints 7–8
ARCS charts 11
Aussenelbe Reede-1 176, 177, 182, 183
Aussenelbe Reede-2 174, 175, 176, 177, 182, 183
Aussenelbe Reede-3 182, 183
Aussenelbe Reede-4 176, 177, 182, 183
auto-steering 6

Bachelors Spit 36, 37
Baden 134, 135
Baidar 113
Ballast Plaat 141
Ballonplate 150, 151
Baltrum 170, 171

Banc à la Ligne 14, 92
Banc Braek 96, 97, 98, 99
Banc Breedt 96, 97
Banc de Mardyck 97
Banc du Snouw 96, 97
Banc Hills 98, 99
Banc Smal 98, 99, 100
Banjaard Shoals 112, 114
Bankje van Zoutelande 106, 107, 108, 109
Bar Flat 86, 87
Barley Picle 74, 75, 76, 77, 78, 79
Barnard 66, 67, 68
Barrow Beacon 32, 33, 34, 35
Barrow Deep 44, 45, 46, 47, 48
Barrow Swatchway 27, 28, 29, 32, 33, 35
Bawd Head 63, 65
Bawdsey 42, 43, 57, 59, 60, 61, 62, 63, 64, 65
Bays, The 82, 83, 84, 85, 86
Beach End 40, 41
Benacre Ness 66, 67, 68
Bench Head 36, 37
Bensersiel 171
Bezeichnet 192
BG2 light beacon 114, 115
Bielshöven Loch 193
Bielshövensand 191
Bink, The 80, 81, 90, 91
Binnenstroombank 100
Black Boy Sand 87
Black Deep 26, 27, 29, 32, 33, 35, 44, 45, 46, 47, 48, 49, 52, 53, 55, 56, 57, 58, 59
Blackman's Head 40, 41, 42, 43
Blackshore Quay 66
Blacktail 27, 28, 29, 30, 31
Blackwater, River 36, 37
Blagzand 128, 132, 133
Blakeney 80, 81

Blakeney Harbour 80, 81
Blakeney Overfalls 78, 79, 80, 81
Blankenberge 102, 103
Blaue Balje 178, 179
Blauort 191, 192, 193,
Blauort Sand 190, 191, 192, 193
Blauwe Slenk 138, 140, 141
Blindes Randzelgat 159
Blyth, River 66, 67
Bob Hall's Sand 80, 81
Bocht van Watum 163
Bokkegat 117
Bollen van Goeree 117
Bollen van het Nieuwe Zand 115
Bollen van Kijkduin 124, 126,
Boomkensdiep 137,
Boorlokatie 161, 163,
Borkum 144, 145, 146, 148, 150, 151, 152, 153, 154, 155, 156, 157, 158, 159, 160, 164, 165
Borkum Kleiner 144, 145, 146, 150, 152, 154, 156, 157, 158, 164, 165
Borkum Riff 165
Borkumriff 152, 153, 154, 155
Borndiep 144
Bornrif 142
Boston 87
Boston Deep 84, 86, 87
Botkil 107, 110, 111
BR buoy 142, 143
Bradwell 36, 37
Brake buoy 16, 18, 19
Brake Sand 14, 16, 18
Brakzand 149
Brancaster 82, 83
Brancaster Road 82, 83, 84, 85
Branderplate 169
Brandgat 142, 144
Brauer platen 165
Breehorn 132, 133
Breewijd 126, 127, 128, 129, 130

Breskens 108, 109
Bridgirdle 82, 83
Brightlingsea 36, 37
Bristol 40, 41
Britannia Pier 70, 71, 72, 73, 74, 75, 76, 77
Broers Bank 98, 99
Brouwersdam 114, 116
Brunsbüttel 184, 190, 194
BS 1 buoy 138, 139, 140, 141
BS11 buoy 140, 141
BS12 buoy 140, 141
BS29 buoy 140, 141
Buitenhaven 112, 116
Buitenstroombank 100
Bull Channel 90, 91
Bull Dog Channel 87
Bull Sand Fort 90, 91
Burnham Deepdale 82, 83
Burnham Flats 82, 83, 84, 85
Burnham Overy Staithe 82, 83
Buschsand 188, 189
Busetief 169
Büsum 190, 191, 192,
Butley, River 65
Buxey Sand 33, 34, 35, 36, 37

CA10 buoy 92, 93, 94, 95
CA3 buoy 92, 93
CA4 buoy 92, 93
CA6 buoy 92, 93
Caister Road 74, 75, 76, 77
Caister Shoal 74, 75, 76, 77
Calais 14, 15, 16, 17, 92, 93, 94, 95, 96
Campen 160, 161, 163
Cant 22, 23
Canvey Island 31
Cap Blanc Nez 14, 15, 17, 92, 93
Cap Gris-Nez 14, 92, 93
Chantry Point 65
Chapel Point 88, 89

chart plotters 9–11
checking waypoints 8–9
Chenal Intermediaire 96, 97
Chequer Shoal 90, 91
Cheyney Spit 30
choosing waypoints 6–9
Clacton-on-Sea 36, 37, 38, 39
Claremont Pier 66, 67, 68, 69, 70, 72
clearing waypoints 7
Clee Ness 90
Cliff Foot 38, 40, 41, 42, 43
Clite Hole Bank 22
Cobbolds Point 43,
Cockle Gatway 74, 75, 76, 77, 78, 79
Cockle Shoal 75, 77, 78
Cockle Strand 81
Colbart 14, 15, 16, 17
College 40, 41
Colne Point 36, 37
Colne, River 36, 37
Columbine Spit 22, 23
Copperas Channel 22, 23
Cork Hole 50, 51
Cork Hole Channel 86, 87
Cork Ledge 43
Cork Sand 38, 39, 42, 43, 50, 51
Corton 70, 71, 72, 73, 74, 75, 76, 77
Corton Road 68, 70, 71, 72, 73
Cromer 78, 79, 82, 84, 86, 88
Cross 50, 51
CROSSMA 16, 18, 92
cross-track error 5–6, 10,
Crouch, River 32, 33, 34, 35
CS5 buoy 52, 53, 55
Cutler 42, 43, 58, 60, 61
Cuxhaven 182, 184, 185, 186, 188

D16 buoy 168, 169
D4 buoy 166, 167, 168, 169
Daseley's Sand 86, 87
data entry 3–4, 9–10

datum of charted positions 11–12
Deal 15, 17
Deben, River 42, 43, 57, 59, 60, 61
Decca 4–5
Delfzijl 146, 148, 160, 162, 163, 164
Den Helder 124, 125, 126, 128, 129, 130, 132, 133, 134, 135
Den Hoorn 130, 131
Den Oever 98, 99, 100, 101, 128, 132, 133, 135
Dengie 36, 37
departure waypoints 7
Deurloo 106, 107, 108, 109
Die Elbe 176, 177, 182, 184, 192
Die Jade 172, 173, 176, 177, 178, 179, 180, 181
Die Weser 172, 176, 177, 178, 179, 180
Dithmarschen 190, 194
DKA buoy 94, 95, 96
DKB buoy 96, 97
DL1 buoy 105, 107
DL2 buoy 104, 106, 107
DL4 buoy 106, 107
DL6 buoy 106, 107
Docking Shoal 88
Doekegat 158, 159, 160, 161
Dogs Head Sands 84, 85
Domburg 111
Domburgerrassen 107
Donna Nook 90, 91
Dornumer-Accumersiel 171
Dove Point 65
Dover 14, 15, 16, 17, 18, 19
Dover Strait 8, 14, 16, 92
Dovercourt 40
Dovetief 166, 167, 168, 169, 170, 171
DR1 buoy 110, 111
DR3 buoy 110, 111
DR5 buoy 110, 111, 112, 113
Drill Stone 52, 53, 55

Droogte van Schooneveld 104, 105
D-Seert 191, 193
dual systems 4–5
Dudgeon Shoal 88
Dukegat Plate 158, 159, 160, 161
Düne 174, 175
Dunkerque 14, 15, 16, 17, 94, 96, 97, 98, 99
DW10 buoy 94, 95
DW11 buoy 95, 96, 97
DW12 buoy 95, 96, 97
DW13 buoy 96, 97
DW14 buoy 96, 97
DW16 buoy 96, 97
DW5 buoy 94, 95
DW6 buoy 94, 95
DW7 buoy 95
DW8 buoy 94, 95
DW9 buoy 94, 95
Dyck East 96, 97
Dyck red buoy 14, 15, 16, 17, 92, 93, 94, 95, 96

E1 buoy 174, 175
E11 buoy 120, 121, 122, 123
E13 buoy 120, 121, 122, 123
E15 buoy 118, 119, 120, 121, 122, 123
E2 buoy 174, 175
E3 buoy 174, 175, 176, 177
Eagle 36, 37
East Barrow 32, 33, 35, 44, 46
East Dyck Bank 94
East Goodwin 14, 15, 16, 17, 18, 19, 52, 53, 55
East Goodwin LANBY 15, 17, 19
East Last buoy 20, 22
East Swin 26, 33, 35, 38, 39, 44, 45, 46, 47, 48, 49, 56, 57, 59
East Tongue 20, 24
Eckwarden 180, 181
Edinburgh 32

Eems, River 144, 146, 150, 152, 156, 158, 160, 162
Eemshaven 144, 150, 152, 156, 158, 159, 160, 161
Eemshorn Plaat 158, 160
Eemskanaal 163
Egmond aan Zee 120, 121, 122, 123
Eider, River 186, 188, 190, 191, 194, 195
Eidersperrwerk 190, 194
Eiderstedt 190, 194
Eierlandsche Gat 134, 135
Eilanderbalg 151
Eilanderbult 149
Elbe 176, 177, 182, 184, 192
Elbe light float 176, 177, 182, 183
Elbow 19, 20, 21, 52, 53, 55
electronic puck 10
Elleboog 109
Emshörn Plate 159
Emshörngat 159
Emshörnrinne 159
Ems-Jade Canal 181
Engelschhoek 137, 139
Engelsmanplaat 146, 147, 148, 149
Esbjerg 206, 207

F16 buoy 164, 165
F2 buoy 52, 53, 55
Falls Head 52, 53, 55
Falsches Tief 186, 187, 188, 189, 190, 192
Fanø 206, 207
Fanø Sandende 207
Felixstowe 41, 42, 43, 50, 51, 58, 62
Felixstowe Ferry 43
Fiegenplate 191, 195
Fischerbalje 157
Fisherman's Gat 24, 44, 45, 47, 48, 52, 58
Fishtoft 86, 87
Flakstjᴪrten 207

Föhr 196, 200, 201
Fort Massac 50, 51
Foulness Point 28, 32
Foulness Sand 33, 34, 35, 36, 37
Four Fathoms 22, 23, 30, 31
Franekergat 139
Fransche Bankje 124, 126
Fransche Gaatje 139
Freeman Channel 86
Friesche Zeegat 145
Frinton-on-Sea 38, 39
Frisian Islands 134, 136, 140, 142, 144,
   150, 166, 168, 170, 176, 186, 188, 192

Gaatje Bocht 163
Galgedyb 206, 207
Galgerevet 207
Galloper 53, 54, 55, 56, 57, 58, 59
Ganges 40, 41
Garrison Point 30, 31
gas rigs 78, 122
Gat Channel 87
Gat Sand 87
Gat van de Stier 132, 133
Gat van Shiermonnikoog 149
GB1 buoy 114, 115
GB2 buoy 114, 115
GB3 buoy 114, 115
GB4 buoy 114, 115
GB5 buoy 114, 115
Gelb Sand 185, 186, 187, 188, 189
German Bight 166, 170, 172, 174, 176
Geul van de Banjaard 112, 113, 114, 115
Gibraltar Point 84, 85
Gieselau 190, 194
Girdler 22, 23, 26, 27, 29
Glaven, River 81
Glinder 149
Global Positioning System, (GPS) 3–10,
   174, 186, 188
Goeree 114, 116, 117, 120, 121

Goldmer Gat 38, 39, 40
Goodwin Fork 19
Goodwin Knoll 16, 18, 19
Goodwin Sands 14, 15, 17, 52, 53, 54, 55
Goote Bank 104, 105
Gore Channel 20, 21, 24, 25
Gore Middle 82, 83, 84, 85, 86
Gore Point 83, 84, 85
Grådyb 206, 207
Grådyb Anduvning 206, 207
Grain Edge 30
Grain Spit 30
Grauw 107
Gravelines 94, 95, 96, 97
Great Yarmouth 70, 71, 72, 73, 74, 75,
   76, 77, 80, 82
Grevelingen Meer 114, 116
Griend 139, 141
Gronden van de Lauwers 151
Gronden van het Plaatgat 147
Gronden van Stortemelk 137, 139
Groningen 162
Groote Plaat 139
Grosser Knechtsand 182
Grosser Vogelsand 182, 183, 184, 185,
   186, 187, 188
Grossputengat 188, 189
Grote Kaap 124, 125, 126, 127, 128
Grote Rede 100, 101, 102, 103
Guard, The 40, 41, 42, 43
Gull 19
Gull Stream 14, 16, 18, 19, 54
Gunfleet 36, 38, 39, 44, 45, 46, 47, 56,
   57, 58, 59

Haaksgat 165
Hafen von Wyk 200
Haile Channel 90
Haile Sand 90, 91
Haisborough Gat 78
Haisborough Sand 78, 79

Haisbro 78, 79
Haken Sand 185
Halliday Rock Flats 40
Ham Gat 22, 23
hand-held GPS 3
Hanerak 141
Happisburgh 78, 79
Haringvliet 116
Haringvlietsluizen 116
Harle 172, 173
Harlesiel 173
Harlingen 136, 138, 140, 141, 146
Harwich 38, 39, 40, 41, 42, 43, 50, 56,
   57, 58, 59, 60, 62
Haut-Fond de Gravelines 94, 95, 96, 97
Haven 50, 51
Haven von List 204
Havengore Creek 31
Havergate Island 65
Havneby 205
Hawke Channel 90, 91
Helgoland 174, 175, 186, 188, 192
Helsdeur 127, 129, 131
Hemsby Hole 74, 75, 76, 77
Herne Bay 22, 23
Het Rif 147, 149
Hever 196, 197
Heverstrom 197
Hewett Gas Field 78, 79
Hinder 116, 117, 118, 119
Hinderplaat 116, 117
Hochsichtsand 195
Hoek van de Bant 149
Hohe Hörn 165
Hoher Rücken 173, 18
Hohes Riff 169
Højer Dyb 204
Holkham Bay 81, 82
Hollesley Bay 64, 65,
Holm Channel 70, 71, 72, 73
Holm Sand 66, 68, 69, 70, 71, 72, 73

Holme-next-the-Sea 82, 83, 84, 86
Holtknobsloch 198, 199, 200, 201
Hompels Shoals 110, 112, 113
Hond Paap 162, 163
Hondengat 115
Hoog Rif 156, 164
Hooge 201
Hook of Holland 118, 119, 120, 121
Hook Spit 20, 22
Hooksiel 180, 181
Hooksielplate 180, 181
Hörnum 198, 200, 201, 202, 203
Hors Onrust 125, 127, 129, 131
Horsborn Plaat 150, 151, 156, 157, 164,
   165
Horsborngat 151
Horsbornzand 157
Horse Channel 22, 23, 24
Horumersiel 181
Hubertgat 144, 145, 146, 147, 150, 151,
   152, 153, 154, 155
Hubertplate 150, 151
Huibertgat 144, 145, 146, 147, 150, 151,
   152, 153, 154, 155, 156, 164, 165
Huisduinen 126, 127, 128, 129
Humber 90, 91
Humber, River 78, 88, 90, 91
Hunstanton 84, 86, 87

IJ1 buoy 120, 121, 122, 123
IJ3 buoy 120, 121, 122, 123
IJ5 buoy 120, 121, 122, 123
IJ7 buoy 120, 121, 122, 123
IJM buoy 120, 121, 122, 123
IJmuiden 120, 121, 122, 123
IJsselmeer 132, 133, 135
Indusbank 118, 119
Ingoldsmells 84, 95, 88, 89
Innenquage 197
Inner Dowsing 84, 85, 88, 89, 90
Inner Dowsing Overfalls 88, 89

Inner Gabbard 56, 57, 58, 59
Inner Ridge 40, 42
Inschot 141
Inter Bank 52, 53, 55
Irrtief 204
Isern Hinnerk 195
Isle of Grain 30, 31
Isle of Sheppey 30

Jacobs Ruggen 139
Jade 2 buoy 172, 173, 176, 177
Jade-Weser buoy 172, 173, 176, 177
Jade-Weser shipping 172
Jappen Sand 181
Japsand 196, 200, 201
Jordsand 205
Jordsands Flak 205
Juist 152, 153, 154, 155, 160, 164, 165, 166, 167, 169
Juisterriff 152, 153, 154, 155, 164, 165
Jungnamensand 199
Juvre 205
Juvre Dyb 206, 207
Juvre Grund 205

Kaap Hoofd 129, 131
Kalfamergat 169
Kalö 145, 147, 153
Kaloo 106, 107, 110, 111
Katchelot Plate 152, 154, 164, 165
Keldsand 206
Kellett Gut 19
Kentish Flats 20, 22, 23
Kentish Knock 48, 49, 52, 53, 55
Kessingland 66, 67, 68
Kiel Canal 184
Kijkduin 125, 126, 126, 127, 128, 129, 130
King's Channel 44
King's Lynn 82, 86
KL buoy 106, 107
Kleine Rede 101

Knob 26, 32
Knob Gat 27, 28, 29
Knock Deep 48, 49, 52, 53, 55, 56, 57, 59
Knock John Channel 27, 33, 35
Knock John Sand 26, 32, 33, 35
Knock John Tower 26, 27, 29, 32, 33, 35
Knoll 36, 37
Knudedyb 206, 207
Kore Sand 207
Kous Shoals 114, 116
Krabengat 115
Kueerens 107, 111
Kuipersplaat 147, 149
Kwade Hoek 116, 117
Kwinte Bank 100, 101

La Barrière 14, 92, 93
La Panne 99
Lamme-lΨger shoals 204
landfall waypoints 6
Landguard 38, 39, 40, 41, 42, 43,
Lange Zand 141
Langeness 201
Langeoog 170, 171, 172, 173
Langli Sand 207
Lauwers 151
Lauwersmeer 146, 148
Lauwersoog 145, 146, 148, 149
Le Rouge Riden 14, 92, 93
Leigh 30, 31
Leitdamm pier 156, 158, 159
Les Quénocs 92, 93
Linnenplate 191
List Ost 204, 205
List West 202, 204, 205
Lister Landtief 202, 203, 204, 205
Lister Tief 202, 204, 205
Little Nore 30, 31
Little Sunk 44, 45, 46, 47, 48, 52, 53, 55, 56, 57, 58, 59

Long Sand 24, 25, 26, 32, 44, 45, 46, 47, 48, 49, 52, 53, 55, 56, 57, 58, 59, 84, 85, 86, 87
Long Sand Head 24, 44, 48, 49, 56, 57, 58, 59
Longnose 20, 21, 24, 52, 53, 55
Loran 3, 4, 5, 6, 7, 8, 9, 10
Lowestoft 66, 67, 68, 69, 70, 71, 72, 73, 78
Lowestoft Ness 68, 69, 70, 71, 72, 73
Lowestoft North Road 68, 69, 70, 71, 72, 73
Lowestoft South Road 68, 69, 70,72
Luechterloch 186, 187
Lütje Hörn 165
Lutjeswaard 132, 133
Lynn Cut 87
Lynn Deeps 87
Lynn Knock 84, 85

Maas 116, 118, 120, 122
Maasgeul 118, 120
Mablethorpe 88, 89, 90, 91
Magne 110, 111
Malzwin 128, 132, 133
Mandø Gyde 207
manual back-up 5
Maplin Sands 27, 28, 29, 30, 31, 32, 33, 35
Maplin Spit 27, 29, 33, 35
Margate 20, 21, 24, 25, 52, 53, 55
Margate Hook 20, 21, 22, 23, 25
Margate Sand 20, 21, 24, 25
Marsdiep 124, 125, 126, 128, 129, 130, 131, 132, 133
Marshchapel 90
Massvlakte 119
MBJ buoy 112, 114, 115
MC buoy 118, 119, 120, 121, 122, 123
MD3 buoy 114, 115
MDW buoy 52, 53, 55

Medem Sand 185
Medusa 38, 39, 40, 50, 57, 58, 59
Medway 22, 23, 30, 31
Meeuwen Staart 156, 157, 158, 159
Mellumplate 178, 179, 180, 181
Memmert 152, 153, 155, 160, 164, 165
Memmertbalje 164
Memmert-Wattfahrwasser 169
Mersea 36, 37
MG buoy 124, 125, 130, 131, 134, 135
MG13 buoy 126, 127, 128, 129, 130, 131
MG14 buoy 126, 127, 128, 129, 130, 131
MG15 buoy 126, 127, 128, 129, 130, 131
MG16 buoy 126, 127, 128, 129, 130, 131
Mid Falls 52, 53, 55
Mid Shingles 26
Middelburg 109
Middelkerke 100, 101
Middelkerke Zuid 100, 101
Middelplaat 133
Middle Bank 82, 83, 84, 85, 86, 87
Middle Deep 32, 33, 35, 36, 37
Middle Sand 23
Middle Shoal 90
Minsener-Oog 176, 178, 179, 180, 181
Mittelhever 196
Mittel-plate 178, 179, 180
Mittelplaten 197
Mittelrinne 178
Mittlegrund 185, 189
MN buoy 114, 115
MN2 buoy 120, 121, 122, 123
MN3 buoy 120, 121, 122, 123
MO buoy 118, 119
Molengat 124, 125, 126, 127, 128, 129, 130, 131, 134, 142, 144
Molenhoofd 107
Molenrak 141
Monden van de Eems 145
Mouse 27, 28, 29
MOW0 light tower 105

MOW1 light tower 102, 103
MOW2 light tower 109
MOW4 light tower 109
MOW5 light tower 105
MR buoy 124, 125, 126, 128, 130, 134, 135
MV buoy 118, 119
MVN buoy 118, 119,
MW5 buoy 118, 119, 120, 121, 122, 123
MW6 buoy 120, 121, 122, 123

Nass 36, 37
Nassauhafen Marina 180
Nathurn 174
Nautica Ena wreck 102
Navtex 6
Naze, The 57, 59
NBJ buoy 112, 114, 115
NE Spit 52, 53, 55
Nebel 198, 200, 201
Negenvaam 100
Nene, River 86
Nes Harbour 142, 144
Nessmersiel 171
Neue Weser 172, 173
Neue Weser Reede 176, 177, 178, 179
Neues Brack 173, 181
Neuhaningersiel 173
Neuwerk 184, 185, 188
New Cut 87
New Sand Hole 90, 91
Newcome Sand 66, 67, 68, 69, 70, 71, 72, 73
NH buoy 124, 125, 126, 128, 130, 134, 135
Nieuwe Sluis 108, 109
Nieuwpoort 9, 10, 100, 101
Nieuwpoort Bank 98, 99, 100, 101
Nolleplaat Shoal 108, 109
Noord Hinder shipping lanes 54
Noord Meep 139

Noorderhaaks 124, 125, 126, 127, 128, 129, 130, 131, 134, 135
Noordland 110, 112, 113
Noordpas 98, 99, 100, 101
Noordpolderzijl 145
Noordvijk aan Zee 120, 121, 122, 123
Noordwest Gronden 137
Noordzee Kanaal 122
Nordby 207
Norddeich 168
Norddorf 200, 201
Norder Gründe 176, 177, 179, 182
Norderaue 200, 201
Norderelbe 182, 183, 186, 187, 188, 189
Nordergründe 171
Norderhever 196, 197, 201
Norderhoofd 107
Norderney 146, 148, 160, 164, 166, 167, 168, 169, 170, 171
Norderneyer Seegat 166, 167, 168, 169, 170
Norderneyer Wattfahr- wasser 170
Norderoog Sand 196, 200, 201
Norderpiep 190, 191, 192, 193
Norderquage 196, 197
Norderriff 171, 173
Nordfeld 190, 194
Nordmarsch 200, 201
Nord-Ostsee Kanal 190, 194
Nore Swatch 30, 31
North Docking 88, 89
North East Cross Sand 74, 75, 76, 77, 78, 79
North East Spit 20, 21
North Edinburgh Channel 24, 25, 27, 29, 32, 34, 44, 45, 46, 47, 48, 52, 58
North Falls 53, 55
North Foreland 18, 19, 20, 21, 24, 25, 52, 53, 55
North Frisian Islands 198, 200, 202, 204, 206

North Ridge 88
North Shelf 40, 41, 42
North Shingles 26, 27, 29
North Somercotes 90, 91
North Tongue 20
North Well 84, 85, 86
Northcoates Point 91
North-east Channel 100, 101

Oaze 22, 23, 30, 31
ODAS buoys 191, 197, 199, 202, 203, 204, 205, 206, 207
OG1 buoy 106, 107, 110, 111
OG-WG buoy 111
Old Lynn Channel 86
Oldoogrinne 178, 179, 180, 181
Oost Dyck 9, 10
Oost Vlieland 134, 136, 137, 138, 142
Oostende 94, 96, 98, 100, 101, 102, 103
Oostendebank 100, 101, 102, 103
Ooster 114, 115, 116, 117
Ooster Buitengronden 147
Oosterschelde 110, 112, 114
Oostfriesche Gaatje 163
Oostgat 106, 107, 108, 109
Oostkapelle 110, 111, 112
OR buoy 112, 113
OR2 buoy 110, 111
Ording 197
Ore, River 65
Orford Haven 60, 64, 65
Orford Ness 64, 65
Orwell 40, 41, 43
Orwell, River 57, 59
OS14 light beacon 115,
Osterems 152, 153, 154, 155, 160, 164, 165
Osterriede 169
Osterriff 169
Otto 135, 137, 143
Otzumer Balje 170, 171, 172, 173

Oude Inschot 141
Oude Roompot 110, 111, 112, 113
Oude Westereems 156, 157, 158, 159
Oudeschild 132, 133
Outer Gabbard 57, 58, 59
Outer Ratel 9, 10
Outer Tongue 24, 25, 52, 53, 55
Outer Westmark Knock 86

Pakefield Road 66, 68, 69, 70, 72
Pan Sand 22, 23
Pandora Sand 86
Passe de l'Est 98
Passe de l'Ouest 96, 97
Passe de Zuycoote 98, 99
Pegwell Bay 19
Pellworm 196, 197
Pennyhole Bay 40
Pepys 40, 41
Peter Heyer Sand 207
Petroleumbol 115
Pettemer Polder 124, 125
Petten 120, 122, 124, 125
Pitching Ground 38, 39, 42, 43
Plaat van Breskens 109
Plaatgat 146, 147, 148
Platters 42, 43
Pollard Spit 22, 23
Pollendam training wall 140
Port Ouest 96, 97
Princes Channel 20, 21, 23, 24, 26, 28
Protector 90, 91
Pye End 38, 39, 40, 41, 42, 43
Pye Sand 39, 40

Quage bank 196
Queens Channel 20, 21, 22, 23, 24, 25
Quénocs, Les 14
Quern 16, 18, 19

Raan Shoal 106, 107, 108, 109

Race Bank 88
Rade de Dunkerque 96, 97, 98
Rak van Scheelhoek 117
Ramsgate 16, 18, 19, 52, 53, 54, 55, 96
Randzel 160, 164
Randzel Sands 158, 159
Randzelgat 144, 150, 152, 156, 157, 158, 159, 160
Rassen Shoal 106, 107
Ray Sand Channel 34, 36, 37
RCE buoy 94, 95
Reculvers 21, 22, 23
Red Sand Towers 22, 23, 26, 27, 29
Rhine 116
Ribben 116, 117
Ribzand 105
Richel 136, 137, 138, 139
Ridens de la Rade 14, 92, 94, 95
Riffgat 144, 145, 148, 150, 151, 152, 153
Roaring Middle 84, 85, 86, 87
Robberplate 169, 171
Rochelsteert 190, 191, 194, 196, 197
Røde Klit Sand 204, 205
Roger Sand 86, 87
Rolling Ground 40
Rømø 202, 204, 205, 206, 207
Rømø Dyb 204, 205
Roompot 110, 111, 112, 113, 114
Roompotsluis 112
Rosse Spit 90, 91
Roter Grund 178, 179
Roter Sand 178, 179
Rotterdam 54, 121, 123
Rottumeroog 151, 153, 155, 157
Rottumerplaat 151, 153, 155
Rough 50, 51
Rough Shoals 51
Roughs Tower 50, 51, 57, 58, 59
Rummelloch 201
Rütergat 198, 199, 200, 201
Ruytingen 14, 15, 16, 17, 92, 93

S1 buoy 166, 167, 168, 169
sailplan 6, 9, 10, 11
Sales Point 36, 37
Salzsand 202, 204
Sand End 22, 23
Sander Watt 181
Sandettié 14, 15, 16, 17 52, 53, 55
Schaar van Spijkerplaat 108, 109
Schapesand 165
Scharhörn 182, 183, 184, 185, 186, 188
Scharhörn Riff 182, 183, 184
Scharhörnriff 176, 177, 182, 183, 184
Scheur 104, 105, 108, 109
Scheur-Wiel 109
Scheur-Zand 105
Scheveningen 120, 121, 122, 123
Schiermonnikoog 144, 145, 146, 147, 148, 149, 151, 153, 155
Schilbolsnol 128, 129, 130, 131, 132
Schildgronden 165
Schillplate 165
Schleswig-Holstein 190, 194
Schluchter 166, 167, 168, 169
Schlüsseltonne 172, 173, 176, 177, 182, 184
Schmaltief 196, 197, 200, 201
Schooneveld 105
Schuiten Sand 159
Schuitengat 136, 137, 138, 139
Schulpengat 124, 125, 126, 127, 128, 130, 134
Scolt Head 82, 83
Scott Patch 84, 85, 88, 89
Scroby 70, 71, 72, 73, 74, 75, 76, 77, 78
Scroby Elbow 70, 71, 72, 73, 74, 76
scrolling 10
Scullridge 87
SD4 buoy 114, 115
Seal Sand 86, 87
seamark waypoints 7
Segre 109
Sellebrunn 174, 175

SG buoy 116, 117, 124, 125, 126, 127
SG1 buoy 139
Sheerness 30, 31
Shell Ness 23,
Sheringham Shoal 78, 79, 80, 81,
Shingles Bank 20
Shingles Patch 24, 25, 26, 27, 29, 32, 44, 46
Shiphead 50, 51
shipping 28, 40, 42, 50, 54, 56, 62, 92, 94, 96, 102, 104, 106, 108, 110, 118, 120, 134, 136, 142, 144, 150, 152, 156, 158, 160, 166, 174, 176, 180, 182, 184, 186, 188, 206
Shipwash 50, 51, 56, 57, 58, 59, 62, 63, 64, 65
Shipway 50, 51, 57, 58, 59, 60, 61, 62, 63, 64, 65
Shivering Sand Towers 22, 23, 26, 27, 29
Shoebury Ness 28, 30, 31, 32
Shotley Point Marina 40, 41
Shotley Spit 40, 41
Simonzand 151
Skallingen 206, 207
Skegness 84, 85, 86
Sledway 58, 60, 61, 62, 63, 64, 65, 82, 83, 84, 85, 86
Slenk 139
Slijkgat 116, 117
SM buoy 136, 137
software 11
SΩnderho 207
Songa 108, 109
South Brake 14, 18, 19
South Channel 20, 24, 42, 43
South Cross 70, 71, 72, 73, 74, 75, 76, 77
South Edinburgh Channel 25, 27, 29
South Falls 14, 15, 16, 17
South Foreland 15, 17, 19
South Goodwin 14, 15, 16, 17, 18, 19

South Goodwin LANBY 14, 15, 16, 17, 18, 19
South Shingles 20, 24
South West Reach 27, 28, 29
Southend 30, 31
Southwold 66, 67
Spaniard 22, 23
Spaniergat 169,
Spiekeroog 170, 171, 172, 173
Spile 22, 23, 30, 31
Spleet Shoal 106, 107, 108, 109
Spurn Head 90, 91
St Edmund's Point 83 85, 86, 87
St Peter 191, 197
St Peter's Flats 36, 37
St Peter-Ording 197
Stanford Channel 66, 67, 68, 69, 70, 72
Steenbanken 110, 111
Steenodde 200
Steingrund 174, 175
Steinplate 169, 171
Stelle Hoek 116, 117
Stellendam 116
Stiffkey Overfalls 81, 82, 83
Stolzenfels 134, 135, 142, 143
Stone Banks 38, 39
storm surge barrier 110, 112, 113, 114
Stortemelk 134, 136, 137, 138, 139, 142
Stour, River 40, 41, 43, 57, 59
Strand-plate 178
Stroombank 100
Studhill Bay 22
Süderaue 200, 201,
Süderhever 190, 191, 194, 196, 197
Süderoog 197, 201
Süderoogsand 196, 197, 200, 201
Süderpiep 190, 191, 192, 193
Südfahrwasser 191, 193
Südfall 197
Sunk Head 53, 54, 55
Sunk Head Tower 36, 48, 49, 57, 58, 59

Sunk Sand 26, 32, 33, 44, 48, 49, 52, 57, 58, 59, 84, 85, 86, 87
Sunken Buxey 34, 36
Sunken Pye 40, 41
SW Sunk 26, 27, 28, 29, 32, 33, 35, 44, 45, 46, 47
Swale 22, 23
Swallow Tail 34, 36, 37
Swin Spitway 33, 34, 35, 36, 37
Sylt 198, 200, 202, 203, 204, 205
SZ-N buoy 172, 173, 176, 177

TE1 buoy 142, 143
TE11 buoy 144, 145
TE13 buoy 152, 153, 154, 155
TE3 buoy 142, 143
TE5 buoy 142, 143
TE7 buoy 142, 143
TE9 buoy 142, 143
Teetotal Channel 86, 87
Tegeler Plate 179, 181
Tegeler Rinne 179
Terschelling 134, 135, 136, 137, 138, 139, 142, 143, 166, 170, 172, 176
Terschelling Gronden 134, 136, 137
Terschelling Sands 134, 136, 142
Tertiussand 190, 191, 192, 193
Tetney Monobuoy 91
Texel 124, 126, 128, 129, 130, 131, 132, 133, 134, 135
Texelstroom 128, 132
TG buoy 134, 135, 136, 137, 142, 143
TG1/Ems buoy 152, 153, 154, 155
TG11 buoy 170, 171
TG13 buoy 170, 171
TG15 buoy 170, 171
TG17/Weser 1 buoy 170, 171
TG19/Weser 2 buoy 176, 177, 172, 173
TG3 buoy 152, 153, 154, 155
TG5 buoy 152, 153, 154, 155
TG7 buoy 152, 153, 154, 155

TG9 buoy 166, 167
Thames Estuary 20, 48, 52, 54, 56, 58, 96
Theddlethorpe 90
Theeknobs 198, 199, 201, 202, 203
Theeknobsrinne 199
Thief Sand 87
Thirslet 36, 37
Thornham 82, 83, 84
Thornton 104, 105
Threshold 50, 51
Titchwell 82, 83, 84
Tizard 33
Tojaro 107, 111
Tollesbury Yacht Harbour 37
Tongue Sand 20, 22, 24, 26, 27, 29
Tongue Sand Tower 20, 21, 22, 24, 25
Traffic Separation Scheme 15, 16, 17, 18, 19, 54, 92, 93, 134, 136, 142, 144, 166, 170, 172
Trap, The 87
Trapegeer 98, 99
Trawl 108, 109
Trial Bank 86, 87
Trinity 53, 54, 55, 56, 57, 59
Trischen 189, 193
TS buoy 142, 143

Uithuizerwad 159
using waypoints 5–9

Varne 14, 15, 16, 17
VHF 6, 118, 120, 180
Vinca G 120, 121, 122, 123
VL1 buoy 134, 135
VL2-SGL 139
VL3 buoy 134, 135
VL5 buoy 134, 135, 138, 139
VL6 buoy 138, 139
VL7 buoy 134, 135, 136, 137
VL9 buoy 134, 135, 142, 143
Vlakte van de Raan 104, 105, 106

Vlieland 134, 135, 136, 137, 138, 139, 142, 143
Vlieree 137
Vliestroom 138, 139, 140
Vlissingen 104, 106, 108, 109
Voorentief 165
Voorne 121, 123
Vortrapptief 198, 199, 200, 201
Voslapp 180, 181

W10 buoy 108, 109
WA buoy 142, 143
Waddenzee 140, 146, 148
Wadgate Ledge 42, 43, 58
Walcheren 106, 108, 110, 112
Walde 94, 95
Wallet 38, 39
Wallet Spitway 36, 37, 44, 45, 46, 47
Walton Backwaters 38, 39, 40
Walvischstraat 106
Wandelaar 102, 103
Wangerooge 172, 173, 178, 179, 180, 181
Wangerooger Fahrwasser 172, 173, 178, 179, 180
Warp, The 26, 27, 28, 29, 32
Wash, The 78, 80, 82, 84, 85, 86, 87
Washington 42, 43, 58, 60, 61
Well, The 86, 87
Welland Cut 87
Wells-next-the-Sea 80, 81
Wenduine Bank 102, 103
Weser 1a buoy 170, 171, 172, 173, 176, 177
Weser 1b/Jade 1 buoy 172, 173, 176, 177
Weser 2a buoy 172, 173, 176, 177
Weser 4 buoy 172, 173, 176, 177
Weser 4a buoy 172, 173, 176, 177, 178, 179
Wesselburen 191
Wesselburener Loch 191, 193
West Aleta 137
West Barrow 27, 28, 29, 32, 33, 35

West Hook Middle 34, 36
West Meep 138, 13
West Ridge 88, 89
West Rocks 38
West Sands 80, 81
West Schouwen 114, 115
West Stones 86
West Swin 27, 28, 29, 32, 33, 35
West Terschelling 136, 137, 138, 140
Westdiep 98, 100, 101
Westerbalje 170, 171, 172
Westereems 144, 145, 150, 151, 152, 153, 154, 155, 156, 158, 160, 164, 165
Westerheversand 196, 197
Westerland 202, 203
Westerplate 191, 195
Westerriff 171, 173
Westerschelde 8, 104, 106, 108
Westertill 176, 177, 182, 183, 184
Westgat 110, 111, 112, 113, 125, 127, 142, 144, 146, 147
Westhoofd 117
Westkapelle 106, 107, 108, 110
Westpit 106, 107
Weststroombank 100, 101
WG buoy 144, 146, 147, 148
WG4 light beacon 110, 111, 112, 113
WG-GB buoy 110, 111, 112, 113
Whitaker 33, 34, 35, 36
Whitaker Channel 33, 34, 35, 36, 37
White Ness 20, 21, 24, 25
Whiting Bank 64, 65
Whiting Hook 65
Whitstable Street 22, 23
Wichter Ee 170, 171
Wielingen Sluis 109,
Wielingen Zand 102, 103, 104, 105
Wierbalg 132, 133
Wierumer Gronden 144, 146, 147
Wilhelmshaven 180, 181
Winterton Overfalls 75, 77

Winterton-on-Sea 78, 79
Wisbech Channel 86, 87
WM1 buoy 138, 139
WM9/ ZM2 buoy 138, 139
Woodbridge Haven 42, 43, 58, 60, 61
Woolpack 82, 83, 84, 85
Would 78, 79
WR13 buoy 124, 125, 135
Wrangle Flats 87
WRG buoy 144, 145, 146, 147
Wriakhörn 200, 201

Yantlet 30, 31
Yarmouth Road 70, 71, 72, 73, 74, 75, 76,
    77

Zand 102, 103, 104, 105
ZBJ buoy 110, 111
ZC2 buoy 92, 93
Zeebrugge 102, 103, 104
Zeegat van Ameland 142, 143, 144
Zeegat van Terschelling 134, 135, 136
Zeegat van Texel 124, 125, 126, 128,
    130, 134, 135
Zeehondenplaat 115
Zehnerloch 188, 189
ZH buoy 124, 125, 135
Zoutkamperlaag 146, 148, 149
ZS Bank 136, 137
ZS13/VS2 buoy 136, 137
ZS15 buoy 136, 138, 139
ZS20 buoy 136, 137, 138, 139
Zuid Meep 139
Zuider Haaks 124, 125, 126, 127, 128
Zuider Stortemelk 136, 137
Zuiderduintjes 157
Zuidstroombank 100, 101
Zwarte Hoek 117

Notes